GLOSSARY OF OLD AKKADIAN

MATERIALS FOR THE ASSYRIAN DICTIONARY

NO. 3

GLOSSARY OF OLD AKKADIAN

BY

I. J. GELB

THE UNIVERSITY OF CHICAGO PRESS

CHICAGO, ILLINOIS

International Standard Book Number: 0-226-62307-6

THE UNIVERSITY OF CHICAGO PRESS, CHICAGO 60637
The University of Chicago Press, Ltd. London

Second Impression 1973. Printed by Cushing-Malloy, Inc.,
Ann Arbor, Michigan, United States of America

TABLE OF CONTENTS

PREFACE

The publication of the _Glossary of Old Akkadian_, announced in 1952, at the time when volumes I and II of the _Materials for the Assyrian Dictionary_ were being issued, has been delayed until now for two main reasons, which have forced me to set aside, at least temporarily, the work on the present volume. The first reason, growing out of my preoccupation with the initial stages of publication of the _Assyrian Dictionary_, needs no further elaboration. The second reason is connected with the steadily growing mountain of new material, either published or made available to me through the kind cooperation of scholars everywhere, which had been accumulating while I was occupied by pressing duties with a higher priority.

The _Glossary_ presents a picture of the Old Akkadian lexicographical material from the oldest times down to the end of the third Dynasty of Ur. Two terms need an explanation. The term "glossary" means exactly what the term normally implies and no more. The _Glossary_ contains words collected for the use of the Assyrian Dictionary, ordered according to form and rough semantic grouping, with translations intended solely to serve as a guide to future investigators of the meanings. The term "Akkadian" embraces probably more than the term implies since the _Glossary_ includes a number of entries used as loan words in Sumerian, which may have been borrowed not from Akkadian but from other Semitic languages spoken in Mesopotamia or in the neighboring areas. Similarly, in order not to prejudice the matter of their linguistic affiliation, all the non-Sumerian names marked as MAR.TU ("Amorite") have been included, as well as some names, such as _I-la-ša-ma-ar_ or _Mar-da-ba-an_, which may be Amorite even through they are attested without the MAR.TU designation. The occurrence or lack of the designation MAR.TU is regularly marked in the _Glossary_.

Three types of sources have been included in the _Glossary_. The primary sources, consisting of Akkadian words occurring in the Akkadian texts, and the secondary sources, consisting of Akkadian loan words in Sumerian and of Akkadian words which occur as elements in proper names in either Akkadian or Sumerian texts.

The _Glossary_ does not give a complete picture of the Old Akkadian lexicon as it can be reconstructed from the available sources, in that it has no entries which are written logographically only and for which no known syllabic spellings can be attested or safely reconstructed. I did collect for the use of the Assyrian Dictionary all the logographic spellings occurring in Old Akkadian, but have decided not to include them in the present Glossary as they would have required a different type of listing and would have doubled the size of this volume.

Certain qualifications should be made in respect to the completeness of coverage of the Old Akkadian onomastic material. Originally, my plan was to excerpt completely all the Akkadian material found in personal names of the Pre-Sargonic and Sargonic sources, but to leave out the comparative material in the Ur III Period, relying on Schneider's publication in Orientalia XXIII-XXIV to take care of this portion of the Old Akkadian lexicon. This turned out to be impossible, however. So many important corrections and additions had to be made to the Schneider publication that in the middle of my work I was forced to revise my original plans and to collect the Ur III materials independently. Due to the immense number of the Ur III sources, it would have been impossible for me to collect the Ur III personal names as completely as I did the Pre-Sargonic and Sargonic names. Some short cut had to be made, and I have decided not to collect completely such common elements as abum, ilum, nadānum, for which ample documentation is attested. Thus the onomastic material is quoted fully for the Pre-Sargonic and Sargonic Periods but is quoted in selection in the Ur III Period when it was thought that the additional examples add nothing of importance to our knowledge of Akkadian in the Ur III Period.

While personal names excerpted from the texts found in the Diyala region, Gasur, Susa in Elam, and from the Maništušu Obelisk are quoted simply with reference to D (and FM), G, E, and MO, it must be clearly understood that they have been collected directly from the respective text publications and not from the lists of personal names. The quotation of the lists of personal names, while it is a short-cut, is useful since the lists often quote many more references than are given in the Glossary. The specific sources are quoted fully in the case of readings which differ substantially from those found in the published lists of personal names.

While words occurring in Old Akkadian sources are quoted with complete references, the personal names usually bear only one reference from each of the three periods of Old Akkadian, only in exceptional cases two or more. The + symbol after a reference means that there are more references which I have collected but have not quoted in the Glossary. This symbol is reliable in the case of Pre-Sargonic and

Sargonic materials, which I have collected fully. Owing to my somewhat unsystematic method of collecting the Ur III onomastic material, I have the feeling that the + symbol will have to be added in many more instances of Ur III quotations than are so marked. This is also true of some very common Akkadian loan words occurring in the Ur III texts, which add nothing of lexical importance to the instances quoted in the Glossary.

The three periods of Old Akkadian are distinguished, whenever necessary, by symbols "PSarg." for Pre-Sargonic, "Sarg." for Sargonic, and "U" or "Ur III" for Ur III. The symbol "PSarg." is regularly used with all occurrences of the Pre-Sargonic Period; the symbol "Sarg." is written only when needed in the discussion, it being taken for granted that lack of any symbol means that the occurrence is dated to the Sargonic Period. Since the majority of occurrences are from the Sargonic Period, it is important for the users of the Glossary to mark this point well. "U" or "Ur III" is used regularly with Ur III references, except in the cases of U followed by a number, which refer to Ur III personal names quoted after Schneider, Orientalia XXIII-XXIV. Comparative materials from later periods are regularly marked by abbreviations denoting periods, such as OB, OA, MB, etc.

Additional information is often found with references, giving the place of origin of the sources, such as Mari or Chagar Bazar. The Elamite sources are not marked because they can be easily recognized from the MDP references in which they were published. The "CM" abbreviation (for Cruciform Monument) is given regularly after the reference to warn the readers of the spurious character of this source (cf. Gelb in JNES VIII 346ff.). The symbol "copy" after a reference means that the source is known only from a late copy and it may not reproduce correctly the older form of the language. Generally, this symbol is omitted in the case of such well-known texts as the royal inscriptions published in PBS V 34 + XV 41 and UET I 274-276. For important distinctions between different types of later copies of the Sargonic royal inscriptions, cf. MAD II 11. Two types of sources, one marked "Dêr" (inscriptions from Dêr) and the other "Voc. prat." (Vocabulaire pratique published in RA XVIII 49-78), have been included in the Glossary, even though they may have been composed in the early OB Period, because they contain materials linking them with the Ur III Period. A warning is also in order about the three texts published as Ur III in BE III 76-78 and included in the Glossary, even though their Ur III date, rather than early OB, may be in question.

Personal names used for PSarg., Sarg., Gutian, etc. kings have no references since they can be easily found with the full critical apparatus in Jacobsen, *The Sumerian King List* (= *AS* XI). Ur III dates are quoted generally after Ungnad, "Datenlisten" in *Reallexikon der Assyriologie* II 136ff. Only one, main, text is quoted in the case of the royal inscriptions, omitting the sometimes quite numerous duplicates.

The entries in the *Glossary* are preceded by what normally would be called "roots," but what actually should be considered as a kind of consonantal skeleton, which is used to help in grouping related entries and in cross referencing. Thus while the "root" of *qaqqadum* is QDQD (or reduplicated QD) or, with vowels, *qadqad*, the consonantal skeleton given in the *Glossary* is QQD, reproducing the three occurring consonants of *qaqqadum*. Similarly *anta* is placed under the consonantal skeleton of ʾ$_1$NT and not ʾ$_1$N or *ʾan*.

Due to typographical difficulties, the transliteration of Sumerian could not be distinguished as carefully from that of Akkadian as it would have been in a printed volume. Sumerian logograms in Akkadian texts are regularly in roman capitals. However, Sumerian elements in Sumerian texts are also given in roman capitals (and are not in spaced roman) to distinguish them clearly from Akkadian elements quoted in small roman minuscules. The only exception are long Sumerian quotations and Akkadian loan words in Sumerian ending in *-um*, such as *ar-ga-núm*, *ḫa-za-núm*, which must be considered as foreign words in Sumerian. In both cases small roman minuscules are used.

Often no line references are quoted, mainly due to the difficulty of finding the correct number of the quoted line in large texts with several columns. Occasionally, such expressions as top, middle, end, or bottom are used to help in finding the quoted reference in texts with many lines in a column. Commas are often added to separate phrases in longer quotations, even though they do not reproduce the the original. This departure from the standard transliteration procedure was introduced to enable scholars to follow complicated Akkadian or Sumerian contexts more easily.

Throughout the long process of preparation of this volume I have enjoyed the most helpful cooperation of scholars throughout the world, which I feel a pleasant duty to acknowledge here. In the first place I should like to mention institutions and scholars who have either provided me with photographs or copies of unpublished materials or have made it possible for me to study the texts in their museums:

Ann Arbor, Michigan. University of Michigan. Kelsey Museum of

Archaeology. Sargonic and Ur III texts of unknown origin, symbolized as "Univ. Michigan." Transliterated in Ann Arbor over twenty years ago with the permission of Professor Leroy Waterman and in the summer of 1956 with the permission of the authorities of the Kelsey Museum of Archaeology.

Baghdad. Iraq Museum. Sargonic texts from the Diyala region, now published in MAD I, and unpublished Sargonic texts of unknown origin, symbolized as "Iraq Mus." Transliterated in Baghdad in the summer of 1947 with the permission of Dr. Naji al Asil, Director-General of Antiquities. A few unpublished Ur III texts are quoted from the transliterations of the late F. W. Geers.

Baltimore, Md. Walters Art Gallery. Pre-Sargonic text of unknown origin, symbolized as "Walters Art Gall." Transliterated from photographs furnished by Miss Dorothy Hill.

Baltimore, Md. Johns Hopkins University. Ur III texts of unknown origin, symbolized as "Johns Hopkins." Transliterated by Professor A. L. Oppenheim.

Berlin. Staatliche Museen. Vorderasiatische Abteilung. Sargonic texts from Assur, symbolized as "VAT." Transliterated from photographs furnished by Professor Walter Andrae with the cooperation of Professor Adam Falkenstein.

Chicago, Ill. University, Oriental Institute. Sargonic texts from the Diyala region, now published in MAD I, unpublished Sargonic and Ur III texts from Tell Asmar, Khafaje, and Nippur, symbolized as "TA," "Kh.," and "NT" respectively, and Sargonic and Ur III texts from Adab and of unknown origin, symbolized as "A."

Chicago, Ill. Chicago Natural History Museum. Sargonic texts from the Diyala region, now published in FM. Transliterated from originals and copies with the permission of Colonel Clifford C. Gregg, the Director of the Museum, and cooperation of Dr. Paul S. Martin and Mr. Richard Martin. Scattered unpublished Ur III and OB texts are quoted from my transliterations.

Chicago, Illinois. Ur III texts in the possession of the late Milton Yondorf, symbolized as "Yondorf."

Copenhagen. Nationalmuseet. Antiksamlingen. Sargonic texts of unknown origin, symbolized as "Cop." Transliterated from photographs furnished by Dr. Niels Breitenstein with the cooperation of Professor

Thorkild Jacobsen.

Geneva. Musée d'Art et d'Histoire. Sargonic texts of unknown origin, symbolized as "Geneva MAH." Transliterated from copies and photographs furnished by Dr. Edmond Sollberger.

Istanbul. Museum. Sargonic and Ur III texts from Adab, Lagash, and Nippur, symbolized as "Ist. Mus." Transliterated in Istanbul in the summer of 1947 with the permission of the authorities and cooperation of Professor F. R. Kraus.

Leiden. Collection de Liagre Böhl. Sargonic texts of unknown origin, symbolized as "LB." Transliterated in Leiden in the summers of 1950 and 1954 with the permission of Professor F. M. T. de Liagre Böhl and Dr. A. A. Kampman.

London. British Museum. Sargonic texts of unknown origin, symbolized as "BM." Transliterated in London in the summer of 1954 with the permission of Professor C. J. Gadd and Mr. D. J. Wiseman.

New Haven, Conn. Yale University. Nies Babylonian Collection. Pre-Sargonic and Sargonic texts of unknown origin, symbolized as "*BIN* VIII." Transliterated in the spring of 1949 from the originals and from the hand-copies of Dr. George G. Hackman with the permission and cooperation of Dr. Hackman, Professor Ferris J. Stephens, and Professor Albrecht Goetze. Texts to be published by Dr. Hackman in *BIN* VIII. A small, additional, number of Sargonic and Ur III texts transliterated in the spring of 1949 are quoted under the symbol "NBC."

Oxford. Ashmolean Museum. Sargonic texts from Kish, symbolized as "Kish." Transliterated in the summer of 1950 from the originals and from the hand-copies of Professor P. van der Meer with the permission of Professor van der Meer and cooperation of Professor T. Jacobsen, who collated for me some difficult passages in the autumn of 1953. Texts to be published by Professor van der Meer in *OECT*.

Paris. Louvre. Late Sargonic texts of unknown origin, symbolized as "Louvre AO." Transliterated in the summer of 1950 with the permission of Mr. Jean Nougayrol and the authorities of the Louvre Museum.

Philadelphia, Pa. University of Pennsylvania. University Museum. Sargonic texts from Nippur, symbolized as "N." Transliterated from photographs furnished by Professor S. N. Kramer. The large tablet containing the copies of the royal Sargonic inscriptions (PBS V 34 + XV 41) was collated by myself in the spring of 1951.

Urbana, Ill. University of Illinois. Oriental Museum. Ur III texts of unknown origin, symbolized as "Univ. Illinois." Transliterated in the summer of 1940 with the permission of the University authorities.

A small number of additional unpublished texts culled from single sources of varied provenience are quoted in the main body of the *Glossary*.

Here, at home I have received much valuable help from my colleagues in the Oriental Institute. I have enjoyed close collaboration with Professor Thorkild Jacobsen especially in the early stages, while I was still working on the transliteration of the vast Diyala material. Professor A. Leo Oppenheim read an early draft of the manuscript and offered many valuable suggestions. I had the good fortune of being able to discuss with Professor B. Landsberger some of the difficult problems of Old Akkadian lexicography. To all these scholars I owe more than can be expressed in words or gleaned from a casual perusal of the volume.

The recognition of my indebtedness must include the names of François Thureau-Dangin and Arthur Ungnad, whose pioneer work in the early phases of the Mesopotamian civilization serves and will remain to serve as an ideal model for future generations.

I. J. Gelb
November, 1956

ABBREVIATIONS

A — Unpubl. texts in the Oriental Institute, University of Chicago.

AAA — Annals of Archaeology and Anthropology.

ABL — R. F. Harper, Assyrian and Babylonian Letters Belonging to the Kouyunjik Collection of the British Museum (14 vols.; Chicago, 1892-1914).

AJA — American Journal of Archaeology.

AJSL — American Journal of Semitic Languages and Literatures.

AnOr — Analecta Orientalia.

AO — Der alte Orient.

AOB — Altorientalische Bibliothek.

AOF — Archiv für Orientforschung.

AOr — Archiv orientální.

APAW — Abhandlungen der Preussischen Akademie der Wissenschaften.

ARMT — G. Dossin et al., Archives royales de Mari (7 vols., texts in translit.; Paris, 1950-).

Arnold, ABTR — W. R. Arnold, Ancient-Babylonian Temple Records in the Columbia University Library (New York, 1896).

AS — Assyriological Studies.

BA — Beiträge zur Assyriologie und semitischen Sprachwissenschaft.

Bab. — Babyloniaca.

Barton, HLC — G. A. Barton, The Haverford Library Collection of Cuneiform Tablets or Documents from the Temple Archives of Telloh (3 vols.; Philadelphia, 1905-1915).

Barton, MBI — G. A. Barton, Miscellaneous Babylonian Inscriptions (New Haven, 1918).

Barton, RISA — G. A. Barton, The Royal Inscriptions of Sumer and Akkad (New Haven, 1929).

BASOR — Bulletin of the American Schools of Oriental Research.

BE — The Babylonian Expedition of the University of Pennsylvania.

Bedale, STU — C. L. Bedale, Sumerian Tablets from Umma in the John Rylands Library, Manchester (Manchester, 1915).

BER — The Babylonian Expedition of the University of Pennsyl-

	vania. Researches and Treatises.
BIN	Babylonian Inscriptions in the Collection of James B. Nies.
BM	Unpubl. texts in the British Museum.
BMQ	British Museum Quarterly.
BO	Bibliotheca Orientalis.
Boson, TCS	G. Boson, Tavolette cuneiformi sumere degli archivi di Drehem e di Djoha .... (Milano, 1936).
BRM	Babylonian Records in the Library of J. Pierpont Morgan.
BS.	Bûr-Sin.
Cameron, HEI	G. G. Cameron, History of Early Iran (Chicago, 1936).
CCT	Sidney Smith, Cuneiform Texts from Cappadocian Tablets in the British Museum (4 vols.; 1921-1927).
Chiera, STA	E. Chiera, Selected Temple Accounts from Telloh Yokha and Drehem. Cuneiform Tablets in the Library of Princeton University (Princeton, 1922).
Clay, PNCP	A. T. Clay, Personal Names from Cuneiform Inscriptions of the Cassite Period (YOSR I; New Haven, 1912).
CM	Cruciform Monument (CT XXXII 1-4).
Coll. De Clercq	Collection de Clercq par De Clercq avec la collaboration de J. Ménant (7 vols.; Paris, 1888-1911).
Contenau, CHÉU	G. Contenau, Contribution à l'histoire économique d'Umma (Paris, 1915).
Contenau, UDU	G. Contenau, Umma sous la dynastie d'Ur (Paris, 1916).
Cop.	Unpubl. texts in the Antiksamlingen of the Nationalmuseet in Copenhagen.
CRAI	Académie des Inscriptions et Belles-Lettres. Comptes rendus.
Cros, NFT	G. Cros et al., Nouvelles fouilles de Tello (Paris, 1910-1914).
CT	Cuneiform Texts from Babylonian Tablets, etc. in the British Museum.
D	I. J. Gelb, Sargonic Texts from the Diyala Region (MAD I; Chicago, 1952).
D.	Dudu.
Dantinne, QTSU	E. Dantinne, Quelques tablettes sumériennes d'Ur (Huy, no date).
Deimel, PB	A. Deimel, Pantheon Babylonicum (Roma, 1914).
Delaporte, CCBN	L. Delaporte, Catalogue des cylindres orientaux .... de la Bibliothèque Nationale (Paris, 1910).

Delaporte, CCL	L. Delaporte, Catalogue des cylindres .... Louvre (2 vols.; Paris, 1920-1923).
Delitzsch, AHWB	Friedrich Delitzsch, Assyrisches Handwörterbuch (Leipzig, 1896).
DN	Divine name.
DP	Allotte de la Fuÿe, Documents présargoniques (3 vols.; Paris, 1908-1920).
E	Sargonic personal names in MDP XIV (cf. index on pp. 127-131).
EK I-IV	S. Langdon et al., Excavations at Kish (3 vols.; Paris, 1924-1934).
EL	G. Eisser and J. Lewy, Die altassyrischen Rechtsurkunden vom Kültepe (2 vols.; MVAG XXXIII [1928], XXXV/3 [1930]).
Fara	A. Deimel, Die Inschriften von Fara (3 vols.; WVDOG XL [1922], XLIII [1923], XLV [1924]).
Fish, CST	T. Fish, Catalogue of Sumerian Tablets in the John Rylands Library (Manchester, 1932).
FM	I. J. Gelb, Old Akkadian Inscriptions in Chicago Natural History Museum (Fieldiana: Anthropology Vol. 44 Number 2; Chicago, 1955).
FN	Field name.
Frank, SKT	C. Frank, Strassburger Keilschrifttexte in sumerischer und babylonischer Sprache (Berlin and Leipzig, 1928).
Frankfort, CS	H. Frankfort, Cylinder Seals (London, 1939).
G	Sargonic personal names in HSS X (cf. index on pp. xxvii-xliii).
Gadd, EDSA	C. J. Gadd, The Early Dynasties of Sumer and Akkad (London, 1921).
GCCI	Goucher College Cuneiform Inscriptions.
Gelb, HS	I. J. Gelb, Hurrians and Subarians (SAOC XXII; Chicago, 1944).
Gemser, BPN	B. Gemser, De Beteekenis der Persoonsnamen .... (Wageningen, 1924).
Geneva	Unpubl. texts in the Musée d'Art et d'Histoire in Geneva.
De Genouillac, FT	H. de Genouillac, Fouilles de Tello (2 vols.; Paris, 1934-1936).
De Genouillac, Kich	H. de Genouillac, Fouilles françaises d'el-ʾAkhymer. Premières recherches archéologiques à Kich (2 vols.; Paris, 1924-1925).

De Genouillac, TD	H. de Genouillac, La trouvaille de Dréhem .... (Paris, 1911).
De Genouillac, TSA	H. de Genouillac, Tablettes sumériennes archaïques .... (Paris, 1909).
Gesenius, HWAT	W. Gesenius, Hebräisches und aramäisches Handwörterbuch über das Alte Testament (17th ed.; Leipzig, 1921).
GN	Geographic name.
Gordon, SCT	C. H. Gordon, Smith College Tablets .... (Northampton, Mass., 1952).
HSS	Harvard Semitic Series.
IAMN	Istanbul Asariatika Müzeleri neşriyati.
Iraq Mus.	Unpubl. texts in the Iraq Museum.
IS.	Ibbî-Sin.
Ist. Mus. Adab	Unpubl. texts from Adab in the Istanbul Museum.
Ist. Mus. Lagash	Unpubl. texts from Lagash in the Istanbul Museum.
Ist. Mus. Nippur	Unpubl. texts from Nippur in the Istanbul Museum.
ITT I-V	F. Thureau-Dangin et al., Inventaire des tablettes de Tello conservées au Musée Impérial Ottoman (5 vols.; Paris, 1910-1921).
Jacobsen, CTC	T. Jacobsen, Cuneiform Texts in the National Museum, Copenhagen .... (Leiden, 1939).
Janneau, DC	C.-G. Janneau, Une dynastie chaldéenne. Les rois d'Ur (Paris, 1911).
JAOS	Journal of the American Oriental Society.
JCS	Journal of Cuneiform Studies.
Jean, ŠA	C. F. Jean, Šumer et Akkad .... (Paris, 1923).
Jestin, TSŠ	R. Jestin, Tablettes sumériennes de Šuruppak conservées au Musée de Stamboul (Paris, 1937).
JNES	Journal of Near Eastern Studies.
Johns, ADD	C. H. W. Johns, Assyrian Deeds and Documents Recording the Transfer of Property (4 vols., Cambridge and London, 1898-1923).
Johns Hopkins	Unpubl. texts in the Johns Hopkins University in Baltimore.
JRAS	Journal of the Royal Asiatic Society of Great Britain and Ireland.
KAH I-II	L. Messerschmidt, O. Schroeder, Keilschrifttexte aus Assur historischen Inhalts (2 vols.; WVDOG XVI [1911],

	XXVII [1922]).
KAJ	E. Ebeling, Keilschrifttexte aus Assur juristischen Inhalts (WVDOG I [1927]).
KAR	E. Ebeling, Keilschrifttexte aus Assur religiösen Inhalts (2 vols.; WVDOG XXVIII [1919], XXXIV [1923]).
KAV	O. Schroeder, Keilschrifttexte aus Assur verschiedenen Inhalts (WVDOG XXXV [1920]).
Kh.	Unpubl. texts from Khafaje in the Oriental Institute, University of Chicago.
Kish	Unpubl. texts from Kish in the Ashmolean Museum in Oxford.
Krausz, GNBSL	J. Krausz, Die Götternamen in den babylonischen Siegelcylinderlegenden (Leipzig, 1911).
Landsberger, Ana ittišu	B. Landsberger, Die Serie ana ittišu (MSL I; Roma 1937).
Landsberger, Fauna	B. Landsberger, Die Fauna des alten Mesopotamiens. (Abh. d. Sächsischen Akad. d. Wiss. XLII No. VI; Leipzig, 1934).
Langdon, BM	S. H. Langdon, Babylonian Menologies and the Semitic Calendars (London, 1934).
Langdon, TAD	S. Langdon, Tablets from the Archives of Drehem .... (Paris, 1911).
Lau, OBTR	R. J. Lau, Old Babylonian Temple Records (New York, 1906).
LB	Unpubl. texts in the Collection De Liagre Böhl in Leiden.
Legrain, CCC	L. Legrain, Catalogue des cylindres orientaux de la collection Louis Cugnin (Paris, 1911).
Legrain, TRU	L. Legrain, Le temps des rois d'Ur .... (Paris, 1912).
Legrain, UE X	L. Legrain, Seal Cylinders (UE X; Oxford, 1951).
Lenormant, CTC	F. Lenormant, Choix de texts cunéiformes .... (Paris, 1873).
Louvre	Unpubl. texts in the Louvre.
LTBA I-II	L. Matouš, W. von Soden, Die lexikalischen Tafelserien der Babylonier und Assyrer in den Berliner Museen (2 vols.; Berlin, 1933).
lw.	loan word.
M xxviff.	Inscriptions of Man-ištušu in PBS V 34.
MA	Middle Assyrian.
MAD	I. J. Gelb, Materials for the Assyrian Dictionary

	(Chicago, 1952-).
MAOG	Mitteilungen der Altorientalischen Gesellschaft.
Margolis, STD	E. Margolis, Sumerian Temple Documents (New York, 1915).
MAW	Mededeelingen der K. Akademie van Wetenschappen. Afdeeling Letterkunde.
MB	Middle Babylonian.
MCS	Manchester Cuneiform Series.
MDOG	Mitteilungen der Deutschen Orient-Gesellschaft.
MDP	Mémoires de la Délégation en Perse.
Mém.	= MDP (used in MAD II only).
Mi.	Man-ištušu.
MJ	Museum Journal.
MN	Month name.
MO	Man-ištušu Obelisk (MDP II, cf. index on pp. 41-52).
MoN	Mountain name.
Moortgat, VARS	A. Moortgat, Vorderasiatische Rollsiegel. Staatliche Museen zu Berlin (Berlin, 1940).
Morgan, MSP	J. J. M. de Morgan, Mission scientifique en Perse (5 vols.; Paris, 1894-1905).
MSL	Materialien zum sumerischen Lexikon.
MVAG	Mitteilungen der Vorderasiatisch-Aegyptischen Gesellschaft.
N	Unpubl. texts from Nippur in the University Museum, Philadelphia.
NA	New Assyrian.
NB	New Babylonian.
Nakahara, STIUK	Y. Nakahara, The Sumerian Tablets in the Imperial University of Kyoto (Tokyo, 1928).
NBC	Unpubl. texts in the Nies Babylonian Collection, Yale University.
Nesbit, SRD	W. M. Nesbit, Sumerian Records from Drehem (New York, 1914).
Nies, UDT	J. B. Nies, Ur Dynasty Tablets .... (Leipzig, 1920).
Nikolski, Dok.	M. V. Nikolski, Dokumenty khoziaistvennoi otchetnosti .... (2 vols.; Moskva, 1908-1915).
NPN	I. J. Gelb, P. M. Purves, and A. A. MacRae, Nuzi Personal Names (OIP LVII; Chicago, 1943).
NS.	Narâm-Sin.
NT	Unpubl. texts excavated at Nippur after the Second World War, now in the Oriental Institute, University of

	Chicago.
OA	Old Assyrian.
OB	Old Babylonian.
OECT	Oxford Editions of Cuneiform Texts.
OIP	Oriental Institute Publications.
OLZ	Orientalistische Literaturzeitung.
Oppenheim, CCTE	A. L. Oppenheim, Catalogue of the Cuneiform Tablets of the Wilberforce Eames Collation in the New York Public Library (American Oriental Series XXXII; New Haven, 1948).
Orient.	Orientalia.
PBS	Publications of the Babylonian Section of the University of Pennsylvania Museum.
PDTI	M. Ciǧ, H. Kizilyay, A. Salonen, Die Puzriš-Dagan-Texte der Istanbuler Archäologischen Museen I (Annales Academiae Scientiarum Fennicae B 92; Helsinki, 1954).
Pinches, AT	T. G. Pinches, The Amherst Tablets .... (London, 1908).
Pinches, BTBC	T. G. Pinches, The Babylonian Tablets of the Berens Collection (London, 1915).
PN	Personal name.
Pope, SPA	A. U. Pope, A Survey of Persian Art from Prehistoric Times to the Present (6 vols.; London and New York, 1938-1939).
Porada, CPML	E. Porada, The Collection of the Pierpont Morgan Library (2 vols.; New York, 1948).
PS	= PSarg. (used in MAD II only).
PŠ.	Puzur-Inšušinak.
PSarg.	Pre-Sargonic.
PSBA	Proceedings of the Society of Biblical Archaeology.
R xviff.	Inscriptions of Rîmuš in PBS V 34 + PBS XV 41.
R.	Rîmuš.
RA	Revue d'assyriologie et d'archéologie orientale.
Radau, EBH	H. Radau, Early Babylonian History down to the End of the Third Dynasty of Ur (New York, 1899).
Ranke, EBPN	H. Ranke, Early Babylonian Personal Names .... (BER III; Philadelphia, 1905).
Reisner, TUT	G. Reisner, Tempelurkunden aus Tello (Berlin, 1901).
Riftin, SVIAD	A. P. Riftin, Staro-vavilonskie iuridicheskie i administrativnie dokumenty v sobraniakh SSSR (Moskva, 1937).
RLA	Reallexikon der Assyriologie (2 vols.; Berlin, 1928-).

RN	River name.
RO	Rocznik orientalistyczny.
RS	Revue sémitique d'épigraphie et d'histoire ancienne.
RSO	Rivista degli studi orientali.
RT	Recueil des travaux relatifs à la philologie et à l'archéologie égyptiennes et assyriennes.
RTC	F. Thureau-Dangin, Recueil de tablettes chaldéennes (Paris, 1903).
S iff.	Inscriptions of Sargon in PBS V 34 + PBS XV 41.
S.	Sargon of Akkad.
Š.	Šulgi.
SAOC	Studies in Ancient Oriental Civilization.
Sarg.	Sargonic.
De Sarzec, DC	Ernest de Sarzec et al., Découvertes en Chaldée (2 vols.; Paris, 1884-1912).
ŠD.	Šu-Durul.
Škš.	Šar-kali-šarrī.
ŠL	A. Deimel, Šumerisches Lexikon (Roma, 1930-).
SLB	W. F. Leemans et al., Studia ad tabulas cuneiformas collectas ab De Liagre Böhl pertinentia (Leiden, 1952-).
SO	Studia Orientialia.
von Soden, AS	W. von Soden, Das akkadische Syllabar (Analecta Orientalia XXVII; Roma, 1948).
Speleers, CIMC	L. Speleers, Catalogue des intailles et empreintes orientaux des Musées royaux du Cinquantenaire (Bruxelles, 1917).
Speleers, RIAA	L. Speleers, Recueil des inscriptions de l'Asie Antérieure des Musées royaux du Cinquantaire à Bruxelles (Bruxelles, 1925).
ŠS.	Šu-Sin.
Stamm, ANG	J. J. Stamm, Die akkadische Namengebung (MVAG XLIV; Leipzig, 1939).
Stephens, PNC	F. J. Stephens, Personal Names from Cuneiform Inscriptions of Cappadocia (YOSR XIII/1; New Haven, 1928).
TA	Unpubl. texts from Tell Asmar in the Oriental Institute, University of Chicago.
Tallqvist, AGE	K. L. Tallqvist, Akkadische Götterepitheta (SO VII; Helsingfors, 1938).
Tallqvist, APN	K. L. Tallqvist, Assyrian Personal Names (Helsingfors, 1914).

Tallqvist, NBN	K. L. Tallqvist, Neubabylonisches Namenbuch .... (Helsingfors, 1905).
TCL	Musée du Louvre. Textes cunéiformes.
Thompson, DAB	R. Campbell Thompson, A Dictionary of Assyrian Botany (London, 1949).
Thureau-Dangin, RÉC	F. Thureau-Dangin, Recherches sur l'origine de l'écriture cunéiforme (Paris, 1898-1899).
Thureau-Dangin, SAKI	F. Thureau-Dangin, Die sumerischen und akkadischen Königsinschriften (Leipzig, 1907).
TMH	J. Lewy et al., Texte und Materialien der Frau Professor Hilprecht Collection of Babylonian Antiquities im Eigentum der Universität Jena (Leipzig, 1932-).
TN	Temple name.
TTKB	Türk Tarih Kurumu. Belleten.
U	Ur III.
U 1ff.	Ur III personal names in Orient. XXIII-XXIV (Roma, 1927).
UCP	University of California Publications in Semitic Philology.
UE	Joint Expedition of the British Museum and of the Museum of the University of Pennsylvania to Mesopotamia. Ur Excavations.
UET	Ditto. Ur Excavations. Texts.
Ungnad, MAS	A. Ungnad, Materialien zur altakkadischen Sprache (MVAG XX/2; Leipzig, 1916).
Univ. Illinois	Unpubl. texts in the University of Illinois.
Univ. Michigan	Unpubl. texts in the University of Michigan.
VAS	Vorderasiatische Schriftdenkmäler der königlichen Museen zu Berlin.
VAT	Unpubl. texts in the Berlin Museum.
Virolleaud, CC	C. Virolleaud, Comptabilité chaldéenne (Poitiers, 1903).
Walters Art Gall.	Unpubl. PSarg. text in the Walters Art Gallery in Baltimore.
Ward, CPM	W. H. Ward, Cylinders and Other Ancient Cylinder Seals in the Library of J. Pierpont Morgan (New York, 1909).
Ward, SCWA	W. H. Ward, The Seal Cylinders of Western Asia (Washington, 1910).
Winckler, AOF	H. Winckler, Altorientalische Forschungen (3 vols.; Leipzig, 1897-1906).
Wiseman, Alalakh	D. J. Wiseman, The Alalakh Tablets (Occasional Publica-

	tions of the British Institute of Archaeology at Ankara II; London, 1953).
WO	Die Welt des Orients.
Woolley, UE II	C. L. Woolley, The Royal Cemetery (UE II; Oxford, 1934).
WVDOG	Wissenschaftliche Veröffentlichungen der Deutschen Orient-Gesellschaft.
WZKM	Wiener Zeitschrift für die Kunde des Morgenlandes.
Yondorf	Unpubl. texts belonging to the late Milton Yondorf of Chicago.
YOS	Yale Oriental Series.
YOSR	Yale Oriental Series. Researches.
ZA	Zeitschrift für Assyriologie.
ZDMG	Zeitschrift der Deutschen Morgenländischen Gesellschaft.

GLOSSARY

ʾ$_{1-7}$

ʾ$_6$ <u>u</u> "and." See also Lʾ$_1$ ulâ.

Written ù, rarely ú.

Between nouns and phrases:

GN$_1$ ù GN$_2$ (BE I 5)

DN$_1$ ù DN$_2$ (YOS I 10 ii)

bi-ri-šu ú šu-um-šu (Morgan, MSP IV 158, Lullubum)

be-lí ù a-bí (D 191)

SUḪUŠ-su li-zu-ḫa ù ŠE.NUMUN-su li-il-gu-da (BE I 2). Variant ú in AOF III 112, Mari

in KAS+X GN iš$_x$-ar ù URU^{KI} SAG.GIŠ.RA ù BÀD-su Ì.GUL.GUL (S ii)

iš-tum KAS+X.KAS+X su$_4$-nu-ti iš$_x$-ar-ru ù sar-rí-su-nu 3 i-ik-mi-ma (YOS I 10)

PN$_1$ PN$_2$ ù PN$_3$ (D 298)

PN$_1$ ù PN$_2$ ù PN$_3$ (HSS X 206)

DN$_1$ ù DN$_2$ ù DN$_3$ (BE I 1)

1 PN ù 1 DAM-zu ù 2 DUMU-su (D 246).

Beginning a sentence:

ù LA.BUR.ŠIR^{KI} a-ti-ma ti-a-am-tim SAG.GIŠ.RA (S ii, viii)

ù ba-ni ENGAR.ENGAR li-zu-ur-ma (HSS X 5 rev. and elsewhere in this text).

ʾ$_7$ <u>iaum</u> "mine."

Sarg. and Ur III PN's:

Li-bu-uš-ì-a-um "may mine (i.e. my child) breathe" (De Sarzec, DC II Pl. LII). Parallels: Lippuš-ilum and Luppuš-ilum "may he / I breathe, O god!," quoted in Stamm, ANG p. 172. Interpr. as -ni-a-um also possible

| I-a-um MAR.TU (UET III 566, U)

| Ià-a-um MAR.TU (ibid. 1678).

ʾ$_1$ʾ$_6$ <u>û</u>, see L ûlū.

ʾ$_1$ʾ$_7$ <u>aj</u>, <u>ê</u> with verb forming a Prohibitive "may not ....."

aj, written A before a vowel (in reality, weak consonant):

a i-ti-in /ajiddin/ "may he not give" (HSS X 5:21)

[a] i-ti-na-šum (R xviii, xxiv; UET I 274 iv, NS.; 276 ii, NS.)

a ib-ra "may it not hunger" (Cop. 10055)

a i-si-ir (ZA IV 406, Gutium)

a e-ru-ub (HSS X 12:9)

a! u-sa-zi-iq (UET I 275 iv, NS.)

a u-gi-il (UET I 276 ii, NS.)

a [u]?-si-si-ra (ibid.)

a el-bi-ma (ibid.). Meaning unknown

a GUB /ajizziz/ (UET I 276 ii). See also e GUB below

a ù-[....] (MDP IV Pl. 2 v).

ê, written E before a consonant:

e tal-li-ik (D 315:14)

e da-ti-in (D 315:20).

Exceptions:

a daq-bí (JRAS 1932 p. 296:10)

e GUB (PBS V 34 x, Lugalzagesi; S ix, xi; R xviii, xxiv; UET I 274 iv, NS., all in late copies). See also a GUB above.

aj "where?"

Sarg. and Ur III PN's:

A-a-pum (Geneva MAH 16459 rev. i)

Á-a-pum or [X]-id-a-pum (Kish 1930, 177g)

A-a-bí (Louvre AO 11337; 11345)

A-a-bi (BE III 90:10, U)

PN ši A-a-be (D)

What is the meaning of Maš-maš-a-a-bi translit. in ITT IV p. 77, 7847, U?

NU.BANDA IGI A-i-ti-su /Aj-iddinšu/ (ITT I 1439 rev.). For NU.BANDA IGI cf. RTC 127 iii etc.

$ʾ_2ʾ_6ʾ_7$? awājum "to speak."

Sarg. and Ur III PN's:

I-wi-DINGIR (MDP XXVIII 524). Cf. also PN's with I-mi- under $ʾ_xMʾ_7$

I-wi-mu-ti MAR.TU (A 5508, U).

awatum "word."

be-lí ʾà-wa-a-ti (Pl.) li-[iš?-m]e? (A 708)

e-ni ʾà-wa-at-zu i-ti-iš i-da-ḫa-az (Ist. Mus. Lagash 11001). Context ununderstandable.

$ʾ_1ʾ_7$B ajjābiš "inimically."

ì-n[u] ŠU.NIGÍN ma-[ta-tim] .... [a]-a-bi-iš [ib]-ba-al-ki-da-an-ni-ma (CT XXXII 1 ii, CM).

$ʾ_6ʾ_3$D wêdum "single," "unique."

Sarg. and Ur III PN's:

We-tum (D 100). Interpr. as a PN doubtful, but cf. PN We-e-tum in an unpubl. OB tablet TA 1930, 610. For wêdum, wêdūtum in OA and Mari cf. discussion in ARMT VI p. 123

We-du-um-li-bur (ZA XII 345, U).

ʾ$_1$ʾ$_2$L <u>âlum</u> "city."

Written logographically as URU$^{(KI)}$ or syllabically.

Kiš^{KI} a-ša-rí-su i-ni (ù) URU^{KI}-lam$_x$(LAM+KUR) u-sa-ḫi-su-ni "he restored Kiš to its place (and) caused them to settle the city" (S iv, ix)

a-na URU^{KI}-lim zu-da-rí-ib (JRAS 1932 p. 296:20)

a-na-lim-ma ki a-la-kam "when I will come to the city" (JRAS 1932 p. 296:34)

[a-na] URU$^{⌈KI⌉?}$-lim (A 708)

x ŠE in a-lí-im PN ú-šu-ri-dam (Louvre AO 8959). Interpr. uncertain

URU^{KI}.URU^{KI}-su-nu (R xvii; RA VII 104, Mi.)

URU^{KI}.URU^{KI}-su-ni (R xix)

URU^{KI}-su-ni (R xx, xxi)

in URU^{KI}-su-ni (R xix, xxi)

in a-ša-ar URU (R xxiii, xxv)

in URU^{KI}-su (MDP IV Pl. 2 iv)

URU^{KI} UNUG^{KI} (S ii)

URU^{KI}-lam Si?-ku?-ma-núm KI-su e-ni (UET I 275 v, NS.)

a-na A-ga-dè^{KI} URU^{KI}-su (MDP VI Pl. 1, 1, NS.).

Compounds:

For abu âlim cf. under abum

PN LÚ.URU (Fish, CST 5; ITT V p. 37, 9383)

x GIŠ.GIGIR URU^{KI} (HSS X 38 iii x+9; similarly in HSS X 65:4; etc.)

x TÚG.A.SU URU (RTC 208 twice)

PN UGULA URU (FM 4:10; 6:1).

Sarg. and Ur III GN's:

in m[i]-iḫ-rí URU-Gi-tim "(field) in front of the city Kite" (FM 25:9). Cf. URU-Ki-dè^{KI} in Sumer III 52 No. 61, OB geogr. lists

A-al-^{d}Šu-^{d}EN.ZU (RA V 99 ii, U)

Cf. ŠRK šarrākum.

PSarg., Sarg., and Ur III PN's:

PN's of the type listed below have been the subject of much discussion. Schneider, Muséon LIX 68ff. and Oppenheim, CCTE p. 180 n. 6 take for granted that the element alī and the like stands for ilī and the like. Stamm, ANG pp. 165, 285f., 314 interprets the great majority of PN's with the elements alum, ali, al by translating them as "where?"; only on pp. 88, 90 does he consider the possibility that âlum "city" occurs in some of the PN's. For other opinions cf. Stamm, ANG p. 286, also Nyberg in Archiv für Religionswissenschaft XXXV (1938) 328ff., 386, who operates with a divine element ᶜal(um). Actually, a large proportion of PN's listed by Stamm and below, esp. those with ali, must be interpreted by taking the element in question to mean "where?." The clearest of these is the PN A-li-šu-ni (below) which must mean "where are they?" (on -šuni = -šunu cf. MAD II 173) on the basis of comparison with a-li šu-nu, a-li šu-ú, a-li at-ta, etc. (Delitzsch, AHWB p. 66). On the other side, a separate group of PN's must be interpreted as containing the element âlum, âlī, âl "(deified) city." Cf. Lú-^{d}A-lí (below); A-lí-li-bur (below) with A-lí-lu-mu-ur (Stamm, ANG p. 86, OB), URU-lu-mur (ibid., NB), and A-li-a-mur (MDP XVIII 31, OB); I-bí-^{d}URU^{KI} (below); A-lu-a-lí (below); A-lu-ì-lum (below); ^{d}Šul-gi-a-al (below) with ^{d}Šul-gi-URU.MU (U 915 passim); Ia-ku-un-a-li (Bauer, Die Ostkanaanäer p. 92) with Ia-ku-un-A-šar (ibid.) and A-li-a-sar (below); Be-lí-a-lí (below) with Ì-lí-a-li (A 21884, OB) and Ì-lí-a-lí (UET V 165, OB); Šu-um-ru-uṣ-a-li (UCP X p. 169:12, OB) with Šu-um-ru-uṣ-Sin (p. 94:23). The PN's in our lists are not subdivided into two groups because of the difficulties in assigning some PN's to one group or another.

Written alum.

PSarg., Sarg., and Ur III PN's:

Ab-ba-a-lum (UET III 1096, U)

A-lu-ì-lum (JRAS 1930 p. 602, PSarg.)

A-lum-BA (DP 116 v+, PSarg.)

A-lum-BÀD (EK IV Pl. XLV iv, PSarg.)

A-lum-DÙG (CT XXXII 7 iv, PSarg.). Cf. A-lí-DÙG (below) and A-al-DÙG (Stephens, PNC p. 12)

A-lum-dan (DP 116, PSarg.)

Pi_x(KA+KÁR)-ša-ḫa-lum /Pišaḫ-alum/ or PÙ.ŠA-ḫa-lum /Puzur-ḫâlum/ (RTC 397 i, U)

Bí-ša-ḫa?(wr. za)-lum (U 559 = Orient. IV p. 59, translit. only)

Da-ti-na-LUM (Legrain, CCC No. 55). Unexplainable

Ga-zu-a-lum (D+). Cf. Ga-zu-^{d}MES (Oppenheim, CCTE p. 187, U)

Ì-lí-a-lum (Barton, HLC III p. 47+, U). Cf. Ì-lí-a-lí (UET V 165:13 OB)

Ku-ku-a-lum (ITT IV p. 87, 8023, U). For ^{d}Ku-ku cf. AnOr XIX No. 251

Nu-ḫa-lum (Pinches, AT p. 180+, U). Cf. Nu-ḫi-lum (U 2406)

ZU-a-lum (D).

Written ali.

Sarg. and Ur III PN's:

A-bí-a-lí (U 59+)

A-ḫi-a-lí (Nikolski, Dok. II p. 133, U)

A-ḫu-a-lí (ITT II p. 48, 933, U)

A-ḫu-wa-lí (ITT II p. 10, 650, U). Cf. Šu-wa-li

A-lí-a-bí (BE III 134, U)

A-lí-a-aḫ (MDP XVIII 31)

A-li-aḫ (Nies, UDT 15, U)

A-lí-a-aḫ (OIP XXXVII 50, U)

A-lí-aḫ (Jean, ŠA CLVI rev., U)

A-li-a-ḫu (D+)

A-lí-a-ḫi (UET III 1041 ii, U)

A-li-A-sar (G)

A-li-be-lí (D). Cf. Al-be-lí in Stephens, PNC p. 12

A-lí-DÙG (MDP XIV 72 iv; BIN V 302:37, U; CT XXXII 34 ii, U)

A-li-en-ni (D)

A-li-KUG.BABBAR-si (D)

A-lí-li-bur (AnOr I 292:8, U)

A-lí-ni-su (Nies, UDT 45 rev., U)

A-lí-ni-šu (U 192+)

A-li-šu-ni (Oppenheim, CCTE p. 180, U). Cf. A-lí-šu-nu in UET V p. 30, OB

A-lí-šu-ni (Nikolski, Dok. II 364, U)

A-li-tu-ru-uḫ (D+)

A-lí-ú-bí (TCL V 6038 rev. iii, U)

A-li-ú-da (G+)

A-lí-ú-da (ITT II/1 p. 6, 618, U)

A-li-um-mi (Reisner, TUT 159 iii, U)

A-lu-a-lí (3 NT 796 i, U)

A-na-ḫa-lí (RTC 290, U; ITT II/1 p. 21, 748 twice, U)

A-ŠI-a-lí (D)

Be-lí-a-lí (VAT 16441 i)

Pi_x(KA+KÁR)-ša-ḫa-li /Pišaḫ-ali/ or PÙ.ŠA-ḫa-li /Puzur-ḫâli/ (Pinches, AT 61, U)

Pi_x-ša-ḫa-lí (TCL II 5498 ii, U; Fish, CST p. 159 i, U)

I-sar-a-lí-iš-zu (A 5600). Parallel to [I]-sar-ma-ti-iš-zu (E)

Lú-^{d}A-lí (Nies, UDT 58:159, U)

PÙ.ŠA-a-lí (Orient. XVIII 27, U)

Rí-a-li(m)-zu, cf. under $R^{\prime}_{4}{}^{\prime}_{7}$

Šu-wa-li (UET III 936, U). Cf. A-ḫu-wa-lí.

Written al.

PSarg., Sarg., and Ur III PN's:

Al-ì-lí (D). Cf. A-al-DÙG (Stephens, PNC p. 12)

Al-ì-li (BIN VIII 46 i, PSarg.)

^{d}Šul-gi-a-al (TMH n.F. I/II 157). Cf. ^{d}Šul-gi-URU.MU in U 915 passim.

Written URU.

Sarg. PN:

I-bí-^{d}URU$^{\ulcorner KI \urcorner}$ (G). Cf. also GN I-bí-URU^{KI} in MO A xv etc.

ʾ$_1$ʾ$_6$L <u>awīlum</u>, <u>abīlum</u> "man" (homo).

Written logographically as LÚ or syllabically.

The interpretation of abīlum as awīlum "man" rather than aplum "heir" is based on the w/b interchange in the Ur III PN's. For this phonetic change cf. MAD II 165.

a-bi-lum a-na a-mu-te ù-la e-bi-iš? "a man should not make (the statue) into columns?" (MDP II p. 63 ii; XIV p. 20 ii). Doubtful

LÚ?-lam na-ga-ra-am (UET I 276 i, NS.)

LÚ-lam? lam-nam (MDP XIV 90 rev.)

PN la ḫa-bi-el a-wi-lim "the non-oppressor of man" (YOS IX 62, Dêr)

x LÚ in KAS+X i-ik-mi (PBS V 36 x+iii, NS.).

Sarg. PN's:

A-bìl-dan (MO)

A-bìl-GI (MO+).

Ur III PN's:

A-bìl-DÍM (CT I 2 ii, U). Or A-bìl-kin$_x$

A-bìl-ki-in (A 5646, U)

Á-bí-la (U 69; Barton, HLC III p. 13)

Á-bí-la-a (U 70; Barton, HLC III p. 13)

Á-bí-la-núm (U 72; Barton, HLC III p. 13). Doubtful

Á-KA-la-núm (Barton, HLC III p. 12). Cf. A-wi-la-núm (TA 1930, 641, OB) and A-wi-la-nu-um (TA 1931, 263, OB). Doubtful

Á-bí-la-ša (U 73+)

Á-wi-la-ša (UET III p. 5)

A-wi-la-ša (Barton, HLC Pl. 12, 52 rev. twice)

Á-bí-la-ti (Reisner, TUT 212)

Á-bí-la-tum (U 74)

Á-bí-lum (U 75; Barton, HLC III p. 13)

A-bi-il-ì-lí (Boson, TCS 371)

Á-bí-lí (U 77+; UET III p. 5)

A-wi-lí (UET III 1410)

Á-wi-lí (UET III 1109)

| Á-bí-lí-a (U 78+; UET III p. 5)
| A-wi-lí-a (AnOr I 295 iv).

ʾ$_7$ʾ$_6$^{M} <u>ûmum</u> "day."

Written logographically as UD or syllabically.

in UD 1 (MDP XIV p. 12 v)

šu 1 UD (D 229 passim)

Á UD.1.KAM (ITT I 1306)

Á 24 UD (ITT I 1450)

KASKAL^{KI} ⌈UD⌉-su (ZA IV 406, Gutium). Cf. ḫa-ra-an ú-ma-ka-al in RA VIII 65 ii 7, OB

u-me-iš-ša = ûmiš-ša "in her day," "then she ...." (Kish 1930, 143 rev., in difficult context).

<u>inûme/i</u> = in ûme/i in Constr. St., "on the day that ....," "when."

Writing with ì not expected, probably in imitation of ì-nu "when":

ì-nu-me GN's i-gi-ru-uš (MDP XIV p. 10 i)

ì-nu-mi PN PA.TE.SI-ki Iš-nun^{KI} "when PN was ensi of I.," literally "on the day of PN the ensi of I." (UCP IX p. 205, 83 iii)

i-nu-mi Za-ri-ku-um PA.TE.SI (MDP XVIII 219 rev., U).

<u>inûmišu</u> = in ûmišu "in his day," "then he ....":

iš-tum KAS+X.KAS+X su$_4$-nu-ti iš$_x$-ar-ru .... in u-mi-su .... ib-ni "after he won these battles .... then he built (a temple)" (YOS I 10 ii, NS.)

in UD-mi-šu-ma "then" (CT XXXII 2 iv, CM)

In the same context we find ì-nu-šu, under ʾ$_4$N inum.

Ur III PN:

ì-nu-me (ITT IV p. 12, 7125).

<u>ûmišam</u> "daily."

ù-mi-sá-am ú-gi-in-šum "(sacrifices) daily he established for him" (MDP IV Pl. 2 ii).

<u>ûmšum</u> "daily."

5400 GURUŠ u-um!-šum NINDA KÚ "x men daily eat bread" (S vi, collated).

[ʾ$_1$ʾ$_7$^{N} <u>ajjânum</u>.]

Ur III PN:

A-a-nu-um ensi of Umma (RA XXXII 130). Almost surely a mistake for A-a-kal-la.

ʾ$_4$ʾ$_7$^{N} <u>ênum</u> "eye."

1 ....-tum ša-at e-nim "(an object) for the eye" (MDP XIV 7 rev.). Translation doubtful

e-nam la-?tim-dam (MDP XIV 90). Doubtful

a-ti e-ni-a la da-mu-ru "as long as you have not seen me" (RA XXIII 25 i 77).

<u>nišî ênim</u> "favored."

Sarg. PN's:

Ni-se$_{11}$-e-ni-sa (RA XXIV 96+)

Ni-se$_{11}$-e-ni-su (D+).

ʾ$_1$ʾ$_6$R <u>urrum</u> "morning," "light."

ur-rí tam-ḫi-e "mornings and evenings" (MDP IV Pl. 2 ii).

Sarg. and Ur III PN's:

Ba-za-ú-ri (ITT II 2 p. 44, 5751, U). For ^{d}Ba-za cf. Kur-ti-^{d}Ba-za (U 1863)

| Da-an-ú-ri (ITT I p. 18, 1277)

| Dan-úr-ri (RA XIX 42 No. 86 rev., U)

Ú-da-ur$_4$-ra (HSS IV 32 rev., U).

ʾ$_1$ʾ$_7$R <u>ajarum</u> "flower." Cf. also below.

Sarg. PN's:

A-ar-DINGIR (MO+)

A-ar-É-a (MO+)

Be-lí-a-ar (D+)

^{d}EN.ZU-a-ar (MO).

ʾ$_1$ʾ$_7$R? <u>ejarum</u>?

Sarg. PN:

E-ar-DINGIR (D). Is this a scribal error or a dialectal form of ajarum? See above.

ʾ$_6$ʾ$_x$R <u>wuʾurum</u> "to send," "to command."

a-ti PA.TE.SI la ù-wa-e-ru-uš "as long as I have not sent the ensi" (HSS X 12:11). Interpr. as 1st pers. is more plausible than as 3rd pers. because of the spelling with ù- (not u-).

<u>tîrtum</u> "command."

i-na ti-ir-ti DN be-lí-šu (Speleers, RIAA 4 ii, Dêr).

ʾ$_x$ʾ$_6$R.

Sarg. and Ur III PN's:

E-wa-ri (A 5847, U). Cf. È-ba-ri

I-wa-ru-um (D+). Cf. I-ba-ru-um.

ʾ$_x$ʾ$_x$R?

Ur III RN:

ÍD E-ur-tum (PBS XV 28:1, 3).

ʾ$_1$ʾ$_1$S <u>aʾâsum</u> "myrtle." Cf. Arabic ʾâsum "myrtle."

x (MA.NA) ŠIM a-á-zum (D 286:4). Cf. ʾ$_x$Sʾ$_x$ asaʾum?.

ʾ$_6$ʾ$_6$T?

Ur III PN's:

Wa-wa-tum (Fish, CST p. 74)

Wa-wa-ti (Fish, CST 328; TCL II 5572). Cf. Ba-ba-ti.

ʾ$_1$B abum "father."

Written syllabically and very rarely logographically as AB.BA, AD.DA, and AD.

maḫ-rí-iš ^{d}En-líl á-bí-su (Böhl, MAW Letterkunde 76B No. 9 p. 12)

a-bi [Sa]r-ru-GI (CT XXXII 1 ii, CM)

a-na PN be-lí ù a-bí (D 191)

a-na PN a-bí ù be-lí (A 4746)

PN? a-pù-su (FM 36:28). Doubtful

ù-la a-bí ad-da (EK III Pl. XI W. 1929, 160).

Ur III GN's:

A-bí-ba-na^{KI} (CT XXXII 19 i)

Maš-gán-a-bí^{KI} (CT XXXII 20 i; 21 vi; 22 vi).

PSarg. and Sarg. PN's:

A-a-pum (Geneva MAH 16459 rev. i). For similar PN's cf. under ʾ$_1$ʾ$_7$ aj "where?"

A-bí-AN.NA (BE I Pl. VII ix)

A-bí-ap-sum$_6$(=šum) (CT I 1a)

A-bí-DA (TMH V p. 14+, PSarg.; MO+)

A-bí-URUDU (TMH V 35 ii, PSarg.)

A-bí-DÍM (RTC 137 i). Or A-bí-kin$_x$

A-bí-DINGIR-su (RTC 230)

A-bí-DÙG (D+)

A-bí-ì-lí (D)

A-bi-ì-lí (ITT II/2 p. 20, 4360, translit. only)

A-bí-i-sar (RTC 169)

A-bí-KUR (E)

A-bí-la-za-ar (D). Doubtful

⌈A⌉-bí-NUMUN-Ba-si-in (D). Doubtful

⌈A⌉?-bí-sa-[liq]? (D)

A-bí-^{d}Tišpak (D+)

A-bí-UR.SAG (D+)

A-bí-za-[ki]? (D)

A-bí-su (D+)

A-bu-a (G)

A-bu-a-bi (ITT II/2 p. 21, 4366, translit. only)

A-pù-BÀD (BE I Pl. VII vii)

A-bu-BALA (Nikolski, Dok. II 35 ii)

A-pù-DÙG (E)

A-bu-GABA (E). Cf. also AD.DA-GABA below

A-pù-GABA (OIP XIV 24, PSarg.)

A-pù-ì-lum (BE I Pl. VII iiif.+)

A-bu-li (G)

A-bu-lum (G+)

A-pù-lum (G+)

A-pù-DINGIR (G+)

A-bu-na (D)

A-pù-sa-tu (D+)

Be-lí-a-pum (D+)

Ì?-lí-a-bí (FM)

I-ti-na-pum (BIN VIII 166)

Pù-^{d}A-bi (LB 972 ii)

Pù-A-bi (E). Cf. Pù-AD below

PÙ.ŠA-^{d}A-bi (D). Cf. also PÙ.ŠA-AD.DA below

PU.ŠA-A-bi (D; U 451+; UET III p. 8, U)

PÙ.ŠA-ra-bí (HSS IV 86, U)

PÙ.ŠA-ra-a-bí (Reisner, TUT 204, U)

Su?-gír-a-bí (E)

Ur-^{d}A-bi (D).

Selected Ur III PN's:

A-bí-a-mu-ti MAR.TU (Legrain, TRU 267 twice)

A-bí-a-ti (TCL V 6047 i passim)

A-bí-e-lum (U 71)

A-bí-DINGIR (U 61)

A-bí-iš-ki-in MAR.TU (TCL II 5508 i)

A-bi-^{d}UTU-ši (UET III 1034 rev. i)

A-bu-um-^{d}AMAR-^{d}EN.ZU (PDTI 541)

A-bu-DINGIR (U 48; PDTI 556)

A-bu-um-DINGIR (U 52+)

A-bu-ì-lum (RTC 388)

A-bu-um-ì-lum (RTC 386 rev.)

A-bu-um-DINGIR.RA (PDTI 407)

A-bu-um-DINGIR-lum (ITT II/1 868 rev.)

A-bu-DÙG (U 50)

A-KA-da-ab (ITT IV p. 63, 7610)

Ab-bu-na (ITT III 5044)

A-bu-ni (U 53+)

A-pù-ni (Reisner, TUT 208 rev.)

A-bu-um (U 51+)
A-pum (UET III 291+)
A-bu-šu-ni (BE III 135 rev.)
DINGIR-ma-a-bí? (A 4979)
^{d}EN.ZU-a-bí-šu (AnOr VII p. 23)
^{d}EN.ZU-a-bu-šu (AnOr VII p. 23+; U 990)
^{d}EN.ZU-a-bu-um (UET III p. 13)
^{d}EN.ZU-a-bu (ibid.)
PÙ.ŠA-a-bi, see under Sarg. PN's.

Written a-ba in Sarg. and Ur III PN's:

A-ba-^{d}Da-di (Ist. Mus. Adab 771; Nies, UDT 58:196, U)
A-ba-Da-di (Reisner, TUT 152 iii 1; 159 ii 11, U)
A-ba-DINGIR (E; ITT V p. 39, 9450)
A-ba-e_{11}-lí (ITT II/1 p. 16, 721, U)
A-ba-GAL (Contenau, CHÉU 100 ii, U)
A-ba-GI (G+). Cf. also ^{d}A-ba-ZI/GI in BIN IX 387:2, OB
A-ba-GI_{4} (Pinches, AT p. 15)
A-ba-na-da (YOS IV 14, U)
A-ba-na-ak-túm (UET III 1394, U)
A-ba-šu-na (Barton, HLC II 60 iv, U; CT III 6 vi, U)
A-ba-^{d}UTU (Reisner, TUT 160 vi, U)
DINGIR-a-ba (G+)
DINGIR-su-a-ba (G+)
$Eš_{4}$-dar?-a-ba (BIN VIII 259)
Nu-úr-a-ba (RA XIX 40 No. 35, U)
Šu-a-ba (Fish, CST p. 159 ii, U). Cf. below.

Written AB.BA.

Ur III PN's:

AB.BA-ga-da (Oppenheim, CCTE p. 181). Cf. possibly AD.DA-ga-da below
Šu-AB.BA (Contenau, CHÉU 38 rev.; PDTI 180). Cf. above.

Written AD.DA.

Sarg. and Ur III PN's:

AD.DA-GABA MAR.TU (Fish, CST 728 i, U). Cf. also A-bu-GABA above
AD.DA-ga-da (U 227+). Cf. possibly AB.BA-ga-da above
AD.DA-na-wi-ir (ITT V 6787, U)
AD.DA-na-bi-ir (U 232; BIN V 106:3, U)
AD.DA-na-bìr (HSS IV 65, U)
AD.DA-na-PIRIG (CT VII 34, 18409 rev.; X 28 ii, U)
PÙ.ŠA-AD.DA (G+). Cf. also PÙ.ŠA-^{d}A-bi above.

Written AD.

PSarg., Sarg., and Ur III PN's:

Nu-úr-AD (Reisner, TUT 157 ii, U). Or Nûr-Ad(ad)

Pù-AD (Woolley, UE II Pl. 191 U 10939, PSarg.). Misread as Shub-ad and the like. Cf. Pù-A-bi above

Šu-AD.MU (MO; Delaporte, CCL II A 206, U)

^{d}Šul-gi-AD.MU (U 911).

abu âlim "elder of a city."

PN$_1$ DUMU PN$_2$ a-bi URU NIM^{KI} (MO D xii)

Cf. PN AB.BA URU of Lagaš (ITT I p. 29, 1461; II/2 p. 34, 4616; 4624, U; similarly V 9320, U)

Cf. PN AD.DA URU (UET II Pl. XLVII 25 ii, PSarg.)

Cf. also n. on šîbum.

ʾ$_x$B abum (meaning unknown).

Ur III MN:

NÍG.DÍB A-bu-um-MA (UET III 244; Univ. Illinois 48)

NÍG.EZEM.MA A-bu-um-MA (UET III 1015)

^{ITI}A-bi (UET III 20). Cf. ^{ITI}A-bi-i in A 21935, OB.

ʾ$_x$B? abîtum (a plant).

Sarg. and Ur III PN:

A-bí-tum (D)
A-bi-tum (UET III 1241, U; 1498 rev. i, U)
Á-bí-tum (AnOr VII 70 rev., U) = Á-bí-la-tum in No. 71 rev.?

ʾ$_x$B? abutum? (a leather object).

^{KUŠ}a-bu-tum (RA XVIII 62, Voc. Prat.).

ʾ$_{3-5}$BB, see DBB? dubbubum?

ʾ$_6$BD, see ʾ$_6$BT?

ʾ$_x$BD?

Ur III Amorite PN:

E-bi-da-nu-um (UET III 566).

ʾ$_6$BG?

wa-ba-g[u?-um]? (D 274 rev., school text?). Very doubtful.

ʾ$_x$BḪ nâbiḫum (an ornament).

Akk. lw. in Ur III Sum.:

na-bí-ḫu-um of gold (UET III p. 133 passim). Also in TA 1930, 694, OB.

nêbaḫum (a girdle).

1 TÚG ne-ba-ḫu-um (MDP XXVIII 526 passim, U?). Cf. NB nêbeḫu.

ʾ$_x$BK?

Ur III PN:

I-bu-ku-um (UET III 11)

| I-bu-kum (MDP XXVIII 410 rev.).

$^{\text{ʾ}}_{1}$BL, see $^{\text{ʾ}}_{1}{}^{\text{ʾ}}_{6}$L awīlum.

$^{\text{ʾ}}_{1}$BL? <u>šâbulum</u> "dry."

Ur III PN:

Ša-bu-lum (JCS VII 106 ii 16 = A 2790 ii). Cf. also NPN p. 315.

$^{\text{ʾ}}_{6}$BL <u>wabālum</u> "to carry hither," "to bring." See also TBL tabālum.

wabālum grain, flour, garments, trees, chariots, etc.:

u-bíl (HSS X 65:7; 92:6; 94:4; 108:20; 112 x+8; 118:7; 150:3?; 160 iv x+4; D 169 ii; 318:13; MDP XIV 8; BIN VIII 215; 216; 220; 247)

u-bí-lam (FM 33:52)

a-na GN u-bí-lam-ma (MDP VI Pl. 1, 1, NS.)

u-ub-lam (A 708)

ù-bi-lam (Louvre AO 8960 rev.)

u-ub-lu, Subj. (D 169 iii)

ù-bi-lu-nim, Pl. (Louvre AO 8960 rev.)

u-ub?-lu (BIN VIII 122)

ub-lu (HSS X 168 rev. x+18)

u-ba-al (HSS X 71:5)

PN wa-bíl-si-in (FM 36:21)

PN [w]a-bíl-su (FM 36:23).

<u>šûbulum</u> "to send":

li-se$_{11}$-bi-lam (HSS X 10:14; 11:6)

ni-se$_{11}$-bí-lam (D 290 rev. x+7)

lu-sa?-bí-la?-kum and lu-sa-[bí?-la]?-kum (EK III Pl. XI W. 1929, 160). Doubtful

[su]-bí-lam, Impv. (ITT I 1080)

su-bí-lim, Impv. (D 185)

x MA.NA KUG.BABBAR .... šu-bi-lam .... la du-ša-ba-lam (NBC 5378, U, soon to be published by Sollberger).

<u>panî wabālum</u> "to give pardon":

ma-ma-na ba-ni-su ù-la u-ba-al "he does not give pardon to anybody" (S xii, xv).

Sarg. and Ur III PN's:

DINGIR-wa-bíl (Fish, CST p. 160 ix, U)

| ì-lí-bi-la-ni (D+)
| ì-lí-bí-la-ni (RTC 245; U 1623)

| U-bíl-Eš$_{4}$-dar (CT XXI 1+)
| Ù-bil-Eš$_{4}$-dar, f.n. (ITT III 6564, U)

U-bìl-ga-zu (MO+).

<u>muttabbilum</u>.

Sarg. and Ur III PN's:

Be-lí-mu-da-bíl (2 NT 618)
DINGIR-mu-da-bíl (Delaporte, CCBN No. 91, U; OIP XLIII 142, U)
DINGIR-mu-ta-bíl (CT XXI 1c, Dêr)
DINGIR-mu-tab-bíl (TCL II 5498 ii, U).

ʾ$_x$BL á-bíl-tum, see TPL? tapiltum?

ʾ$_x$BL abullum "gate."

Ur III GN:

A-bu-la-AD^{KI} (MDP X 125). To be interpreted perhaps as /Abull-Ad/ "gate of Adad" on comparison with KÁ.GAL-Ad^{KI} ḪUR.SAG Ki-maš-KA (Thureau-Dangin, SAKI p. 70 vi 21, Gudea) and KÁ.GAL-^{d}U (KAV 92:14f.).

ʾ$_1$BN abnum "stone."

Written logographically only.

sa-tu-e a-bar-ti ti-a-am-tim sa-bil-tim NA$_4$.NA$_4$-su-nu MI i-bu-l[am-ma] (M xxvi)

in sa-tu-su-nu NA$_4$.NA$_4$ E.SIG-im? i-bu-lam-ma (MDP VI Pl. 1, 1, NS.)

Elsewhere only NA$_4$ occurs

Cf. also NA$_4$ KUG.BABBAR "stone of silver" used for measuring (FM 36:19).

ʾ$_4$BR šûburum "to cause to cross."

ti-a-am-tim sa-bil-tim MÁ.MÁ GIŠ.LA-e u-sa-PI-ir (M xxvii; UET I 274 iv, NS.). This use of PI not expected in Ur; read perhaps u-sa-wi-ir and cf. Šʾ$_6$R.

abartum "the other side."

URU^{KI}.URU^{KI} a-bar-ti ti-a-am-tim (RA VII 104, Mi.)

sa-tu-e a-bar-ti ti-a-am-tim (M xxvi).

Sarg. GN:

in A-⌈bar⌉-tim (HSS X 25 ii).

nêberum "crossing."

Ur III GN's:

Ne-bi-ru-um^{KI} (Orient. XLVII 17)

Ne-bi-ir-^{d}Šul-gi^{KI} (BE III 36; cf. also translit. "Ne-bi-ir-dingir!-^{d}Šul-gi-ra" in PDTI 407).

ʾ$_6$BR ubarum "friend."

Sarg. and Ur III PN's:

U-bar (U 1107; UET III p. 29, U; Fish, CST p. 159 iii, v, U)
U-bar-um (U 1109+)
U-ba-ru-um (D+)
U-bar-ru-um (D+)

U-bar-A-a (BE III 103 ii, U)

U-bar-É-a (UET III p. 29, U)
U-bar-^{d}EN.ZU (ITT II 1 p. 9, 638, U)
U-bar-Eš$_{4}$-dar (UET III p. 29, U)
U-bar-ni (Reisner, TUT 204 rev.+, U)
U-bar-ni-a (TMH n.F. I/II 170, U).

ubartum "friend" (Fem.).
Sarg. and Ur III PN's:
U-bar-tum (D+; U 1110+)
U-bar-ti RA.GABA (Pinches, BTBC p. 93:15, U).

ʾ$_{6}$BR wubburum.
Ur III PN:
Wu-bu-ru-um (U 2533). Cf. Ubburu in Holma, Die assyrisch-babyl. Personennamen der Form Quttulu p. 23
Wu-bu-ru (Nikolski, Dok. II 476 rev.; Orient. XVIII 7:10).

ʾ$_{x}$BR? abrum?
Akk. lw. in Ur III Sum.:
áb-ru-um-ŠÈ (UET III 905)
áb-ru-MA DÍB.BA (Oppenheim, CCTE N 4)
"áb-ru-um-ma-ba-⌈an⌉" (PDTI 560 rev., thus translit.).

ʾ$_{x}$BR? nâbarum (a garment). Cf. also ʾ$_{x}$MR nâmarum and ḪBR naḫbarum.
x TÚG na-ba-ru-um (4 NT 56). Read possibly na-<áš>-ba-ru-um and cf. ŠPR našparum.

ʾ$_{x}$BR? ibārum? Cf. ʾ$_{x}$ʾ$_{6}$R.
Sarg. and Ur III PN's:
Ì-ba-rí-im, Gen. (MO)
I-ba-ru-um (E)
È-ba-ri (Nies, UDT 85, U).

ʾ$_{x}$BR? ibrijum?
x za-bí-um, x TUM-rí-um, also x DUR.GI.BÀD, DUR.GI.ÙR, DUR.GI.TUR.TUR, SIG$_{4}$.ZIKUM.MA (ITT V 9261). If read as íb-rí-um, we may compare perhaps i-ib-ri-a-am in YOS II 41:16, OB, and i-ib-ri-am in UET V 12:16, OB, both occurring in connection with KA.LUM "dates."

ʾ$_{1}$BRK abaraktum (a profession).
a-ba-ra-ak-ti DN (D 192).

ʾ$_{1}$BT?
Ur III PN:
I-bí-it-Ìr-ra (Legrain, TRU 67:3).

ʾ$_{6}$BT?
Sarg. and Ur III PN's:
Gi-núm-u-ba-at (D)

Wa-ba-ad/t-ì-lí (U 2532; Fish, CST p. 160 viii, U). Cf. Wa-ba-at-Tu-uk-ri-iš^{KI} in RA XXXII 171 vi 19.

ʾ$_{6}$BZ? wubbuzum?

Ur III? PN:

Wu-bu-zu-um (Speleers, CIMC p. 134 No. 476).

ʾ$_{x}$BZ?

Sarg. and Ur III PN's:

ʾÀ-ba-za (U 1035; Nies, UDT 91 iv, U)

ʾÀ-ba-zum (OIP XIV 110).

ʾ$_{4}$D adi, adima, adum "up to," "until," "as long as."

Preposition adi(ma) with geogr. expressions:

a-ti-ma ti-a-am-tim (S ii, viii)

a-ti-ma bu-ti ti-a-am-tim (S vi)

a-ti-ma GIŠ.TIR GIŠ.ERIN (S vi; UET I 274 ii, NS.)

a-t[i-ma] ti-a-am-[tim] sa-bíl-tim (R xvii)

a-ti-⌈ma⌉ ḫu-rí KUG (M xxvi)

a-ti-ma Ba-ra-aḫ-sum^{KI} (UET I 274 i, NS.)

iš-tum-ma GN$_1$ a-ti-ma GN$_2$ (UET I 275 ii, NS.)

iš-tum GN$_1$ a-ti GN$_2$ (CT XXXII 2 iv, CM).

Subjunction adi(ma) with temporal expressions:

a-ti e-ni-a la da-mu-ru .... ù [a]-ti la dag-ru-s[a]?-am "as long as you have not seen me .... and as long as you have not .... to me" (RA XXIII 25)

a-ti PA.TE.SI la ù-wa-e-ru-uš "as long as I have not sent the ensi" (HSS X 12:10)

[a]-ti-ma [a]-la-kam "until I shall come" (HSS X 10:9).

adi-matum "until when?," "how long?."

Ur III PN's:

A-ti-ma-tum (U 203; AnOr VII p. 19)

⌈A⌉-ti-ma-at (TMH n.F. I/II 338).

adi .... adi "including .... including," "be it .... be it":

ŠU.NIGÍN 9624 GURUŠ.GURUŠ a-ti mi-gi$_{4}$-tim a-ti LÚ+ŠU "total of x men, including killed and captive" (R xxiii).

adum minim "why?":

á-tum mi-nim la è-e-sa-ru (D 290 rev. x+10). Verb ununderstandable

⌈á⌉?-tum mi-nim i-na-na [....-k]am-m[a ....] (Ist. Mus. Lagash 11001).

Varia:

a-ti da-ni-iš "in great force" (HSS X 5:11)

a-ti si-dar KI-šu (AOF III 112 end, Mari). Meaning unknown.

ʾ$_{7}$D idum "arm," "strength."

i-da-su "his 2 arms" (Kish 1930, 143 rev.).

Sarg. and Ur III PN's:

^{d}EN.ZU-i-ti (UET III 871, U)

I-da-ri-ik (RTC 243) = Id-arik

I-da-rí-ik (ITT IV p. 10, 7102, U)

I-da-sa (D; MDP XVIII 72, U)

I-du-a (TCL II 5499 rev. iii, U)

ì-du-um-e-ti (MDP XXVIII 526 rev., U?)

ì-ti-DINGIR (E+)

I-tum-be-lí (D)

ì-tum-Gá-gá (TCL V 6170 rev., U)

ì-du-na (Contenau, UDU 68, U)

⌈I⌉-tu-sa (D)

I-za-ri-ik (U 1598+) = Issa-arik

I-za-rí-ik (U 1599)

I-zu-a-rí-ik (U 1601+)

I-zu-ri-ik (U 1604)

I-zu-GÍD (G+)

I-zu-a-GÍD (Ist. Mus. Adab 82)

I-zu-sa-bar (PDTI 559 rev., U; CT XXXII 50:13, U). Interpr. doubtful

Li-bur-ì-du-ni (TCL II 5484, U)

LUGAL-ì-ti (Langdon, TAD 51:15, U; UET III p. 23+, U)

NIN-i-ti (Chiera, STA 16 i+, U).

ʾ$_7$Dʾ$_4$ <u>wadāʾum</u> "to know."

mu-bi? lu ti-da "my instructions?/orders? may you know" (JRAS 1932 p. 296:41). Or "truly you know"

i-da (MCS IV 13 rev., in difficult context).

PSarg.?, Sarg., and Ur III PN's:

In all cases the interpretation from Nʾ$_1$D (Impv.) could also be considered.

DINGIR-i-d⌈a⌉ (E)

I-da-be-lí (G+; TCL II 5549, U)

I-da-bí-ì-li (D+; FM). Cf. I-da-bí-DINGIR in BIN IX 316:24, OB

I-da-DINGIR (D+)

I-da-^{d}EN.ZU (FM). Same PN in A 21938, OB

I-da-GIŠ.TUKUL-ki (ITT V 9275)

I-da-ì-lum (TMH V 31 ii, PSarg.?)

[....]-su$_4$-i-da (HSS X 203 rev.).

Ur III RN:

ÍD I-ta-Um-ma (TMH I/II 133)

ÍD I-da-Um-ma (ZA LI Pl. I after p. 74 ii 8).

mûdaʾum "knowing."

Sarg. and Ur III PN's:

Be-lí-mu-da (D+)

DINGIR-mu-da (D+; ITT III 6577, U)

É-a-mu-da (OIP XIV 101)

^{d}EN.ZU-mu-da (D+)

Eš$_4$-dar-mu-d[a?-....] (D)

Ḫ̮I.AN-mu-da (D)

Ìr-ra-mu-da (U 1764)

Sar-ru-mu-da (Nikolski, Dok. II 35+)

Su$_4$-a-tum-mu-da (MO+)

^{d}UTU-mu-da (Louvre AO 11272). Cf. ^{d}UTU-mu-di in Ranke, EBPN p. 146 OB.

In the following PN's possibly GAL.ZU = mûdaʾum:

Be-lí-GAL.ZU (D+)

DINGIR-GAL.ZU (Kish 1930, 148)

^{d}En-líl-GAL.ZU (ZA XII 332)

GAL.ZU (D+)

GAL.ZU-DI.TAR (ZA XII 335)

GAL.ZU-DINGIR (MO+)

GAL.ZU-Lu-lu (UET III 1198, U)

Sar-ru-GAL.ZU (ZA XII 335)

^{d}Šul-gi-GAL.ZU (PDTI 456, U)

^{d}UTU-GAL.ZU (ZA XII 332).

$ʾ_6Dʾ_7$ wuddûm "to consign?"

^{d}UTU u-sa-za-za-su$_4$ GIŠ.TUK.PI ⌈ú-wa-ti-x-šum⌉ (BE I 12, unknown king). Cf. (countries) a-na ri-it-ti-šu lu-wa-di-a-am in UET I 146 iv, OB.

$ʾ_xDʾ_x$? wadaʾum? (a bronze object).

Akk. lw. in Ur III Sum.:

1 wa-da-um UD.KA.BAR KI.LAL.BI 1/3 MA.NA LAL 3 GÍN (BIN V 1:16).

$ʾ_xDʾ_x$.

Ur III Amorite PN:

| A-ù-da-Il MAR.TU (A 4648)
| A-wu-te-Il MAR.TU (PDTI 28).

$ʾ_x$DD.

DN Adad.

Written syllabically in Ur III PN's:

En-ni-ma-da-ad (TMH n.F. I/II 285 rev. twice). = Ennī-ma-Adad

I-ti-na-da-ad (Nikolski, Dok. II 386)

Zé-la-da-ad (RA XIX 41 No. XLVII rev.).

Written logographically as IM in Sarg. and Ur III PN's:

^{d}IM-sar (Kish 1930, 170d)

PÙ.ŠA-^{d}IM (MO+)

Rí-iš-^{d}IM (UET I 275 iii, NS.)

Šu-^{d}IM (G+)

Passim in Ur III (Schneider, AnOr XIX No. 14).

The foll. Ur III PN's may have a different interpr.:

En-ni-ma-Ad (UET III passim). Or Ennī-ma-abī or Ennī-maʾad

Nu-úr-Ad (Reisner, TUT 157 ii). Or Nûr-abī

For GN A-bu-la-AD^{KI} see ʾ$_x$BL abullum.

ʾ$_x$DD?

Sarg. and Ur III PN's:

A-da-da (Orient. XLVII 484, U)

A-da-tum (U 168+)

A-ti-da (TCL II 5525 i, U). Cf. A-di-du-um in BA VI/5 p. 121, OB

I-da-tum (MO). Cf. I-da-du-um in Ranke, EBPN p. 95

Ú-da-da (E)

Ú-da-dum (D+)

Ú-du-da (D+).

ʾ$_6$DL? <u>wadaltum</u>, <u>badaltum</u>.

A location in Ur III texts:

ŠÀ wa-da-al-tum (Legrain, TRU 221; 226; Fish, CST 204, 233; Nesbit, SRD 13; Univ. Illinois 131; PDTI 670)

KI wa-da-al-tum (Boson, TCS 235; 344)

[wa]-da-al-tum SÁ.DUG$_4$ .... (Nikolski, Dok. II 498)

wa-da-al-tum (RA IX 46f.)

GIŠ.SAR ba-da-al-tum (Oppenheim, CCTE C 1 iv).

ʾ$_x$DM <u>adammum</u> (a garment).

TÚG ʾà-dam-mu-um (HSS X 217 x+5)

6 TÚG ʾà-dam-mu 10 TÚG.TUM.GUNU ʾà-dam-mu 3 TÚG.TUM.GUNU ʾà-dam-m<u>-ù (BE I 11).

Sarg. PN:

A-da-mu (ZA XII 337; LB 1847)

ʾÀ-da-mu (Kish 1930, 406 iii, rev. i+)

A-dam-u (D+).

ʾ$_x$DM, see NDN nadānum.

ʾ$_x$DM?

1 MA.NA 5 GÍN e-da-mu (Kish 1930, 175e twice). Perhaps a PN.

ʾ$_x$DN.

Sarg. PN:

Á-⌈dan⌉-núm (RTC 248).

$^{\supset}{}_1$DR adārum.

Ur III MN:

A-da-ru-um (MDP XVIII 79; XXVIII 410 rev.).

$^{\supset}{}_1$DR? adrum? "dark."

a-na u-su$_4$-a-im a-ti-ir (UET I 275 iv, NS.). Doubtful.

$^{\supset}{}_3$DR? adūrum (a location).

The Sum. logogram É.A = ᵓÀ.DUR$_5$ may go back to a Sem. word of the root ḪDR "to surround." Cf. e.g.:

ᵓÀ.DUR$_5$-Me-me (CT XXXII 8 i, PSarg.) besides ᵓÀ.DUR-Me-me^{KI} (Fish, CST 20)

ᵓÀ.DUR$_5$-PA.AL^{KI} (ITT I 1099)

ᵓÀ.DUR$_5$-PA.TE.SI-KA^{KI} (ITT I 1182+).

$^{\supset}{}_x$DRKL?

Ur III PN:

A-dar-ku-LUM (CT VII 7 iii).

$^{\supset}{}_3$DŠ uddušum "to renovate."

É.BABBAR lu u-ud-di-iš (CT XXXII 1 iii, CM).

eššiš "anew."

ni-se$_{11}$ ša-at DN BÍL-iš i-ki-su-šum (UET I 275 ii, NS.). Doubtful, but cf. same spelling in BIN II 34:7.

eddešumma "anew."

e-dè-šum-ma É DN i-bu-uš "he made anew the temple" (MDP II p. 58). The form may be compared with eddešī-ma, for which cf. id-di-ši-ma BÀD GAL ša Kiš^{KI} lu e-pu-uš (RA VIII 65 ii 37, Asduni-erim and similarly in CT XXXVI 4) and pa-la-a-am id-di-ša-am (<eddešiįam) "a renewing rule" (AAA XIX Pl. LXXXI iii 8, Šamšī-Adad I).

$^{\supset}{}_x$G?

Ur III PN's:

A-ga-tum (BE III 135)

A-ga-ti (BE III 135 rev.).

$^{\supset}{}_x$G$^{\supset}{}_x$ agijum (a garment).

Akk. lw. in Ur III Sum.:

NÍG.DÍB ^{TÚG}a-gi$_4$-um LUGAL (Chiera, STA 23 ii end).

$^{\supset}{}_x$GḪ aguḫḫum (a garment).

Akk. lw. in Ur III Sum.:

x TÚG á-gu(d)-ḫu-um (Reisner, TUT 126 ii; Pinches, AT p. 47; AnOr VII 155; Oppenheim, CCTE p. 65; UET III p. 171+; RA XVIII 53 i, Voc. prat.; MDP XXVII 188 v, ibid. also SAGŠU á-gu(d)-ḫu-um)

x MA.NA SÍG TÚG á-gu(d)-ḫu-um LUGAL (De Genouillac, FT II Pl. LXIX

AO 12987)

It seems tempting to explain 12 TÚG ʾà-ku-ḫi-na· (BE I 11, list of garments) as containing aguḫḫum plus the Hurrian -ḫina suffix (cf. lines 1, 2, 4, 8).

ʾ$_x$GL?

Sarg. and Ur III PN's:

A-ga-la (Iraq V 177 No. 30, U)

ʾÀ-ga-lum (G+).

ʾ$_x$GL?

Ur III PN:

E-gu-LUM (Barton, HLC I Pl. 43, 217 obv.).

ʾ$_6$GM? wuggumum?

ki GURUŠ.GURUŠ u-wa-ga-mu ti-bu-dam li-se$_{11}$-ù-ni-kum-ma "when the workers will ...., may they help you" (JRAS 1932 p. 296:17).

ʾ$_1$Ḫ aḫum "brother."

Written logographically or syllabically.

PN ŠEŠ-su (RA IX 34 rev. v, NS.?; D 241)

PN ŠEŠ-šu (Boson, TCS 371, U)

PN$_1$ ŠEŠ PN$_2$ (HSS X 39:4; 153 iv 18; etc.)

PN's ŠEŠ be-lu GÁN, see under Bʾ$_4$L bêlum

A-bí-bí a-ḫu NU.BANDA (FM 13:4). Cf. PN$_1$ a-ḫu-ú PN$_2$ in EL 9:1, OA.

PSarg. and Sarg. PN's:

A-ḫa-ar-ši (G+)

A-ḫa-KUG.BABBAR-sa (FM)

A-ḫu-a (MDP XXVIII 526)

A-ḫu-ba-lik (MO)

A-ḫu-DINGIR (G+)

A-ḫu-ì-lum (BE I Pl. VII ii+)

A-ḫu-DÙG (G+)

A-ḫu-GIŠ.RÍN (G+)

A-ḫu-i-sar (BIN VIII 144)

A-ḫu-li-bur-ra (D)

A-ḫu-ma (G)

A-ḫu-mu-bí (MO+)

ŠEŠ-mu-bí (RTC 84)

A-ḫu-ni (E)

A-ḫu-ni-sa? (Kish 1930, 177n)

A-ḫu-si-na (ITT I 1379)

A-ḫu-šè-na (ITT II/2 p. 35, 4640)

A-ḫu-si-ra (D)

A-ḫu-su_4-ni (D)
A-ḫu-su_4-nu (D+)
A-ḫu-su-nu (D+)
A-ḫu-šu-ni (Ist. Mus. Nippur 2614+)
A-ḫu-um (RTC 243+)
A-li-a-aḫ (MDP XVIII 31)
A-li-a-ḫu (D+)
Ar-ši-aḫ (RTC 249 rev. i)
Ar-ši-a-ḫa (G+)
Ba-na-aḫ (Coll. De Clercq I 71)
Be-lí-a-aḫ (VAT 16441 i)
Bí-bí-a-ḫi? (TMH V 194 ii, PSarg.?)
DINGIR-a-ḫa (MO+)
DINGIR-su-a-ḫa (D+)
DÙG-a-ḫi (D+)
Ì-lí-a-ḫi (D+)
Ì-lum-a-ḫa (BIN VIII 11 iv, PSarg.)
I-sar-a-ḫi (D+)
I-su-a-ḫu (G+)
Ma-ma-ḫu (MO+). Doubtful
Ma-núm-a-ḫi (BIN VIII 151)
Sá-lim-a-ḫu (D+)
ŠEŠ-za-ḫír/ḫar (G)
Ú-da-aḫ (D+).

Selected Ur III PN's:

A-ḫa-am-ar-ši (U 123)
A-ḫa-an-ni-šu (U 125)
A-ḫa-ni-šu (U 127)
A-ḫu-ni-šu (U 142)
A-ḫi-MI-lum (Pinches, AT 77)
A-ḫu-ki-in (Yondorf b)
A-ḫu-mi-lum (AnOr I 97). Or Aḫu-ṣillum
A-ḫu-um-DINGIR (CT V 40 ii+)
A-ḫu-na (MDP XVIII 79 seal)
A-ḫu-šu-ni (Fish, CST p. 61+)
A-ḫu-šù-ni (BE III 64; Coll. De Clercq I 109, U?)
A-ḫu-u-ni (RTC 373 rev.+)
A-ḫu-wa-gàr (U 136+)
A-lí-a-aḫ (OIP XXXVII 50)
Ar-ši-aḫ (U 355+)

Ì-lí-ki-aḫ (RTC 346)

I-ti-in-a-ḫu-um (3 NT 796 i)

| Ša-al-maḫ (U 2584+)

| Ša-lim-a-ḫu-um (U 2596+).

<u>aḫatum</u> "sister."

SI.A-tum a-ḫa-at Bí-bí (A 30794, seal).

PSarg., Sarg., and Ur III PN's:

A-ḫa-ti (Nikolski, Dok. I viii, PSarg.; U 129+)

A-ḫa-tum (D+; U 128).

$^{\prime}{}_{x}$ḪD? <u>aḫidātum</u>, see ṢḪT? ṣāḫitum.

$^{\prime}{}_{x}$ḪLB <u>aḫulab</u> "woe!"

Ur III PN:

A-ḫu-lá-bi "woe to me!" (ITT IV 7099). For spelling with b cf. a-ḫu-la-(a)-bi-(ia) in KAR 73 rev. 12, 14 and 175 rev. 23; for use as PN cf. ^{I}A-ḫu-lab-ia in YOS VI 82:7.

$^{\prime}{}_{1}$ḪN <u>uḫinnum</u> (a type of date).

Sum. Ù.ḪU.IN may be a lw. from Akk. For Semitic etymologies cf. Thompson, DAB p. 310.

x Ù.ḪU.IN GUR.LUGAL (Pinches, AT p. 54)

x Ù.ḪU.IN GUR (UET III 1081 ii, U)

x KA.LUM Ù.ḪU.IN GUR (UET III 1098)

x(QA) Ù.ḪU.IN (UET III 1105 twice)

Ù.ḪU.IN (UET III 546). An ornament made of gold.

$^{\prime}{}_{1}$ḪR <u>uḫḫurum</u> "to change?"

This meaning is not attested elsewhere. For the semantic change cf. šunnûm "to make second," "to change." Ungnad, MAS p. 31 translates uḫḫurum as "hintenansetzen," "verachten."

ma-ma-na DÙL su_4-a u-a-ḫa-ru ^{d}En-líl MU-su li-a-$ḫir_x$? "whoever changes? this statue, (then) his name Enlil may change?" (PBS V 34 x, Lugalzagesi; S ix, xi)

šu-ut IN.TU.RA U-Ù-ḫi-ru-un li-ḫu-$uš_x$(EŠ) (RTC 77 rev.). Difficult.

<u>uḫḫurum</u> "left behind."

x GURUŠ, DAM, and DUMU.ARAD ù-ḫu-ru-tum (D 207).

$^{\prime}{}_{1}$ḪZ <u>aḫāzum</u> "to take (possession)."

1) 7 GÍN KUG.BABBAR 2) PN 3) a-na SAG 4) SAG ù-la a-ḫu-uz (BM 54309 i)

ḫa-ra-nam a-ḫu-z[a-a]m "I have taken the road" (FM 53:9). Uncertain

x É, ŠÁM-su-nu x KUG.BABBAR, iš-dè PN_1 ù PN_2 PN_3 i-ḫu-uz (JCS X 26 i)

animals MÁŠ.DA.RI.A PN i-ḫu-ùz (BIN VIII 146)

(something) PN i-ḫu-uz (Kish 1930, 170c)

e-ni ʾà-wa-at-zu i-ti-iš i-da-ḫa-az (Ist. Mus. Lagash 11001). Context doubtful.

Akk. PN:

A-ḫa-zé-iš (E+).

<u>šûḫuzum</u> "to cause to dwell."

Kiš^{KI} a-ša-rí-su i-ni (ù) URU^{KI}-lam$_x$ u-sá-ḫi-su-ni "he restored Kiš to its place (and) caused them to settle the city." Sum. Kiš^{KI} ki-bi bi-gi$_4$ uru-bi ki-gub e-na-ba (S iv, ix).

<u>tâḫazum</u> "battle," "campaign."

Written logographically only.

in KAS+X GN iš$_x$(LAM+KUR)-ar (S ii, vii; R passim)

PN (Acc.) in KAS+X ŠU.DU$_8$.A (S ii, viii)

34 KAS+X iš$_x$-ar (S vi)

in GN KAS+X iš-ni-a-ma iš-gu-na-ma iš$_x$-ar (S vii)

GN$_1$ ù GN$_2$ .... a-na KAS+X ip-ḫu-ru-nim-ma (R xxii; RA VII 104, Mi.)

NS. ša-ir 10 LAL 1 KAS+X (YOS I 10; MDP VI Pl. 1, 1 i)

iš-tum KAS+X.KAS+X su$_4$-nu-ti iš$_x$-ar-ru (ibid.)

KAS+X u-ga-e (PBS V 36 x+iv, NS.)

KAS+X-e iš$_x$-a-ru-ni (RA IX 34 i, NS.?, copy)

(KAS+)X GN saʾārum (passim in dates of NS. in D 217; 220; 231; 236 and of Škš. in D 268; RTC 130; ITT I 1115; cf. also ITT V 9265 rev.)

KAS+X .... (MDP II p. 53 ii)

1 X PN and 1 GIŠ.GIGIR PN (D 249 passim).

ʾ$_x$Kʾ$_x$?

Sarg. and Ur III PN's:

For the divinity ^{d}A-ku cf. Deimel, PB No. 61 and ^{d}A-ku-ra-bi in VAS VIII 14:40, OB.

A-gu-a-lí (U 83+)

A-gu-a-nu-rí (UET III 754 ii, U)

A-gu-a-ti (Oppenheim, CCTE p. 179, U). Cf. A-gu-ú-a-ti and A-gu-ú-a-IGI-ma-ti in PBS XI/3 p. 244, OB

A-gu-a-zi-im-ti (RA X 65 No. 29, U)

A-gu-ni (Reisner, TUT 56 rev., U)

A-gu-tim (MO)

A-ku-a (U 152+)

A-gu-a (U 82+)

A-ku-a-ḪA.MA.TI (U 153)

A-ku-É-a (MO)

A-ku-ì-lum (MO+)

A-ku-um-mi (BIN V 32, U)

A-ku?-zi-li (Orient. XLVII 40:45, U).

ʾ$_x$Kʾ$_x$.

Sarg. and Ur III PN's:

A-ki-a-ti (UET III 17, U)

A-ki-ša-ar (Reisner, TUT 165, U)

A-ki-sar (TCL V 5674 i, U)

^{d}EN.KI-ʾà-ki (ITT II/2 p. 51, 5876)

Cf. also GÁN ša-at ʾÀ-ki-im (MO D viii).

ʾ$_x$Kʾ$_x$ akītum.

Akk. lw. in Sum.:

Á-ki-ti, month and festival from PSarg. (UET II Pl. XLIX 44) through Sarg. to Ur III

Á-ki-tum (MDP XXII 144 rev., U).

ʾ$_x$KBR? ikbarum?

x+5 gu(d)-za-rí-ku?! /kusarikkū/ 2 la-aḫ-ma-an KUG.GI iš-mu-tu ù ik-ba-ri? ìr-ku-zu "they plucked down? (melted?) x+5 kusarikkum(-figurines) and 2 laḫmum(-figurines) of gold and tied (in their place?) ikbarum" (PBS IX 30).

ʾ$_x$KK?

Sarg. and Ur III PN:

A-ku-ku-ni (MDP XXVIII p. 4). But cf. MDP VI p. 15

A-gu-gu-ni (De Genouillac, TD 59, U).

ʾ$_x$KK? akukūtum.

Ur III PN:

A-gu-gu-tum (YOS IV 246 i).

ʾ$_1$KL akālum "to eat."

Written logographically only.

35 UDU a-na KÚ-šu-nu (Louvre AO 11254 ii)

barley a-na KÚ UDU (HSS X 83:7)

x GURUŠ be-lu GÁN KÚ KUG.BABBAR "sellers" (MO A iv etc.)

x GURUŠ .... NINDA KÚ (S vi)

x AB+ÁŠ.AB+ÁŠ in É PN NINDA KÚ (JCS X 26 L.E.).

šâkultum "meal" (or the like).

Akk. lw. in Ur III Sum.:

x GUD ZI.GA ša-gu-ul-tum ^{d}Innin (Univ. Illinois 209).

ʾ$_6$KL.

Sum. UGULA possibly a lw. from Akk. ʾ$_6$KL ukula < ukla < wakla.

Sarg. and Ur III PN's:

Ú-gu-la ensi Kiš (TCL II 5490 rev.+, U) = UGULA ensi Kiš (5617)

Ú-gul-la-ni-su (Kish 1930, 170c). Cf. ^{d}Ù-gul-lá in OIP XLIII 184, OB.

ʾ$_x$KL ʾakallum "palace."

Lw. from Sum. É.GAL.

Sarg. and Ur III PN's:

PÙ.ŠA-É.GAL (G+; CT XXXII 34 ii, U)

Um-mi-É.GAL SAL (Bab. VII Pl. XXI No. 13, U).

ʾ$_x$KM, see ʾ$_6$GM?

ʾ$_x$KR ikkarum "plowman," "peasant."

Lw. from Sum. ENGAR.

Written normally ENGAR, or ENGAR.ENGAR in Pl.

Ur III PN:

I-ga-ru-um (De Genouillac, TD p. 6).

ʾ$_x$KR? ekurum?

Akk. lw. in Sum.:

[x GIŠ]? e-ku-ru-um (ITT V 9273, in a list of garments, woods, bronze). A small wooden ekurrum?

ʾ$_x$KR? ukurum? (a type of brick?).

Akk. lw. in Ur III Sum.:

x SAR SIG$_4$ ù-ku-ru-um (RA XII 166 i, ii; XXXII 127f.)

ʾ$_x$KṢ?

Sarg. and Ur III PN's:

A-gu-za-na (U 90; YOS IV 2, U)

A-gú-zi (RTC 244).

ʾ$_x$KṢ? ikṣum.

ik-zum šu GUR$_7$ wa-ar-ki-im (D 270, tag). Inscription complete. Cf. x ŠE.GUR šu GUR$_7$ BÍL (D 327).

Sarg. MN:

Ik-ṣum (D). Ikṣûm "cold?" Cf. likṣî lu ba-ḫir "let it cool, steam off" in Langdon, BM p. 16.

ʾ$_x$KṢ? ukkuṣum.

Sarg. PN:

Ù-ku-za-at (Iraq Mus. 30350).

ʾ$_1$L ilum, elum "god," "divinity."

Written syllabically or logographically as DINGIR.

maḫ-rí-iš ì-lí-su (R xviii, xxiv; UET I 274 iv, NS.; UET I 276 ii, NS.)

^{d}A-ba$_4$ il-su (S vi)

il?!-su "his god" (UET I 275 iv, NS.)

da-iš ì-li (R xxvii). Very doubtful

ì-lu ra-bí-ù-tum (PBS V 36 rev. iv, NS.)

DINGIR ra-bí-ù-tum (UET I 276 ii, NS.)

i-lu ra-b[í-ù-tum] (Morgan, MSP IV 161 ii, Lullubum)

DINGIR Gu-ti-im (ZA IV 406, Gutium)

NS. DINGIR A-ga-dè^{KI} (AO XVII/XVIII No. 229; RTC 165; 166; 169; 170; 171; etc.)

DINGIR A-ga-dè^{KI} (RTC 173)

É DINGIR A-ga-dè^{KI} (ITT V 9289)

Škš. DINGIR UR.SAG A-ga-dè^{KI} (Ist. Mus. Adab 767)

Škš. da-núm DINGIR ma-ti X^{KI} (Pope, SPA I 281).

Written ilum (and ilu) almost exclusively in PSarg., MO, and BE I Pls. VIIff.:

A-pù-ì-lum (BE I Pl. VII iiif.+)

A-bu-LUM (G+)

A-pù-LUM (G+)

A-ḫu-ì-lum (BE I Pl. VII ii+)

A-ku-ì-lum (MO+)

A-lu-ì-lum (JRAS 1930 p. 602, PSarg.)

Ba-ba-LUM (D)

BALA?-ì-lum (BE I Pl. VI viii)

Ba-ni-lum (E)

Da-da-ì-lum (UET I 11, PSarg.)

Dan-ma-lum (Nikolski, Dok. II 48 rev.)

E-bi-ir-ì-lum (MO)

En-na-LUM (G+)

En-ni-LUM (Ist. Mus. Nippur 2614)

I-bí-ì-lum (MO)

I-bi-ì-lum (TMH V 11 iv, PSarg.?)

I-da-ì-lum (TMH V 31 ii, PSarg.?)

I-ki-LUM (MO+)

Ì-lum-BE (YOS IX 2, PSarg.)

I-lu-DINGIR (JCS X 26 vi)

Ì-lu-ga-sa-ad (RA VIII 158 AO 5659)

Ì-lum-a-ḫa (BIN VIII 11 iv, PSarg.)

Ì-lum-a-zu (BE I Pl. VII iii)

Ì-lum-ba-ni (TMH V 104 iii, PSarg.?)

Ì-lum-dan (HSS III 27 v, PSarg.; BE I Pl. VIII 17)

Ì-lum-GÀR (DP 2 i, PSarg.)

Ì-lum-GIŠ.RÍN (BE I Pl. VII vi+)

Ì-lum-gur-ad (UET II Pl. XLVII 19+, PSarg.)

Ì-lum-i-pi (TMH V 170 i, PSarg.?)

Ì-lum-LA (A 25412 v, PSarg.)

È-lu-ME-ir (RTC 127 rev. vi+)

I-lu-ME-ir (ITT V p. 36, 9377). Cf. DINGIR-Me-ir, an OA king, in JNES I 268

ì-lum-ra-bí (BIN VIII 11 iv, vi, PSarg.)

ì-lu-ra-bí (OIP XIV 61 i, PSarg.)

ì-lum-sa(g)-ir /šā'ir?/ (EK IV Pl. XL, PSarg.)

ì-lum-SAR (BE I Pl. VII vii)

I-mi-ì-lum (BE I Pl. VI iv)

I-pù-úr?-Il (Jestin, TSŠ 479 i, PSarg.)

Iš-má-ì-lum (BE I Pl. VI i+)

Iš-me-ì-lum (A 25412, PSarg.; Walters Art Gall. 41.107 passim, PSarg.)

Iš-me-lum (TMH V 9 rev. v+, PSarg.)

Iš-ni-lum (TMH V 97 ii, PSarg.?)

I-ti-LUM (D+)

I-zi-LUM (D+)

Ku-lí-LUM (G)

Me-zé-ì-lum (MO)

Ra-bí-ì-lum (CT XXXII 8 i A+, PSarg.)

Ra-bí-LUM (Nikolski, Dok. II 48+)

Sar-ma-ì-lum (OIP LIII 147 No. 5, PSarg.)

SIG_5-ì-lum (MO)

Su-tu-ì-lum (OIP XIV 51 v, PSarg.)

U-li-id-ì-lum (MO).

Written il standing for DN Il or il, the predicate state of ilum.

PSarg. and Sarg. PN's:

Ap-ra-il (MO+). Cf. West Semitic ʿApr(a)ʾel discussed by Albright in JAOS LXXIV 225 and 233

BÀD-il (MO)

En-na-Il (A 25412 xvii, PSarg.; G+)

EN.TI-il (RA XXXI 143, PSarg.)

Ib-lul-Il (TMH V 31 ii, PSarg.)

I-ku-⌈Il⌉ (CT V 3 iv, PSarg.). Or I-ku-tum

íl-be-lí (D)

íl-ib-gi (G)

Iš-dup-Il (CY XXXII 8 iii, PSarg.; A 25412 i, PSarg.)

Iš-lul-Il (TMH V 31 ii, PSarg.)

I-šu-Il (PSarg. king)

I-zi-íl? (BIN VIII 11 ii, PSarg.)

Ra-bí-Il (OIP XIV 51 vii, PSarg.)

Sa-rí-Il? (D 269).

Written ilī "my god."

PSarg. and Sarg. PN's:

A-bí-ì-lí (D)
A-bi-ì-lí (ITT II/2 p. 20, 4360)
A-bu-li (G)
Al-ì-lí (D)
Al-ì-li (BIN VIII 46 i, PSarg.)
A-rí-ik-ì-li (ITT II/2 p. 14, 3072)
A-zu-NI (D)
DAM.GÀR-ì-lí (MDP XXVIII 526)
Dan-ì-lí (FM+)
Dan-ì-li (MO)
Da-ni-lí (ITT II/2 p. 16, 3117)
DI.TAR-ì-li (A 1100)
É-a-ì-lí (FM)
En-ni-lí (D+)
En-num-ì-lí (E)
EN-ì-lí (D+)
Ga-lí-ì-li (MO)
I-da-bí-ì-li (D+; FM)
I-gu-ì-lí (Walters Art Gall. 41.107 vi, PSarg.)
Ì?-lí-a-bí (FM)
Ì-lí-a-ḫi (D+)
Ì-lí-ASARU (Nikolski, Dok. II 43+)
Ì-li-ASARU (TMH V 35 ii, PSarg.)
Ì-lí-ba-lik (BIN VIII 249)
Ì-lí-ba-ni (FM)
Ì-lí-BE (D+)
Ì-lí-be-lí (G+)
Ì-lí-EN (G)
Ì-lí-pi-lí (Nikolski, Dok. II 14; 22+)
Ì-lí-bí (D+)
Ì-lí-bi-la-ni (D+)
Ì-lí-bí-la-ni (RTC 245)
Ì-lí-dan (D+)
I-lí-lí (G+)
Ì-lí-lí (G+)
Ì-lí-DIRIG (FM)
Ì-lí-DÙG (TMH V 174 i, PSarg.?)
Ì-lí-en-núm (D+)
Ì-lí-^{d}EN.ZU (Kish 1931, 122 i)
Ì-lí-Eš$_4$-dar (Ward, SCWA No. 387)

Ì-lí-GAL (FM+)

Ì-lí-Il-la-at (E). Cf. also E-la-^{d}Il-at

Ì-lí-íl-la-at (ITT II/2 p. 15, 3093)

Ì-lí-ìl-la-at (E)

Ì-lí-iš (RTC 92+). Cf. also E-li-iš

Ì-lí-iš-da-gal (D+)

Ì-lí-iš-i-sar (ITT II/2 p. 37, 4664+)

Ì-lí-iš-ma-ni (D+). Cf. also E-li-iš-ma-ni

Ì-lí-iš-me-ni (ITT II/2 p. 5, 2899)

Ì-lí-kára-bí (FM)

Ì-lí-maḫ-rí (D+)

Ì-lí-me-šum (G)

Ì-lí-nu-uḫ-si (D)

Ì-lí-Rí-mu-uš (ITT I 1096)

Ì-lí-sa-liq (D+)

Ì-lí-sar-ru (MO)

Ì-lí-su (TMH V 185 rev. v, PSarg.?)

Ì-lí-SUKKAL (D+)

Ì-lí-TAB.BA (D+)

[Ì]-lí-tu-gul-ti (RTC 127 v)

Ì-lí-du-gul-ti (Kish 1930, 139)

Ì-lí-tum-ki (D)

GÀR-ì-li (E)

GÀR-ì-lí (JAOS LII 113)

Ku-ra-ti-ì-lí (Coll. De Clercq I 105)

La-ba-DINGIR (ZA XII 332)

Li-bí-it-ì-li (YOS I 10)

Na-ra-me-ì-li (RTC 127 rev. iv)

Na-zi-ir-ì-lí (FM+)

Pi-ì-lí (TMH V 16+)

Pù-ì-lí (D+)

Pù?-ì-li (D)

Pù-su-lí (D)

PÙ.ŠA-ì-li (MO)

PÙ.ŠA-ì-lí (E)

Sar-ru-GI-ì-lí (MO)

Sar-ru-ì-lí (MO+)

Šu-ì-li (MO). Cf. also Šu-e-li

Šu-ì-lí (ITT II/2 p. 5, 2899)

Tab-ì-lí (FM)

Ù-ì-lí (G+). Cf. also Ú-e-li

Ù-mu-ì-lí (OIP XIV 51 iv+, PSarg.)

Wa-dar-ì-li (Louvre AO 8638 rev.)

ZAG.MU-ì-lí (PBS IX 98 rev.).

Written ilšu, ilišu.

PSarg. and Sarg. PN's:

A-bí-DINGIR-su (RTC 230)

ARÁD-ì-lí-[su]? (Kish 1930, 406 rev. i)

d?Da-gan-DINGIR-su (RTC 127 rev. ii)

DINGIR-su (RTC 133)

DINGIR-su-a-ba (G+)

DINGIR-su-a-ḫa (D+)

DINGIR-su-dan (D+)

DINGIR-su-⌈DÙG⌉ (ITT I 1372)

DINGIR-su-GÀR (MO+)

DINGIR-su-la-ba (MO)

DINGIR-su-ra-bí (MO+)

| Ḫa-ti-ì-lí-su (D). = Ḫadî-iliššu

| Ḫa-ti-ì-[lí]-iš-[su] (D)

Il_x-su(d)-GÀR (BIN VIII 11 ii, PSarg.)

Il-su-Ma-lik (UET II Pl. XXXVI 308, PSarg.)

Šu-ì-lí-su (D+).

Written ilū (= ilu(m)?)

Sarg. PN's:

Ì-lu-dam-ku (D+)

Ì-lu-da-nu (D+).

Written DINGIR.

PSarg. (very rare) and Sarg. PN's:

A-ar-DINGIR (MO+)

A-ba-DINGIR (E)

A-pù-DINGIR (G+)

A-ḫu-DINGIR (G+)

A-mur-DINGIR (D+)

A-sur-DINGIR (E+)

A-ti-DINGIR (CT I 1c)

A-zu-DINGIR (D+)

Ba-ba-DINGIR (G)

| Ba-ša-aḫ-DINGIR (MO+)

| Ba-sa-aḫ-DINGIR (Iraq Mus. 43612)

Be-lí-DINGIR (G+)

Bí-bí-DINGIR (D+)

DA-DINGIR (E)

Dar-ba-DINGIR (E)

DINGIR-a-ba (G+)

DINGIR-AB.GU (Iraq Mus. 44025)

DINGIR-a-ḫa (MO+)

DINGIR-al-su (D+)

DINGIR-a-ma (D)

DINGIR-a-zu (D+)

DINGIR-BALA (D)

DINGIR-ba-na (MO)

DINGIR-ba-ni (D+)

DINGIR-b[e?-l]í? (D)

DINGIR-BU (UET I 12, PSarg., and Jacobsen, AS XI 103)

DINGIR-da-ti (ZA XII 332)

DINGIR-dan (D+)

DINGIR-DÙG (D+)

DINGIR-É (D+)

DINGIR-en-ni (Walters Art Gall. 41.107 passim, PSarg.)

DINGIR-e-ri-iš (E)

DINGIR-GAL.ZU (Kish 1930, 148)

DINGIR-ga-lí (MO)

DINGIR-GI (FM+)

DINGIR-gi-ma-at (D+)

DINGIR-GIŠ.RÍN (G)

DINGIR-GÚ (D+)

DINGIR-gu-l[í] (G)

DINGIR-ku-lí (D)

DINGIR-i-d⌈a⌉ (E)

DINGIR-IGI.D[U]? (D)

DINGIR-il-la-at (Fish, CST 17+)

DINGIR-il-la-zu (D+)

DINGIR-KÁR (Kish 1930, 148)

DINGIR-GÀR (D+)

DINGIR-la-ba (G+)

DINGIR-la-la (D)

DINGIR-ma (Iraq Mus. 43612)

DINGIR-ma-ru-[....] (E)

DINGIR-mu-da (D+)

DINGIR-na-zi-ir (D+)

DINGIR-nu-id (MO+)

DINGIR-ra-bí (D; Kish 1930, 559e)

DINGIR-SAR (D)

DINGIR-SIG$_5$ (D+)

DINGIR-SIPA (D+)

DINGIR-SUKKAL (RTC 95)

DINGIR-su-su (MO). Cf. DINGIR-zu-zu

DINGIR-ŠUM (G)

DINGIR-TAB.BA (D+)

DINGIR-TI.LA (G+)

DINGIR-UR.SAG (D+)

DINGIR-zu-zu (RTC 122+). Cf. DINGIR-su-su

DU-DINGIR (E+)

DÙG?-DINGIR (Kish 1930, 149)

E-ar-DINGIR (D)

En-na-DINGIR (G+)

En-bu-DINGIR (G)

GAL.ZU-DINGIR (MO+)

GAL-DINGIR (E)

Gi-ba-DINGIR (D)

Gu-lí-DINGIR (G+)

Ku-lí-DINGIR (E)

Ḫu-zu-us-DINGIR (Kish 1930, 406 rev. ii)

I-bí-DINGIR (D+)

Ib-lul-DINGIR (MO+)

Ib-ni-DINGIR (G+)

I-da-DINGIR (D+)

I-din-DINGIR (D+)

Id-lul-DINGIR (BIN VIII 259)

Ik-ru-ub-DINGIR (MO+)

I-ki-DINGIR (G)

Ì-lí-DINGIR (G+)

I-lu-DINGIR (JCS X 26 vi)

I-lul-DINGIR (D+)

I-mi-DINGIR (D+)

Ip-ti-DINGIR (D+)

Iq-bí-DINGIR (D+)

Ìr-am-D[INGIR] (G)

I-rí-DINGIR (G)

I-sar-ì-lí (RA XXIII 18 No. 9)

I-si-im-DINGIR (MO)

I-su-DINGIR (MO+)

Iš-dup-DINGIR (MO+)

Iš-kun_x(KUM)-DINGIR (MO)

Iš-lul-DINGIR (D+)

Iš-má-DINGIR (D+)

Iš-me-DINGIR (Ist. Mus. Adab 325)

Iš-rí-DINGIR (RA XIII Pl. I opp. p. 8 No. 5 seal)

I-ti-DINGIR (D+)

I-wi-DINGIR (MDP XXVIII 524)

KA-ma-DINGIR (ITT I 1365+)

KIL-DINGIR (D+)

ME-DINGIR (D)

Me-ra-DINGIR (A 5232+)

Nir-ra-DINGIR (A 5232)

Ni-ti-DINGIR (E+). = Ì-ti-DINGIR /Idī-ilum/

Ra-bí-DINGIR (G+)

Rí-is-DINGIR (PSBA XX Pl. I ii, PSarg.+)

Sar-ru-DINGIR (DP 246 iv, PSarg.+)

Sa-aṭ-pi-DINGIR (RTC 78)

Sa-aṭ-be-DINGIR (E+)

Ša-aṭ-be-DINGIR (D+)

Sa-tu-DINGIR (G+)

SIG_5-DINGIR (D+)

Su_4-ma-DINGIR (G+)

Ša-DINGIR (D+)

Ša-ki-DINGIR (E+)

Ša-rí-DINGIR (G+)

TE.NA-DINGIR (D+)

Ú-bí-DINGIR (De Genouillac, TSA 12 rev. ii, PSarg.)

U-li-DINGIR (JCS X 26 vi)

Ú-si-DINGIR (E).

Written DINGIR.DINGIR; probably = ^{d}Anum because ilū or ilān is impossible with verbs in Sg.

PSarg. and Sarg. PN's:

Iš-dup-DINGIR.DINGIR (CT XXXII 8 i A, PSarg.)

I-ti-DINGIR.DINGIR (MO)

Ku-ru-ub-DINGIR.DINGIR (D+)

Me-gir-DINGIR.DINGIR (D).

Written AN.NA.

Sarg. and Ur III PN's:

A-bi-AN.NA (BE I Pl. VII ix)

Im-ti-AN.NA (ITT V p. 48, 9660, U).

Written elum, elī, etc.

PSarg., Sarg., and Ur III PN's:

A-ba-e_{11}-lí (ITT II/1 p. 16, 721, U, translit. only)

A-bí-e-lum (Fish, CST p. 159 iii, U)

Ba-ba-e-lí (D)

DINGIR-é-il MAR.TU (SO IX/1 No. 21, U)

E-la-^{d}Il-at (ITT I 1460)

E-li-$Eš_{4}$-dar (UET III 923, U)

E-li-iš (Nikolski, Dok. II 72). Cf. also Ì-lí-iš

E-li-iš-ma-ni (OIP XIV 102). Cf. also Ì-li-iš-ma-ni

E-lí-ni-šu (Barton, HLC Pl. 12, 52 rev., U)

E-lu-ba-ni (TMH n.F. I/II 56, U). Cf. also DINGIR-ba-ni

E-lu-da-an (ITT IV p. 69, 7694, U)

È-lu-Me-ir (RTC 127 rev. vi+). Cf. also I-lu-Me-ir

^{d}EN.ZU-e-li (Barton, HLC I Pl. 43, 217 rev., U)

Ši-e-lí (UET III 1041 ii, U)

Šu-e-li (RTC 143+; Barton, HLC I Pl. 47, 237, U). Cf. also Šu-ì-lí

Šu-e-lum (G)

Ú-e-li (Barton, HLC III Pl. 132, 335:5, U). Cf. also Ù-ì-lí

Ur-^{d}E-lum (Fara III 35 vi; TMH V 78 iii, PSarg.).

Written ela, ila.

Sarg. and Ur III PN's:

DINGIR-la-il MAR.TU (SO IX/1 No. 21 rev., U)

E-la-DINGIR (ZA XII 334)

E-la-GÀR (HSS IV 86, U)

E-la-ga-ra-ad (Pinches, BTBC p. 93 rev. 6, U)

E-la-^{d}Il-at (ITT I 1460). Cf. also Ì-lí-Il-la-at

I-la-ap-ti-il MAR.TU (SO IX/1 No. 21 rev., U)

I-la-ša-ma-ar (A 2964:12, U).

Selected Ur III PN's:

A-bu-DINGIR (U 48; PDTI 556)

A-bu-ì-lum (RTC 388)

A-bu-um-DINGIR (U 52+)

A-bu-um-DINGIR.RA (PDTI 407)

A-bu-um-DINGIR-lum (ITT II/1 868 rev.)

A-bu-um-ì-lum (RTC 386)

Ba-ba-LUM (U 398)

DINGIR-DINGIR-su (Nies, UDT 119:4)

DINGIR-il-su (TCL II 5498 rev. i). Both DINGIR-il-su and DINGIR-DINGIR-su in PDTI 507

DINGIR-ni (Lau, OBTR 1)

DINGIR-ni-ra-bí (ITT IV p. 12, 7120)

DINGIR-su-ra-bí (AnOr I 24:10; Reisner, TUT 154 ii)

DINGIR-šu-ra-bí (YOS IV 246 rev. v)

DINGIR-šu-ba-ni (AnOr I 220)

DINGIR-ba-ni (TMH n.F. I/II p. 20)

DINGIR-lu-ba-ni (ibid.)

^{d}EN.ZU-il-šu (Barton, HLC III Pl. 102, 155 rev.)

Eš$_4$-dar-DINGIR-šu (TCL II 5504 ii)

Eš$_4$-dar-il-šu (Nies, UDT 91 vi)

ì-an-bí-ì-lum MAR.TU (TCL II 5508 i)

ì-lí-DINGIR-lum (TMH n.F. I/II 259)

ì-lí-Eš$_4$-dar (Orient. n.s. V 130+)

I!-lí-is-da-gal (BIN V 1:19)

ì-lí-Ma-ma (Reisner, TUT 99a rev.)

ì-lí-su-ra-bí (UET III p. 17+)

Il-šu-ba-ni (RA XIX 41 No. 57 rev.)

ì-lum-a-ḫi (Fish, CST p. 12)

ì-lum-mi-sár (Barton, HLC II Pl. 75 ii)

I-lu?-ni-ìr-ra (YOS IV 16)

Il-zi-lí (RA XIX 43 No. 92)

I-mi-ì-lum (RA XIX 40 No. 30)

^{d}ìr-ra-ìl-mi-ti (SO IX/1 No. 31 rev. 1)

Šu-ì-li (PBS XIII 28)

Šu-ì-lí (U 719+)

Ta-ki-il-ì-lí-šu (De Genouillac, Kich II D 60 rev.)

For other names cf. Schneider in Muséon LIX 73-9.

Ur III RN:

ÍD DINGIR-ba-ni (ZA LI Pl. I after p. 74 ii 6).

<u>iltum</u> "goddess."

Ur III PN's:

Šu-il-tum (ITT II/1 p. 28, 803)

Šu-íl-tum (Pinches, BTBC p. 89:3; p. 93 rev. 11, 14)

Il-da-num (CT III 35 i). Cf. Iltānum in Ranke, EBPN p. 188.

ʾ$_4$L <u>al</u> "upon."

al DÙL Rí-mu-uš (R xviii, xxiv; similarly UET I 276 i, NS.)

al-su-nu (R xxiii, xxv)

al PN i-ba-šè "(so much barley) is upon PN" = "PN owes (so much barley)" (HSS X 46:3; 50 iii x+5; 51 iv 4; 109:22; 110:6; BIN VIII 125; A 5423)

al-su-ni i-ba-šè (HSS X 59:9)

ši-[nothing?]-tum al-[nothing?]-su i-ba-se_{11} (FM 9:28)

al GN i-ba-šè (Fish, CST 7)

al PN iš-ku-un (RTC 119:7)

al-su (Ist. Mus. Lagash 11001 rev.)

PN_1 al PN_2 (11 times, each time different names, in Kish 1930, 140).

PSarg., Sarg., and Ur III PN's:

^{d}A-ba_4-al-su! (ITT II/2 p. 27, 4491)

Al-su-da-ad (E). Formation like Sar-ru-da-ad

Dan-al-su (UET III 15, U)

DINGIR-al-su (D+)

^{d}EN.ZU-al-su (MO)

^{d}EN.ZU-al-šu (U 992)

$Eš_4$-dar-al-su (MO+)

GIŠ.TUKUL-ga-su-al-si-in /Kakkašu-alšin/ (MO)

Ìr-ra-al-su (E)

^{d}Nisaba-al-su (E)

Sar-ru-al-si-in (D).

ʾ$_x$L *ali*, *alum*, see ʾ$_1$ʾ$_2$L âlum.

ʾ$_x$L *alum* (a type of sheep).

Akk. lw. in Ur III Sum.:

GANAM a-lum, UDU a-lum, and $SILA_4$ a-lum (passim in Ur III; cf. Orient. XXII 10f., 24, 36).

ʾ$_x$L?

U.LUM in du!-a-rí-su GN na-ki-ir-ma SAG.GIŠ.RA (R xvii). Von Soden, ZA XL 99: ullum "später." The passage was collated; the sign U very doubtful.

ʾ$_4$Lʾ$_7$ *alājum* "to come up."

li-li-am "may he come up" (HSS X 7:6).

aljum "upper."

ma-dam a-lí-dam (S vi, xiv)

ti-a-am-dam a-lí-dam ù sa-bil-dam (S iv, viii, xii; R xxv)

ti-a-am-dam a-lí-dam (UET I 275 i, NS.; IAMN XII Pl. IV, NS.)

ti-am-[tum]? e-li-t[um]? (Morgan, MSP IV 161 ii, Lullubum).

alijātum "upper (regions)."

EN.EN a-lí-a-tim "the lords of the upper (regions)" (UET I 274 ii, NS.).

ʾ$_x$Lʾ$_x$N, see ʾ$_x$Rʾ$_x$N iriānum.

ʾ$_6$LD walādum "to bear children," "to beget."

DN in ma-ti-su a-la-da-am li-ip-ru-us "may DN withhold child-birth in his land" (CT XXXII 4 xii, CM).

Sarg. and Ur III PN's:

A-lí-id-^{d}EN.ZU (UET III 1431, U). Doubtful

Tu-li-id-da-nam (MO)

Tu-li-id!-Ma-ma (BIN V 300:1, U)

Tu-li-^{d}UTU (MDP XIV 78) = Tu-li-<id>-^{d}UTU?

Tu-li-id-^{d}UTU (Fish, CST p. 16, U)

Tu-lí-id-^{d}UTU (PDTI 555 iv, U)

Tu-li-id-^{d}UTU-ši (Nikolski, Dok. II 464 rev., U; Boson, TCS p. 28, U)

U-li-id-ì-lum (MO)

Wa-al-ti-lum (unpubl., U).

littum "child."

Sarg. PN:

Li-da-at-GI (D).

ʾ$_x$LḪR allaḫarum, alluḫarum (a plant?).

Akk. lw. in Ur III Sum.:

x QA al-la-ḫa-ru (RTC 229 rev. i; TCL V 5680 iv, rev. i; AnOr I 34; Nikolski, Dok. II 438; RA XVI 19f. iii, iv, viii, xi; Chiera, STA 23 v; ITT IV p. 83 7954; UET III 259; 1498 rev. iv; etc.)

x QA ni-ik-tum al-la-ḫa-ru (TCL V 6037 rev. vi). Cf. x MA.NA a-al-la-ḫa-ru ni-ik-tum in BIN IX 83, OB

1 al-la-ḫa-ru GUR (UET III 1767 rev. ii)

al-lu-ḫa-ru-um (RA XVIII 63, Voc. prat.)

Cf. a-al-la-ḫa-ru and al-la-ḫa-ru in BIN IX 80, 81, 82, 104, 105, 467, 470, OB.

ʾ$_2$LK alākum "to go."

Written syllabically.

a-na-lim-ma ki a-la-kam "as I shall come to the city" (JRAS 1932 p. 296:34)

[a]-la-kam (HSS X 10:10)

è-la-kam "he will come" (HSS X 6:6)

i-la-ak (ITT V 6682)

10 GEMÉ a-na GN i-la-gu "they will go" (HSS X 200:13)

.... lu il-la-gu (CT XXXII 2 v, CM)

su-ma e-la-ga-LAM+KUR "if (the two fugitives) come" (Kish 1930, 768). We expect ellakā-nim or ellakā-nikkim

al-li-ku (UET I 275 iv, NS., in difficult context)

e tal-li-ik (D 315:14)

ma-na-ma la i-lí-ik (UET I 274 ii, NS.)

PN i-lí-ik-ma (ibid.)

PN i-li-ik-ma (MDP XIV p. 10 i)

PN il-li-kam-ma (MDP XIV p. 12 v)

li-li-ik (ITT V 6682)

li-li-kam?-me (Kish 1930, 170c)

al-kam-ma "come!" (FM 10:11)

^{d}U.MEŠ á-lí-ik maḫ-rí-su (R xix twice)

a-la-kam aq-bí-si-im "I told her to go" (D 315:13, also 5?, 18)

ì-nu PN a-na GN i-li-ku (BIN VIII 129). With a-na "to"

[ì]-nu a-na GN a-li-ku (BIN VIII 135). With a-na "to"

ì-nu PN in GN i-li-g⌈a-ni⌉ (BIN VIII 146). With in "to"

[ì]-nu PN in GN i-li-kam (BIN VIII 146). With in "to"

ì-nu PN's i-li-ga-ni (BIN VIII 265, Dual)

ì-nu .... i-lí-ku (UET I 274 ii, NS.)

[i]n 1 [MU] NS. .... i-li-[ku] (Ist. Mus. Adab 404, date)

ni?-is-ku-su a-na? UNUG^{KI} lu it-tal-ku "truly they went" (Ist. Mus. Lagash 11001 rev.).

ilkum "corvée."

⌈i⌉-li-ik-šu-nu la iḫ-ši-ḫu (CT XXXII 2 v, CM).

$^{\prime}{}_{x}$LK? allikum? (a plant or a tree).

Akk. lw. in Ur III Sum.:

x QA al-lí-ku-um (Chiera, STA 11 ii). Read simply al-ni-ku-um?

x QA NUMUN al-lí-ku-um (ibid.).

$^{\prime}{}_{1}$LL? allānum (a plant or a tree).

Akk. lw. in Sum.:

al-la-núm (UET III 513, U; 558). A gold ornament

3 KIL GIŠ.ŠUB al-la-núm (UET III 812, U; 1498 rev. i, copied al-la-tum)

a-la-núm (YOS I 11 v, in a list including trees or woods).

$^{\prime}{}_{1}$LL illatum "power?" or "family?" (Stamm, ANG pp. 299f.).

Written syllabically and logographically as KASKAL.KUR.

In some cases Illat is a DN.

PSarg., Sarg., and Ur III PN's:

Be-lí-ìl-la-at (D)

DINGIR-Il-la-at (Fish, CST 17+)

E-la-^{d}Il-at (ITT I 1460)

ì-lí-Il-la-at (E)

ì-lí-íl-la-at (ITT II/2 p. 15, 3093)

ì-lí-ìl-la-at (E)

ì-lí-la-at (3 NT 796 iii, U)

DINGIR-il-la-zu (D+)

DINGIR-šu-KASKAL.KUR (ITT V 6767 rev., U)

E-la-túm (TCL V 6039 ii, rev. iii, U)

^{d}EN.ZU-KASKAL.KUR (TMH n.F. I/II 129, U)

Eš$_{4}$-dar-ìl-la-at (D)

ì-lí-mi-la-at (3 NT 796 iii, U)

Il-la-at (D)

Il-la-at-zu (E+)

Il$_{x}$-la-zu (U 1733)

^{d}IM-il-la-at (U 869)

^{d}IM-KASKAL.KUR (U 871+)

Iš-dup-Il?-at? (TMH V 5, PSarg.?)

^{d}UTU-il-at (RTC 180)

^{d}UTU-il-la-at (RTC 108)

^{d}UTU-ìl-[la?-at]? (D)

^{d}UTU-ši-la-at (Lau, OBTR 22, U).

ʾ$_{1}$LL ulālum "weak."

Sarg. and Ur III PN's:

Ù-la-lum (G+)

Ú-la-lum (CT VII 7 i, U).

ʾ$_{3-5}$LL ullulum "to purify."

[....] ù EN.LÍL^{KI} a-na ^{d}En-líl u-li-il (S x).

ellum "pure," "refined."

x KUG.BABBAR el-lum (D 303:1). Cf. KUG.BABBAR UD in Oppenheim, CCTE p. 24, U

20(QA)? NI KUG "pure oil" (MDP IV Pl. 2 iii).

Sarg. and Ur III PN's:

E-la-nu-um MAR.TU (Legrain, TRU 295 rev., U). Cf. Ellānum in Iraq VII 37, Chagar Bazar

El-lum (D+).

ʾ$_{x}$LL alālum "to rejoice."

Sarg. PN's:

I-lul-DINGIR (D+)

LI-lu-ul-dan, king of Akkad (AOF X 281). Possibly to be identified with Elulu; cf. MAD II 12.

ʾ$_{x}$LL ullum "joy?"

Ur III PN's:

Ìr-ra-ul-li (De Genouillac, TD 60)

Ìr-ra-ul-lí<<-lí>> (ibid.; probably the same person, cf. Šu-ab-ba ibid.)

Ul-lí-be-lu-ug (RA XIX 192 No. 10). Ununderstandable

Ul-li-be-lu-ug (Nies, UDT 91:166; Fish, CST p. 55 No. 507, translit. as Ul-li-ša-be-lu-úg.

ʾLL?

Sarg. PN:

U-li-DINGIR (JCS X 26 vi).

ʾ$_x$LL allum "hoe."

Akk. lw. in Sum.:

1 ^{GIŠ}al-lum (FM 33:16)

x ^{GIŠ}al-lum (HSS IV 6 ii, U)

23 GIŠ.AL and 4 AL (BIN VIII 271:5 and 9).

Sarg.?! PN:

Al-lum (AnOr VII 372).

ʾ$_x$LL allalum?

Ur III PN:

Á-la-lum (HSS IV 78 rev.).

ʾ$_x$LL allatum.

Ur III DN:

^{d}Al-la-tum (Schneider, AnOr XIX No. 20)

Cf. possibly the old Arabic goddess Allāt discussed under Lāt in Encycl. of Islam III 18f. and under Alilat in I 300.

ʾ$_x$LL.

Ur III PN:

Ì-la-lum (U 2425 = RA IX 56, translit. only)

Ì-là(l)-lum (U 2426+).

ʾ$_x$LMK elammakum, elimmakum (a tree).

Akk. lw. in Ur III Sum. For the reading cf. Falkenstein in JAOS LXXII 44:

ŠÀ ^{GIŠ}ZAG.BAR e-lam!-ma-gúm-TA (UET III 1498 vi bottom)

ŠÀ ZAG.BAR ^{GIŠ}e-lam-ma-[gúm-TA] (UET III 816)

1 GIŠ.BANŠUR e-lam-ma-gúm (Orient. XLVII 37)

3 GIŠ.BANŠUR e-li-ma-gúm (UET III 828)

Cf. ^{GIŠ}e-lam-ma-kum in YOS I 36 ii 23, Anam of Uruk.

ʾ$_x$LN? elunum (a festival).

Akk. lw. in Ur III Sum.:

è-lu-núm (YOS IV 240; AnOr VII 67)

é-lu-núm (RA XIX 192 No. 4)

Cf. UD e-lu-nu-um-ŠÈ in TA 1931, 326, OB; é/e-lu-nu-um ^{d}Nin-gal in UET V p. 69, OB and è-lu-núm ^{d}Innin in BIN IX 331, OB.

ʾ$_1$LP *alappum "ship."

Written logographically only.

ti-a-am-tim sa-bil-tim MÁ.MÁ GIŠ.LA-e u-sa-PI-ir (M xxvi)

in MÁ.MÁ i-za-na-ma (UET I 274 v, Mi.)

MÁ of various countries in ga-rí-im ši A-ga-dè^{KI} ìr-ku-us (S vi, xiv)

1 MÁ ša-at 30(GUR) TA (BIN VIII 151). Of Fem. gender.

ʾ$_x$LR.

Ur III PN's:

A-la-ru-um (U 158; TCL II 4682)

Al-la-ru (Nies, UDT 91 viii).

ʾ$_1$M ummum "mother."

um-ma-su (TA 1931, unpubl.).

PSarg., Sarg., and Ur III PN's:

A-li-um-mi (Reisner, TUT 159 iii, U)

Eš$_4$-dar-um-mi (G+; U 1780+)

Eš$_4$-dar-um-me (RTC 53 ii+, PSarg.)

Ma-ma-um-mi (D+)

Si-um-me (Nikolski, Dok. I 104+, PSarg.)

Si-um-mi (D)

Um-mi-DÙG (D+; U 1161)

Um-mi-da-bàt (Chiera, STA p. 32, U)

Um-mi-da-bat$_5$ (TMH n.F. I/II p. 24+, U)

Um-mi-É.GAL SAL (Bab. VII Pl. XXI 13, U)

Um-mi-Eš$_4$-dar (FM+)

Um-mi-Ma-ma (D+)

Um-mi-mi (D+)

Um-mi-Nu-nu (UET III 1357 rev., U)

Um-mi-^{d}UTU (D+). Cf. UTU-AMA.MU (HSS III 21 vi 22, PSarg.).

In the following cases the logogram AMA may be read in Akk.:

AMA-Ga-zur$_x$(SAG) (FM)

AMA-^{d}Innin (D)

AMA-^{d}EN.ZU (MO).

ʾ$_1$M amtum "slave girl," "woman worker."

Written GEMÉ, very rarely syllabically.

The word amtum has the meaning "slave girl" in texts pertaining to sales of slave girls, such as D 43; A 815. It means simply "woman worker," parallel to GURUŠ "man worker," in such texts as D 163; MDP XIV 71 rev. iii; etc. Cf. also SAL contrasted with GURUŠ in ITT I 1099.

Sarg. and Ur III PN's:

A-ma-at-É-a (UET III 1033, U)

GEMÉ-^{d}Innin (FM+)

GEMÉ-tum (ITT I p. 18, 1285)

GEMÉ-za (Ward, SCWA p. 81 No. 217)

GEMÉ-zu (FM)

GEMÉ-zu-ni (D+)

Passim in Ur III (U 660ff.).

ʾ$_4$M *ammum* "paternal uncle."

Interpr. as ʾ$_4$M ammum "paternal uncle" rather than as ʾ$_3$M amum "father-in-law" is necessitated by parallels in Amorite and South Semitic onomastic usage.

Sarg. and Ur III PN's:

Be-lí-a-mi (MO+)

DINGIR-a-ma (D)

PÙ.ŠA-a-mi (Orient. XVIII 28 rev., U). Cf. Puzur-ḫâli under ḫâlum.

ʾ$_6$M?

Ur III PN:

Wa-me-ti (Nikolski, Dok. II 458 rev.).

ʾ$_x$M?

Ur III PN?:

^{d}Nin-líl-e-mu-tu-ut (UET III 754 ii). Ununderstandable.

ʾ$_6$Mʾ$_1$ *wamāʾum* "to swear"; see also TMʾ$_1$ tamāʾum.

Normally followed by Subjunctive.

by DN's ú-má "I swear" (R xxiii, xxvi; RA VIII 136, R; RA VII 105, Mi.; M xxvii; Ist. Mus. Lagash 11001 rev.)

BÀD A-ga-dè^{KI} ù-[nothing?]-ma (FM 9:17)

⌈e⌉?-ni na-ʾà-áš ^{d}Šar-ga-lí-LUGAL-rí ù-má "behold?, by the life of Škš. I swear" (JRAS 1932 p. 296:29)

na-ʾà-áš-su ù-má (A 708, referring to [LUG]AL?).

mammîtum "oath."

Ur III MN:

^{ITI}Ma-mi-a-tum (RA XIII 133)

^{ITI}Ma-mi-a-tim (RA XIII 133)

^{ITI}Ma-mi-tum (RA XXXII 190)

^{ITI}[Ma]-mi-tum (TA 1931, 366)

This MN appears also in OB texts from Mari and Diyala.

Ur III PN:

Ma-me-at (ITT II/1 p. 19, 737).

DN in Ur III PN's:

Šu-Ma-mi-tum (UET III p. 15+)

Šu-^{d}Ma-mi-tum (Aegyptus XXVI 176)
Šu-^{d}Ba-mi-tum (RA X 208b rev.). Doubtful

Cf. Deimel, PB Nos. 2043f.

ʾ$_x$Mʾ$_7$ amājum.

Sarg. and Ur III PN's:

ì-me-Dur-ùl (FM). For the spelling cf. ì-bí-^{d}En-líl

I-mi-DINGIR (D+). Cf. also I-wi-DINGIR under ʾ$_2$6ʾ$_7$? awājum

I-mi-^{d}EN.ZU (MO+; U 1642)

I-mi-lum (RTC 391 rev., U)
I-mi-ì-lum (BE I Pl. VI iv; RA XIX 40 No. 30, U)

I-me-ìr-ra (RT XIX 48)
I-mi-ìr-ra (ZA XII 333; UET III p. 16, U)

I-mi-sar-ru (JCS X 26 iv)

I-mi-^{d}UTU (RTC 246)

I-mi-ZU (D+).

ʾ$_4$MD amādum "to stand by?"

e-dam-da /eʾtamdā/ (Kish 1930, 143 rev.). Interpr. doubtful.

šûmudum "to let stand," "to set up," "to place," "to procure." Von Soden's doubts in WO I 356f. about the translation of šûmudum are difficult to follow.

MU-su u-sa-mi-id = Sum. me-te-ni ì-ŠID "R. set up his name" (R xxvii; RA VIII 139, R.)

ŠE .... a-na ŠE.NUMUN li-sa-me-id-ma li-ti-in "the barley for seed may he procure and give" (HSS X 5:7).

Ur III PN:

Su-mi-id-DINGIR (TCL II 4681+)
Su-me-id-DINGIR (ITT V p. 55, 9838)
Zu(m)-mi-id-DINGIR (2 NT 601; PDTI 556 rev.).

amūdum? "column?"

a-bi-lum a-na a-mu-te ù-la e-bi-iš? "a man should not make (the statue) into columns?" (MDP II p. 63 ii; XIV p. 20 ii). Very doubtful.

imdum "support."

Sarg. and Ur III PN's:

Eš$_4$-dar-im-ti (U 1782)

I-mi-id-^{d}EN.ZU (U 1642+)

I-mi-id-^{d}Eš$_4$-dar (BE III 93, U)

I-mi-id-DINGIR (AnOr VII p. 25, U)

Im-ti-AN.NA (ITT V p. 48, 9660, U)

Im-ti-li-bur (D+)

Im-ti-lum (ITT V 6887, U)

Im-tum (MO)

dNIN.LÍL-tum-im-ti (A 5535, U).

imittum "support."

Sarg. and Ur III PN's:

Eš$_4$-dar-i-mi-ti (FM)

|Ì-lí-mi-ti (U 1634+)

|DINGIR-mi-ti (BIN V 346:21, U).

nêmedum? "stand?"

Akk. lw. in Ur III Sum.?:

ne-me-tum (MDP XXVIII p. 13 No. 11, Votive).

$^{\supset}{}_{x}$ML.

Sarg. PN:

A-ma-lim, Gen. (D+).

$^{\supset}{}_{x}$ML?

Akk. lw. in Sum.:

10(QA) ZÍD ù-ma-al-tum (Reisner, TUT 121 xiv)

Cf. 12 GIŠ ù-má-al-[....] (UET III 805:1).

[$^{\supset}{}_{x}$MM ummatum.]

Ur III PN:

Um-ma-zi-na (Reisner, TUT 160 v 21), read Um-ma-gi-na.

$^{\supset}{}_{x}$MM ummānum, Fem., "army."

ma-ḫi-iṣ ga-ga-ad um-ma-an GN's (CT XXI 1c, Dêr)

(ì-nu ....) ga-ga-ad um-ma-nim si-a-ti im-ḫa-zu-na (Speleers, RIAA 4 ii, Dêr)

[ŠU.NIGÍN] um-ma-[ni]-ì-a (CT XXXII 1 ii) = nap-ḫar um-ma-ni-ia (RA VII 180) in CM.

ummānum "craftsman."

ŠU.NIGÍN 30 LAL 3 ti-ru IGI.GAR ("inspection") um-ma-nim (MDP XIV 24 end).

Sarg. and Ur III PN's:

Um-ma-núm (RTC 237)

|Ù-ma-ni (TMH V p. 22+; TCL V 5666 i, U)

|Ú-ma-an-ni (UET I 17).

$^{\supset}{}_{7}$MN imnum "right (hand)."

Sarg. and Ur III PN's:

Im-ni-dIM (Orient. XLVII 423, U). Or MN$^{\supset}{}_{7}$ manājum

Im-num (ITT II/2 p. 53, 5897).

Ur III RN:

ÍD Im-ni-a (ZA LI Pl. I after p. 74 ii 9, 11).

ʾ$_x$MN.

Sarg. PN's:

A-ma-an-Eš$_4$-dar, f.n. (Ward, SCWA No. 217)

E-ma-an-Eš$_4$-dar (D). Cf. OB names E-ma-an-^{d}EN.ZU in Kh. 1935, 29; same, f.n., in TA 1930, 542; E-ma-^{d}Tišpak in TA 1931, 463 i

E-ma-num (UCP IX p. 205, 83 iii).

ʾ$_x$MN umunum?

Sarg. and Ur III PN's:

Ù-mu-NI (CT I 1, 91-5-9, 589)

Ú-mu-nu-um (ITT III 5255, U).

ʾ$_4$MQ amūqum, emūqum "strength."

Sarg. and Ur III PN's:

ʾÀ-mu-ku[m] (D)

Ma-nu-um-e-mu-uq (Fish, CST p. 160 ix, U).

ʾ$_1$MR amārum "to see," "to inspect." See also NMR? namārum?

da-mu-ur-ma "you saw" (HSS X 8:5)

a-ti e-ni-a la da-mu-ru "as long as you have not seen me" (RA XXIII 25:12)

ma-na-ma la i-mu-ru (Subj.) "nobody saw" (PBS V 36 x+ii, NS.)

6 persons i-mu-ru (D 336:20). Witnesses inspected

6 persons e-mu-ru (FM 6:10).

Sarg. and Ur III PN's:

A-ma-rí-iš (D)

A-ma-ru-um (D+)

A-mi-ir-DINGIR (Orient. XLVII 136:15, U)

A-mi-ir-^{d}Šul-gi (TCL II 5500 ii, U)

A-mur-a-DINGIR (De Genouillac, TD 54 ii, U). Ununderstandable

A-mur-a-LUGAL (TCL II 5567, U). Ununderstandable

A-mur-DINGIR (D+; U 172+)

A-mur-Eš$_4$-dar (RTC 127 rev. iv)

A-mur-KAL.LA (E)

A-mur-la-ba (RTC 197; 198)

A-mur-^{d}Šul-gi (BIN V p. 5, U)

A-mur-^{d}UTU (Kish 1930, 144a ii; ITT II/1 p. 49, 939, U)

Ḫa-áš-ḫa-me-ir (CT XXI 6, 89126, U).

ʾ$_1$MR immerum "sheep."

Logogram UDU is used regularly not only for sheep, but also for goats; cf. ITT I 1047, where x UDU and x ÚZ are summed up as x UDU.ḪI.A.

Ur III PN:

Im-me-ir (UET III p. 17+).

ʾ$_3$MR imārum "donkey."

Logogram ANŠE includes various types of equids, such as ANŠE.LIBIR, ANŠE.BAR.AN, ANŠE.EDIN (PBS IX 38; A 3012; A 3397).

Sarg. and Ur III PN:

I-ma-ru-um (OIP XIV 149+)
E-ma-ru-um (CT VII 20b rev. 19, U)

ʾ$_x$MR? nâmarum (a garment). Cf. na-ma-rum = ṣu-ba-tu in Malku VI 30 and ʾ$_x$BR? nâbarum and ḪBR? naḫbarum.

Akk. lw. in Ur III Sum.:

2 TÚG na-ma-ru-um TUR.TUR (YOS IV 296:36)
1 TÚG na-ma-ru-um KA.AḪ (l. 38)
1 TÚG na-ma-ru-um 3.KAM UŠ (UET III 1750).

ʾ$_x$MTḪŠ? imtuḫšum?, intuḫšum? (a container).

Akk. lw. in Ur III Sum.:

GÁ.DUB.BA im-duḫ-ZUM ù KUŠ.DÙG.GAN (Reisner, TUT 164[4])
20 in-daḫ-šu-um (ITT IV p. 6, 7059; translit. DAḪ probably for DUḪ)
2 GUR.DUB TUR 275 in-duḫ-šu-um (TCL II 5578)
30 in-duḫ-šum (BE III 55 rev.)
Instead of duḫ, reading du$_8$ (or gaba) can also be considered.

ʾ$_1$N anni "now."

a-ni-me mim-ma-su la ti-su "now nothing of it thou hast" (FM 8:14).

annijum "this."

za-al-mi-in an-ni-in (Morgan, MSP IV 161, Lullubum).

Ur III PN:

An-ni-tum (TCL V 6039 i, ii).

ʾ$_2$N enma, umma "thus."

Written en-ma in Sarg., um-ma in Ur III.

en-ma PN$_1$ a-na PN$_2$ ki-bí-ma "thus (says) PN$_1$, say to PN$_2$" (passim in letters)
en-ma PN$_1$ a-na PN$_2$ è-ga-bi (BM 54318 rev.)
PN's AB+ÁŠ en-ma PN$_1$ a-na PN$_2$ (FM 8:8; 9:13; 10:5; [11:6]; [12:17])
en-ma LUGAL a-na PN (RTC 77:4, in middle of text)
en-ma PN (MDP XIV 7, in middle of text; 32)
en-ma NS. (UET I 275 iii)
um-ma PN (MDP XXVIII 424 rev., U)
um-ma sar-ru-um-ma a-na PN ki-bí-ma (RA XXIV 44, U)
um-ma PN ni-iš LUGAL it-ma (Yondorf a, U).

ʾ$_4$N inum "time," "when."

Inum is originally a noun as best evidenced by:

ì-nu NS. da-nim "at the time of NS., the mighty" (PBS V 36 rev.

x+ii), comparable with i-nu-ma da-wi-di-im (Syria XIX 110) and i-nu-ma te-bi-ib-tim (Iraq VII 26), both from Mari

ki DN .... i-ti-nam-ma ì-nu-šu dam-si-[lí] ab-ni "when DN gave me ...., then I made my image" (UET I 275 iii, NS.). Construction parallel to in-ûmišu, under ʾ$_7$ʾ$_6$M ûmum.

In all other cases ì-nu functions as a conjunction with the meaning "when," construed with Subj. (or without it when verb is in Allative):

ì-nu GN SAG.GIŠ.RA-ni (BE I 5, R.; UET I 10, R.; R xxiv; M xxvi)

ì-nu ^{d}En-líl DI.TAR-su i-ti-nu-ma (PBS V 36 rev. x+iii, NS.)

[ì]-nu .... i-lí-ku (UET I 274 i, NS.)

ì-nu .... i-ti-nu-ma (UET I 275 ii, NS.)

ì-nu PN .... IN.DA.LAL-ni (RA VIII 200 i, NS., copy)

ì-nu .... ip-te-ù (MDP IV Pl. 2 ii)

ì-nu ma-at A-wa?-an ú-te-ra/ru (Morgan, MSP IV 158, Lullubum)

ì-n[u] ŠU.NIGÍN ma-[ta-tim] .... [a]-a-bi-iš [ib]-ba-al-ki-da-an-ni-ma (CT XXXII 1 i) = ia-š[i] ib-b[al-ki-tu] (RA VII 180 i) in CM

ì-nu PN a-na GN i-li-ku (BIN VIII 129)

ì-nu LUGAL u-ur-da-ni (BIN VIII 134)

[ì]-nu a-na GN a-li-ku (BIN VIII 135)

ì-nu PN in GN i-li-g⌈a-ni⌉ (BIN VIII 146)

[ì]-nu PN in GN i-li-kam (BIN VIII 146)

ì-nu PN's i-li-ga-ni (BIN VIII 265).

ittum "time," "term."

PN a-na it-ti-šu ITI Ma-mi-a-tim na-da-ni-iš ga-bi (RA XIII 133, U).

ʾ$_x$N ana "to," "for," etc.

en-ma PN$_1$ a-na PN$_2$ ki-bí-ma "thus (says) PN$_1$, say to PN$_2$" (passim in letters)

ŠE šu a-na ŠE.BA a-si-tu "barley which I left over for rations" (HSS X 5:4)

a-na ŠE.BA É (D 322:5)

a-na ŠE.NUMUN li-sa-me-id-ma "may he place for seed barley" (HSS X 5:6)

a-na ŠÁM DUN "for the price of pig" (HSS X 105 i x+9; 106:5; 107:12; etc.)

a-na GN i-la-gu (HSS X 200:12)

a-na GN wabālum (D 318:12)

a-na 15 ŠE.GUR "for 15 GUR of barley" (HSS X 210:1)

a-na ḫu-bu-lim maḫārum "to receive on loan" (D 291:3)

a-na TÚG.ŠAG$_4$.GA.DÙ ga-ba-zi-im "for bleaching a garment" (D 258) a-na NÍG.KI.GAR É grain, oil, etc. a-na NI.ZAG PN i-ti-in (JCS X 26 ii, iii)

a-na za-bi-im "for the workers" (JCS X 29 No. 8 rev., U)

grain a-na ḫa-ša-lim (HSS X 132:2, 12)

a-na ŠE nadānum (FM 8:13)

a-na ŠÁM ŠE šadādum (FM 8:17)

a-na ur-ki-im "in the back" (FM 11:10) and a-na ra-si-im "in the front" (FM 11:12)

ì-nu PN a-na ŠE.BA a-na GN i-li-ku "when PN went to GN concerning the barley rations" (BIN VIII 129)

[a]-na DI.TI.LA Na-ra-am-^{d}EN.ZU "according to the decision of NS." (UCP IX p. 205, 83 iv)

a-na 10 ŠE.GUR ù-la da-ki-ba-an-ni "with 10 GUR of barley you did not trust me" (EK III Pl. XI W. 1929, 160)

a-na na-si LUGAL "for the life of the king" (BIN VIII 121)

a-na-ʾà-si-su a-na-ʾà-si PN (Iraq I Pl. IXb)

a-na-lim-ma "to the city" (JRAS 1932 p. 296:34)

a-na PN_1 GEMÉ a-na PN_2 la a-ra-ga-mu "(he swore:) concerning PN_1, the slave girl, I will not make a claim against PN_2" (RA XXXII 190, U)

Cf. a-ru-gi-ma, possibly for ar-rûqimma, discussed under rašājum

⌈a⌉-na ^{d}A-a (CT XXXII 1 i) = an ^{d}A-a (RA VII 180, NB) in CM.

ʾ$_x$N in, ina "in," "to," "from," etc. See also ʾ$_7$ʾ$_6$M ûmum.

Written in in PSarg. and Sarg., but both in and i-na in Ur III.

In PSarg. and Sarg.:

in GN (CT XXXII 7 ii, 8 i; PSBA XX Pl. I; DP 2 ii; A 25412; all PSarg.; HSS X 20 rev.; etc.)

in 1 MU (HSS X 72 iv 8)

[i]n DUB li-iš-tu-ru-nim (D 290 rev.)

ì-nu PN in GN i-li-kam (BIN VIII 146) compared with ì-nu a-na GN a-li-ku (BIN VIII 135)

in É PN (JCS X 26 L.E.)

in ki-ib-ra-tim ar-ba-im (BE I 120 ii, NS.)

in ŠU.NIGÍN-su-nu (PBS V 36 rev. iv, NS.; UET I 276 ii NS.)

in NAM.RA.AG GN A.MU.RU "from the booty of GN he offered" (BE I 5, R.; UET I 10, R.)

in sa-la-ti GN A.MU.RU (KAH II 1, Ititi)

SUḪUŠ GN_1 in UKÙ GN_2 i-zu-uḫ-ma "from the people of GN_2" (R [xxiii], xxv)

in kir-bí-su "from it(s midst)" (HSS X 5:13)

in ga-ti-ku-ni "in your hands" (Cop. 10055)

in na-ap-ḫa-rí-su-nu "in totality" (Cop. 10055)

in bu-bu-tim "in hunger" (MCS IV 13 rev.)

in E.SI DÙL-su ib-ni-ma "of E.SI stone" (UET I 275 iii, NS.)

in ra-ma-ni-ga "yourself" (JRAS 1932 p. 296:32)

in 1 GÍN TA "at 1 shekel each" (MDP XIV 86+)

so much grain in 30(QA) LUGAL (HSS X 72 ii 5)

so much grain in 30(QA) DINGIR (HSS X 72 iii 5)

4 GUR in 40(QA) (HSS X 107:1)

so much grain in ši 40(QA) (HSS X 116:2)

KUG.BABBAR-su 25 MA.NA in 3 MA.NA TA (ITT II/2 5798)

KUG.BABBAR-su 50 MA.NA in 2(PI) 30(QA) TA (ITT II/2 5893 i)

A difficult case: 1 ANŠE.BAR.AN Ab-ba in NU.BANDA Amar-šè (ITT I 1431) translated as "Abba qui est dans (la section) du nu-banda Amar-si" by Thureau-Dangin in ITT I p. 28.

Sarg. PN:

In-su-mi-su-da-nu (MO).

In Ur III:

i-na mu-ši-im (UET III 270 iv, post-Ur III)

i-na ^{ITI}Ma-mi-a-tum (RA XIII 133)

i-na ti-ir-ti DN (Speleers, RIAA 4 ii, Dêr)

i-na ša-du-im Ba-ti-ir (Morgan, MSP IV 161 ii, Lullubum)

ì-na GN and ì-na MÁ (MDP XXII 144)

I seized him ki gal-bi-im ì-na ki-ša-ti-šu, ki me-ra-ni-im ì-na pi-ir-ti-šu (3 NT 30, cf. ṣabātum)

in GN (ZA III 94; AS VI 22f.). Royal inscriptions; therefore the use of in is perhaps anachronic in Ur III.

ʾ$_{x}$N <u>entum</u> (a priestess).

Tu-da-na-ap-šum e-na-⌈at⌉ ^{d}En-líl (Ward, SCWA No. 217).

ʾ$_{x}$Nʾ$_{x}$? <u>enûm</u>? "utensils?"

e-nu (FM 7:21). Including garments, objects of skin, bronze, flour, etc.

^{GIŠ}e-ni Ù.RÍ.A (FM 33:42). Or ^{GIŠ}e-ni-ù RÍ.A?. Very doubtful

1 ....-tum ša-at e-nim (MDP XIV 7). Perhaps "eye."

ʾ$_{x}$Nʾ$_{x}$.

Akk. lw. in Ur III Sum.:

2 QA NI.NUN e-ni-tum-ŠÈ (PDTI 430). Cf. also No. 471 in difficult context. Cf. um-mi e-ni-tum in King, Chronicles II p. 88:2.

ʾ$_{x}$Nʾ$_{x}$.

Sarg. PN:

È-ni-um (FM)

| I-ni-um (FM).

$^{\supset}{}_{x}N^{\supset}{}_{x}$ unuātum? (type of bread).

Akk. lw. in Ur III Sum.:

2 5/6 MA.NA GAR u-nu-a-tum (AnOr I 165).

$^{\supset}{}_{4}$NB enbum "fruit."

PSarg., Sarg., and Ur III PN's:

En-bí-Eš$_{4}$-dar (BE I 104 and 105, PSarg.)

En-bu-DINGIR (G+)

En-bu-LUGAL (G)

Nu-úr-en-ba (ITT IV p. 74, 7789, U). Doubtful

^{d}Šu-^{d}EN.ZU-ì-ni-ib?-Eš$_{4}$-dar (UET III 1357, U).

$^{\supset}{}_{4}$NB?

Ur III Amorite PN:

I-na-ba-nu-um MAR.TU (A 2868).

$^{\supset}{}_{x}$NDL andullum "protection" (or the like).

Sarg. and Ur III PN's:

Be-lí-AN.DÙL (E+)

| DINGIR-AN.DÙL (UET III 43, U)
| Ì-lí-AN.DÙL (U 1619+).

$^{\supset}{}_{x}$NG?

Ur III PN:

In-gi-tum (YOS IV 254 ii).

$^{\supset}{}_{1}$NḪ anāḫum "to sigh."

Sarg. and Ur III PN's:

A-da-na-aḫ (MO+; U 107)

A-na-aḫ-ì-lí (U 179+)

A-na-ḫa-lí (RTC 290, U; ITT II/1 p. 21, 748 twice, U).

$^{\supset}{}_{1}$NK anāku "I."

a-na-gu a-ga-sa-ar (HSS X 5:15)

a-na-gu mi-ma ù-la a-ga-bi (JRAS 1932 p. 296:25)

en-ma a-na-gu-ma (Ist. Mus. Lagash 11001)

a-na-gu .... ki-iṣ-ri-su [....] "I [shall pay]? his hire" (BM 54318 rev.)

a-na-ku-ú lu GEMÉ (Yondorf a, U).

$^{\supset}{}_{3}$NN unnīnum "prayer."

Ur III PN:

Ú-ne-nu-um (A 2790 iii).

$^{\supset}{}_{x}$NN.

The form ennī "my request," "please," could go back to $^{\supset}{}_{3}$NN "to request," "to pray." Possibly even the form ennum in such PN's as

Ennum-ilī could be explained as "request, (O my god!)." But the form ennam in such PN's as Ennam-ilī cannot be derived from a noun. We may have to reckon possibly with a demonstrative element going back to $^{\supset}{}_{2}$N, as in en-ma.

e-ni e tal-li-ik "please?, do not go" (D 315:14)

⌈e⌉?-ni na-ʾà-áš ^{d}Šar-ga-lí-LUGAL-rí ù-má "behold?, (upon) the life of Škš. I swear" (JRAS 1932 p. 296:27)

e-ni ʾà-wa-at-zu i-ti-iš i-da-ḫa-az (Ist. Mus. Lagash 11001, doubtful).

PSarg., Sarg., and Ur III PN's:

A-li-en-ni (D)

DINGIR-en-ni (Walters Art Gall. 41.107 passim, PSarg.)

E-na-ba-d[an]? (D)

E-na-be-lí (E+)

E-na-^{d}EN.ZU (D+)

En-na-DINGIR (G+)

En-na-Il (A 25412 xvii, PSarg.; G+)

En-na-É-a (MO+)

[En]-na-LUGAL (G)

En-nam-^{d}EN.ZU (U 1091)

En-nam-ì-lí (UET III p. 13+, U)

En-nam-^{d}Šul-gi (U 1090+; Nesbit, SRD 23, U)

En-^{d}Šul-gi (Nesbit, SRD 23 seal, U)

En-na-nu (D+)

En-na-LUM (D+)

En-na-na (D+)

En-ni-a-ti (ZA XXV 206, U)

En-ni-íl-la (OIP XIV 143)

En-ni-lí (D+)

En-ni-lu (ITT I 1156+)

En-ni-LÚ (ITT II/2 p. 48, 5812)

En-ni-LUM (Ist. Mus. Nippur 2614)

En-ni-ma-da-ad (TMH n.F. I/II 285 twice, U). Enni-ma-Adad

En-ni-ma-ad (UET III p. 13+, U). Enni-ma-Ad(ad) or Enni-ma-abī or Enni-maʾad

En-ni-Mà-mi (Yondorf a, U)

En-ni-mu-um (UET III p. 13, U)

En-ni-na (E)

En-ni-na-da(n) (Cf. $N^{\supset}{}_{1}D$)

En-nu-a (OIP XIV 6)

En-um-É-a (JRAS 1937 p. 472 No. 4, U+)

En-num-ì-lí (E)

En-núm-ì-lí (U 1092)

En-um-ì-lí (U 1085+)

En-ú-mi-lí (RA XIX 39 VI rev., U; RTC 373 rev., U)

En-ú-mi-ì-lí (RA XIX 44 No. 10543 rev., U)

En-um-mi-ì-lí (A 5568, U)

En-nu-um-mi-lí (2 NT 672, U)

En-nu-ì-lí (Coll. De Clercq I 109, U?)

En-um-^{d}EN.ZU (UET III p. 13+, U)

En-um-Eš$_{4}$-dar (U 1086)

En-núm-Eš$_{4}$-dar (U 1093)

En-um-^{d}IM (U 1084+)

Ì-lí-en-núm (D+)

Ma-da-en-nam (UET III 1449 rev. i, U).

ʾ$_{x}$NN.

Ur III PN's:

A-na-na-num (Barton, HLC II Pl. 88 iv)

Á-na-núm (CT VII 7 iii).

ʾ$_{x}$NN.

Sarg. PN:

A-nin-u (FM+).

ʾ$_{x}$NN.

Sarg. PN:

I-nin-um (E+)

I-nin-núm (FM+)

ʾ$_{x}$NN <u>inanna</u> "now."

i-na-na (Ist. Mus. Lagash 11001, in broken context).

ʾ$_{x}$NN.

Sarg. and Ur III PN's:

Ì-na-ni (G+). Cf. Innanni/u in Clay, PNCP pp. 89f.

I-na-núm (A 2790 iii, U).

ʾ$_{x}$NN <u>inūnum</u> "punishment."

Sarg. PN:

I-nu-sa-tu (BIN VIII 298 rev.). Cf. I-nun-É-a (RA VIII 69:5, OB).

ʾ$_{1}$NP <u>appum</u> "branch (of a tree)?"

ab-bi ^{GIŠ}A.TU.GAB.LIŠ (Kish 1930, 143 rev.).

ʾ$_{4}$NQ? <u>anqum</u>? "ring?," "handle (of a container)?"

a-ni-iq GUR (FM 43 rev.).

ʾ$_{x}$NR?

Ur III PN:

Ù-nu-ru-um (RA XIX 40 No. XXV). = Ù-<zi>-nu-ru-um?

ʾ$_{x}$NSM ansammum (a container).

Perhaps a lw. from Sum.:

1 an-za-mu?! (FM 34:3). Listed among containers

x ^{GIŠ}AN.ZA.AM LAM and MES (Pinches, BTBC p. 106 ii, U)

1 AN.ZA.AM KA (BIN V 2:36, U)

^{NA_4}AN.ZA.AM ŠIR.GAL (UET III p. 187a top, U and others on p. 89)

Cf. also x AN.ZA.AM! UD.KA.BAR and KUG.BABBAR (MDP XVIII 94:13 and 100 rev. 12, OB).

Sarg. PN:

GÁN An-za-ma-tim (MO D ix).

ʾ$_{1}$NŠ aššatum "wife."

Sarg. PN:

Si-a-sa-at (D).

In all other cases the word is written logographically as DAM or SAL:

DAM PN (HSS X 55:2f.; 135:3; 154 iii 19, v x+14; 155 v 1; 157 i x+9, iii 1; D 331; 56; FM 16:1; CT I 1a)

PN$_1$ DAM PN$_2$ (HSS X 137:6; 139 x+5; 155 iii x+8, v 13; MDP XXIV 342 twice)

GURUŠ, DAM, DUMU.ARAD (D 207)

1 PN ù 1 DAM-zu ù 2 DUMU-su (D 246)

GURUŠ, DAM, DUMU.ARAD, DUMU.SAL, GABA (D 255)

PN$_1$, PN$_2$ DAM-zu (Iraq Mus. 43612)

Šu-a-tum ù Da-da SAL (FM 20:4)

SAL EN-li (HSS X 153 viii 6).

ʾ$_{3-5}$NŠ anāšum "to become weak."

Ur III PN's:

La-ì-ni-iš (JCS X 30 No. 10 rev.)

La-te-ni-iš (UET III 1215 vi)

La-te-in-iš(-E) (TCL V 6163)

Ú-la-e-ni-iš (Univ. Illinois 147)

Ú-la-ì-ni-iš (U 1128+)

Ú-li-ì-ni-iš (Nies, UDT 97:11)

Ú-la-ni-iš (PDTI 579 rev.).

enšum "weak."

PSarg. PN:

En-šu (RTC 54+). Doubtful because no mimation.

ʾ$_{1}$NT atta "thou" (Masc.).

ù-la a-bí ad-da (EK III Pl. XI W. 1929, 160)

ad-da ARÁD da-sa-am-ma "you will buy the slave" (BM 54318 rev.)

ad-da GÁN-lam ʾà-ru-uš (JRAS 1932 p. 296:14)
ad-da MÁŠ.ANŠE ù-la da-na-za-ar (ibid. 1. 36).

atti "thou" (Fem.).
at-ti ... ti-ni "give!" (MDP XIV p. 19).

ʾ$_x$NTḪŠ? antaḫšum (a plant).
Akk. lw. in Ur III Sum.:
10(QA) an-daḫ-šum (BE III 77 rev.).

ʾ$_x$NTḪŠ? intuḫšum, see ʾ$_x$MTḪŠ?

ʾ$_x$NZB.
Sarg. PN:
In-zi-ba-num (D).

ʾ$_x$NZR? anzārum?
Ur III PN:
An-za-ru-um RA.GABA (RA XIX 30, translit. only).

ʾ$_x$P aptum "window."
na-ak-da-ma-at ap-tim "covers for the window" (FM 41:1).

ʾ$_x$P aptum, see ʾ$_x$ŠT? eštum?

ʾ$_6$Pʾ$_x$ wuppûm?
PSarg., Sarg., and Ur III PN's:
A-lí-ú-bí (TCL V 6038 rev. iii, U)
Dan-ú-pi (Delaporte, CCL I T 220+, U)
Da-an-ú-bi (ITT II/1 4159, U)
DINGIR-ú-bi (ITT V Pl. III 10032+, U)
Ú-bí-DINGIR (De Genouillac, TSA 12 rev. ii, PSarg.)
Ú-bí-BÍ (OIP XIV 48 i, PSarg.)
Ú-KA-ma-tum (D)
Ù-bi-mu-ú-tum (U 1112 = YOS IV 2).

mûpium.
PSarg. and Sarg. PN's:
Is Mu-bí a DN?
A-ḫu-mu-bí (MO+)
ŠEŠ-mu-bí (RTC 84)
ARÁD-mu-bí (ITT I 1119)
BÀD-mu-bí (BIN VIII 118; 273)
E-bi-ir-mu-bí (MO)
E-bir$_5$-mu-bí (E+)
E-mu-te-mu-bí (D+). Ununderstandable
Gi-nu-mu-bí (BIN VIII 144 rev. iv). Or Kînum-ûpî
Íl-e-mu-bí (Iraq Mus. 43612)
Na-id-mu-bí (ITT I p. 30, 1466)
Sar-ru-um-Dilmun-mu-bí (UET II Pl. L No. 50 rev., PSarg.)

Zi-gur-mu-bí (MO)

Cf. also NBʾ$_1$? mubbiʾum.

<u>šûpium</u> "resplendent?"

Sarg. PN's:

Su-pi-um (PBS IX 4 iv+)

Šu-bí-^{d}Nin-[....] (MDP XIV 32). Doubtful.

ʾ$_x$PḪ? Derivation from ʾ$_6$PḪ or ʾ$_7$PḪ (J. Lewy in Hebrew Union College Annual XVIII 459ff.) impossible since the expected older forms would have to be wapiḫ, ûpiḫ, îpiḫ, or the like.

Ur III GN:

EN.TI^{KI} (RA X 65 No. 76; ITT V 8233; etc.).

Deified GN in Ur III PN's:

A-bí-A-bi-iḫ (TCL II 5552 rev.; Fish, CST 329)

A-bi-A-bi-iḫ (De Genouillac, TD p. 4, translit. only)

A-bí-A-bí-iḫ and A-bi-A-bi-iḫ (PDTI 609)

A-bí-A-pi-iḫ (BIN V 31 rev.)

PÙ.ŠA-A-bi-iḫ (CT XXXII 19 ii).

Before Ur III written logographically:

EN.TI-il (RA XXXI 143, PSarg.)

EN.TI-ni-bí (ITT II/2 4362)

Ìr-e-^{d}EN.TI (G+)

Ur-^{d}EN.TI (PBS IX 9:7).

ʾ$_1$PL <u>apālum</u>?

in É ši uš-da-a-bí-la (FM 10:8). Meaning doubtful.

ʾ$_1$PL <u>aplum</u> "heir."

Ur III Amorite PN:

Ap-lum and Ap-lum MAR.TU (Boson, TCS 371)

Cf. also note on ʾ$_1$ʾ$_6$L abīlum.

ʾ$_x$PN? <u>appunama</u> "exceedingly?," "in large numbers."

a-bu-na-ma Gu-ti-um-ma-me (JRAS 1932 p. 296:6). Landsberger, ZA XLIII 73: "ausserdem," "obendrein," "mit Bestimmtheit." But cf. the interpr. of ap-pu-na-ma as ma-aʾ-diš in a commentary (V R 47:54f.), which seems to fit our text.

ʾ$_x$PP <u>uppum</u> "door-handle?"

ub-bu (FM 43:15). The interpr. of ub-bu as door-handle (not drum) should be preferred here if the interpr. of DA.NAGAR šu-ga-e in FM 43:16 as part of a door is correct.

ʾ$_x$PQ <u>ipqum</u> (or <u>epqum</u>?). See also NPQ napāqum.

Sarg. and Ur III PN's:

Íl-ip-gi (G)

Ip-kum (D+)

Ip-ku-sa (TMH n.F. I/II 7, U)

Ip-ku-ša (U 1691; TMH n.F. I/II 82, U)

E-ip-ku-ša (Oppenheim, CCTE p. 186, U)

^{d}Nisaba?-ip-ki (D).

ʾ$_{x}^{PQ}$ upīqum.

Sarg. PN:

U-bi-kum (E).

ʾ$_{3-5}^{PR}$ apārum "to provide (with food)."

Sarg. PN's:

E-bi-ir-ì-lum (MO). Cf. E-pír-^{d}IM in KAV 19 rev. 11

E-bi-ir-mu-bí (MO)

E-bir$_{5}$-mu-bí (E+). Not Enammune, as read by Scheil and other scholars.

aprum

DN in PSarg. and Sarg. PN's:

Ap-ra-il (MO+). Cf. West Semitic PN ʿApr(a)ʾel discussed by Albright in JAOS LXXIV 225 and 233

Ur-Ap-ra (CT XXXII 7 iv+, PSarg.).

ʾ$_{x}^{PS}$ apsûm "sweet-water sea."

Lw. from Sum. apsu.

Sarg. and Ur III PN's:

A-bí-ap-sum$_{6}$(=šum) (CT I 1a)

Ap-za-núm (Pinches, AT p. 186, U). Interpr. doubtful

I-bí-ZU.AB (MO)

Ur-ZU.AB (MO).

ʾ$_{x}^{PSS}$ apsasûm (an ox-like animal).

9 ga-nu-nu a-na áp-za-za-tim GIŠ.SAG.GUL (PBS IX 21 twice). Here part of a door in form of an apsasûm.

ʾ$_{3-5}^{PŠ}$ apāšum "to make."

a-bi-lum a-na a-mu-te ù-la e-bi-iš? (MDP II p. 63 ii; XIV p. 20 ii)

ZÍD.BA-su ù-la e-bí-iš "he will not make his flour ration" (FM 53:15)

GIŠ.TUR.ŠÈ i-bu-uš (MDP X Pl. 3, 2)

GIŠ.TUR.ŠÈ NA$_{4}$ i-bu-uš (MDP X Pl. 3, 1a and 1b)

É .... i-bu-uš (KAH II 2, BS.)

e-dè-šum-ma É DN i-bu-uš (MDP II p. 58)

Mi. [e]-bi-iš [z]u-uk-ki-im (CT XXXII 1 i) = e-piš suk-ki (RA VII 180) in CM

lu e-bu-uš (ibid.).

epšum "wise?"

PN ri URU? ip-šum "the wise? shepherd? of the city?" (RA IX Pl. 1 opp. p. 1, Urkiš and Nawar). Cf. rēʾû itpišu in Delitzsch, AHWB p. 119b.

Sarg. PN:

Ip-šum (Kish 1930, 140+).

$ʾ_x$PŠ.

Sarg. PN:

Ì-bí-sa (G+). Cf. I-bi-ša in Cappadocian (OIP XXVII 55:21) and OB (BIN VII 68:20).

$ʾ_x$PT aptum, see $ʾ_x$ŠT? eštum?

$ʾ_6$Q$ʾ_7$? wuqqûm? "to establish?," "to ordain?"

animals etc. KIN UD.1.KAM ug_5-gi_4 (CT XXXII 1 v, vi etc., CM)

lu ug_5-gi_4 (ibid. iii, xii).

$ʾ_3$QL eqlum "field."

Written logographically as GÁN or A.ŠÀ, with or without phonetic indicators.

GÁN-lam (JRAS 1932 p. 296:4, 8, 15).

It is evidently Fem. to judge from: x (GÁN) GÁN.SAR.A ša-at A-za-la (HSS X 1), GÁN ša-at ʾÀ-ki-im ù Zi-ma-na-ak (MO D viii), and similarly in ša-at Gu-lí-zi (B vi), ša-at Bar-rí-im^{KI} (C xii, xviii), ša-at Sar-ra-tum^{KI} (BE I Pl. VII vii). Cf. also A.ŠÀ ša-at ^{d}Šu-^{d}EN.ZU (TMH n.F. I/II 171 rev., U) with A.ŠÀ ^{d}Šu-^{d}EN.ZU (ibid. No. 96).

In the following cases šu may refer not to eqlum specifically but to the whole measured area:

x GÁN šu É (D 119 x+ii)

x GÁN šu li-ip-tim etc. (D 332). May refer to ŠE

x GÁN šu Zu-ra-rí-tim (MDP XIV 32 rev. i)

GÁN su_4-a-ti and GÁN su_4-a-tu are found in CM (CT XXXII 2 iv), in a period which does not distinguish between genders of the Demonstr. Pron.

While GÁN means "field," A.ŠÀ denotes usually the "area of the field," as in HSS X 16; 19; 21; etc.; RTC 142; 148; etc. Still note that A.ŠÀ-su (MDP XIV 45) = GÁN-su (MDP XIV 10) and A.ŠÀ.BI (OIP XIV 116) = GÁN.BI (OIP XIV 163).

$ʾ_6$QR waqrum "dear."

Ur III PN's:

A-ḫu-a-gàr (U 132; Jean, ŠA p. 75)

A-ḫu-ba-gàr (U 133+)

A-ḫu-wa-gàr (U 136+)

Wa-gàr-^{d}Šu-^{d}EN.ZU (De Genouillac, TD 87)

Wa-gàr-tum, f.n. (UET III 1383+)

Ba-gàr-tum, f.n. (Delaporte, CCL II A 255).

<u>šûqurum</u> "to make dear."

Sarg. and Ur III PN's:

Su?-gír-a-bí (MDP XIV 6 rev.). Interpr. doubtful. Cf. [Šu]?!-ki-ir-^{d}Ma-ma in PBS XI/1 No. 386, OB

Si?-da-ag-su-kir (MDP XIV 27). Interpr. unknown

E-la-ag-šu-kir (U 1055; SO IX/1 No. 31 rev., U; TCL II 5483, U)

I-la-ag-šu-kir (PDTI 556, U)

E-la-ag-šu-gìr (Nikolski, Dok. II 481 i, U).

ᵓ$_{x}$QṢ, see ᵓ$_{x}$KṢ.

ᵓ$_{6}$R, see MR?

ᵓ$_{6}$R?

Sarg. PN:

Si-wa-ra (D+)

Si-wa-ra-at (G).

ᵓ$_{x}$R <u>erum</u> (a plant?).

Akk. lw. in Sum.:

x ZÍD e-ru (RTC 221 rev. v; 222 rev. iii; 225 rev. i; 229 rev. iii)

Cf. Thompson, DAB pp. 298ff.: "laurel." Read ÉŠ for ZÍD?

ᵓ$_{x}$R? <u>erum</u>?

Akk. lw. in Ur III Sum.:

UD e-ru-um ^{d}NIN-dar-ra-ba-an (TA 1931, 261). Here a festival?

Ur III PN's:

DINGIR-šu-e-ir (Johns Hopkins T 494). Cf. also BIN IX p. 27+, OB

E-ir-DINGIR (AnOr XII 278 v)

E-ir-^{d}EN.LÍL.(LÁ) (RT XIX 54 No. XXVII; ZA XII 344).

ᵓ$_{x}$R <u>irtum</u> "breast."

NS. .... na-e [i]r-tim (BE I 120 ii)

na-e e-ir-tim (PBS V 36 rev. x+iii, NS.).

ᵓ$_{6}$Rᵓ$_{6}$ <u>warāwum</u> "to bring." See also TRᵓ$_{6}$ tarāwum.

PN (acc.) in si-ga(r)-rìm a-na KÁ ^{d}En-líl u-ru-uš (S ii, vii)

PN a-na GN u-ru (HSS X 171:9)

gold, copper, slaves u-ru-a-am-ma (R xxiv)

x GIŠ.TUKUL PN u-ru-am (MDP XIV 33 ii). Opposite of ŠU.DU$_{8}$?

[....] u-ru (D 127)

men and animals li-ru-ù-nim (ITT I 1057; 1471)

a person li-ru-nim (ITT I 1103; Kish 1930, 170e)

sheep nu-ru-am (D 159)

an animal li-si-rí-àm (MDP XIV 7)

[....] li-se$_{11}$-rí-am (HSS X 6 rev.)

pigs li-su-rí-am (ITT I p. 17, 1265).

muttarrijum "care-taker?," "leader?"

[NS.]? mu-dar-rí ERIM URU? (RA IX 34 ii, copy).

ʾ$_6$Rʾ$_x$ werium? "bronze."

According to Thureau-Dangin, RA VIII 93, referring to ITT I 1422, the relationship of URUDU to silver was 240:1.

Written logographically.

objects of URUDU (passim)

URUDU-e (MDP IV Pl. 2 ii)

URUDU-su-nu (MDP XIV 86 rev. ii).

ʾ$_6$Rʾ$_x$ warûm (a garment).

Akk. lw. in Ur III Sum.:

1 TÚG wa-ru-um (2 NT 644). Cf. a-ru-u listed among garments in KAR 40:1.

ʾ$_x$Rʾ$_x$ arʾum.

3240? ŠE.GUR šu GUR$_7$ BÍL 54? ŠE.GUR šu ar-i-im (D 327:4). The word ar-i-im (ši-ri-i-im not plausible) looks like opposite of BÍL; cf. also ik-zum šu GUR$_7$ wa-ar-ki-im in D 270.

ʾ$_x$Rʾ$_x$.

a-rí-im (FM 40:15, 18).

Sarg. PN's:

A-ra?!-im (BE I Pl. VI v). Read probably thus rather than A-ku-si-im

Ar-rí-im (MO)

A-ru-um (D).

ʾ$_x$Rʾ$_x$ urûm "beam for the roof."

Apparently a lw. from Sum.:

GIŠ.ŠUBUR GIŠ u-rí-i[m] (FM 39:2)

Elsewhere regularly written GIŠ.ÙR.

ʾ$_1$Rʾ$_6$ʾ$_7$ arwijum "gazelle."

PSarg. and Ur III PN:

| Ar-bí-um (ITT II/1 p. 48, 933, U)
| Ar-wi-um (PSarg. king).

arwîtum "female gazelle."

Ur III PN:

| Ar-bí-tum (U 352). Cf. Ar-wi-tum in Ranke, EBPN p. 184
| Ar-bi-tum (Legrain, TRU 41; PDTI 525).

ʾ$_x$Rʾ$_x$M irʾemum.

Cf. irîmum discussed by von Soden in ZA XLIV 38.

^{d}EN.KI ir-e-ma-am è-ra-a-am-su "DN loves i." (Kish 1930, 143:1)

ir-e-mu-um DUMU ^{d}Innin (ibid. l. 3)

ir-e-mu ú-da-bi-bu-si-ma "the ir'emū have ....ed her" (ibid. rev. 30).

$'_{x}R'_{x}N$ iri'ānum, eli'ānum (a tree).

Akk. lw. in Sum.:

1 GIŠ.NAD GIŠ.MES i-rí-a-núm (RTC 221 iv)

1 GIŠ.NAD GIŠ.GUR$_8$ i-rí-a-núm (ibid.)

1 GIŠ.NAD GIŠ.GURUN i-rí-a-núm (ibid.)

1 GIŠ.NAD UMBIN GUD i-rí-a-núm KUG.GI GAR.RA (RTC 222 ii; 223 i)

1 GIŠ.NAD i-rí-a-núm (RTC 222 iv)

1 GIŠ.NIM e-li-a-núm (Orient. XVI 14 VAT 4722 ii, PSarg.). Cf. ^{GIŠ}i-li-a-nu-um in BIN II 65, OB.

$'_{3}$RB arābum "to combat." Root following Arabic ḤRB "to combat."

Sarg. and Ur III PN's:

La-á-ra-ab (FM). Formation like lâ-maḫār, lâ-šanān, lâ-gamāl

La-'à-ra-ab (D+)

La-'à-ra-bu-um (Gutian king)

La-ra-bu-um (AnOr VII 42 rev., U).

$'_{5}$RB arābum "to enter."

a e-ru-ub "may he not enter" (HSS X 12:9)

x ZÍD.ŠE šu PN a-na É.ÙR.BU è-ru-ub "flour of PN entered into É...." (A 5235)

x GÚ GI a-na É.ÙR ši PA NAR è-ru-ub (A 5899)

SUM and SA šu Ur-mes a-na É.KIŠIB.BA è-ru-ub (A 5926)

[ù]?-la a-na sa-li-iš-tim ni-e-ra?-[ab]? (D 126).

šûrubum "to cause to enter."

kings maḫ-rí-iš ^{d}En-líl u-sa-rí-ib (YOS I 10, NS.)

lords ŠUK.^{d}INNIN maḫ-rí-[su] u-sa-rí-[bu] (UET I 274 ii, NS.)

šar-rí-si-in in ga-mi-e u-sá-rí-ib (CT XXXII 5, 98917, unknown king)

[u]?-⌈sá?-rí⌉-ba, Subj. (FM 36:30)

MÁŠ.ANŠE a-na URU^{KI}-lim zu-da-rí-ib, Impv. (JRAS 1932 p. 296:21).

erbum "gift."

e-ri-ib-su ú-la ip-ru-us "his (god's) gift he did not withhold" (MDP IV Pl. 2 iv)

it-ti ìr-bi ù ⌈ki-š⌉a-a-tim (CT XXXII 1 ii) = it-ti ir-bi ù ki-ša-a-ti (RA VII 180) in CM.

Sarg. PN's:

Ir-bí-a (D)

Iš-dup-ir-pum? (BE I Pl. VII ix).

erūbatum (a festival?).

Akk. lw. in Ur III Sum.:

UD è-ru-ba-tum-KA (AnOr VII 167)

UD e-ru-ba-tum ᵈGu(d)-gu(d)-KA (Fish, CST 41).

nârabtum "entrance."

ì-nu .... su_4-ma da-li na-ra-ab-ti-su i-ik-mi-ù-su_4? "when .... at the door jambs of his entrance he bound him" (UET I 275 iii, NS.).

nêrebum.

Akk. lw. in Ur III Sum.:

MU ᴳᴵŠne-ri-bu-um-ŠÈ (UET III 817).

$ʾ_x$RB.

Sarg. PN:

Ìr-ru-pum (Ist. Mus. Nippur 2614).

$ʾ_x$RB.

Sarg. PN:

Ar-ba-AN (HSS X 25 i 10, read as Ar-ba-ilum ibid. p. xxviii; 187 i 3; read as [E]-ri-ba-ilî ibid. p. xxx).

$ʾ_1$RB$ʾ_4$ arbaʾum "four."

PN LUGAL ki-ib-ra-tim ar-ba-im (passim, NS.; Enridawizir; Š.; BS.; ŠS.)

ki-ib-ra-tum ar-ba-um (IAMN XII Pl. IV, NS.; PBS V 36 rev. x+ii, NS.)

ki-ib-ra-tim ar-ba-im [....] (MDP X Pl. 3, 1a)

in ki-ib-ra-tim ar-ba-im (BE I 120 ii, NS.).

$ʾ_6$RD warādum "to go down."

ì-nu LUGAL u-ur-da-ni (BIN VIII 134).

šûrudum "to bring down."

PN ù-šu-rí-id DN (Acc.) a-na KÁ GN (RA XXXIII 178, Mari)

in a-lí-im PN ú-šu-ri-dam (Louvre AO 8959).

wardum "slave."

Written almost exclusively ARÁD, i.e. ARAD+KUR. The sign ARAD is used for "male" in such combinations as UDU.ARAD, DUMU.ARAD, GUD.ARAD, etc. The spelling ARAD.LUGAL (HSS X 94:3) as against ARÁD.LUGAL (HSS X 32:3; 66:23; 201:5; 206:5; 208:5) may be due to an error of the scribe or the copyist. In the Ur III period ARÁD and ARAD are used interchangeably.

PN ARÁD-zu (RTC 78 rev.)

PN ARÁD PN (HSS X 119:2; D 252, also ARÁD PN)

ŠE.BA ARÁD (D 299; 334)

PN ARÁD DN (D 336; FM 8:4, among witnesses)

PN NAGAR ARÁD PN (FM 9:10, witness).

Sarg. and Ur III PN's:

ARAD-Ba-dan (Orient. XLVII 105, U)

ARAD-da-pum (D+). Should be read Ìr-da-pum in Sarg., but cf. ARAD-DÙG in 2 NT 689, U, for the writing, and Wardu-kênu in NPN p. 173, for the meaning

ARAD-da?-bu-um (Arnold, ABTR 9, U)

ARÁD-da-ni = /Wardani/? (HSS IV 10 rev. i, U; 49 ii, U)

ARAD-É-a (De Genouillac, TD 60 rev., U)

ARÁD-ì-lí-[su]? (Kish 1930, 406 rev. i)

ARÁD-^{d}Innin (D)

ARÁD-mu-bí (ITT I 1119)

ARÁD-^{d}Tišpak (D)

ARÁD-tum (D)

⌈ARÁD⌉-Tu-tu (D)

ARÁD-zu-dan (AnOr XII 278 iv, U)

ARÁD-zu-ni (D+)

Ar-ti-a (RTC 392, U)

Ú-ar-ti-a (Reisner, TUT 210 ii, U).

ʾ$_{x}$RD.

Ur III PN:

U-ra-tum (Boson, TCS 300).

ʾ$_{x}$RGN <u>arganum</u> (a resinous plant). See also below.

Akk. lw. in Ur III Sum.:

x MA.NA ^{ŠIM}ar-ga-núm (UET III 1117)

x MA.NA ar-ga-núm (Chiera, STA 1 ii; BIN V 292; TCL V 5680 ii, v; 6042 i, ii; etc.).

ʾ$_{x}$RGN?

Since measures used with the word below are different from those used with arganum (above) the two words ought to be kept separate.

10(QA) ar-KUR-nam (MDP XIV 8). KUR = gìn/kìn?

ŠU.NIGÍN 9(GUR) 2(PI) 30(QA) ar-KUR-nam PN im-ḫur (MDP XIV 76)

Cf. ar-gi-nu-u = [gi-šim]-ma-ru in CT XVIII 2:69.

ʾ$_{1}$RḪ <u>arḫiš</u> "quickly."

[ar]?-ḫi-iš [su]-bí-lam (ITT I 1080)

ar-ḫi-iš? (MCS IV 13 rev., in difficult context).

ʾ$_{x}$RḪ <u>arḫum</u> (a type of brick). Meissner, OLZ XXV 241f.: "Halbziegel."

Akk. lw. in Sum.:

20 SIG$_{4}$ ar-ḫu (ITT V 9322).

ʾ$_{x}$RḪ.

Ur III RN:

A-ra-aḫ-tum (BE III 84 iii).

ʾ$_1$RK *arākum* "to be long."

Sarg. PN:

BALA-su-li-rí-ik (D).

arkum "long."

Written syllabically or logographically.

Sarg. and Ur III PN's:

Ar-kum (D+)

A-ri-ik-ì-li (ITT II/2 p. 14, 3072)

Be-lí-a-rí-ik (U 508+)

Be-lí-a-ri-ik (TA 1931, 220, U)

Be-lí-á-rí-ik (RA XXV 20 ii, U)

I-da-ri-ik (RTC 243)

I-da-rí-ik (ITT IV p. 10, 7102, U)

I-za-ri-ik (U 1598+)

I-za-rí-ik (U 1599)

I-zu-a-rí-ik (U 1601+)

I-zu-ri-ik (U 1604)

I-zu-GÍD (G+)

I-zu-a-GÍD (Ist. Mus. Adab 82).

ʾ$_6$RK *warkijum* "later."

[....] wa-ar-ki-um (HSS X 68 rev. x+1)

ŠE wa-ar-ki-um (HSS X 69:5)

ik-zum šu GUR$_7$ wa-ar-ki-im (D 270:3)

wa-ar-gi$_4$-um (D 229). Distribution of KAŠ and ZÍD.

urkum "back," "rear."

a-na ur-ki-im "in the back" opposite of a-na ra-si-im "in the front" (FM 11:10).

urkijum "later."

Ur III PN:

Ur-ki-um (RTC 322; 323)

Ur-ki (ITT IV p. 62, 7592).

ʾ$_x$RK? *urkum?*

a-ḫu-uš$_x$(EŠ) ur$_4$-ki ša ši-na-tim "I gave the .... of urine?" (Kish 1930, 143:15).

ʾ$_x$RK *urākum* (an implement).

Akk. lw. in Ur III Sum.:

3 and 6 u-ra-ku-um (TCL V 6044 rev. i, ii).

ʾ$_x$RKD *urkidānum* (a tree?).

Akk. lw. in Sum.:

x GIŠ.TIM ur-ki-da-núm (RTC 221 rev. v).

ʾ$_x$RL? <u>aralum</u>?

Akk. lw. in Ur III Sum.:

x GÍN URUDU a-ra-LUM (Cros, NFT p. 185 AO 4210 rev.).

ʾ$_x$RL? <u>erālum</u> or <u>erānum</u> (a tree).

Akk. lw. in Sum.:

^{GIŠ}e-ra-LUM (Thureau-Dangin, SAKI p. 106 xv 33, Gudea).

ʾ$_x$RM <u>armatum</u> (object of bronze).

Akk. lw. in Ur III Sum.:

x MA.NA x GÍN URUDU ar-ma-tum (AnOr VII 245; A 2620; Nikolski, Dok. II 419)

2 MA.NA 16 1/2 GÍN ar-ma-tum URUDU DU$_8$.A (RA XLIX 93 No. 38).

ʾ$_x$RM?

Ur III PN:

Ur-ma-LUM (CT VII 7 ii).

ʾ$_x$RN <u>arnum</u> "sin."

Ur III PN:

Mi-na-ar-ni "what is my sin?" (Chiera, STA 29 vi). Cf. ^{f}Am-mi-ni-an-ni in PBS II/2 53:31, MB.

ʾ$_1$RN <u>irinum</u> "cedar."

a-za GURUN i-ri-nim in bu-ti-su (Kish 1930, 143 rev.).

ʾ$_x$RN? <u>arinum</u> (an object or stone?).

Akk. lw. in Ur III Sum.:

a-rí-núm UD (UET III 441; 1498 ii end)

a-rí-núm (UET III 474; 548).

ʾ$_x$RN <u>urānum</u> (a plant?).

Akk. lw. in Sum.:

5 KUŠ.ŠUḪÚB u-ra-núm É.BA.AN (RTC 217 rev.)

70 u-ra-[núm] (RTC 229 rev. i)

NA$_4$ ZA.KA+SA u-ra-núm (UET III 733 i, U).

ʾ$_x$RN <u>urnum</u> (a tree).

Akk. lw. in Ur III Sum.:

1 GIŠ.IG DÍB ur-núm and its measurements (UET III 826 i twice; written GIŠ ur-núm in 1498 rev. i end)

1 GIŠ.APIN? IG Ù.KU MU GIŠ.IG DÍB ur-núm-ŠÈ (UET III 1347; 1498 rev. i)

Cf. 1 ^{GIŠ}úr-na-am in TCL XXVII 63 rev. 5, Mari, and Kupper, ARMT VI p. 122.

ʾ$_1$RNB <u>arnabum</u> "hare."

Sarg. PN:

Ar-na-ba (Louvre AO 8642).

ʾ$_x$RNN.

Sarg. and Ur III PN:

| Ir-na-núm (ITT IV p. 91, 8103, U)
| Ìr!-na!-[nothing?-]núm (Kish 1930, 406 rev. i).

ʾ$_7$RQ? aruqum? "green?"

Sarg. PN:

Á-ru-kum (FM).

ʾ$_1$RR arārum "to curse."

DN's ar-ra-dam [l]a?-mu-ut-dam li-ru-ru-uš (PBS V 36 rev. iv, NS.)

DN's ar-ra-dam la-mu-dam li-ru-ru-uš (UET I 276 ii, NS.)

DN's ir-ra-dam li-mu-dam li-ru-ru-uš (Morgan, MSP IV 161 ii, Lullubum).

arratum, erratum "curse."

DN's ar-ra-dam [l]a?-mu-ut-dam li-ru-ru-uš (PBS V 36 rev. iv, NS.)

DN's ar-ra-dam la-mu-dam li-ru-ru-uš (UET I 276 ii, NS.)

DN's ir-ra-dam li-mu-dam li-ru-ru-uš (Morgan, MSP IV 161 ii, Lullubum).

ʾ$_x$RR.

Sarg. PN:

I-ra-ru-um (Gutian king).

ʾ$_4$RS arsānum "barley groats." Transl. in accordance with Talm. ʿarsān "barley groats." Sum. AR.ZA.NA is apparently a lw. from Sem.

1 QA ar-za-ni! (MDP XIV 68)

UTUL ar-za-nu-um (RA XVIII 59 vi, Voc. prat.). A soup

x QA AR.ZA.NA (A 947; TMH n.F. I/II 121, U; ITT II 892 ii, U; ITT IV 8019 rev.; Chiera, STA 29 v, U; UET III p. 65, U)

ŠE AR.ZA.NA (Ist. Mus. Adab 108, U).

ʾ$_1$RṢ? arṣatum? "earth."

Ur III DN:

^{d}Nin-tul-ar-za-tum (Nikolski, Dok. II 236 i; BIN V 277:35). It is tempting to assume that arṣatum is the old form of erṣetum "earth."

ʾ$_3$RŠ erāšum "to plough."

šum-ma e-ra-si-iš na-tu "if (it) is suitable for plowing" (HSS X 5:23)

GÁN-lam ʾà-ru-uš, Impv. (JRAS 1932 p. 296:4)

ad-da GÁN-lam ʾà-ru-uš (JRAS 1932 p. 296:15)

GÁN-lam ù-la a-ru-uš (JRAS 1932 p. 296:9).

arrāšum, errēšum "ploughman."

Sarg. and Ur III PN:

| ʾÀ-ra-sum (G)
| ʾÀ-ra-śum (E+)

Ìr-ri-šum (U 1772+)
Ìr-ri-šu-um (Jacobsen, CTC 48 rev., U)
E-ir-ri-šu-um (MDP XXVIII 526, U).

ersum "cultivation."

e-ri-su-nu li-zu-ru da-ni-iš "strongly may they watch their cultivation" (HSS X 5:18)

[e?-ri?-s]u-nu [l]i-iṣ-ba-at (HSS X 11:11).

irištum "cultivation."

Sarg. MN:

I-rí-sa-at (D+).

ʾ₄₋₅RŠ erāšum "to wish," "to request."

su-tu-uḫ-ḫa-tim ù-lu ki-sa-ma-ri te-ir-rí-iš "thou requests .... or ...." (FM 52:8)

iš-bi-gi gi-nu-tim a-rí-iš-ga "I requested from you the regular grain accumulations" (JRAS 1932 p. 296:40)

šum-ma KUG.BABBAR è-ri-šu!-ga "if they request silver from you" (EK III Pl. XI W. 1929, 160).

Sarg. and Ur III PN's:

ʾÀ-rí-iš (E+)

DINGIR-e-ri-iš (E)

Nu-um-e-ri-eš (TMH n.F. I/II p. 23 compared with p. 47, U). Doubtful.

eršum "wise."

Sarg. PN:

Ir-šum (G+).

ʾₓRŠ erīšum.

ŠU.NIR KUG.BABBAR ù KUG.GI è-ri-sá-am A.MU.NA.RU (MDP IV Pl. 2 iii).

ʾₓRŠ?

Ur III FN:

A.ŠÀ Ar-ša-ti-a (CT VII 24, 15310; IX 32 i; 38 ii+).

ʾₓRŠ?

Sarg. PN's:

PN šu Ir-sa-tim (Pope, SPA I 281)

Irsutum (ibid., Sarg. tablet from Kish)

Ìr-su-ti-a (Fish, CST 4, 6, 17).

Ur III canal:

PA_5 Ìr-šum-ma (ZA LI Pl. IV after p. 74 iv 19, 20).

ʾₓRŠ?

Ur III RN:

ÍD Ur-ša-tum (ZA LI Pl. 3 after p. 74 i 28).

ʾₓRŠ uršānum "hero" (or the like).

A lw. from Sum. UR.SAG ursang:

Škš. DINGIR UR.SAG A-ga-dè^{KI} (Ist. Mus. Adab 767).

Sarg. and Ur III PN's:

A-bí-UR.SAG (D+)

Be-lí-UR.SAG (D+)

DINGIR-UR.SAG (D+)

^{d}EN.ZU-UR.SAG (D+)

Eš$_{4}$-dar-UR.SAG (FM+)

Ìr-ra-UR.SAG (RTC 127 rev. v; U 1761+)

^{d}Ìr-ra-UR.SAG (U 952+)

LUGAL-UR.SAG (U 2120)

Šar-ru-UR.SAG (Orient. n.s. XXIII Pl. XXI 1)

Šá-gán-UR.SAG (G). Sum. name?

^{d}Ša-gan-UR.SAG (EK IV Pl. XLIII No. 3 i, PSarg.)

UR.SAG-UD.KIB.NUN^{KI} (MO+)

Ur-sa(g)-num (D 187 i). Cf. Ur-ša-(a-)nu-um in UET VI 174:11 and seal, OB

Ur-sa(g)-núm (MO).

ʾ$_{x}$RZ <u>arzatum</u>, see ʾ$_{1}$RṢ? arṣatum?

ʾ$_{x}$RZ?

Sarg. PN:

Ìr-ru-zum (MO A xiii).

ʾ$_{x}$Sʾ$_{x}$ <u>asûm</u> "physician."

A lw. from Sum. A.ZU azu.

There is a strong possibility that instead of a-zu /asū/ we should read A.ZU. Note that with fem. divinities we should expect a form as(u)wat or the like.

Sarg. and Ur III PN's:

A-zu-DINGIR (D+)

A-zu-lí (D). Or ʾ$_{x}$ZN

Be-lí-a-zu (D; U 507+)

DINGIR-a-zu (D+)

Eš$_{4}$-dar-a-zu (D)

Eš$_{4}$-dar-AZU.A (E). See below

Ì-lum-a-zu (BE I Pl. VII vii)

Ma-ma-a-zu (D+).

Instead of A.ZU an artificial spelling A.ZU$_{5}$(AZU) and even AZU.A (see above) sometimes appears, as in:

PN A.ZU$_{5}$ (Kish 1930, 144a rev. ii)

A.ZU$_{5}$ among professions (MDP XIV 18; 25; HSS X 222 iii).

ʾ$_x$Sʾ$_x$? <u>asaʾum</u>?

2 ^{GIŠ}a-za-an (FM 33:5). Cf. ʾ$_1$ʾ$_1$S aʾāsum

a-za GURUN  in ga-ti-su (Kish 1930, 143 rev.)

a-za GURUN i-ri-nim in bu-ti-su (Kish 1930, 143 rev.).

ʾ$_6$SM <u>wusmum</u> "ornament."

Ur III PN:

^{d}Šu-^{d}EN.ZU-wu-zu-um (Orient. XLVII 36). Cf. DINGIR-wu-zum (PBS XI/2 No. 452) and ^{d}UTU-wu-zum (No. 557).

<u>wussumum</u> "ornate."

Sarg. PN's:

Wu-zum-tum (D+)

Wu-zu(m)-mu-um (Kish 1930, 144a rev. iii).

<u>simtum</u> "ornament," "jewel."

Akk. lw. in Ur III Sum.:

zi-im-tum PN (YOS IV 227 twice).

Sarg. and Ur III PN's:

A-ab-ba-zi-im-ti (U 18)

A-bí-zi-im-ti (U 67+)

A-bí-zi-im-dè (UET III 1504 viii, U)

A-gu-a-zi-im-ti (RA X 65 No. 29, U)

Be-lí-zi-im-ti (A 3304, U)

Dam-ku-zi-ma-zu (Langdon, TAD 40:4, U)

^{d}La-az-zi-im-ti (RT XIX opp. p. 47 No. 8)

Li-bur-zi-im-ti (AnOr VII p. 26, U)

Lu-zi-im-[ti]? (Cop. 10059)

^{d}Šul-gi-zi-im-ti (U 917+)

^{d}Šul-gi-zi-im-tum (U 916+)

Zi-im-tum (D+).

ʾ$_x$SM, see ʾ$_x$NSM ansammum.

ʾ$_x$SN <u>isinnum</u> "festival."

Sarg. and Ur III PN's:

EZEN (FM)

EZEN.NA (E)

E-zi-ni-iš (MDP XXVIII 524)

Ì-zi-na (FM+; Reisner, TUT 159 iv, U; PDTI 525, U)

I-zi-na (HSS IV 47, U)

I-zi-LUM (D+).

ʾ$_6$Ṣʾ$_1$ <u>waṣāʾum</u> "to go out."

so much grain wu-zu-iš "for going out" (HSS X 186:6). Cf. ḫu-zu-zi-iš (HSS X 197:13)

<u>šûṣuʾum</u> "to cause to go out," "to sell?"

[u]-su-zé "he sold?" (HSS X 210:7)

u-su-zé-[ma] (HSS X 8:8)

li-su-zé-áš-su-ni "may he cause them to go out" (RTC 78:12)

grain li-⌈se_{11}⌉-zi-ù-nim-ma (Cop. 10055 rev.)

2 fields PN ú-se_{11}-zi (BIN VIII 144 end)

x GURUŠ.GURUŠ in URU^{KI}.URU^{KI} Šu-me-rí-im u-su-zi-am-ma (R xvii, xix, xxi twice)

⌈ÍD⌉ [in] qir-bí-su u-su-zi "he withdrew" (PBS V 36 x+iii, v, NS.).

PSarg., Sarg., and Ur III PN's:

No clear evidence that i-zi represents an allomorph of ù-zi etc. For problems in West Semitic cf. Bauer, Die Oskanaanäer p. 75.

I-zé-mi-sar (Orient. XLVII 423:19, U)

I-zi-^{d}DA (G)

I-zi-^{d}Da-gan (MDOG LIV 23, Mari)

I-zi-íl? (BIN VII 11 ii, PSarg.)

I-zi-Ra-sa-ap! (MDP XIV 72 ii)

Bu-ḫi-lí-zi (Jean, ŠA LIII rev., U)

U-za-si-na-at (MO)

U-zé-a (ITT II/2 4439)

Ú-zé-a (2 NT 71, U)

Ú-zé-da-num (OIP XLIII 145, Diyala, U)

U-zé-i-sar (E)

U-zé-^{d}Ma-lik (De Sarzec, DC II p. LVII)

U-zé-me-num (E). Meaning unknown

U-zé-um (D+; AnOr VII 372 iv, Sarg.?!)

Ù-zi-na-wi-ir (Nikolski, Dok. II 523 rev., U)

Ù-zi-nu-ri (U 1126+)

Ú-zi-nu-ru-um (Delaporte, CCL II A 266, U)

Ù-zi-wa-dar (PSarg. king)

Ù-zu-ḫa-lum (RTC 247 end). Doubtful

Ù-zu-nu-ru-um (RA XIX 39 No. I twice, U). Doubtful.

ṣîtum.

GÁN su_4-a-tu a-na UD? za-a-ti lu u-te-ìr "forever" (CT XXXII 2 iv, CM). Doubtful.

$ʾ_3$ṢD aṣādum "to reap."

Ur III PN's:

^{d}EN.ZU-e-zé-id (UET III 1037)

E-zi-tum (UET III 1398).

$ʾ_{6-7}$ṢP wuṣṣupum "to add."

fields A.NAG a-na PN_1 PN_2 u-zi-ip (HSS X 14:8)

⸢ù⸣?-da-za-bu (FM 9:25). Doubtful

Ur III PN's:

Zi-ip-mi-sar (TCL V 6039 ii). Cf. Zi-pa-am-ì-lí in BA VI/5 125, OB

Zi-ip-za-zu (TCL V 6039 iii). Meaning?

ʾ₃ṢR uṣārum "court" (or the like).

The Ur III GN's Ú-za-ar-Ba-ba-ti[KI] (TCL V 6041 ii), Ú-za-ar-Šul!-gi (ibid. rev. i), Ú-za-ar-I-mi-DINGIR[KI] (ibid.), Ú-za-ar-Gar-ša-na[KI] (SAKI pp. 148f. No. 22:16) are explained by Gelb in AJSL LV 84f. as containing uṣar, a Constr. St. of uṣrum, from a Semitic root ḤṢR. In view of aṣārum (see below) the formation uṣārum is preferred to uṣrum. Some post-Ur III GN's composed with uṣār are listed in the above mentioned article. The Ur III uṣārum is probably identical with OA i-za-ri, Mari (ᵈNIN-)ḫi-za-ri; cf. Hehn, MAOG IV 70ff., Dossin, Studia Mariana pp. 44 and 49, and differently Landsberger, TTKB XIV 237f. For i>u in iṣārum>uṣārum cf. MAD II 168.

Ur III FN:

A.ŠÀ Ú-za-ar-x-x (UET III 1357 rev.).

aṣārum "court."

In the following Ur III GN's the formation aṣārum appears as a variant of uṣārum (see above). Cf. also ḫaṣārum for some kind of enclosure in late Bab. and at Mari (ARMT XV 205):

A-za-ar-ᵈŠul-gi (RA XXV 5, 15, 21 vi)

Nergal A-za-ru-um-Šul-gi (Nikolski, Dok. II 236 i; AnOr I 88 viii; copied everywhere as DA, not ŠUL)

Nergal A-za-ru-um-Šul-gi[KI] (Orient. XLVII 347; BIN V 277 i; copied everywhere as DA)

A-za-ru-um-Šul-gi (Fish, CST 688 rev., copied as DA)

A-za-ru-um-A-ùr-ra[KI] (UET III 1065 ii; Oppenheim, CCTE KK 25)

A-za-ru-um-Wa-ar-ga[KI] (UET III 1410)

Cf. also GN's A-za-ra (BE I Pl. VII i), A-zar (ZA LI Pl. II after p. 74 iii 25, 26, U), and discussion of Kraus in ZA LI 69 on A-zar-la.

ʾ₃ṢR? aṣārum?

Sarg. PN:

ʾÀ-za-rí-tum (D).

ʾₓṢR? uṣārum.

Sarg. and Ur III PN's:

Ú-za-ru-um (Orient. XLVII 481:17, U)

Ú-za-ar-ni (ITT II/2 p. 28, 4512). Cf. Ú-za-ri-a in Stephens, PNC p. 69 and ma-da Ú-za-ru-um in TCL X 79:10, OB.

ʾ$_x$ṢṢ uṣāṣum.

Sarg. PN:

Ú-za-zum (D+).

ʾ$_1$Š išum "fire."

DN in PSarg., Sarg., and Ur III PN's:

I-šu-um-DINGIR (U 1661)

I-šum-ba-ni (U 1662)

I-din-I-šum (U 1683)

PÙ.ŠA-Ì-šum (Mount Holyoke Alumnae Quarterly I 212 seal, U)

Šum-su-Ì-šum (BIN VIII 265)

Ur-Ì-šum (OIP XIV 48 ii, PSarg.).

ʾ$_x$Š?

Sarg. and Ur III PN's:

A-ŠI-a-lí (D)

A-ŠI-DINGIR (U 1750+)

A-ŠI-ga-la (G+)

A-ŠI-gu-ru-ud (MO)

A-ŠI-sar (Jean, ŠA LXVI ii, U)

ʾ$_x$Š?

3 ú-ša-at KI PN (Ur III tablet belonging to Miss Leake of the Winona State Teachers College). The phrase occurs 3 times in a list of ZÍD, ZÍD.KAL, ZÍD.GU, A.TIR, KA.LUM.

ʾ$_7$Šʾ$_6$ išû "to have."

la ti-su "thou hast not" (FM 8:15)

so much ŠE of different persons PN i-ti Zi-ra-si i-su (MDP XIV 49)

ŠE PN$_1$ al PN$_2$ i-su (Kish 1930, 170d).

PSarg., Sarg., and Ur III PN's:

I-su-a-ḫu (G+)

I-su-DINGIR (MO+)

I-su-GI (FM+)

I-šu-dan (ITT IV p. 64, 7619, U)

I-šu-Il (PSarg. king)

Ni-su-dan-nam (Kish 1930, 148+).

For the type of PN's listed below cf. Stamm, ANG p. 130:

Some of the names below may have a different interpr.

A-a-ni-šu (U 13)

A-bu-ni-šu (ITT II p. 48, 933, U)

A-ḫa-an-ni-šu (U 125+)

A-ḫa-ni-šu (U 127+)

A-ḫu-ni-šu (U 142; PDTI 724 twice, U)

Al-la-ni-su (Fish, CST p. 159 v, U)

A-lí-ni-su (Nies, UDT 45 rev., U). But cf. Ali-nišūa etc. in Stamm, ANG p. 285

A-lí-ni-šu (U 192)

^{d}Ba-ú-ni-su (De Genouillac, TSA 10 vii+, PSarg.)

DINGIR-ni-su (UET III 15, U; MCS VI 55 H 6196, U = p. 85)

E-lí-ni-šu (Barton, HLC Pl. 12, 52 rev., U)

^{d}EN.ZU-ni-šu (ITT IV p. 68, 7690, U)

Eš$_4$-dar-ni-su (BIN VIII 143 rev.)

Ma-la-ni-su (MO+)

PÙ.ŠA-ni-šu (U 484)

Ú-gul-la-ni-su (Kish 1930, 170c). Cf. ^{d}Ù-gul-lá in OIP XLIII 184, OB

Úr-ra-ni-šu (U 1431).

ʾ$_x$Šʾ$_x$ <u>ašium?</u>

NI ù a-si-su (FM 43:18).

ʾ$_x$Šʾ$_x$ <u>ešium</u> "dolerite."

In all cases E.SI and E.SIG may be logograms for ešium, like BAR.SI and BAR.SIG for paršigum

in sa-tu-su-nu NA$_4$.NA$_4$ E.SIG-im? i-bu-lam-ma (MDP VI Pl. 1, 1, NS.). Cf. NA$_4$.NA$_4$-su-nu MI (M xxvi); dolerite is black

in E.SI DÙL-su ib-ni-ma (UET I 275 iii, NS.)

E.SIG ZÉ in GIŠ.SAR i-da-ba-aḫ-si (MDP XIV 90). Interpr. unknown.

ʾ$_x$Šʾ$_x$? <u>ušuʾāʾum?</u>

a-na u-su$_4$-a-im a-ti-ir (UET I 275 iv, NS.).

ʾ$_x$Šʾ$_x$? <u>têšîtum?</u>

Sarg. PN:

Te-si-tum (FM)

Te-ši-[tum]? (D).

ʾ$_6$ŠB <u>wašābum</u> "to sit," "to stay."

in ^{GIŠ}GU.ZA la tu-sa-bu "(may you be conjured) that you will not sit on the chair" (RA XXIII 25:16)

in GN u-ša-bu (ITT I 1103; 1256)

in maš-ga-ni PA.TE.SI .... u-ša-ab (ITT I 1468)

PN iš-dè PA.TE.SI .... u-ša-ab (ITT I 1471; II/2 4362)

PN iš-dè PN u-ša-ab (Kish 1930, 170e rev.)

PN in É ki-šè-ir-tim .... li-iš-bu (HSS X 10:11)

la u-šu-b[u] for la u-ša?-b[u]?, Subj. Pl. (A 708).

<u>šušubum</u> "to settle."

a-na 1/2? DA.NA TA ma-ag-ga-ti zu-si-ib-ma (JRAS 1932 p. 296:13). Meaning doubtful.

wašibum "dweller," "renter?"

PN's wa-si-bu (Kish 1930, 150 rev.; 177n).

šubtum "dwelling."

[....] da šu-ub-tum (UET III 1498 vi middle, U). Meaning unknown; read possibly Da-šu-ub-tum.

Ur III PN:

Da-bu-šu-ba-at (AnOr VII 262 rev. iii; CT XXXII 34 i). Interpr. doubtful, but cf. Ṭâb-ašābšu in BA VI/5 p. 124, OB.

$^{\supset}_{x}$ŠB? ašb/patum.

Akk. lw. in Ur III Sum.:

1 aš-ba-tum SIG_5 PN TÚG.DU_8 MU.DU (BIN V 51). An object made by TÚG.DU_8.

$^{\supset}_{x}$ŠB? ešbum?

Possibly a profession:

PN LÚ éš-pum (RA XXXI 142, PSarg.)

PN [éš]?-pum (Banks, Bismya p. 145, NS.).

Sarg. PN's:

Éš-ba (G)

| $Eš_4$-pum (E+)
| Iš-pum (G+)
| Iš-pù-um (G)

Iš-bu-a (FM).

$^{\supset}_{x}$ŠB?

uš-bi-ma MÁŠ.ANŠE-me Gu-ti-ù it-ru-ù (JRAS 1932 p. 296:22). Meaning unknown.

$^{\supset}_{x}$ŠD išdum "foundation," "root" (originally part of body).

Written logographically as SUḪUŠ and DU (once). Cf. also Š$^{\supset}_{x}$P šêpum and ŠRŠ šuršum.

2 DN's SUḪUŠ-su li-zu-ḫa ù ŠE.NUMUN-su li-il-gu-da (PBS V 34 x, Lugalzagesi; RA XXI 66 and 71, S.; S ix, xi twice, xv; R xviii twice, xix, xx, xxi twice, xxiv, xxv, xxvi, xxvii; RA VIII 136; 139, Mi.; NS.; Škš.)

DN SUḪUŠ-su li-zu-uḫ ù ŠE.NUMUN-su li-il-gu-ut (S iv)

DN's SUḪUŠ-su li-zu-ḫu ù ŠE.NUMUN-su li-il-gu-du (BE I 120, NS.)

DN's SUḪUŠ-ti-[su] li-iš-ba-al-ki-du (MDP II p. 63 ii)

SUḪUŠ GN in UKÙ GN i-zu-uḫ-ma (R xxiii; xxv)

DN's DU-su li-zu-ḫa ù ŠE.NUMUN!-su li-il-gu-da (ZA IV 406, Gutium). Here DU is written in place of the normal SUḪUŠ

Cf. also 8 SUḪUŠ URUDU GIŠ.GÁN (PBS IX 30).

$^{\supset}_{x}$ŠG? išgijum? (object of wood).

Akk. lw. in Sum. or vice versa:

iš-[gi$_4$]-um (FM 44:10, school text?)

1 ^{GIŠ}iš-gi$_4$-u[m] LIŠ? (ITT II/2 4646)

Cf. also 3 ^{GIŠ}ŠE.ḪI ^{GIŠ}IŠ.GI$_4$ (DP 418 ii, PSarg.) and 1 TÚG.BAR.DÍB IŠ.GI$_4$ (RTC 203).

ʾ$_x$ŠGL?

Ur III PN:

Iš-ga-LUM (CT VII 7 i).

ʾ$_x$ŠḪL ašḫallum (a container?).

Akk. lw. in Ur III Sum.:

1 aš-ḫal-lum UD.KA.BAR KI.LAL.BI 1 MA.NA 10 GÍN+ (Reisner, TUT 124 viii)

1 ^{GIŠ}aš-ḫal-lum ḪA.LU.ÚB GÍN.BA KA.AM.SI GAR.RA (HSS IV 5 iv)

Cf. 6 ^{GI}aš-ḫa-lum in BIN IX 355, OB.

ʾ$_x$ŠK iššiakkum "governor."

Lw. from Sum. ensi:

Written logographically as PA.TE.SI (passim).

Ur and PA.TE.SI.PA.TE.SI-su (R xvii)

ì-nu-mi PN PA.TE.SI-ki Iš-nun^{KI} "when PN was ensi of I." (UCP IX p. 205, 83 iii).

iššiakkūtum "governorship."

DUMU.DUMU A-ga-dè^{KI} PA.TE.SI-gu-a-(a-)tim u-ga-lú (S iv, ix).

ʾ$_x$ŠKD, see ʾ$_x$ŠQD.

ʾ$_x$ŠKR eškurum "wax."

Akk. lw. in Ur III Sum.:

2 MA.NA 10 GÍN! eš-ku-ru-um KUG.BI ("its price") 1 GÍN 15 ŠE (TCL V 6037 rev. vii).

ʾ$_x$ŠKR iškarum "allotment."

Written as logogram ÉŠ.GÀR in HSS X 26; 27; 28; 64; 132; etc.

ʾ$_1$ŠL ašlum (a plant).

Akk. lw. in Ur III Sum.:

1 áš-lum (UET III 770; 1498 i, here an object in form of ašlum).

ʾ$_x$ŠL ušallum "meadow."

PSarg. GN:

in Ú-sá-la?-tim (PSBA XX Pl. I i).

ʾ$_x$ŠL?

Sarg. PN:

U-sa-LUM (ITT II/2 p. 7, 2925).

ʾ$_x$ŠLL?

Sarg. PN:

Áš-lul-tum, f.n. (YOS I 7). An older form of aššultum (a plant)?

ʾ$_x$ŠM?

Sarg. PN:

Áš-ma-tum (FM).

ʾ$_x$ŠN.

PSarg. and Ur III PN's:

Áš-ni-tum (De Genouillac, TSA 12 iv+, PSarg.; U 371)

Uš-ni-tum (De Genouillac, TSA 10 iv+, PSarg.).

ʾ$_x$ŠP išippum, see Mʾ$_x$ mûm?

ʾ$_x$ŠP išpatum "quiver."

Akk. lw. in Ur III Sum.:

2 ^{KUŠ}iš-ba-tum (BE III 76:30).

ʾ$_x$ŠQD ašqudum. Cf. asqudum "hamster?" and OB PN Asqudānum discussed by Landsberger, Fauna p. 109.

Ur III PN:

Aš-ku-da-núm (UET III 1582 rev. iv)
Áš-ku-da-núm (RA XIX 43 No. 113 rev.).

ʾ$_1$ŠR ašārum.

Sarg. and Ur III PN's:

EN-a-ši-ra-ni (RTC 131)

Ì-lí-aš-ra-ni (U 1620; UET III p. 17, U).

ʾ$_1$ŠR.

DN in Sarg. PN:

A-sur-DINGIR (E+). Doubtful.

Sarg. GN:

A-ŠIR^{KI} (HSS X passim).

ʾ$_1$ŠR?

DN in Sarg. and Ur III PN's:

A-ḫu-A-sár (UET III 10, U)

A-li-A-sar (G)

GEMÉ-^{d}A-sár (Chiera, STA 14 i, 16 i, U)

LÚ-^{d}A-sár (AnOr VII 373, U)

Ur-^{d}A-sár (U 1222+)

Cf. also ^{d}A-sar (UET I 12) and PN's Ša-lim-^{d}A-šar, A-šar-ì-lí-šu (Studia Mariana pp. 54 and 69, Mari), I-zi-A-šar (TCL I 62:3, OB), and Ia-ku-un-A-šar (Bauer, Die Ostkanaanäer p. 92).

ʾ$_1$ŠR ašarum "place."

Written syllabically or logographically as KI.

Kiš^{KI} a-ša-rí-su i-ni (ù) URU^{KI}-lam$_x$ u-sá-ḫi-su-ni = Sum. Kiš^{KI} ki-bi bí-gi$_4$ uru-bi ki-gub e-na-ba "he restored Kiš to its place and caused them to settle the city" (S iv, ix)

URU^{KI}-lam Si?-ku?-ma-núm^{KI} KI-su e-ni (UET I 275 v, NS.)

a-ti si-dar KI-šu (AOF III 112 end, Mari). Ununderstandable

NE.RU-dam in a-ša-ar URU al-su-nu iš-bu-uk (R xxiii, xxv).

ʾ$_{1}$ŠR? ašriš?

PN im-ḫur [á]š?-rí-iš  -za-am-ì-li (MDP XIV 13).

ʾ$_{6-7}$ŠR jašārum "to be right," "to succeed."

KASKAL KI.⌜UD⌝-su a i-si-ir (ZA IV 406, Gutium). Cf. ḪRR ḫarrānum.

uššurum "to release."

x URU^{KI}.URU^{KI} a-na ^{d}UTU lu uš-šu-ru "were released" (CT XXXII 2 v, CM).

šûšurum "to make right," "to direct."

DN's his .... a [u]?-si-si-ra (UET I 276 ii, NS.)

mu-uš-ti-ši-⌜ir⌝ ḫa-ab-lim ù ḫa-bi-el-tim (YOS IX 62, Dêr).

Sarg. PN's:

Su-si-ra (E)

Ù-a-še-ir-Da-ga-an (ITT V 6718). Cf. Wa-še-ir-bi-tu in MDP XXIII 312:12, OB. Doubtful.

U-su-si-ir-ti-ni (ITT I 1465+).

išarum "righteous."

Sarg. and Ur III PN's:

In many cases Išar may be a DN; cf. Sa-am-su-^{d}I-[s]ar in ARMT VI 14:13.

A-bí-i-sar (RTC 169)

A-pum-i-sar (ITT IV 7449)

A-bu-um-mi-LUGAL (ITT III 6062 rev., U)

A-ḫu-i-sar (BIN VIII 144)

Be-lí-i-sar (U 514+)

DINGIR-i-sar (RA XXXIII 178, Mari)

Gal-iš-i-sar (ITT II/2 5885 ii)

Ì-lí-iš-i-sar (ITT II/2 p. 37 No. 4664+)

I-sar-a-ḫi (D+; U 1644)

I-sar-ra-ḫi (AJSL XXIX 133 No. 1 rev., U; Barton, HLC Pl. 94, 105, U)

I-sar-a-lí-iš-zu (A 5600, U)

I-sar-ba-dan (U 1645+)

I-sar-pa-da-an (AnOr I 228 i 10, U)

I-sar-be-lí (G+; U 1646+)

I-sar-DI.TAR-ni (Pope, SPA I 281)

I-sar-DÍM (RTC 249 i). Or I-sar-kin$_{x}$

I-sar-^{d}EN.ZU (Porada, CPML No. 287, U)

I-sar-ì-lí (RA XXIII 18 No. 9, U+)

Ì-sar-ì-lí (ITT II 2643, U)

I-sar-^{d}IM (ITT II/1 p. 25, 772, U)

I-sar-i[š-d]a-gal (G)

I-sar-iš-^{d}EN.ZU (Iraq V 178 CBS 9165, U)

I-sar-ki-^{d}UTU (Jean, ŠA CXIII rev., U). Cf. I-sar-ki-ma-^{d}UTU in OECT IV 155 ii 39, OB

I-sar-ki-in (U 1652+)

I-sar-kur-ba-aš (U 1650)

I-sar-la-e (TMH n.F. I/II 7:12, U)

I-sar-la-ì (YOS IV 224, U)

I-sar-li-i (PDTI 186, U)

I-sar-li-bur (D+; PDTI 561, U)

I-sar-li-bu-ur (BIN VIII 142)

I-sar-lu-ba-lí-it (UET III 28, U)

I-sar-lú-ba-lí-⌈iṭ⌉ (UET III 49, U)

I-sar-ma-ti-iš-su (E)

I-sar-ni-ḫi-sa-am (Kish 1930, 144a). Interpr. unknown

I-sar-ni-si (BE III 46 rev., U)

I-sar-ra-ma-aš (U 1654+)

I-sar-sar-rí (RTC 127 rev. iv)

I-sar-tu[m]? (PBS IX 69, PSarg.?)

I-sar-ru-um (G+; U 1656)

I-sar-ru (U 1655)

I-sa-ru-um (D+)

I-sa-ru (E)

I-sar-um (U 1648+)

Sar-ru-i-sar (RTC 127 rev. v)

U-zé-i-sar (E).

<u>mêšarum</u>, <u>mîšarum</u> "justice."

DI.TAR me-sar-im (MDP IV Pl. 2 iv)

[ba]-da-an [m]i-sar-im (CT XXXII 2 iv, CM)

PN ša-ki-in me-ša-ri-im (YOS IX 62, Dêr).

Sarg. PN:

Me-sar (G+).

Ur III PN's:

In some cases the element Mi-sar is deified; cf. ^{d}Mi-šar-rum-ga-mil in TCL I 181:6, OB.

DINGIR-mi-sar (Orient. XXI 88 IB 180)

DI.TAR-mi-sar (U 860+)

I-ku-me-sar (ITT II/1 p. 52, 966)

I-ku-mi-sar (U 1608+; De Genouillac, TD 73)

Ì-lum-mi-sár (Barton, HLC II Pl. 75 ii)

I-za-az-mi-sar (UET III 1034 ii)

I-zé-mi-sar (Orient. XLVII 423:19)

NI.UŠ-mi-sar (Orient. XLVII 494 rev.). Interpr. unknown

| dŠul-gi-mi-sar (U 927+)
| dŠul-gi-mi-sár (Jean, ŠA CLI)
| dŠul-gi-me-sar (ZA XII 338)

| Ú-da-mi-sar-ra-am (U 1122+)
| Ú-ta-mi-sar-ra-am (U 1141)
| Ú-da-mi-sar-am (Legrain, TRU 229)
| Ù-da-mi-ša-ra-am (Nies, UDT 44)

Zi-ip-mi-sar (TCL V 6039 ii). Cf. wuṣṣupum.

mêšartum "justice."

Sarg. PN:

Me-sar-tum (Speleers, RIAA 54).

ʾxŠR.

á-tum mi-nim la è-e-sa-ru (D 290 rev. x+11). Meaning unknown

[....] la i-e-sa-ru (ibid. l. 13).

ʾxŠR.

so many breads ŠILIG ù-su-ri (MDP XIV 9).

Ur III GN's:

Maš-gán-ú-šu-ri[KI] (CT XXXII 20 iv)

Cf. also Ur III RN ÍDÙ-sur (ITT II 766; 893; III 5972; RS XI 77 No. IV), ÍDÙ-sur-ra (ITT V p. 61, 9980), and ÍDÙ-sar-ra (ITT V p. 47, 9638, translit. only).

ʾxŠRD asarīdum "leader" (or the like).

Sarg. and Ur III PN's:

A-ša-rí-id, ensi of Kazallu (R xvii+)

A-ši-rí-da (Oppenheim, CCTE H 45, U). Doubtful.

ʾ1ŠŠ uššum "foundation."

uš-se11 É (RTC 86; 106; 144, date of NS.; RTC 87, date of Škš.)

Sarg. and Ur III PN's:

| Uš-si-gi-in (D)
| Uš-šu-ki-in (U 1441)

Gi-nu-mu-si = Kînum-uššī? (A 2736; YOS IV 53, U)

| Gi-nu-uš-sa-am = Kîn-uššam "make firm the foundation!" (G)
| Gi-in-uš-sa-am (ZA XII 333+).

ʾxŠŠ? ašāšum?

Sarg. PN:

A-ša-su-GIŠ.RÍN (BE I Pl. VI iv). "His ašāʾum?" or "his ašāšum?"

ʾ$_6$ŠT *ište*, *ištu* "with," "from."

Meaning "with":

animals iš-dè PN (D 236)

ŠE iš-dè PN (HSS X 64:4; 72; 96:4; MDP XIV 26; FM 15 rev.; 32 rev.)

PN$_1$ iš-dè PN$_2$ .... u-ša-ab (ITT I 1471)

iš-dè PN i-ba-šè (D 267; BIN VIII 138; 140; 145; A 910, 4796)

iš-dè-su i-ba-šè (MCS IV 13 rev., cf. also obv.)

PN's iš-dè PN (D 212; 219)

1 animal iš-dè PN ḫu-bu-da-tum (FM 32 rev.)

ŠE iš-dè PN (ḫu-bu-lum) (HSS X 111:2)

animals iš-dè PN ru-ù-ba-um (HSS X 175 iii 7)

x iš-dè PN (D 283; RTC 1465)

iš-dè-su (HSS X 6:3).

Sarg. and Ur III PN's and deified PN:

Ma-an-iš-tu-su (Sarg. king)

Ma-an-iš-t[i-su]^{KI} (OIP XIV 114 rev., collated)

Ma-an-iš-ti-su (JRAS 1920 pp. 21ff., U). Doubtful

^{d}Ma-ni-iš-ti-su (Speleers, CIMC p. 116 No. 594)

^{d}Ma-ni-iš-di(n)-su (Oppenheim, CCTE p. 13, 133, U)

Ur-^{d}Ma-an-iš-di(n)-su (YOS IV 232 i, U; TCL II 5674 iii, rev. viii, U).

Meaning "from":

iš-dè PN maḫārum (HSS X 42:3; 81 x+9; 99:6; 107:3; 120:2, 4; 126 x+5; PBS IX 122; A 748; MDP XIV 13)

x É, ŠÁM-su-nu x KUG.BABBAR, iš-dè PN$_1$ ù PN$_2$ PN$_3$ i-ḫu-uz (JCS X 26 i)

PN's iš-dè PN li-su-zé-aš-su-ni (RTC 78 rev.)

iš-dè-šù PN [ŠU].BA.TI (A 803 in broken context).

ištum "from," "after."

Preposition "from" with a noun:

iš-tum ti-a-am-tim sa-bil-tim (S iv, ix)

iš-tum da-ar si-ki?-ti ni-se$_{11}$ (UET I 275 i, NS.)

iš-tum-ma GN$_1$ a-ti-ma GN$_2$ (UET I 275 ii, NS.)

iš-tum BÀD .... a-na BÀD .... (UET I 275 ivff.)

iš-tum GN$_1$ a-ti GN$_2$ (CT XXXII 2 iv, CM).

Conjunction "after" with a verb:

iš-tu[m] PN .... BA.ÚŠ "after PN .... died" (HSS X 176:12)

iš-tum PN PA.TE.SI "after PN (became) ensi" (BIN VIII 144)

iš-tum KAS+X.KAS+X iš$_x$-ar-ru "after he had won the battles" (YOS I 10, NS.; MDP VI Pl. 1, 1 i).

ʾ$_x$ŠT *ištiniš* "together."

[ki-i]b-ra-tum ar-ba-um iš-ti-ni-[iš] [i-ba-al-ki-tu-nim-ma] (IAMN XII Pl. IV, NS.)

GA.LUL-ma /kaluma?/ ki-ib-ra-tu[m] ar-ba-um iš-ti-ni-iš i-ḫa-ni-su$_4$-ma (PBS V 36 rev. x+ii, NS.).

ʾ$_x$ŠT? eštum? "straw" (or the like).

Akk. lw. in Ur III Sum.:

x GUR èš-tum (Reisner, TUT 121 vi; YOS IV 298:34; ITT V 6905; RA XVI 19f. ii, iv, vi, xi). Since in all cases the word AP-tum occurs in connection with words for "straw," Dr. Landsberger suggests to read AB-tum as èš-tum and to compare it with iltu "eine Art Stroh" in Delitzsch, AHWB p. 77a.

ʾ$_6$ŠṬ waštum "hard," "powerful."

Sarg. PN:

Ù-áš-ti-a (RTC 249 rev. i). Cf. also Ba-áš-ti-a under Bʾ$_6$Š.

ʾ$_1$T itti "with," "from."

it-ti ìr-bi ù ⌈ki-š⌉a-a-tim (CT XXXII 1 ii) = it-ti ir-bi ù ki-ša-a-ti (RA VII 180) in CM

x ŠE of different persons PN$_1$ i-ti PN$_2$ i-su (MDP XIV 49)

x ŠE i-ti PN$_1$ PN$_2$ i-ša-am "PN$_2$ bought x ŠE from PN$_1$" (Yondorf b, U).

Ur III PN:

^{d}Šu-^{d}EN.ZU-i-ti-ì-lí-UR.UR (JCS X 28 No. 5 rev. and p. 24).

ittiš "together?"

e-ni ʾà-wa-at-zu i-ti-iš i-da-ḫa-az (Ist. Mus. Lagash 11001, in difficult context).

ʾ$_x$T itum "side."

è-da-su ^{IM}MAR.TU, è-da-su ^{IM}sa-ti-um (DP 2 ii, PSarg.).

ʾ$_x$T.

Akk. lw. in Ur III Sum.:

ì-tum (PDTI 543, in difficult context).

ʾ$_x$T etum?

Akk. lw. in Sum.:

2 DUG NI.DUN (E)RÍN e-tum ŠE (OIP XIV 95).

ʾ$_x$T itum?

ŠE.ḪAR.AN PN$_1$ šu PN$_2$ in i-te-su ik-su$_4$-ra (FM 36:8).

ʾ$_6$Tʾ$_x$ watāʾum "to find."

Sarg. and Ur III PN's:

As against several examples with TA in OB (quoted below), spelling with DA occurs in ^{d}UTU-ú-da (VAS IX 98:10, OB) and Nu-úr-šu-ú-da (MDP XXVIII 442:25, OB?).

| A-li-ú-da (G+)

A-lí-ú-da (ITT II/1 p. 6, 618, U). Cf. A-lí-ú-ta in UET V p. 30 passim, OB

Ú-da-aḫ (D+)

Ú-da-a-ḫi-i? (TA 1931, 463 iii, U?). Cf. Ú-ta-a-ḫi and Ú-ta-a-bi in De Genouillac, Kich II A 463 bis, school text

Ú-da-be-lí (BIN VIII 142 rev.)

Ú-da-mi-sar-ra-am (U 1122+)

Ú-da-mi-sar-am (Legrain, TRU 229, U)

Ú-ta-mi-sar-ra-am (U 1141+)

Ù-da-mi-ša-ra-am (Nies, UDT 44, U)

Ú-da-ur$_4$-ra (HSS IV 32 rev., U).

Interpr. of the following PN's is doubtful:

Tu-da-LUGAL-li-bí-iš (D+)

Tu-da-sar-li-bí-iš (D+)

Tu-da-na-ap-šum (D+).

ʾ$_x$Tʾ$_x$?

Sarg. and Ur III PN's:

A-bí-a-ti (TCL V 6047 i passim, U)

A-gu-a-ti (Oppenheim, CCTE p. 179, U)

A-ḫu-a-ti (UET III 272 i, U)

A-ki-a-ti (UET III 17, U)

A-ti-DINGIR (CT I 1c)

En-ni-a-ti (ZA XXV 206, U)

Ì-lí-a-ti (RA IX 56 SA 232, U). Cf. same PN in PBS XI/1 p. 55, OB.

ʾ$_x$TGR itgurtum "spoon?"

Sarg. GN:

It-gur-da^{KI} (Kish 1930, 147 rev.).

ʾ$_x$TḪ? utuḫum?

Akk. lw. in Ur III Sum.:

2(PI) GAR ù-tu-ḫu-um LUGAL (BIN V 327:1)

flour GAR u$_4$-duḫ-ḫu-um-ŠÈ (UET III 907).

ʾ$_x$TL etellum "heroic" (or the like).

Ur III PN:

E-te-al-pi$_x$(KA+KÁR)-^{d}Da-gan (Bab. VIII Pl. V 17:19; Boson, TCS 241; 243). Sign AL may have the value el$_x$; cf. MAD II 113.

ʾ$_x$TL? utlum "bosom."

Ur III PN:

Ú-túl-Ma-ma (Oppenheim, CCTE p. 202; Nikolski, Dok. II 353 rev.). Cf. Ut-li-Eš$_4$-dar in TCL XXVII 14:11, Mari.

ʾ$_x$TL.

Ur III PN:

Ú-du-lu (Reisner, TUT 56+). Probably Sum. word for cowherd.

$^{\text{ʾ}}{}_{x}$TM? etimtum?

2(PI) NÍG.ḪAR.RA ù e-tim-da-su (D 290 rev. x+6). Evidently part of NÍG.ḪAR.RA, possibly "bran??"

$^{\text{ʾ}}{}_{x}$TN itinnum? "architect."

PN? i-ti-num (FM 40:16).

Sarg. and Ur III PN's:

I-ti-ni (ITT II/1 p. 26, 786, U)

I-ti-LUM (D; ZA XII 333; ITT II/1 721, U).

$^{\text{ʾ}}{}_{x}$TN?

Sarg. PN's:

Ú-du-na (G)

Ú-tu-LUM (UCP IX p. 210, 89). Or Sa?-tu-lum.

$^{\text{ʾ}}{}_{6}$TR watrum "excellent."

PSarg., Sarg., and Ur III PN's:

Ba-da-ru-um (UET III 1048, U). Cf. Wa-da-ru-um below

Ba-da-rí-im, Gen. (D)

É-a-DIRIG (D)

Ì-lí-DIRIG (FM)

Ú-zi-wa-dar (PSarg. king)

Wa-at-ra-at (U 2531)

Wa-at-ra-at-PA-tum (AnOr VII p. 37, U)

Wa-at-ra-at-ḫa-tum (Nikolski, Dok. II 457, U)

⌈Wa-da⌉-ru (E)

Wa-da-ru-um (D; U 2534+). Cf. Ba-da-ru-um above

Wa-at-ru-um (MDP XVIII 78, U)

Wa-at?-rúm (BE I Pl. VI ii). Doubtful

Wa-dar-ì-li (Louvre AO 8638 rev.)

Wa-dur-be-lí (OIP XIV 79+).

Interpr. of foll. Sarg. and Ur III PN's is doubtful:

DIRIG-a (Oppenheim, CCTE p. 208, U). Or Si-a-a comparable with Ši-a-a (TCL II 6163 rev., U; ITT III 5241 rev., U+)

DIRIG-ni (G+). Or Si-a-NI

DIRIG-tum (D+; BE I 15, U). Watartum or Si-a-tum

DIRIG-um (D+; Oppenheim, CCTE p. 208, U). Wat(a)rum or Si-a-um.

In Ur III DN:

^{d}Geštin-an-na-SI.A-tum (TCL II 5514; Orient. XVIII 24 ii).

šûturum "to exceed."

1 ḫa-zi-núm šu 4 EME-su A.MU.NA.RU ù-sa-ti-ir BÀD-si-in KUG.BABBAR

A.MU.NA.RU "he presented 1 ax with 4 "tongues," and he exceeded, (even) their "covers" of silver he presented" (MDP IV Pl. 2 iii).

ʾ$_6$TR? itirtum? (a milk-product).

Looks like a Sum. lw. from Akk. of the type of GU.ZI.DA, DU.TI.DA. A milk-product, perhaps "cream," if derived from *(w)itirtum. Cf. "Oberes" in German for semantics, and Capp. itirtum "overpayment" for the form.

2 QA GA i-ti-ir-da (UET III 1219, U). Among NI.NUN and GA. Cf. also Falkenstein in JAOS LXXII 42ff. for ì-te-ir-da and i-ti-ir-da in post-Ur III examples.

ʾ$_{3-5}$TR aṭārum "to take away."

šu .... ki-iš-da-su i-ti-ru "whoever .... takes away his gift" (MDP IV Pl. 2 iv).

ʾ$_x$ṬL eṭlum "(grown up) man"; "vir," not "homo."

Written logographically as GURUŠ or syllabically.

Meaning "man" ("soldier"):

5400 GURUŠ u-um!-šum NINDA KÚ = Sum. 5400 erín u(d)-šú-šè igi-ni-šè ninda ì-kú-e (S vi)

x GURUŠ.GURUŠ u-sa-am-gi$_4$/ki-it (R xvii, xix, etc.)

x iṭ-lu?-[tim? ŠU.DU$_8$.A] "he took captive x men" (S xiii)

ù iṭ-lu-[tim]? ŠU.[DU$_8$.A] (R xvi).

Sarg. and Ur III PN:

| Iṭ-lum (G)
| Iṭ-lum MAR.TU (Fish, CST 728 iii, U).

Meaning "working man," probably "serf," not "slave":

30 GURUŠ ga-za-ru (HSS X 71:6)

a-na GURUŠ.GURUŠ (HSS X 129 i 12)

GURUŠ.ME (HSS X 188 i 13, etc.; 205:7)

GURUŠ and GEMÉ "working men and women" (D 163 end)

GURUŠ and SAL "working men and women" (ITT I 1099 rev.)

GURUŠ, DAM, DUMU.ARAD (D 207)

GURUŠ, DAM, DUMU.ARAD, DUMU.SAL, GABA (D 255)

GURUŠ includes QA.ŠU.DU$_8$, šūt GIŠ.GIGIR, šūt GIŠ.GU.ZA, šūt GIŠ.É.GIGIR, ŠU.I, LÚ.KIN.GI$_4$.A, GIŠ.TÚG.PI.KAR.DU, MU, NAR (D 226)

GURUŠ includes NAGAR, AŠGAB, AD.KID, SIMUG, TÚG.DU$_8$, MU, LÚ.KISAL, A.ZU, AB (RTC 93)

Thureau-Dangin, ITT I p. 2 n. 2 distinguishes GURUŠ GUB.BA "present," ZI.GA "absent," and ḪA.A "fugitive"

ŠU.NIGÍN 30 LAL 3 GURUŠ ZAG NU.U.ME "total of 27 men not marked" (A 4491) implies the existence of the practice of marking serfs, as also slaves.

ʾ$_4$ZB azābum "to leave."

[ša] a-bi S. [e]-zi-ba-am (CT XXXII 1 ii, CM)

barley li-zi-ib (HSS X 5:24).

šûzubum.

Ur III PN:

Šu-zu-bí (Legrain, TRU 43 rev.).

izbum.

Ur III PN:

Iz-bu-um (ITT V p. 59, 9941). Cf. PN's in Stamm, ANG p. 49.

ʾ$_x$ZB?

Ur III PN:

A-zi-ba?-LUM (Reisner, TUT 16 iii).

ʾ$_x$ZB?

Sarg. PN:

A-za-bí-LUM (ITT V 6867+).

ʾ$_x$ZL? azallûm (a plant).

Akk. lw. in Sum.:

1 GIŠ.NAD ^{GIŠ}a-za-LUM (BIN VIII 260).

ʾ$_x$ZL?

Ur III PN:

Ì-za-li (Fish, CST p. 159 iv end, 160 ix). Cf. ʾ$_x$ZN?

ʾ$_1$ZN uznum "ear."

⌈i⌉n? uz-ni-su [su]?-ub-si (MDP II p. 66)

in uz-ni-ki ⌈su-ub-si⌉? (MDP XIV p. 19).

uznīnum?

Ur III PN:

Ùz-ne-nu-uš (UET III 1486; 1487; 1491; 1495; 1496; UET V 690:31)

Ùz-nin-nu-uš (UET III 1490)

Ùz-ne-nu-⌈um⌉? (YOS IV 254:94). Thus copied.

ʾ$_x$ZN?

Sarg. and Ur III PN's:

A-zi-na-tum (U 118 = TCL V 6163 rev., U)

A-zu-NI (D)

I-za-LUM MAR.TU (TCL II 5503 ii, U). Cf. ʾ$_x$ZL?

Ì-za-LUM (UET III p. 26, U)

I-za-nu-um (UET III 1391 iv, U).

ʾ$_6$ZR wazirijum, see ZRʾ$_x$.

ʾ$_x$ZR?

Ur III PN's:

A-zi-ri (Barton, HLC III Pl. 114 x)

A-zi-rí-lum (Jean, ŠA LXVII iii; Reisner, TUT 16 iii).

$^{\supset}{}_{x}$ZZN?

Ur III PN:

A-zu-zu-nu-um (Fish, CST p. 159 iii). Misread as A-zu-nu-um in U 117.

B

B$^{\supset}{}_{x}$?

Sarg. PN's:

| Bu-e-im (BE I Pl. VII v)
| Bu-im (MO)

Bi-im (MO)

Bi-e-tim (MO).

B$^{\supset}{}_{6}{}^{\supset}{}_{1}$ buā$^{\supset}$um "to come."

Sarg. PN's:

| I-ba-tum (E). Cf. I-ba-tum, Ib-ba-tum in Ranke, EBPN p. 88
| Ib-$^{\supset}$à-tum? (D)

I-ba-um (E). Cf. I-ba-šar-rum in Ward, CPM No. 110, OB.

Sarg. DN:

I-ba-um (Iraq I Pl. IXb). Cf. ^{d}I-ba-um in OIP XLIII 178, OB.

B$^{\supset}{}_{x}$B bâbum "gate."

Written logographically only.

KÁ-su "in his gate," Acc. loci (MDP IV Pl. 2 ii)

a-na KÁ-su du-mu-ki-im (MSP IV Pl. 2 iii)

PN KÁ ^{d}Tišpak it-ma (FM 7:26)

[KÁ] ^{d}Tispak [it]-má-ù (FM 51 rev. x+2).

B$^{\supset}{}_{x}$D b/pûdum (an object).

Akk. lw. in Sum.:

2 bu-tum KUG.GI (OIP XIV 52 ii, PSarg.). Cf. bûdu "e. Werkzeug" in Delitzsch, AHWB p. 161a.

B$^{\supset}{}_{4}$L ba$^{\supset}$ālum "to rule over (a land)."

Rímuš NIM^{KI} i-be-al (R xxiii, xxv). Sign AL perhaps = el$_{x}$

GN's [lu] SAG.GIŠ.RA [l]u e-be-el "I truly conquered" (CT XXXII 1 ii = RA VII 180 ii) in CM.

bêlum "lord," "owner."

Written syllabically or logographically as EN.

DN be-al DÙL su$_{4}$-a (R xviii, xxiv; UET I 274 iv, NS.; 276 i, NS.). Sign AL perhaps = el$_{x}$

DN be-al puḫrim(UKKIN) (AOF III 112 twice, Mari)
a-na DN be-lí-šu (Speleers, RIAA 4 i, ii, Dêr)
in KÁ DN be-lí-su (MDP IV Pl. 2 ii)
a-na DN be-lí-su (MDP IV Pl. 2 i, iii; VI Pl. 2, 1 i etc.; CT III 1 7288, U)
a-na be-lí-[su] (MDP X Pl. 3, 1a)
É DN be-[lí]-su (ZA III 94f., U)
a-na dUTU be-lí-ì-a (CT XXXII 1 i etc., CM)
a-na PN be-lí ù a-bí (D 191)
a-na PN a-bí ù be-lí (A 4746)
a-na be-lí [prob. nothing] (A 708; 830)
be-lí ʾà-wa-a-ti li-[iš-m]e? (A 708)
be-lam? (A 708)
various artisans be-lu ga-da-tim (MDP XIV 71 ii)
be-lu GÁN "owners of the field" (MO A iv etc.; Kish 1930, 138)
ŠEŠ be-lu GÁN not "brothers of the owners of the fields" but probably a compound ŠEŠ-be-lu /aḫbêlū/ with a specific meaning still to be determined (MO A v etc.). Cf. LÚ.ŠEŠ (RTC 15 iv) and LÚ.ŠEŠ.EN (BIN VIII 11) in similar transactions
EN.EN-su-nu (of the cities) u-sa-am-[ki]-it (RA VII 104, Mi.)
Ma-ni-u[m] EN Má-gan[KI] (MDP VI Pl. 1, 1, NS.)
EN.EN a-lí-a-tim "lords of the upper (regions)" (UET I 274 ii, NS.)
Ḫur-ša-ma-ad-ki EN ⌈A-ra⌉-am ù Am (RA VIII 200 i, NS., copy). Doubtful
EN.EN UD.NUNKI-ME (Pinches, AT 10)
GIŠ.SAR EN, GIŠ.SAR SUKKAL.MAḪ (ITT I 1282)
ŠABRA EN (RTC 254 rev. ii, iii).

PSarg. and Sarg. PN's:
A-li-be-lí (D)
Be-lam-nu-bi-iq (A 725; 974)
Be-la-su-nu (BE I Pl. VII ii) = Bêlassunu?
Be-lí (D+)
EN-li (G+)
Be-lí-a-ar (D+)
Be-lí-a-pum (D+)
Be-lí-a-mi (MO+)
Be-lí-AN.DÙL (E+)
Be-lí-a-zu (D)
Be-lí-BÀD (ITT I 1103)
Be-lí-tu-rí (D)

Be-lí-BALA (RTC 127 rev. iv)
Be-lí-ba-liḫ (D+)
Be-lí-ba-lik (D+)
Be-lí-ba-ni (D+)
Be-lí-BÍ (D+)
Be-lí-da-bum$_{x}$(BALAG) (OIP XIV 102)
Be-lí-dan (D+)
Be-l[í?-da?-t]i? (FM)
Be-lí-DINGIR (G+)
Be-lí-DÙG (D+)
Be-lí-du-gul (D)
Be-lí-^{d}EN.ZU (Kish 1930, 149)
Be-lí-GAL.ZU (D+)
Be-lí-GÀR (E+)
Be-lí-GI (D+)
Be-lí-GÚ (MO+)
Be?-lí-GUR$_{7}$ (FM)
Be-lí-ìl-la-a[t] (D)
Be-lí-iš-da-gal (D+)
Be-lí-la-ba (D+)
Be-lí-^{d}Ma-ar (ITT I 1472 ii)
Be-lí-mu-da (D+)
Be-lí-na-ba-áš-ti (D+)
Be-lí-nu-rí (D)
Be-lí-ra-bí (ITT II/2 p. 14, 3072)
Be-lí-sa-tu (G+)
Be-lí-SIPA (D+)
Be-lí-SU[D]? (BIN VIII 122 rev. iii)
Be-lí-tu-gul-ti (ZA XII 332)
Be-lí-tum-ki (D)
Be-lí-UR.SAG (D+)
Be-lí-^{d}UTU-si (D)
Be-lí-za-ki (G+)
Be-lu-GÚ (ITT I 1472 iii)
Bu-be-lí (Delaporte, CCL II A 154)
Pù-be-lí (MO)
K[A]-be-lí (FM)
DINGIR-b[e?-l]í? (D)
É-a-be-lí (CT I 1c)
EN-a-ši-ra-ni (RTC 131)

EN-Bí-bí (Fish, CST 3+)
EN-ì-lí (D+)
EN-ku-li (G+)
EN-lum (G+)
E-na-be-lí (E+)
EN-su-dan (ITT II/2 p. 39, 4700)
^{d}⌈Ḫa⌉?-ri-im-be-lí (Kish 1930, 170c)
I-da-be-lí (G+)
I-tum-be-lí (D)
íl-be-lí (D)
ì-lí-be-lí (G+)
ì-lí-pi-lí (Nikolski, Dok. II 14 i+)
ì-lí-EN (G)
I-rí-iš-be-lí (MO)
I-sar-be-lí (G+)
Li-bur-be-lí (E+)
Lú-be-lu (G+)
Ma?-ki-be-lí (CT VII 4 No. 22451, PSarg.)
Mu-ti-pi-lí (TMH V 29 rev. vi, PSarg.?)
PÙ.ŠA-be-lí (ITT I 1156)
PÙ!.ŠA-pi-lí (TMH V 3 i, PSarg.?)
Sá-lim-be-lí (G+)
Si-be-la (D)
Su$_4$-be-la (G+)
Šu-be-la (G+)
Su$_4$-be-lí (D+)
Su-EN-lí (D)
Šu?-EN-lum (G)
Šu?-be-lum (Iraq VII 66 F 1159)
Su?-pi-lum (Nikolski, Dok. II 31)
Su$_4$-mu-be-lí (A 1087)
Ša-ki-be-lí (AOF VIII 258 Abb. 6a)
U-da-be-lí (BIN VIII 142 rev.)
Ur-^{d}Pi-lí (Nikolski, Dok. II 58 rev.)
Wa-dur-be-lí (OIP XIV 79+).

Selected Ur III PN's:
Be-lí (U 505)
Be-lí-a (U 506)
Be-lí-a-zu (U 507)
Be-lí-a-rí-ik (U 508)

| Be-lí-ba-ni (U 509)
| Be-lí-pa-ni (U 515)
Be-lí-dan (U 510)
Be-lí-DÙG (U 511)
Be-lí-ì-lí (U 512)
Be-lí-i-sar (U 514)
Ša-lim-be-lí (U 2597+)
Ša-lim-be-lí-ni (RTC 342).

PN in Ur III GN:
Me-EN-ì-lí (ZA LI Pl. I after p. 74 ii 2, 4, IV iv 1, 2).

bêlatum "lady."
Written syllabically or logographically as NIN.
É DN be-la-ti-šu (KAH II 2, BS.)
a-na .... DN .... be-lí-ti-ì-a (CT XXXII 1 i, CM)
a-na DN be-el-ti-ì-a (CT XXXII 4 xi, CM)
na-ʾà-áš LUGAL ù na-ʾà-áš NIN (RA XVIII 25)
PN NIN (A 1167).

Sarg. PN:
Be-la-su-nu (BE I Pl. VII ii; su clear on photo, still perhaps miswritten for zu; cf. Be-la-zu-nu in MDP XXVIII 418:22).

In Ur III DN's:
^{d}Be-la-at-Bí-ru (Schenider, AnOr XIX No. 50)
^{d}Be-la-at-Dír-ra-ba-an, etc. (ibid. No. 51). Also ^{d}Be-la-at-Te-ìr-ra-ba-an in Sarg. (MDP XIV p. 20 i, Elam) and ^{d}Be-la-at-Te-ra-ba-an in Ur III (OIP XLIII 143) = ^{d}NIN-Te-ra-ba-an (p. 144)
^{d}Be-la-at-Suḫ-nir, etc. (AnOr XIX No. 52, read as -múš-nir, but cf. Jacobsen, CTC p. 21)
^{d}Be-la-at-Na-gàr (AnOr XIX No. 53) and ^{d}NIN-Na-gàr^{KI} (RA XLII 6 rev.)
^{d}Be-la-at-Ti-tu-ri-im (PDTI 563 i).

DN Bêlatum in Ur III PN:
^{d}NIN.LÍL-tum-im-ti (A 5535). Cf. ^{d}NIN.LÍL-ti-im in Gadd, EDSA Pl. 3:23, Lipit-Ištar of Isin; but Sum. pronunciation is indicated in Nin-líl-iš-gi-in (FM). Cf. also Gemé-Nin-líl, without divine classifier in PDTI 220, U.

baʾūlatum "dominion" or baʾūlātum "dominions."
Škš. .... LUGAL A-ga-dè^{KI} ù ba$_{11}$-ú-la-ti ^{d}En-líl (BE I 2)
Škš. da-núm LUGAL ba$_{11}$-ú-la-ti ^{d}En-líl (MJ III 23).

Bʾ$_{7}$N? biānum?
PN$_{1}$ ù PN$_{2}$ i-bí-na-ma PN$_{2}$ PN$_{3}$ da-áš-zi (BIN VIII 121).
Sarg. PN:
U-bi-in-LUGAL-rí (MO+).

$B^{\circ}{}_{x}N$ bînum "tamarisk."

25 ŠIM SU pi-núm (D 286:2). Spelling PI for pi abnormal in Diyala texts

10 ^{GIŠ}BÍ.NUM = ^{GIŠ}bí-num? (HSS X 38 iii).

Akk. lw. in Ur III Sum.:

1 É bí-NI-tum ^{GIŠ}bi-nu-u[m] (UET III 1027).

$B^{\circ}{}_{3}R$ ba'ārum or bi'ārum "to choose."

šu-ut .[....] i-bi-ru "whom (Pl.) PN? has chosen" (HSS X 184:9)

x men bi-ru "selected" (Kish 1930, 146 rev.; 170a).

$B^{\circ}{}_{6}R$ buārum "to be firm" (as in Capp.).

Stamm, ANG pp. 155f. translates this verb as "klar, heiter sein," v. Soden, Orient. n.s. XVI 443 as "klar sein."

PSarg., Sarg., and Ur III PN's:

A-ḫu-li-bur-ra (D)

A-lí-li-bur (AnOr I 292:8, U)

Da-pù-ra (D)

Da-bu-ra (UET III 1440; 1506 iii, U)

Da-bur-PA-tum (De Genouillac, TD 87, U; PDTI 454, U)

Im-ti-li-bur (D+)

I-pù-úr?-Il (Jestin, TSŠ 479 i, PSarg.)

I-sar-li-bur (D+; PDTI 561, U)

I-sar-li-bu-ur (BIN VIII 142)

Li-bur (FM+; UET III 44, U)

Li-bur-an-ni-^{d}EN.ZU (UET I 90, U)

Li-bur-be-lí (E+; U 2219+)

Li-bur-dum-ki (Iraq Mus. 10625, U)

Li-bur-^{d}EN.ZU (UET III p. 19+, U)

Li-bur-ì-du-ni (TCL II 5484, U)

Li-bur-ì-lí (UET III p. 19+, U)

Li-bur-ki-^{d}En-líl (BIN VIII 203+)

Li-bur-me-šum (Kish 1930, 559c)

Li-pù-ru-um (FM)

Li-bur-ri-im, Gen. (FM)

Li-bur!-ra-a[m], Nom. (TMH n.F. I/II 361 rev., U). Cf. Li-bu-ra-am in Delaporte, CCL II A 519, OB, and Li-bur-ra-am in BE VI/2 10:38, OB

Li-bur-^{d}Šul-gi (U 2220+)

Li-bur-zi-im-ti (AnOr VII p. 26, U)

We-du-um-li-bur (ZA XII 345, U).

$B^{\circ}{}_{x}R$ bûrum "young animal."

Sarg. and Ur III PN's:

Bur-^{d}IM (U 537)

Bur-Ma-ma (RTC 254 rev. ii; U 538+)

In other cases this word is written with logogram AMAR.

<u>bûrānum</u>.

Sarg. PN?:

Bu-ra-ni-e, Gen. (D+).

B'$_x$R? <u>bûrum</u>?

a-ḫu-uš$_x$(EŠ) bu-ra-?ma-ti GN "I gave .... of the land? of GN" (Kish 1930, 143:13).

B'$_x$Ṣ? <u>bûṣum</u>? (an animal).

Sarg. and Ur III PN's:

Bu-zi (Delaporte, CCL II A 211, U)

DINGIR-pù-zi (YOS IV 305 rev., U; TCL V 5666 rev., U)

| KA-zé-a (RTC 107 rev.)
| Pù-zi-a (MDP XVIII 219 rev., U)

Pù-zum (UET III 92, U).

B'$_x$Ṣ? <u>bûṣatum</u>.

Ur III PN's:

Bu-za-ti-a (TMH n.F. I/II 105)

Bu-za-tum (U 524). Cf. Bûṣatum in Stamm, ANG p. 255 n. 2.

B'$_6$Š <u>bâšum</u> "ashamed."

Sarg. PN:

La-ba-a'-šum (Gadd, EDSA Pl. 3). Read by Gadd as La-ba-te-šum. Cf. also BḪŠ? baḫšum. The name of an early king of Uruk, read as "La-ba-a<ḫ? (old lacuna?)>IR" by Jacobsen, AS XI 90f. and n. 136, is almost certainly to be corrected to La-ba-aḫ-[š]um.

<u>bâštum</u> "pudenda," "vigor."

Ur III PN's:

A.AB.BA-ba-áš-ti, f.n. (APAW 1936 Phil.-hist. Kl. Nr. 13 p. 23). Cf. also PDTI 244

Ba-áš-ti-a (UET III 1542). Cf. also Ù-áš-ti-a under '$_6$ŠT

Ìr-ra-ba-aš-ti (Reisner, TUT 210).

B'$_x$Š <u>bûšānum</u>.

Ur III PN's:

| Bu-ša-nu-um (Fish, CST p. 48, 416)
| Pù-ša-núm (TCL II 5610).

B'$_7$T <u>biātum</u> "to pass the night."

al-kam-ma ba-dam "come and pass the night" (FM 10:12). Doubtful.

<u>bîtum</u> "house," "estate."

Written logographically or syllabically (in Ur III).

su-lum É ga-lí-su (D 290 rev. x+3)

šu É-ti PN_1 ši PN_2 (D 280:3)

in É-ti PN (FM 36:10)

a-na É-ti-su_4-nu (FM 36:29)

a-na su-ur-ki É-ti-su (Cop. 10090)

The meaning "estate" for É is clear from such texts as D 163 end.

Ur III PN's:

DÙG-bí-ti-iš-zu (YOS IV 284)

Na-si-bí-tum (Oppenheim, CCTE p. 197). Meaning unknown; Našî-biltum improbable.

Ur III GN:

Bí-tum-ra-bí-um^KI (date of BS. 7).

Apparently deified É in Sarg. and Ur III PN's. Cf. Bi-tum-mu-ba-lí-iṭ in PBS VIII/2 p. 178, OB, and É-ga-mil, É-mu-ba-lí-iṭ, É-ra-bi, É-še-mi in UET V p. 36, OB:

| Ba-luḫ-É (E). Cf. Pa-luḫ-bi-tum in PBS VIII/1 101 ii 5, 14, OB
| Ba-lu-úḫ-É (E)

DINGIR-É (D+; Oppenheim, CCTE UU 16, U). Cf. Ì-lí-É in PBS XI/2 No. 59, OB

^dEN.ZU-É (D+)

$Eš_4$-dar-É (D+)

I-ti-É (MO+)

LUGAL-É (Kish 1930, 138)

$Ni\text{-}se_{11}$-^dÉ (PBS XI/3 No. 55, U)

Ur-É (Iraq Museum 10630)

| ^dUTU-É (D+)
| ^dUTU-SA (D+). For SA = É cf. MAD II 62.

B'_xT?

Sarg. and Ur III PN's:

| Ba-a-ti (G+)
| Ba-a-dè (G+)

Ba-a-a-ti (TMH n.F. I/II 70, U; Orient. XLVII 471, U)

BÀD-ti (BIN VIII 117).

BB? bibbum "wild sheep." Cf. PN's in Stamm, ANG p. 242 and ^dBibbu in Deimel, PB No. 397.

PSarg., Sarg., and Ur III PN's:

Bí-bí (JCS X 26 iii)

Bí-bí-a (RA XIX p. 42 LXXXVIII, U)

Bí-bí-a-ḫi? (TMH V 194 ii, PSarg.?)

Bí-bí-DINGIR (D+)

Bí-bí-ì-lí-DÙG (Barton, HLC I Pl. 26 ii, U)

É-a-bí-bí (RA IX 43 SA 12 and p. 47 SA 79, U)

EN-bí-bí (Fish, CST 3+)

Gur?-bí-bí (FM)

^{d}ÍD-bí-bí (PBS XIII 27 rev. i, PSarg.).

Ur III GN:

ʾÀ.DUR$_5$-Bi-bi-AN.NA (ZA LI Pl. IV after p. 74 iv 11, 12).

BBʾ$_x$ bubûtum "hunger."

ki na-tu-ni-a? in bu-bu-tim ("in hunger") ⌈il?-mu-tu (MCS IV 13 rev.).

Sarg. and Ur III PN's:

Bu-bu-tum (G+)

Pù-pù-da (Reisner, TUT 154 iii, U; CT III 21 i, U)

Pù-pù-ti-a (ITT III 6609, U).

BBT?

Ur III PN:

Ba-ba-ti (BIN V 6:73+). Cf. Wa-wa-ti.

BBT?

Ur III PN:

Bu-ba-ti (BIN V 106:4)

Pù-ba-ti (HSS IV 59).

BD?

Ur III PN:

Bí-da-núm (RA XIX 40 No. 30+).

BDM, see BṬM buṭumtum.

BDR, see ʾ$_6$TR.

BGG, see BQQ.

BGN buginnum (a vessel).

Sarg. PN:

KA-ki-ni-iš (RTC 233 rev.).

BGŠ?

Sarg. and Ur III PN's:

Bu-ga-šum (G+)

Bu-ku-šum (UET III 1582 rev. iii, U). Cf. also BIN IX p. 26+ and Bu-ku-zum under BGZ?

BGZ?

Sarg. PN:

Bu-ku-zum (G). Cf. also Bu-ku-šum under BGŠ?

BḪR baḫīrum "heat?"

Sarg. MN's:

Ba-ḫi-ir IGI and Ba-ḫi-ir EGIR (D pp. 233f.).

BḪŠ? baḫšum?

Ur III PN:

Ba-aḫ-šum (U 384; UET III 1362; Fish, CST p. 159 iv). Cf. also B'$_6$Š bâšum.

BḪZ?

Sarg. PN:

Bu-ḫu-zum (G+).

BKN? bukannum (a wooden instrument).

Akk. lw. in Ur III Sum.:

2 ^{GIŠ}KA-ga-núm (Fish, CST p. 138 No. 581).

BL balum, bal "without."

ba-[lu]?-um PA.TE.SI "without? (the permission?) of the ensi" (HSS X 12:5)

ba-la Ù.URU+A (FM 40:6). Meaning unknown.

Sarg. and Ur III PN's:

Ba-al-È (Orient. XLVII 487:12, U)

Ba-al-ì-lí (Radau, EBH p. 362, U; UET III 43, U)

Pa-al-ì-lí (ITT IV p. 37, 7317, U)

Ma-an-ba-lum-^{d}Da-gan (Ist. Mus. Adab. 111)

Ma-ba-lum-^{d}Da-gan (BM 54318).

BLG balangum (a musical instrument).

Sarg. and Ur III PN's:

Bala-ga (G+). Doubtful

Ba-la-an-gi (BE III 4 rev., U)

Eš$_4$-dar-BALAG? (FM).

BLḪ baluḫḫum, buluḫḫum (a resinous plant).

Akk. lw. in Sum.:

25 ŠIM ⌈SU⌉ ba-lu-ḫum (D 286:3)

x MA.NA ŠIM KA+IM-lu-ḫum (ITT II/2 4461; 5766; V 9293; Reisner, TUT 122 v, viii, U; 131 i, U)

ŠIM KA+IM-lu-ḫu-um (MDP XIV 89, school text)

x MA.NA ŠIM bu-lu-ḫu-um (TMH n.F. I/II 307, U).

BLK ballukkum (a resinous plant).

10 ŠIM ba-⌈lu⌉-kum (D 286:5).

BLKT nabalkutum "to revolt," "to transgress."

ì-n[u] ŠU.NIGÍN ma-[ta-tim] .... [a]-a-bi-iš ib-ba-al-ki-da-an-ni-ma (CT XXXII 1 ii, CM)

[m]u-ba-al-ki-tum [KUG.BAB]BAR? 1 MA.NA [i]-sa?-gal "the transgressor will weigh out? 1 mina of silver?" (UCP IX p. 205, 83 iv)

ib-ba-al-gi-it-ma "if he transgressed" (Louvre AO 8959).

šubalkutum "to strip," "to transgress," "to tear out."

ma-sa-ak-sa ⌈u⌉-uš-ba-la-ga-at-ma "her skin (of sheep) he will strip" (MDP XIV 90)

šu DI.TAR-su uš-ba-la-ga-du (MDP IV Pl. 2 iv)

DN's ŠE.NUMU[N-su] li-i⌈l⌉-gu-[du] SUḪUŠ-ti-[su] li-iš-ba-al-ki-du (MDP II p. 63 ii).

BLL balālum "to pour out" (or the like). Or PLL palālum?

PSarg. and Sarg. PN's:

Ib-lul-DINGIR (MO+)

Ib-lul-ZI-DINGIR (G). Ununderstandable

Ib-lul-Il (TMH V 31 ii, PSarg.?).

BLL? bililum?

DN in Ur III PN's:

DINGIR-Bi-li-li (BE III 56 iii)

DINGIR-Bí-lí-lí (RA X 208b 6)

Šu-^{d}Bí-li-li (BE III 44:3)

Šu-Bi-li-li (BE III 97:16; TCL V 6163+)

Cf. also ....-^{d}Bi-li-e-li in Pinches, BTBC 102 rev. 19, OB, and Be-li-li in Deimel, PB No. 357.

Ur III PN:

Bí-li-li (Reisner, TUT 194 rev.).

BLL? billum?

Sarg. and Ur III GN's:

Bìl-lum-GAL^{KI} (BIN VIII 144 rev. iii). Cf. Bí-lum-GU.LA^{KI} and Bí-lum-TUR.RA^{KI} in geogr. list in Sumer III 77 ii 45f. and 80 ii 1f.

Bí-lum-ŠE.GIŠ.NI-ŠÈ GÍN.NA (RA XIX 41 No. LVII, U).

BLL?

Ur III PN's:

Ba-la-la (ZA XII 342+)

Ba-la-LUM (ibid.).

BLL?

Sarg. PN:

Bí-la-LUM (Kish 1930, 768).

BLL? bulālum (a plant).

Sarg. and Ur III PN's:

Bu-la-LUM (YOS IV 246 iv, U; Orient. XLVII 36, U)

Pù-la-LUM (UET III 29 rev., U)

KA-la-lum (ITT II/1 p. 12, 675, U)

Bu-la-la-tum, f.n. (Legrain, CCC No. 55)

Pù-la-NI (Cros, NFT p. 263 iv).

BLṢ bulluṣum, see PLS.

BLṬ balāṭum "to live."

Written syllabically.

Sarg. and Ur III PN's:

Ba-al-tu!-ša-ru-um (ITT II/1 p. 26, 779, U)

| I-sar-lu-ba-lí-iṭ (UET III 28, U)
| I-sar-lú-ba-lí-⌈iṭ⌉ (UET III 49, U)

Li-ib-lu-uṭ (D+)

Li-ib-lu-uṭ-ni-a-áš (D)

| Lú-ba-lí-iṭ! (Arnold, ABTR 8 rev., U)
| Lu?(wr. KU)-ba-lí-iṭ (UET III 264, U).

bulluṭum "to bring to life."

.... u-ba-li!-iṭ (Ist. Mus. Lagash 11001).

balāṭum "life."

Written syllabically or logographically as TI.LA.

a-na ba-la-ti-šu [ù] ba-la-a[ṭ]! [ma]-ti-⌈šu⌉ (Speleers, RIAA 4 ii, Dêr)

a-na ba-la-ti-šu (KAH II 2, BS.)

a-na ba-la-aṭ PN (ibid.).

Sarg. and Ur III PN's:

Ba-la-ti (UET III p. 7, U; U 438+)

DINGIR-TI.LA (G+)

Šu-TI.LA (G).

BN binum "son."

Sarg. PN's:

| Bi-in-ga-lí-LUGAL-rí (RA IX 82+)
| Bi-ga-lí-LUGAL-rí (RTC 94)

Cf. also Ì-lí-pi-lí, Mu-ti-pi-lí, PÙ!.ŠA-pi-lí, and Ur-dPi-lí under bêlum.

BN'₇ banājum "to build," "to beget."

Written syllabically or logographically as DÍM.

DÙL-su ib-ni-ma (R xviii; UET I 275 iii, NS.)

DÙL KUG.AN la ib-ni (R xxvii)

DÙL-su ša KUG.AN ib-ni-ma (R xxvii)

DÙL-su ib-ni (UET I 274 v, Mi.; MDP VI Pl. 1, 1, NS.)

É .... ib-ni (YOS I 10, NS.; Syria XXI 162ff., Mari)

dam-si-[lí] ab-ni (UET I 275 iii, NS.)

dam-ši-il-su ib-ni-ma (RA VIII 200 ii, NS.)

dam-si-il-su ib-ni-ma (RA IX 34 i, NS.?)

PN BA.DÍM É.KUR (BE I 1 i, 2 i, Škš., etc.)

PN DÍM (RA IX Pl. 1 opp. p. 1, Urkiš and Nawar)

PN DÍM É (ibid.)

PN DÍM sa-ḫu-rí (Syria XXI 159, Mari).

PSarg.?, Sarg., and Ur III PN's:

A(n)-nu-ba-ni-ni (Morgan, MSP IV 161 i, king of Lullubum). Cf. DINGIR-ba-ni-ni in CT XIII 29 i 21, late legend

Ba-ni (FM). Doubtful

Ba-ni-lum (E; Boson, TCS 241, U+)

Ba-ni-tum (U 448)

| Be-lí-ba-ni (D+)

| Be-lí-pa-ni (RA X 208b 7, U)

DINGIR-ba-ni (D+)

É-a-ba-ni (JAOS LII 113)

^{d}EN.ZU-ba-ni (D+)

I-ib-ni-a (ITT IV 7766, U)

Ib-ni-DINGIR (G+; U 1693+)

Ib-ni-^{d}EN.ZU (U 1695+)

| Ib-ni-^{d}IM (U 1694+)

| I-ib-ni-^{d}IM (RA XIX 33, U)

Ib-ni-LUGAL (BIN VIII 151+)

Ì-lí-ba-ni (FM)

Ì-lum-ba-ni (TMH V 104 iii, PSarg.?)

Ìr-ra-ba-ni (UET III p. 18+, U)

PÙ.ŠA-ba-ni (AnOr I 126 rev., U)

Sar-ru-ba-ni (ITT I 1372+)

Su_4-ma-ba-ni (MO)

Tab-ni (FM+).

Reading DÍM or kin_x:

A-bí-DÍM (RTC 137 i)

A-bìl-DÍM (CT I 2 ii, U)

I-sar-DÍM (RTC 249 i).

Ur III RN:

ÍD DINGIR-ba-ni (ZA LI Pl. I after p. 74 ii 6).

<u>nabnijum</u>.

Ur III PN:

^{d}EN.ZU-na-ab-ni (UET III 967; 1582 rev. ii?). Cf. also Tu-tu-na-ab-ni (Speleers, CIMC p. 178 No. 406b) and ^{d}AMAR.UD-na-ab-ni (Krausz, GNBSL p. 97), both OB.

BN$^{\circ}_{7}$? <u>binîtum</u>? (a structure?).

Akk. lw. in Ur III Sum.:

20 GIŠ.Ù.KU bí-NI-tum 7 KÙŠ TA (RA XVI 19 v)

8 GIŠ.GAL 10 KÙŠ TA MI GÍD bi-NI-tum-ŠÈ (ibid.). Woods for making a bí-NI-tum

1 É bí-NI-tum ^{GIŠ}bi-nu-⌈um⌉ (UET III 1027)

GIŠ (for É?) bí-NI-tum (ibid. 1768 rev.).

BNʾ$_x$?

Sarg. and Ur III PN's:

Ba-ba-pa-na (AnOr I 292:32, U)

Ba-na-aḫ (Coll. de Clercq I 71)

Ba-na-Da-da (Barton, HLC III Pl. 118, 249 iv, U)

DINGIR-ba-na (MO)

I-bí-ba-na (ZA XII 333)

| Lú-ba-na (G; Barton, HLC I Pl. 19, 305, U)
| L[u]-ba-na (FM).

Ur III GN:

A-bí-ba-na^{KI} (CT XXXII 19 i).

With metals, all doubtful:

URUDU AN.NA PA.NA (ITT II/2 5728)

AN.NA PA.NA (ITT V 6670; 9276)

x URUDU.⌈GAG⌉ PA.NA (RTC 221 iv)

x KUG.[nothing]? GÍN BA.NA (PBS IX 3 i, PSarg.).

BNḪ?

so much zi-nu-[?], KAŠ.SUR.RA, KAŠ.UŠ.SA, ŠE.GUR [b]an-ḫa-tum PN (D 129).

BQN <u>baqānum</u> "to pluck hair."

Ur III PN:

| Ba-ki-na-tum (UET III 1391 i)
| Ba-gi-na-tum (AnOr I 177).

BQQ <u>baqqum</u> "fly."

a-ḫu-uš$_x$(EŠ) ba-ki ša ru-ga-tim "I gave flies of far-away (places)" (Kish 1930, 143:12)

a-ḫu-uš$_x$(EŠ) ba-ki ša da-ti "I gave flies of my beloved" (l. 32).

Ur III PN:

Ba-gu-um (AnOr VII 8; PDTI 139). Cf. Ba-ak-kum in Ranke, EBPN p. 72.

<u>buqāqum</u> "fly."

Ur III PN:

Bu-ga-ku-um (RTC 428 i). Cf. Bu-qá-qum in TCL XXIII 119:2 and 120:2, Mari.

BQQ?

Ur III PN:

| Ba-ga-ga-núm (UET III 936)
| Ba-ga-ga-nu-um (A 4979).

BQR?

Ur III PN:

Bu-ga-ar (Fish, CST p. 159 v)

Cf. bu-qá-ru translated as "bétail" in ARMT II 131:39, Mari.

BRʾ$_1$ <u>barāʾum</u> "to hunger."

GÁN a ib-ra "may the field not hunger" (Cop. 10055).

BRʾ$_7$ <u>barājum</u> "to see?" (or "to inspect," "to certify").

date PN in GN ib-rí "PN saw? in GN (that this is) the (new year) date" (D 220).

Sarg. PN:

Ib-rí-^{d}MAR.TU (ZA XII 336). But cf. Ur-rí-^{d}MAR.TU (p. 337).

<u>barîtum</u> "between."

in ba-rí-ti GN$_1$ ù GN$_2$ (R xxiii, xxv)

ba-rí-ti GN$_1$ ù GN$_2$ (PBS V 36 x+iv, NS.).

Ur III GN:

Ba-rí-tum^{KI} (Orient. V 55 No. 21).

<u>nabrijum</u> (a festival).

Akk. lw. in Ur III Sum.:

1 GUD.Ú na-bí-rí-um É DN (Legrain, TRU 272)

2 MÁŠ na-ab-rí-um-ŠÈ DN$_1$ ù DN$_2$ (Legrain, TRU 282)

3 UDU.Ú NÍG.BA LUGAL na-ab-rí-(1)um-[ŠÈ] (BRM III 47)

1 UDU.Ú ^{d}Ul-ma-ši-tum UD na-ab-rí-um-KA (PDTI 162).

Ur III MN:

^{ITI}Na-ab-ri-um (TA 1930, 760).

<u>tabrijum.</u>

KUŠ.MUL tab-ri-um IGI ŠABRA.É tab-ri-um IGI AB+ÁŠ URU^{KI} (FM 44:6 f.)

⸢tab?-ri⸣?-um ⸢É⸣?.MU (FM 48:9).

<u>tabrîtum?</u> "picture?"

DÙL KUG.GI ša da-ab?-ri-a-ti tu-un-ni-su ù KAS+X-e "a silver statue (showing) the likeness of his might and battles" (RA IX 34 i, NS.?, copy).

BRʾ$_x$ <u>barjum.</u>

x ŠE.GUR ba-ri-um (and x ŠE.GUR ŠE.SIG$_5$) (D 151).

<u>burrûm</u>

30(BUR) GÁN ÉŠ?.GÀR 5 GIŠ.APIN PN ú-ba-rí (BIN VIII 144)

GÁN šu pù-ru-im (D 332 rev. x+3).

BRʾ$_x$? <u>burutum?</u> (a garment).

1 ^{TÚG}bu-ru-tum (FM 35:7).

BRBR barbarum "wolf" (or the like).

Sarg. and Ur III PN's:

Bar-bar (HSS X 142 rev.; U 498+)

Bar-bar-NI-a (U 499+).

BRD? bir(a)dum (a tree).

[2]? GIŠ bi-ra-da-an, Dual (D 318:7)

1 GIŠ bi?-ir-tum (A 850).

BRḪ? biraḫum "string (of onions)."

60 bi-ra-ḫu SUM (D 313)

Cf. 5 bi-ri-iḫ-ḫu SUM.SAR (BE VI 102:1, OB).

BRK? burkum?, see MBRK meburkum.

BRK?

Sarg. PN's:

Bí-rí-ga (D)

^{d}LUGAL-Bar-ga-at (BE I Pl. VII rev. iv). Or DN.

BRMM? burmāmum (an animal).

Ur III PN:

Bur-ma-àm (RA XIX 42 No. LXXXII; Barton, HLC III Pl. 128, 290; MCS III 87, 105525).

BRR? barrum? (a head-dress).

6 ^{TÚG}bar-ru šu-ut SAG (FM 7:7).

BRR? barrum? "shining."

Sarg. PN:

Ba-ra-tum (D+; AnOr VII 372 rev. iii, Sarg.?!).

BRŠ burāšum? "pine."

Akk. lw. in Ur III Sum.:

1 ^{KUŠ}A.GÁ.LAL bu-ra-šu-um? (BE III 78:5).

BRŠ? burrušum?

Ur III PN:

Bu-ru-šu-um (UE X 347).

BṢN buṣinnum "wick."

pù-zè-num (FM 41:6).

Ur III PN:

Bu-zi-na (Iraq V 171; BE III 56).

BŠ'$_7$ bašāum "to be."

al PN i-ba-šè "(x barley) is upon PN" = "PN owes (x barley)" (HSS X 46:4; 51 iv 4; 59:10; BIN VIII 125; A 5423; PBS IX 126)

al-su i-ba-se$_{11}$ (FM 9:29)

al GN i-ba-šè (Fish, CST 7)

ḫu-bu-lum šu al PN i-ba-šè-ù "the debt which is upon PN" (HSS X 109:23; 110:8)

iš-dè PN i-ba-šè (D 267; 283; JCS I 348b; BIN VIII 138; 140; 145; A 910; 4796)

iš-dè-su i-ba-šè (MCS IV 13 rev.)

16 GÚ GI in ÙR i-ba-šè (A 5899). Sg. like è-ru-ub (ibid.)

i-ba-s⌈e$_{11}$-ù⌉? (D 327)

[....] i-ba-šè-ù (PBS IX 22)

i-ba-šè (HSS X 52 iii 5; 120:8; 145 iv 3; Kish 1930, 138 rev.)

ma-ti-ma .... la i-ba-aš-šu-ú (CT XXXII 2 iv, CM)

ib-ši (D 167, U?)

⌈i⌉n? uz-ni-su [su]?-ub-si (MDP II p. 66).

Sarg. PN:

| Ba-si-um (D)
| Ba-ši-um (G+).

BŠD, see PŠT paštatum.

BŠL see PŠL pašallum.

BŠ[illegible].

Sarg. [illegible] III MoN:

Ba-sa-ar KUR (RTC 124). Cf. Gelb, AJSL LV 73

ḪUR.SAG Ba-ša-ar (RA IX 57, SA 3, U)

Ba$_{11}$-sal-la (Thureau-Dangin, SAKI p. 70 vi 5, Gudea).

BT?

Ur III Amorite PN:

Ba-ta-núm MAR.TU (ITT II/2 3470).

BTBDḪ? (a garment).

Akk. lw. in Ur III Sum.:

Written regularly BA.TAB-duḫ-ḫu-um or BA.TAB-duḫ-um, in which BA.TAB may have an unknown syllabic value.

1 TÚG BA.TAB-duḫ-ḫu-um (Jean, ŠA LXXVII obv. and rev.)

1 TÚG BA.TAB-duḫ-ḫu-um UŠ (ITT V 6858 ii)

Cf. GAD, SÍG, TÚG BA.TAB-duḫ-ḫu-um (UET III p. 67 passim)

x TÚG BA!.TAB!-duḫ!-ḫu-um 3.KAM UŠ (AnOr VII 155:5, read thus against x TÚG ba?-zi-ḫu-um of copy in accordance with BIN V 175)

x SÍG/TÚG BA.TAB-duḫ-ḫu-um (TMH n.F. I/II 181) = -duḫ-um (Nos. 182 twice; 238 twice; 242) = -duḫ-RI-um (Nos. 189; 224; 240; 242 four times). For ḪU = RI cf. MAD II 62

Cf. also TÚG BA.TAB-duḫ-ḫu-um in MDP XXVII 69; 188 v, lex. texts

The spelling 1 TÚG.BA da?-aḫ?-ḫu-um in MDP XXVIII 526:1 (on which the reading dáḫ in MAD II 117 was based) cannot be collated (according to Mr. Nougayrol) and is probably wrong.

BTQ <u>batāqum</u>? "to break," "to cut away."

in 1 MU Škš. [X].SU!.GAL [KAŠ]?.DÉ.A KUG.GI [...]. É ^{d}En-líl [ib]?-tu-ku (OIP XIV 117, date).

BṬʾ$_7$ <u>baṭijum</u> (a container).

Akk. lw. in Ur III Sum.:

1 ba-ti-um of ivory (UET III 760, U; 1498 i)

1 ^{GIŠ}ba-ti-um MES (HSS IV 5 iv)

2 pa(p)-ti-um UD.KA.BAR (BIN V 2:24) compared with 1-en ba-ṭu-ú UD.KA.BAR (Strassmaier, Inschriften von Darius I 301:8)

Cf. alzo x ^{GI}ba-ti-um in BIN IX 339, 387, 452, OB.

BṬM <u>buṭumtum</u> "pistachio-nut."

Sarg. PN:

Bu-tu-um-tum (D). Cf. Bu-du-um-tum in Speleers, CIMC p. 180, OB or later, and bu-uṭ-ma-tim in TCL XXV 42:18, Mari.

BZ?

Sarg. and Ur III PN's:

Bí-za?-t[um] (D). Cf. Bi-za-tum (TA 1930, 356 rev., OB, and NPN p. 323)

Bí-za-ti (PDTI 595 rev., U).

BZ?

Sarg. and Ur III PN's:

Bí-za-num (FM+)

Bi-za-núm (HSS X 219)

Bí-za-nu-um (Oppenheim, CCTE p. 182, U).

BZKL?

Sarg. PN:

Bi-iz-ki-lum (D).

BZZ?

Ur III PN:

Ba-za-zum (UET III 1220 ii). Cf. Ranke, EBPN p. 72.

D

Dʾ$_6$D <u>dâdum</u> "beloved."

Škš. DUMU da-ti ^{d}En-líl /Škš. marʾum dâdi E./ (BE I 2). The interpr. as "beloved" is based on comparison with: Sa-am-su-i-lu-na na-ra-am ^{d}UTU ù ^{d}A-a = da-ti ^{d}UTU ù ^{d}A-a = ki-ág ^{d}UTU ^{d}Šu-nir-da-bi in CT XXXVII 2 ii 63 etc., and on KI.ÁG = da-du in V R 16 iii 34g. The spelling da-ti, instead of da-di, in the Samsu-iluna inscription should be considered an archaism ti-ib da-ad-ga "heal thy beloved!" (Kish 1930, 143:11). Interpr. doubtful

a-ḫu-uš$_{x}$(EŠ) ba-ki ša da-ti (Kish 1930, 143 rev. 32).

PSarg., Sarg., and Ur III PN's:

In some cases below Da-da, Da-ad, Da-di may be a DN. Cf. also Ur-^{d}Da-a-da in PBS XI/3 No. 1058, OB, and PN's cited in Gemser, BPN pp. 104f. and 110. Also ^{d}Da-da in PDTI 645, U.

A-ba-Da-di (Reisner, TUT 152 iii; 159 ii, U). Cf. A-bu-da-di in Ranke, EBPN p. 60

A-ba-^{d}Da-di (Ist. Mus. Adab 771; Nies, UDT 58:196, U)

Al-su-da-ad (D)

Ba-na-da-da (Barton, HLC III Pl. 118, 248 iv, U)

Be-l[í?-da?-t]i? (FM)

Da-da (D+)

Da-da-ga-bi (Fish, CST p. 159 iii 3, U)

Da-da-ḪA.MA.TI (U 781+)

Da-da-ì-lum (UET I 11, PSarg.)

Da-tum (OIP XIV 48 i, PSarg.; U 1458)

Da-tu-um (ITT IV 7128)

Da-ti (D+; U 799+)

Da-a-ti (Barton, HLC III p. 37, U; AnOr I 297, U)

Da-ti-a (U 800+)

DINGIR-da-ti (ZA XII 332)

LUGAL-da-ti (D). See also below

Mi-iš-da-ti (E)

Nu-úr-da-ad (Chiera, STA 33:7, U)

Sar-ru-da-ti (RTC 127 rev. ii). See also above

Sar-ru-da-ad (AnOr I 126, U)

Si-da-da (E+)

Šu-da-ti (MO)

Šu-da-da (G+; PDTI 35, U).

Sarg. GN:

Da-tum^{KI} (Iraq IV 66 F. 1153 rev.).

D'$_{6}$D?

Sarg. and Ur III PN's:

Da-a-da-ni (CT III 9 i; 33 v, U)

Da-da-a-ni (Reisner, TUT 139 iii, U)

Da-da-ni (BIN V 298:12, U; Barton, HLC I Pl. 31 i, U+)

Da-da-núm (MO)

Cf. also Da-da-nu-um in TCL XXII 90:6, 10, Mari, Da-da-nu in

Tallqvist, NBN p. 52, and Da-ad-da-ni in MDP XVIII 156:4, OB.

D'$_{6}$D? dûdum? (a vessel).

Akk. lw. in Sum.?:

[1] ^{GIŠ}DU.DA TUR (MDP XIV 7 rev.). Among utensils and vessels

1 ^{GIŠ}DU.DA URUDU (HSS X 26 iii)

1 $^{\text{NA}_4}$du$_{8}$-du$_{8}$-um UD.KA.BAR GÁ.RA (TCL V 6055 rev. i, U).

D'$_{6}$D?

Sarg. PN:

Du-da-LUM (E). Cf. Du-da-nim, Gen., in Studia Mariana p. 54 and Du-da?-a-nu-um in PBS XI/3 No. 345, OB.

D'$_{7}$N diānum "to judge."

Written syllabically.

dînam diānum:

ì-nu DN DI.TAR-su i-ti-nu-ma (S x; PBS V 36 rev. x+iii, NS.)

ì-nu DN DI.TAR NS. da-nim i-ti-nu-ma (UET I 275 iii, NS.)

DI.TAR-ni ti-ni, Impv. (MDP XIV p. 19)

(DN) DI.TAR me-sar-im in URU^{KI}-su i-din (MDP IV Pl. 2 iv).

dajjānum "judge."

Written syllabically or logographically as DI.TAR.

da-ia-an ki-na-tim (YOS IX 62, Dêr)

Kun-du-pum DI.TAR Ba-ra-aḫ-sum^{KI} (S xii, xvi). The title DI.TAR implies some high function; cf. the Phoenician and Hebrew "judges"

various DI.TAR and their respective PA.RIM$_{4}$ ("bailiffs") (D 228; D 242; BIN VIII 121)

PN DI.TAR (FM 7:27, and PA.RIM$_{4}$; MO A iv, xiii)

2 PN's DI.TAR.ME (ITT I 1472 ii)

3 PA.TE.SI Ga-za-lu^{KI} DI.TAR (BIN VIII 121)

DI.TAR SIPA ANŠE (A 826).

Sarg. and Ur III PN's:

In some cases DI.TAR is a DN; cf. Deimel, PB No. 808.

Da-a-a-ni (U 752+)

DI.TAR-ì-li (A 1100). But cf. DI.NI.NI /Dîn-ilī?/ in YOS IV 208:1, 3, U

DI.TAR-ì-lí (U 859+, U)

DI.TAR-mi-sar (U 860+)

GAL.ZU-DI.TAR (ZA XII 335+)

I-sar-DI.TAR-ni (Pope, SPA I 281).

dînum "judgment."

Written syllabically or logographically as DI.TAR.

šu DI.TAR-su uš-ba-la-ga-du (MDP IV Pl. 2 iv)

For other examples see diānum, above.

Sarg. PN:

U-su-si-ir-ti-ni (ITT I 1465+).

D'$_6$R dârum "cycle," "period," "eternity."

iš-tum da-ar si-ki?-ti ni-se$_{11}$ "since the time of the creation of people" (UET I 275 i, NS.). The expected form is da-rí, Gen. of Constr. St.

Sarg. PN's:

| Su-mu-tar (D+). Cf. A-ḫi-lú-tar in CT VI 49b, OB
| Su-mu-da-ar (D)

Ti-rí-tar (G+)

Zi-mu-dar (PSarg. king; De Genouillac, FT II Pl. LIII AO 13015, U).

Ur III GN:

Zi-mu-dar^{KI} (CT XXXII 20 iii+).

dârijum "eternal."

PSarg., Sarg., and Ur III PN's:

Sum. DA.RÍ probably lw. from Akk.

Da-rí (MDP XVIII 78 i, U)

| Da-rí-sa (D)
| Da-rí-ša MAR.TU.SAL (HSS IV 51 rev.+, U)

Eš$_4$-dar-da-rí (FM)

Lu-da-rí (ITT IV p. 11, 7105, U)

LUGAL-da-rí (ITT II/2 p. 17, 3136)

Ma-zé-da-rí (Barton, HLC II Pl. 67, 32 iii, U)

SIPA-da-rí (RTC 234; Oppenheim, CCTE p. 199, U). Cf. SIPA-da-ar in TA 1931, 630, OB

Šu-da-rí (ITT III 6416, U)

^{d}Šul-gi-SIPA-da-rí (Reisner, TUT p. 46+, U).

dûrum "wall," "fortress."

Written syllabically or logographically as BÀD.

city SAG.GIŠ.RA ù BÀD-su Ì.GUL.GUL (S ii, etc.)

BÀD.BÀD-su-nu Ì.GUL.GUL (R xvii; xxiii)

BÀD.BÀD-su-ni Ì.GUL.GUL (R xix, xxi)

BÀD dannum, BÀD GAL, BÀD ga-da?-im (UET I 275 ivff., NS.)

BÀD A-ga-dè^{KI} ù-ma (FM 9 rev.)

1 ḫa-zi-núm šu 4 EME-su A.MU.NA.RU ù-sa-ti-ir BÀD-si-in KUG.BABBAR A.MU.NA.RU "he presented 1 ax with 4 'tongues,' and he exceeded, (even) their 'covers' of silver he presented" (MDP IV Pl. 2 iii). Reading pàṭ-si-in impossible because the expected spelling would be pàṭ-zi-in.

PSarg., Sarg., and Ur III PN's:

A-a-BÀD (ITT IV 7260, U)

A-lum-BÀD (EK IV Pl. XLV iv, PSarg.)

A-pum-BÀD (BE I Pl. VII vii)

BÀD-il (MO)

BÀD-mu-bí (BIN VIII 118; 273)

BÀD-su-nu (MO)

Be-lí-BÀD (ITT I 1103)

Be-lí-tu-rí (E)

^{d}EN.ZU-BÀD (D)

Ì-lí-BÀD-ri, f.n. (UET III 18, U)

Sar-ru-BÀD (MO)

Sar-ru-tu-rí (OIP XIV 116)

Ši-tu-ri (TCL II 5484 rev., U)

Šu-BÀD (FM)

^{d}Šul-gi-tu-ri (Legrain, TRU 41, U).

Sarg. and Ur III GN's:

Dur-Ib-la^{KI} (Nikolski, Dok. II 10, U; A 3206, U; A 4327, U)

Maš-gán-BÀD-Ib-la (HSS X 1)

Many GN's composed with BÀD in Sarg. and Ur III.

Dʾ$_x$Š? <u>dûšum</u>? (an object of silver).

2+[x]? du-sa-an KUG.BABBAR (PBS IX 22).

DB <u>da-ba-tum</u>, see TPʾ$_x$? tappatum?

DBB? <u>dubbubum</u>?

ir-e-mu ú-da-bi-bu-si-ma ù iš-ku-nu-⸢si⸣! a-na mu-ḫu-tim "the irʾemū have ....ed her and placed her ...." (Kish 1930, 143 rev.).

DBL?

Sarg. PN's:

Da-ba-al (G+)

Da-ba$_4$-la (BE I Pl. VII rev. vi)

Da-ba-la-a (G)

Da-ba-li (D)

Da-ba-LUM (D+)

Da-bi-LUM (FM) = I-da-bí-ì-li in the same text?

Da-ba?-al?-^{d}En-líl DUB.SAR (Speleers, RIAA 218).

PSarg., Sarg., and Ur III GN's:

Da-ba-al^{KI} (D+)

Tu(m)-ba-al^{KI} (CT XXXII 20 iii, U, referring to places in the Diyala region; Univ. Illinois 28, U). This GN cannot be equated with Tummal. To be read perhaps Tub/pal and compared with later Tub/pl-iaš?

(URU) Da-ba-la (Barton, MBI 1 iv twice, PSarg.)

ÍD ⸢D⸣a-ba-al-^{d}A-ba$_4$ (ITT I 1096).

DBN?

Deified RN D/Ṭaban? in Sarg. and Ur III PN's:

KA-Da-ba-an (D). Cf. Šu-^{d}Da-b[a-an] in OIP XLIII 154, OB

⌈Ki⌉?-nam-Da-ba-an? (D)

LUGAL-Da-ba-an (Oppenheim, CCTE p. 194, U; ITT II/1 p. 42, 906, U)

LUGAL-DUB-ba-an (Jean, ŠA LXVI iii, U)

^{d}Šul-gi-Da-ba-an (Fish, CST p. 97 No. 847, U)

Ur-^{d}DUB-an (CT XXXII 8 ii, U).

DBR?

Ur III GN's:

Da-bu-ru-um^{KI} (Reisner, TUT 104 rev.; 127 i)

Da-ab-ru-um-TA (TCL V 5675 rev. v)

DUB-ru-um^{KI} (RA IX 113 iv+; TCL V 6041 rev. i+).

DBŠ dabašinnum (an object of leather).

1 ^{KUŠ}da-ba-si-num (FM 7:14).

DDN?, see D'$_{6}$D? and TDN?

DDN? dudittum (a breast ornament).

1 tu-ti-tum? (MDP XIV 53).

Evidently a lw. from Akk.; cf. GU.ZI.DA = kusîtum.

2 DU.TI.DA UD.KA.BAR.URUDU (OIP XIV 105)

10 DU.TI.DA UD.KA.BAR KI.LAL.BI 1 MA.NA 10 GÍN (YOS IV 296 rev. twice, U)

13 URUDU DU.TI.DA KI.LAL.BI 1/2 MA.NA (ibid.)

x DU.TI.DA UD.KA.BAR (A 5834, U)

1 TU.DI.DA UD.KA.BAR KI.LAL.BI 2 GÍN (Jean, ŠA LXXVII obv. and rev., U)

15 TU.DI.DA UD.KA.BAR KI.LAL.BI 5/6 MA.NA 3 GÍN (TCL V 6055 ii, U)

x TU.DI.DA ZA.GUL (TCL V 6044 rev. i, iii, U)

Many examples of TU.DI.DA of gold and silver in UET III p. 170, U.

DDR?

Sarg. PN:

Du-da-ru-um (ITT I 1472 ii).

DG?

Ur III PN's:

Da-a-ga (U 755+)

Da-ga (U 767+)

Da-a-ga-la-ba (SO IX/1 No. 36:10)

Da-gi (U 773+)

Da-gí (U 774+)

Da-a-gi (U 757+)

Da-a-gi$_4$ (U 758+).

DGL dagālum "to look."

Sarg. and Ur III PN's:

Be-lí-du-gul (D)

Eš$_4$-dar-tu-gul (UET III 919, U)

Sar-ru-du-gul (D).

digālum "jewel" (or the like).

Sarg. PN:

Ti-ga-lum (BIN VIII 235+).

DGN.

DN occurs frequently in Sarg. PN's, as in Iš-ku-un-$^{(d)}$Da-gan (ITT I 1316+; p. 11, 1167), I-ti-^{d}Da-gan (D+), Pù-^{d}Da-gan (MO), Šu-^{d}Da-gan (MO), and in Ur III PN's (Schneider, AnOr XIX No. 66). Cf. also spelling Da-ga-an in Ar-sa-AN-Da-ga-an (MDP XXVIII 524) and Ù-a-še-ir-Da-ga-an (ITT I 1465+), both difficult to explain.

DGN?

Sarg. PN:

Da-gu-na (G+).

DḪB?

Ur III MN:

^{ITI}Da-ḫu-bu-um (Oppenheim, CCTE UU 16 rev.).

DK'$_7$ dakājum "to conscribe (troops)," "to levy."

[....] id-gi-e-su!(wr. zu)-nu-ma (PBS V 36 x+iv, NS., copy).

DKR, see TKR.

DKŠ, see KŠ'$_x$? takšijum?

DL'$_6$ madlaum? "pail?"

ma-ad-lá-um (FM 37:8).

DLB dulubum "plane tree?"

Akk. lw. in Sum.:

^{GIŠ}tu-lu-bu-um (Thureau-Dangin, SAKI p. 70 v 57; p. 106 xv 32, Gudea)

2 GIŠ.BANŠUR [t]u!-lu-bu-um (UET III 828, U).

DLL dalālum "to praise."

ad-lul a-da-la-li (TA 1932, 9, in difficult context).

Sarg. and Ur III PN's:

A-da-làl (U 105+)

Da-ad-lul-tum, f.n. (D+)

Id-lul-DINGIR (BIN VIII 259)

Ì-lu-da-lil?(-E) (Nikolski, Dok. II 13).

DLL? dilīlum?

PSarg. and Sarg. PN:

Ti-li-lum (MO). Cf. Dilīl-Ištar and Dalīl-Ištar in Tallqvist, APN pp. 68, 70. Cf. Ti-ni-ni under DNN

Ti-li-lu(m)-um (BIN VIII 11 iii, PSarg.).

DLL, see DNN?

DM damū, plurale tantum, "blood."

ú-má .... GIŠ.TUKUL da-me al-su la a?-sa-ga-nu (Ist. Mus. Lagash 11001 rev.).

DM? damtum? (some form of destruction).

NE.RU-dam in a-ša-ar URU al-su-nu iš-bu-uk "he poured a blood-bath? upon them within the city" compared with in ir-ṣi-it Kiš^KI dam-tam e-li-šu iš-bu-uk in an inscription of Samsu-iluna discussed by Goetze in AnOr XII 185ff. Cf. also a-na da-am-tim in TCL XXV 86:38, Mari.

DM dimatum, dimtum "pillar," "district." See also LTM.

Ur III GN's:

Written syllabically or logographically as ^dZA.GÀR.

Ti-ma-at-^dEn-líl-lá (ITT V p. 61, 9962; Orient. XLVII 38; Thureau-Dangin, SAKI p. 150+) = ^dZA.GÀR-^dEn-líl^KI (RA XXXII 170 iv 12, OB)

Ti-ma-tum^KI (TCL V 6041 i)

ŠÀ Ti-im-tum^KI Ur-šag$_5$-ga (2 NT 71)

Cf. also ^dZA.GÀR-^dNu-muš-da-ka (ZA LI Pl. I after p. 74 i 1, 11, 17, ii 19), ^dZA.GÀR-ḫur-sag-gá (i 20, 21), ^dZA.GÀR-DUMU.LUGAL-ka (Pl. IV iv 5, 6), ^dZA.GÀR-Ḫu-WI-um-ma (iv 13, 14), and ^dZA.GÀR-DUB.SAR^KI (TCL V 6041 i).

DMQ damqum "good," "beautiful."

Written logographically or syllabically as SIG$_5$.

da-me-iq (Kish 1930, 143, in difficult context)

In other cases written regularly SIG$_5$, as in KAŠ.SIG$_5$, KA.LUM.SIG$_5$, etc.

Sarg. and Ur III PN's:

Da-mi-iq (TCL II 5484, U)

Da-mi-iq?-tum (D). Or Da-mi-ir?-tum

Dam-kum (CT XXXII 22 i, v, U)

Da-am-ku-um (PDTI 252, U)

Dam-ku-um (Barton, HLC III p. 37, U)

Dam-ku-ù (Nikolski, Dok. II 455, U). Read as Dam-qú-ša$_{10}$? by von Soden, ZA XL 213

DINGIR-SIG$_5$ (D+)

É-a-da-me-iq (Delaporte, CCL II A 87)

^dEN.ZU-SIG$_5$ (D)

Eš$_4$-dar-dam-ga-at (D+)

Ì-lu-dam-ku (FM+)

Iq-bí-SIG$_5$ (D). Cf. ^{d}Iq-bi-da-mi-iq in Deimel, PB No. 1585

Šar-ru-SIG$_5$ (E)

| SIG$_5$-DINGIR (D+)

| SIG$_5$-ì-lum (MO)

SIG$_5$-tum (D)

UD-kum if read Dám-kum (D+).

dummuqum "to make beautiful."

a-na KÁ-su du-mu-ki-im "to make his gate beautiful" (MDP IV Pl. 2 iii).

dumāqum "gift."

Sarg. PN:

Du-ma-ga (FM).

dumqum "goodness."

Sarg. and Ur III PN's:

Be-lí-tum-ki (D)

Dam-ku-zi-ma-zu (Langdon, TAD 40:4, U)

É-a-tum-ki (Fish, CST p. 160 viii, U)

Ì-lí-tum-ki (D)

Li-bur-dum-ki (Iraq Mus. 10625, U)

Tu-muk-su (YOS IX 17, U?).

DMR.

Sarg. PN's:

Ad-mar (D+)

Da-mi-ir?-tum or Da-mi-iq?-tum (D). Cf. Da-me-ru-um (RA VIII 69, rev.), Da-mi-ru-um (BIN IX 224:5), and Da-me-rí-im (Kh. 1935, 99), all OB.

DN?

Akk. lw. in Ur III Sum.?:

PISAN da-ni UD.KA.BAR (RA XII 61).

DN?

Akk. lw. in Ur III Sum.?:

1 PISAN MÁ ti-ni-um (RTC 304 iii).

DNK?

Ur III PN's:

DINGIR-id-ni-ik MAR.TU (Nies, UDT 39 rev.; Arnold, ABTR 2). Interpr. DINGIR-á-lí-ik not probable

I-da-ni-ki-ì-li (Univ. Illinois 274)

Cf. also Da-na-ku-um in MDP XVIII 181 iv, OB.

Ur III DN:

^{d}Da-ni-ik-tu (Lau, OBTR p. 53 No. 59, translit. only).

DNN dan̄anum "to be strong."

Ur III PN's:

Id-ni-in-^{d}EN.ZU (Legrain, TRU 300)

Id-ni-^{d}EN.ZU (PDTI 509)

Id-nin-gá-ta (AnOr I p. 29+; AnOr VII p. 25; BIN V 98 rev.).

Interpr. unknown; cf. also Id-AN-gá-ta in CT XXXII 36 ii 1

Id-ni-in-ḪÉ.[GÁL] (UET III 51).

dunnunum "to execute."

PN si-ip-rí li-da-ni-in "may PN execute my order" (BIN VIII 151).

dannum "powerful."

Written syllabically, but for the rare use of the artificial logogram DA.NÚM.

Said of kings:

king da-núm (passim NS., Škš., D., ŠD.)

ì-nu NS. da-nim (PBS V 36 rev. x+ii, copy)

DUMU NS. da-nim (De Sarzec, DC II Pl. LVII = Pl. 26bis Fig. 2)

a-na na-ʾà-si NS. da-nim (MDP VI 6)

PŠ. da-núm (MDP X Pl. 3 No. 2; No. 1a)

E-bir$_{5}$-mu-bí da-núm (MDP XIV p. 5)

En-ri-da-wi-zi-ir da-núm (BER VI pp. 20f.)

La-⌈ʾà-ra-ab⌉ da-núm (ZA IV 406)

A(n)-nu-ba-ni-ni da-núm (Morgan, MSP IV 161 i)

A-bìl-GI da-núm (Syria XXI 159, Mari)

Šul-gi da-núm (CT III 1, 17288; etc.)

ba-da-an NS. DA.NÚM, Gen. (UET I 275 i, copy)

a-na ba-la-aṭ ^{d}AMAR-^{d}EN.ZU DA.⌈NÚM⌉, Gen. (KAH II 2)

^{d}Šu-^{d}EN.ZU .... sar-ru-um dan-núm (MDP IV p. 8).

Said of a god:

a-na ^{d}⌈KA⌉.DI ⌈da!-an⌉!-nim (Speleers, RIAA 4, Dêr).

Said of a wall:

iš-tum BÀD da-ni-im (UET I 275 ivff., NS.).

PSarg. and Sarg. PN's:

A-bìl-dan (MO)

A-lum-dan (DP 116, PSarg.)

Be-lí-dan (D+)

Da-an-ú-ri (ITT I p. 18, 1277)

Da-ni-a (G+)

Dan-ì-lí (FM+)

Dan-ì-li (MO; Louvre AO 8959)

Da-ni-lí (ITT II/2 p. 16, 3117)

Dan-ma-lum (Nikolski, Dok. II 48 rev.)

Dan-Ti-bar (G)

Da-núm (D+)

DINGIR-dan (D+). Cf. below

DINGIR-su-dan (D+)

É-a-dan (RTC 127 vi)

EN-su-dan (ITT II/2 p. 39, 4700)

^{d}EN.ZU-dan (D+)

Eš$_{4}$-dar-dan A.AZU (Kish 1930, 144a rev. ii)

Eš$_{4}$-dar-da-na-at (D+)

Íl-e-da-núm (RTC 203+)

Ì-lí-dan (D+). Cf. above

Ì-lu-da-nu (D+)

Ì-lum-dan (HSS II 27 v, PSarg.; BE I Pl. VIII 17). Cf. above

In-su-mi-su-da-nu (MO)

Li-lu-ul-dan, king of Akkad (AOF X 281)

Lu-da-na-at (MO)

Ni-su-dan-nam (Kish 1930, 148+)

Sar-ru-dan (E+)

Si-da-na-at (E+)

Tu-li-id-da-nam (MO).

Selected Ur III PN's:

ARÁD-zu-dan (AnOr XII 278 iv)

Ba-ba-da(n)-an-na-at SAL (Fish, CST p. 160 ix)

Be-lí-dan (U 510)

Dan-al-su (UET III 15)

Da-ni-lí (ITT IV p. 14, 7137)

Dan-ì-lí (U 815+)

Da(n)-an-ì-lí (Jean, ŠA CXXXIII)

Dan-ki-ì-lí (HSS IV 88)

Dan-La-aḫ-[ma-at] (De Genouillac, TD 62 rev.). Cf. MDP XXVIII 546:5, OB

Dan-La-ma-at (MCS VI 85 AO 10342 rev.)

Dan-^{d}MAR.TU (U 1821)

Dan-^{d}Šul-gi (U 1820)

Da-núm (ITT V 6990; RTC 261 ii)

Dan-núm (AnOr XII 277 i)

Dan-ú-a (AnOr I 277 ii)

Da-núm-ì-lí? (Barton, HLC III Pl. 113 iv)

Dan-úr-ri (RA XIX 42 LXXXVI rev.)

É-a-dan (PDTI 292, U)

|E-lu-da-an (ITT IV p. 69, 7694)
|I-lí-da-an (RA XIX 33, thus translit.)
I-šu-dan (ITT IV p. 64, 7619)
Ma-ma-dan-na-at (Reisner, TUT 159 iv twice)
Ši-da-na-at (UET III 1041 rev. ii)
Ú-zé-da-num (OIP XLIII 145, Diyala).

Ur III GN:
Rí-ig-mu-uš-dan (ZA LI Pl. II after p. 74 iii 8, 9).

dannatum "power."

Ur III PN:
Da-na-ti (Orient. XLVII 122:16).

danniš "strongly."
a-ti da-ni-iš "in great force" (HSS X 5:11)
da-ni-iš "strongly" (HSS X 5:19)
da-ni-iš da-ni-iš (D 298:7, 16).

danninum.

Ur III PN:
Dan-ni-nu-um (RA XIX 30, 34).

dinninum?

Sarg. and Ur III PN's:
Ti-ni-na (FM)
Ti-ni-ni (RTC 290, U). Cf. DLL? dilīlum?

dunninum.

PSarg. PN:
Dun-ne-nu-um (Nikolski, Dok. I 224 rev. i; 232 rev. i; 242 ii).

dunnum "might."
DÙL KUG.GI ša da-ab?-ri-a-ti tu-un-ni-su ù KAS+X-e "a silver statue (showing) the likeness of his might and battles" (RA IX 34 i, NS.?, copy).

Sarg. and Ur III PN's:
|Dun-núm (OIP XLVII 35)
|Du-núm (Barton, HLC II 84 iii, U)
Dun-ni-a (Reisner, TUT 154 vi, U).

DNN?
[....] da-an (S xii, in difficult context).

DNN?
PSarg. and Sarg. PN's:
LUGAL-da-na (Jestin, TSŠ Pl. CXII rev. ii, PSarg.; ZA XII 334; Gordon, SCT 2 ii)
LÚ-da-na (ITT II/2 p. 9, 2954, translit. only).

DNN?

Ur III PN's:

For the formation cf. ^{d}UTU-da-an-ni (PBS VIII/2 233:8, case 10, OB), Lu-lu-dan, Lu-lu-dan-ni (PBS XI/1 No. 7 i, OB) and PN's with -da-bi under ṭâbum.

A?-ḫu-da-ni? (Reisner, TUT 205 rev.)

^{d}IM-da-ni (De Genouillac, TD 54 ii).

DN ^{d}Da-ni in Ur III PN's:

AMAR-^{d}Da-ni (TCL V 6038 rev. ii)

LÚ-^{d}Da-ni (U 1944+)

Ur-^{d}Da-ni (U 1248+).

DNN? (location?).

In the first 2 cases reading NI = lí is possible.

GN_1 ù GN_2 in da-NI GN_3 .... iš$_x$(LAM+KUR)-ar (R xxii). The sign is clearly DA; therefore kab-lí is impossible

ŠE (Acc.) šu PN_1 PN_2 (Nom.) in da-NI GIŠ.SAG.ḪAR ù-bi-lam (Louvre AO 8960 rev.)

If reading ni is correct, then cf.:

PN_1 DUMU PN_2 GN in dan-ni rí-iš-tim (MO A xvi). Cf. also in? NI-ri-iš$_x$(LAM+KUR)-tim (Ist. Mus. Adad 280).

DQQ daqqum "thin."

Sarg. PN:

Da-kum (D+).

DRB?

Sarg. PN's:

Dar-ba-a (D)

Dar-ba-DINGIR (E)

Dar-bi (D).

DRK, see TRK.

DŠḪ?

Ur III FN:

A.ŠÀ Da-si-ḫu-um (Pohl, TMH n.F. I/II 87)

A.ŠÀ Da-še-ḫu-um (Speleers, RIAA 190; Univ. Illinois 273).

DŠM duššumum. Cf. Hebrew DŠN but Arabic DSM "to be fat."

Ur III PN:

Du-šu-mu-um (CT XXXII 34 i; Legrain, TRU 182:9; Fish, CST p. 159 iv). Cf. also BIN IX p. 26, OB.

DŠŠ daššum "he-goat."

Sarg. PN:

Da-áš-si (E+)

Da-si (D).

DTN, see TDN?

G

Gʾ$_x$?

Sarg. MN:

Gi-um (D+).

Gʾ$_x$? gaiûm? "clan?"

Sarg. GN:

Maš-gan?!-Ga-im (D 280)

Cf. ARMT XV 200 under gâʾûm and the occurrences in RA XLVII 122f. and XLIX 16f., Mari.

Gʾ$_7$D gîdānum "sinewy."

Ur III PN:

Gi$_4$-da-núm (Barton, HLC Pl. III 150 ii). Cf. Gi-da-nu-um in BIN VII p. 12 passim, OB

Ki-da-núm (BE III 110 x).

GB?

PSarg., Sarg., and Ur III PN's:

A-bu-GABA (E). Cf. Ab-bu-GABA in MDP XVIII 180 ii, OB

A-pù-GABA (OIP XIV 24, PSarg.)

AD.DA-GABA MAR.TU (Fish, CST 728 i, U)

Mu-úr-ti-ga-ba (Nikolski, Dok. II 476 i, U). Not Semitic?

Mu-úr-di(n)-ga-ba (Legrain, TRU 256 rev. i, U)

Mu-úr-di(n)-GABA (CT XXXII 36 ii, U).

GBB, see KBB kabābum.

GBR, see KBR kabrum.

GD, see QD?

GDD, see QDD.

GG? gagatum.

Akk. lw. in Ur III Sum.:

40 MA PA? GI ("reed"?) ga-ga-tum (UET III 850).

GG? gugutum (a plant).

Akk. lw. in Ur III Sum.:

x(QA) NUMUN gu-gu-tum (RTC 307 iv; ITT II 892 iv; V 6857 ii)

1 SILA$_4$.GA gu-gu-tum (RA VIII 185,No. 3). Suckling lamb, fed with gu-gu-tum?

6 SILA$_4$ gu-gu-tum (PDTI 575).

GGʾ$_x$ gagium "cloister" (or the like).

12(BUR) GÁN [g]a-gi$_4$-a-am zi-ib-zi-ìr ANŠE.ZI.ZI?-im (CT XXXII 1 i = RA VII 180) in CM.

GGL gugallum "canal inspector."

Sum. lw. in Akk.

Ur III PN:

Gu-ga-lum (Nies, UDT 91 vii).

GGR, see KKR? kikurum?

GGZ, see KKS?

GLB gallabum "barber."

Sarg. and Ur III PN's:

Ga-la-ba (ITT I p. 2, 1044+)

| Ga-la-bi (U 568)

| Gal-la-bi (U 585).

GLB? gulbum? (a plant?). Cf. Thompson, DAB pp. 103f.

Ur III Amorite PN:

Gul-ba-nu-um MAR.TU (Fish, CST p. 11).

GLB?

Sarg. PN:

Gul-la-ba (RTC 244 rev.).

GLGL? galgaltum?

x MA.NA A.LÙ.LÙ, x MA.NA GAL+LÁ-GAL+LÁ-tim (MDP XIV 35). Complete text. Read perhaps gal-gal-lá-tim. AN.NA is to G. in proportion of 1 to 8.

GLL? gallatum?

Akk. lw. in Ur III Sum.:

1 GIŠ.IG É.SIG$_5$ SAG gal-la-tum ESIR SU.BA (TCL V 6036 vi).

GLL? gullatum? "ball?" (or the like).

Akk. lw. in Ur III Sum.:

x GIŠ.IG É.KU.BA gul-la-tum SI.GA (UET III 1498 rev. ii)

x GIŠ.IG É.KU.BA ZU gul-la-tum SI.GA (826 ii; 1498 rev. ii). Cf. É Ku-ba-tum in 348:2.

GLL? gillum? (an object of silver).

Akk. lw. in Sum.:

10 KUG.GÍN GI$_4$+GI$_4$-lum, 1 KUG.GÍN PI (PBS IX 45). Value gil$_x$ or kil$_x$ for GI$_4$+GI$_4$ cannot be proved at present.

GLTP? galtappum?

Akk. lw. in Ur III Sum.:

1 SILA$_4$ gal-tab-bu-um GIŠ.DÙ (PDTI 21). Meaning foot-stool does not fit

1 SILA$_4$.GA gal-tab!-bu-um (PDTI 644, collated).

GLZ? gullizum "cowherd" or "cattle-attendant."

Sarg. and Ur III PN's:

Gu-lí-zum (MO+)

Ku-li-zum (Fish, CST p. 159 vi end, U)

ša-at Gu-lí-zi (MO B vi)

Gul-li-iz (YOS IV 212 ii, U).

GLZ?

Ur III PN:

Gul-zum (Fish, CST p. 159 i 6).

GML gamālum "to save."

The forms are igmul, igammal.

DN_1 ù DN_2 ú-má lu a-ga-ma-lu-su$_4$ "by DN's I swear that I shall truly spare him" (Ist. Mus. Lagash 11001 rev.).

Sarg. and Ur III PN's:

^{d}AMAR-^{d}EN.ZU-ga-mi-il (HSS IV 47 rev., U)

^{d}EN.ZU-ga-mi-el (MDP XXVIII 525)

Ig-mul-ìr-ra (U 1705)

Ig-mu-lum (OIP XIV 101; U 1704+).

Sarg. and Ur III DN:

la-ga-ma-al (UET III p. 121, U). Here an ornament of metal

La-ga-ma-al (PBS XIV 138, seal). DN or PN.

GML? gimlum?

Sarg. PN:

Ma-an-ki-im-lu-uš "who is within his ....?" (D). Root KML "to rage?"

GML gamlum (a weapon).

Akk. lw. in Ur III Sum.:

1 ^{GIŠ}kam-lum ḪAR (a wood) (UET III 566; 1498 iv)

1 ^{GIŠ}kam-lum MA.NU (a wood) (UET III 584; 587; 1498 iv)

7 ^{GIŠ}ga-am-lu (BE III 77:4)

Cf. also ^{GIŠ}ga-am-lum in BIN IX 31, 461, OB.

GMM, see KMM kamamtum.

GMM?

Ur III PN:

Ga-ma-ma-nu-um? of Sippar (Iraq Mus. 46306).

GMR gamārum "to conquer" (or the like).

A-ma-nam SA.TU GIŠ.ERIN i-ig-mu-ur "(NS.) conquered? A., the cedar mountains" (UET I 275 ii). For parallels cf. ga-me-er GÚ ÍD.UD.KIB.NUN in RA XXXIII 49:7 and ki-ša-ad Bu-ra-tim ig-mu-ur-ma in Syria XXXII 15:4, both Mari.

gamīrum "complete," "perfect."

Sarg. PN:

| Ga-me-ru-um (D+)
| Ga-mi-ru-um (FM).

GNN? ganūnum? (material for doors and their parts).

13 1/2 ga-nu-nu a-na 1 GIŠ.SAG.GUL ("lock") GAL.UŠUM (PBS IX 20)

1 1/2 ga-nu-nu a-na za-ḫa-ar-tim (ṣaḫartum = part of a door) (PBS IX 20)

5 (or 3 1/2) ga-nu-nu a-na GAG KÁ (PBS IX 20; 21)

9 ga-nu-nu a-na 1 áp-za-za-tim GIŠ.SAG.GUL (PBS IX 21)

2 ga-nu-nu(sic) a-na TUR.TUR (part of a door) (PBS IX 21)

1 ga-nu-núm a-na rí-su-ti 1 si-im-ti KÁ.GAL (PBS IX 21)

several occurrences of x ga-[nu-nu] occur in broken context in PBS IX 123).

GNN?

Ur III PN's:

Ga-na-na (U 574+)

Ga-na-núm (U 573)

Ga-na-ni-im (U 575). F.n., not Gen.

Cf. Ga-na-nu-um (TA 1930, 605, OB).

GNN, see KNN kannum.

GNN, see KNN kunnunum.

GNT?

Sarg. PN:

Gu-nu-tum (Kish 1930, 406 iii).

GPŠ gapšum "thick."

Ur III PN:

Ga-ap-šu-um (MDP XXII 144). Cf. also Ga-ap-šum in XXVIII 528 and Ga-ap-ši-im in 529, OB.

GRʾ$_7$ garjum "opponent," "enemy."

Sarg. and Ur III PN's:

Ga-rí (G+)

Ga-rí-um (RTC 110)

Ga-ri-DINGIR (Oppenheim, CCTE p. 186, U).

girjum "opposition," "opponent."

Ur III PN:

Ma-an-gi-ìr (CT XXXII 34 ii).

GRD? gurrudum "bald."

Sarg. PN:

Ku-ru-da (D).

GRDP? gurdappum (a container for measuring, of variable size, like the

American bushel basket).

Lw. from Sum. GUR.DUB.

8 DUG 2 gur-da-b[u]? and 7 DUG 3 gur-da-b[u]? (HSS X 170:1 and 6, in a list of containers)

1 DUG zi-bí-bí-a-núm 1 GUR.DUB zi-bí-bí-a-núm (BIN VIII 132 iii). A measure

1 GUR.DUB (of 30 QA or of 1 PI etc.) (TCL II 5530, U; V 6036 passim, U)

1 GIGUR.DUB (of 1 PI) (Boson, TCS 361, U; TCL V 6036 iv, U; BIN V 273, U)

Cf. gu-ur-du-up-pi (TCL XI 161 passim, OB).

Ur III PN:

Gur-da-bi (CT XXXII 19 iii; 21 v).

GRM, see ṢRM?

GRN magrattum "threshing-ground" (or the like).

Ur III GN:

Ma-ag-ra-tumKI (TCL V 6041 i).

GRR girrānum "lamentation?"

Akk. lw. in Ur III Sum.:

gi-ra-núm DN (Orient. XVIII pp. 20f.; AnOr VII p. 44+; Fish, CST 170; 467; Jacobsen, CTC 9; Nesbit, SRD 12; PDTI 61; 645)

gi-ra-núm-ŠÈ (CT XXXII 49 obv. and rev.)

Cf. also gi_4-ír-ra-an-um in Hilprecht Anniversary Volume Pl. 16 v 14, OB.

GRŠ? garāšum? (a verb of movement?).

[a]-ti la dag-ru-⌈sa⌉?-am "as long as you have not .... to me" (RA XXIII 25:14). Thureau-Dangin: "tant que tu ne m'auras pas parlé," comparing Arabic ǰarasa "rendre un (faible) son," "parler (à voix basse)." Note, however, that a verb of movement is suggested by context, and cf. ig-ru-uš, parallel to iq-ra-ab, in RA VII 18 ii 8 (where interpr. ik-ru-uš "l'invita" was proposed)

Cf. also ig?-ru-sa-am (D 172).

GŠM?

Ur III PN:

Ú-ša-ag-šim (BE III 128; 149 twice). Sign ŠIM clear. For the formation cf. Ušaklil under KLL.

GŠR? gašārum (some agricultural activity in connection with grain).

a-na-gu a-ga-sa-ar (HSS X 5:15). Object ŠE

[....] ik-su-ra (FM 14:30)

10 ŠE.GUR ŠE.ḪAR.AN PN ik-sur (FM 36:2)

ŠE.ḪAR.AN PN šu PN in i-te-su ik-su_4-ra (FM 36:9).

GŠR gašrum "strong," "mighty."

Ur III PN:

Ìr-ra-ga-še-ir (U 1758; Fish, CST p. 159 iii)
Ìr-ra-ga-ši-ir (TMH n.F. I/II p. 20).

GŠR? tagšīrum "strengthening."

Akk. lw. in Ur III Sum.:

da-ag-ši-ru-um "(workers for) strengthening (of a building)" (TMH n.F. I/II 174)

Cf. also tak/g-ši-ru-um "repair?" in BIN IX 228 rev.; 376; 377+, OB. Root most probably KŠR.

GŠR? giširtum?

in É ki-ši$_4$-ir-tim .... li-iš-bu "may they stay in ...." (HSS X 10:8).

GŠR? gušurrā'um "agreement?," "transaction?"

PN's AB+ÁŠ-bu-ut ("witnesses") ⌈gu⌉?-su-ra-im (FM 4 end)
PN's AB+ÁŠ.AB+ÁŠ gu-su$_4$-ra-im (Louvre AO 8638 end)
ŠU.NIGÍN 7 AB+ÁŠ-bu-ut gu-su[r-r]a-im (D 179 end).

GŠRN gišrinnum "scale."

Lw. from Sum.

In some cases $^{(d)}$GIŠ.RÍN is a deified symbol:

^{d}GIŠ.RÍN (Woolley, UE II Pl. 191 U 9567)
4 GIŠ.RÍN (BIN VIII 20).

Sarg. and Ur III PN's:

A-ḫu-GIŠ.RÍN (G+)
A-ša-su-GIŠ.RÍN (BE I Pl. VI iv)
DINGIR-GIŠ.RÍN (G)
^{d}EN.ZU-GIŠ.RÍN (MO)
Ì-lum-GIŠ.RÍN (BE I Pl. VII vi+)
PÙ.ŠA-^{d}GIŠ.RÍN (A 3312, U).
Cf. Meek in RA XXXIV 59f.

GZ, see K'$_x$Ṣ? kâṣum.

GZB, see KSP kusiptum.

GZL?, see also GZN?

Sarg. PN:

Ku-za-lu (D+).

GZL? guzullum.

Ur III PN:

Gu-zu-LUM (Nikolski, Dok. II 454 rev.; De Genouillac, TD 81 rev.)
Cf. Ku-zu-ul-lum in YOS V p. 31+, OB.

GZN?

Ur III PN:

Gu-zi-na (TCL V 6039 iv twice).

GZN?, see also GZL?

Ur III PN's:

Gu-za-na (HSS IV p. 30; Chiera, STA p. 20); Gu-za-na = Gu-za-ni (Oppenheim, CCTE S 1 case and tablet)

Gu-za-NI (U 622+)

Gu-za-LUM (UET III 1585 rev. iv).

GZZ gazāzum "to shear."

2 persons za-nam /ṣaʾnam/ li-ig-zu-zu (Cop. 10055 rev.).

GZZ? gizzum or kizzum (type of goat).

30 UDU šu-ut É.MAR.URU$_5$, 20 MÁŠ ki-zu-tu[m] ša-[at]? Pù-zu-zu MU.DU (MDP XIV 14). Cf. JNES IV 166 n. 123.

H

Ḫʾ$_x$? ḫaʾum (a chair cover?).

Akk. lw. in Ur III Sum.:

x TÚG ḫa-um GIŠ.GU.ZA ZAG.BI UŠ LUGAL (UET III 1612)

x TÚG ḫa-um GIŠ.GU.ZA ŠU.NIGÍN LUGAL (UET III 1612; 1753; 1754). ŠU.NIGÍN not BARAG, cf. both with GIŠ.GU.ZA in Pinches, BTBC p. 106 i

x TÚG ḫa-um GIŠ.GU.ZA ŠEŠ.AB^{KI} LUGAL (UET III 1612)

x TÚG ḫa-bu-um GIŠ.GU.ZA (YOS IV 296:37; JCS VII 31b). On intervocalic w > b cf. MAD II 165 and foll. word.

Ḫʾ$_x$? ḫaʾum (kind of clay).

Akk. lw. in Sum.?:

IM ḫa-um imported by Gudea (Thureau-Dangin, SAKI p. 70 vi 57). Cf. ḫa-a-bu equated with IM.GÚ.EN.NA, IM.DARA$_4$, etc. in lexical texts. For intervocalic w > b see prec. word. Cf. also MÁ ḫa-ù-na in SAKI p. 106 xvi 7.

Ḫʾ$_6$ʾ$_7$? ḫuwium.

PN in Ur III GN:

^{d}ZA.GÀR-Ḫu-WI-um-ma (ZA LI Pl. IV after p. 74 iv 13, 14).

ḪʾL, see ḪL?

Ḫʾ$_6$Š ḫuāšum "to give" (or the like).

The meaning "to give" is derived from the synonym lists, where we find ḫa-a-šu = na-da-nu (CT XVIII 29, 11233:9 + Pl. 23, 13681:5) or ḫa-a-šú = na-da-nu (A 3407), besides ḫa-a-šu = a-la-a-ku (CT XVIII 6:56).

1 MÁŠ (Acc.) PN i-ḫu-uš$_x$(EŠ) (D 127)

PN$_1$ (Acc.) PN$_2$ (Nom.) [li]-ḫu-uš$_x$ (D 278)

PN (Acc.) li-ḫu-uš$_x$ (RTC 77 rev.)

a-ḫu-uš$_x$ various things (Kish 1930, 143 passim).

Ḫ'$_7$T, see NḪD?

Ḫ'$_6$Z maḫâzum "city" (in some specific sense).

Ur III GN:

Ma-ḫa-zum^KI (Nies, UDT 91 xi 341).

ḪB? (an animal).

Akk. lw. in Ur III Sum.:

x ḫa-bu-um (BRM II 38; UCP IX p. 242 No. 43; PDTI 526 i, iii; A 3312; Boson, TCS 365). Listed with small cattle, etc.

ḪB? (a cloth), see Ḫ'$_x$.

ḪB?

Sarg. and Ur III PN:

Ḫa-pum (E; UET III 350, U).

ḪB?

Sarg. PN:

Ḫi-pum (E).

ḪB, see ḪP ḫuppum.

ḪB'$_x$, see ḪBT? naḫbatum.

ḪBB.

Ur III PN's:

Ḫa-bí-ba-tum (Orient. XLVII 47; CT XXXII 30 i, ii)

Ḫa-ba-ba-tum (U 1512+).

ḪBD? (an implement of bronze). "Hacke" according to Landsberger, JNES VIII 275. Cf. also ḪBT?

Evidently an Akk. lw. in Sum.:

x ^URUDU ḪA.PÙ.DA (RTC 210 iii; UET III p. 183, U; RA XII 20f., U; many references quoted by Landsberger, op. cit.). For weights cf. MCS I 47

x ḪA.PÙ.DA^URUDU (OIP XIV 60 i, ii, PSarg.)

x ^URUDU ḪA.BU$_x$(=Ú).DA (Orient. XVI 39 VAT 4856, PSarg.).

ḪBL ḫabālum, see ḪBN? ḫabānum?

ḪBL ḫabālum "to rob," with double Acc., "to oppress."

SAL.ME su$_4$-a-ti GÁN su$_4$-[a-ti] la iḫ-bi-lu-ši-ma "they have not taken away this field from this priestess" (CT XXXII 2 iv, CM)

PN la ḫa-bi-el a-wi-lim "the non-oppressor of man" (YOS IX 62, Dêr).

Ur III PN:

Iḫ-bu-lum (Contenau, UDU 91). Note iḫbul against iḫbil above.

ḫablum "oppressed."

PN mu-uš-ti-ši-ṛirˀ ḫa-ab-lim ù ḫa-bi-el-tim "the one who guides the oppressed" (YOS IX 62, Dêr).

Sarg. and Ur III PN's:

Ḫa-ab-lum (Gutian king)

Ḫa-bí-lum (RTC 246; Pinches, BTBC No. 75, U)

Ḫa-bil-ki?-in (Gutian king).

ḫabulum.

Sarg. PN:

Ḫa-bu-l[um] (G).

ḫibiltum "ruin," "oppression."

Ur III GN:

Ḫi-bí-la-at^{KI} (A 4397 quoted in Gelb, HS p. 112; also PDTI 548)

Ḫi-bí-la-ti (Jean, ŠA XXX).

ḫubilum.

Sarg. PN:

Ḫu-bi-lum (D+).

ḫubullum "debt (on interest)."

Refers to loans of grain, oil, silver.

ḫu-bu-lum šu al PN i-ba-šè-ù "the loan which is upon PN" or "the loan which PN owes" (HSS X 109:21; 110:5)

barley šu PN ḫu-bu-lam im-ḫu-ru (D 110)

silver and barley a-na ḫu-bu-lim PN im-ḫur (D 291)

a-na ḫu-bu-lim nadānum (MDP XXIV 342 twice)

DUB ḫu-bu-lim ši GN_1 ù GN_2 (D 148, tag)

barley šu ḫu-bu-lim šu GN (D 17). Perhaps PN Ḫubbulum

ḫu-bu-lum (HSS X 111:7; 197:12; D 105; D 280, perhaps PN Ḫubbulum; D 321 x+5; D 322:17; D 334:12).

ḫubbulum.

Sarg.? and Ur III PN's:

Ḫu-bu-lim, Gen. (D 17) and Ḫu-bu-lum (D 280) may represent word ḫubullum

Ḫu-bu-ul (TCL V 6039 v, U).

ḪBL?

Sarg. PN:

Ḫa-ba-LUM (ZA XII 335).

ḪBN? ḫabānum? (an object of wood).

Akk. lw. in Ur III Sum.:

2 ^{GIŠ}ḫa-ba-LUM KI.LÁL.BI 1 GÚ 40 [MA.NA] (UET III 790). Read possibly za!-ba-lum and cf. SPL.

ḪBR ḫibarītum "morass."

Ur III GN:

Ḫi-ba-rí-tum (ZA LI Pl. I after p. 74 ii 26, 30, 32, Pl. II iv 12, 13, 16).

ḪBR?

Ur III PN's, perhaps not Akk.:

Ḫa-ab-ru-ša (TCL II 5504 ii)

Ḫa-ab-ru (YOS IV 289)

Ḫa-ab-ru-še-ir (Nies, UDT 91 x).

ḪBR? nahbarum (a garment). For the root and meaning cf. possibly Hebrew maḥberet "coupling of a dress" (Ex. 28:27; 39:20). Cf. also ʾ$_x$BR? nâbarum and ʾ$_x$MR? nâmarum.

1 TÚG na-aḫ-ba-[ru-um] (D 169)

1 TÚG na-aḫ-ba-ar TÚG.GAD (ibid.).

ḪBR? ḫabburum?

Akk. lw. in Sum. or vice versa:

^{GI}ḪA.PÙ.ÚR (Thureau-Dangin, SAKI p. 132 xii 2, Gudea).

ḪBṢ.

Sarg. and Ur III PN's:

Ḫa-ba-za (ITT I 1090)

Ḫi-ba-zum (D)

Ḫu-ba-za (D)

Ḫa-ba-za-tum (Orient. XLVII 36, U).

ḪBṢN?

Ur III PN:

Ḫa-ba-zi-in (Nikolski, Dok. I 444). Same writing in Chicago Natural History Museum No. 15608 rev. 2, OB.

ḪBṢR ḫabaṣīrum (a mouse).

Ur III PN:

Ḫa-ba-zi-ri (ZA XII 342). Cf. Ḫa-ba-ṣi-ru in YOS VI 73:5, NB, GCCI II 128:2, NB, etc., but Ḫa-ba-zi-ru apparently in Thompson, The Prisms of Esarhaddon p. 22:68.

ḪBŠ taḫabaštum.

Akk. lw. in Ur III Sum.:

1 GI da-ḫa-ba-áš-tum (TCL V 6036 x). Cf. later Akk. taḫabšum.

naḫbaštum. Cf. naḫbašum (an implement).

Akk. lw. in Ur III Sum.:

ŠU.NIGÍN 1 GI na-aḫ-ba-áš-tum (TCL V 6036 rev. iv).

ḪBT ḫabtum "run-away (slave)," "fugitive."

ŠU.NIGÍN 3 GURUŠ ARÁD LUGAL in BÀD.LUGAL^{KI} ši Za-bi-im ḫa-ab-tu (HSS X 201:8).

Ur III PN:

Ḫa-ab-túm (Reisner, TUT 164^{15} v end).

ḫubbutum.

animals a-na PN na-zi-iḫ in DUB-su ù-la ḫu-bu-ut (BIN VIII 141)

a-na ....? la ḫu-bu-t⌈u⌉ (Fish, CST 19 end).

ḪBT?

Sarg. and Ur III PN's:

DINGIR-ḫa-bi-it (Oppenheim, CCTE p. 189, U)

[....]-ḫa?-bi-da (D 126).

ḫubuttàtum "debt (free of interest)."

1 $SILA_4$.SAL iš-dè PN ḫu-bu-da-tum (FM 32:4).

ḪBT?

Ur III PN's:

Ḫu-bu-ti-a (U 1550; Oppenheim, CCTE p. 188; YOS IV 254 i)

Ḫu-ba-ti-a (HSS IV 56)

Ḫa-ba-ti-a (RA XIX 32)

Possibly from ḪBD/Ṭ, cf. Ḫu-bu-du-um in PBS VIII/2 177:8, 11, OB, Porada, CPML No. 446, OB, and Ḫu-bu-di-ia in TCL X 33:11, OB.

ḪBT? naḫbatum, nabḫatum (a sheath for swords, a box, etoui, made of wood or leather).

Akk. lw. in Ur III Sum.:

3 ^{KUŠ}na-aḫ-ba-tum (RA VIII 184 No. 2). For GÍR "sword"

1 GIŠ.GÁN na-aḫ-ba-tum (Pinches, BTBC p. 108 rev. i)

1 ^{GIŠ}na-aḫ-ba-tum DA (UET III 795)

^{KUŠ}na-aḫ-ba-tum (UET III 1289; YOS IV 137)

na-aḫ-ba-tum (Nies, UDT 170)

^{GIŠ}n. and ^{KUŠ}n. occur in BIN IX 38; 127 rev.; 333; 355+, OB.

The word nabḫatum is probably identical with naḫbatum:

GIŠ.KU ^{GIŠ}na-ab-ḫa-tum (ITT V 6972). Copied KU instead of TÚG(-tree)?

2 ^{GIŠ}na-ab-ḫa-tum TUR (Reisner, TUT 126 vii).

ḪBT?

Sarg. and Ur III PN's:

Ḫa-ba-at (UET III p. 16+, U)

Ḫa-ba-tum (JAOS LII 113).

ḪDʾ$_6$ ḫadāwum "to rejoice."

aḫ-da-tu? (Ist. Mus. Lagash 11001). Very doubtful.

Sarg. and Ur III PN's:

Ḫa-ti-ì-lí-su (D)

Ḫa-ti-ì-[lí]-iš-[su] (D)

Ḫa-ti-um (D; Ward, SCWA No. 163, U).

ḫedûtum, ḫidûtum "joy."

Ur III PN's:

Ḫé-du-ut-^{d}AMAR-^{d}EN.ZU (RA VIII 192 No. 14)

Ḫi-du-tum (Langdon, TAD 7 rev.).

ḪDR?

Akk. lw. in Ur III Sum.

Perhaps Akk. ḫattarû, a profession.

Nin-kug-zu ḫa-da-ru-um ^{d}Na-na-a (Jean, ŠA LXXVII rev.). Not clear.

ḪḪB? ḫuḫbum.

Akk. lw. in Sum.:

ḫu-úḫ-bu-um UD.KA.BAR (MDP XXVII 57 ii, U or later)

Cf. also MDP XVIII 101 rev. 12, UET V 795:11; 882:24, OB.

ḪL? ḫalum?

Cf. perhaps Arabic ḫâlun "maternal uncle." The word seems to occur only in PN's, since Lú-^{d}Šara ḫa-a-lum (Orient. VI 60 No. 11, U) may have to be interpr. as L. ḫa-za!-núm. Cf. also Šalim-ḫalum, Ilī-ḫalum (quoted in Stamm, ANG p. 286, n. 3), and Abum-ḫalum (Porada, CPML No. 326, OB; YOS VIII 98:47, OB). This word deified occurs in PN's DUMU.SAL-^{d}Ḫa-li (BE VI/1 p. 62, OB) and ^{d}Ḫa-li-ma-ra-aṣ (De Genouillac, Kich I p. 57 No. 219, OB, besides Ḫa-NI-ma-lik on the same seal) and is different from ^{d}Ḫa-NI which is to be read as Ḫa-ià in accordance with Tallqvist, AGE p. 320 and an unpublished text from Nippur quoted by Jacobsen, JCS VII 38 n. 17.

Sarg. and Ur III PN's:

Ḫa-li-a (JAOS LII 113)

Ḫa-lum (MO)

PÙ.ŠA-ḫa-lí (TCL II 5498 ii, U; Fish, CST p. 159 i, U+). Cf. also Puzur-ammī. Read perhaps Pi$_x$(KA+KÁR)-ša-ḫa-lí /Pišaḫ-ali/

PÙ.ŠA-ḫa-li (Pinches, AT 61, U). Also in Ranke, EBPN p. 115

PÙ.ŠA-ḫa-lum (RTC 397 i, U). Apparently also in ITT V p. 56, 9857 where translit. as "Bá-ša ḫa-num." Read perhaps Pi$_x$(KA+KÁR)-ša-ḫa-lum /Pišaḫ-alum/.

ḪLʾ$_7$ ḫuljum (a mouse).

Sarg. PN:

Ḫu-li-um (D+; AnOr VII 372, Sarg.?!).

ḪLʾ$_x$ ḫalaʾum (a garment).

Akk. lw. in PSarg. Sum.:

x ^{TÚG}ḫa-la-um (TMH V 103; 104 ii)

x ḫa-la-um^{TÚG} (TMH V 106; 107; 114; JCS X 26 ii).

ḪLḪL ḫalḫallum (a grain?; object for a chariot).

Akk. lw. in Ur III Sum.:

60 PISAN+GI ḫa-al-ḫa-lu (Pinches, AT 7). Also MUN and ŠE.LI

2 SÍG ḫal-ḫal-lum (ITT V 6875, U). For a chariot.

ḪLḪL.

Ur III PN:

Ḫal-ḫal-la (ITT II/1 p. 41, 904)

Cf. Ḫa-al-ḫa-lum in Riftin, SVIAD 44:19, OB.

ḪLL? ḫillatum (a kind of wool).

Akk. lw. in Sum.:

SÍG ḫi-la-tum (ITT I p. 18, 1283). Cf. x MA.NA ḫi-il-la-tum in Strassmaier, Inschriften von Nabonidus 664:5, with other kinds of wool.

ḪLL? ḫallūtum?

Sarg. MN:

Ḫa-lu(l)-ut (D+).

ḪLL ḫulālum (a precious stone).

Ur III PN's:

Ḫu-la-lí (De Genouillac, TD 59 rev.)

Ḫu-la-al (CT XXXII 36 i)

Ḫu-la-la (UCP IX p. 192, 64:9)

Ḫu-la-lum (ITT IV p. 42, 7368). Cf. Ḫu-la-lum in Ranke, EBPN p. 87 and elsewhere.

ḪLLʾ$_x$ ḫallulaja? (an insect).

Akk. lw. in Ur III Sum.:

ḫa-lu-la-[a]? (UET III 828 rev.). An object or figurine.

ḪLP? neḫlaptum? (a garment).

1 ne-eḫ-la-<ap>?-du-um (MDP XXVIII 526 rev., U?). Listed among garments. Writing with ne influenced perhaps by ne-ba-ḫu-um in the same text.

ḪLP ḫaluppum (a tree).

Akk. lw. in Sum.:

(GIŠ)ḪA.LU.ÚB (Thureau-Dangin, SAKI p. 70 vi 46, 47, p. 104 xv 16, Gudea; MDP XIV 90; RTC 221 iv, v, rev. ii, U; etc.). Also SAKI p. 30 b iii 2, Enannatum.

ḪLQ ḫalāqum "to destroy."

Sarg. PN:

Iḫ-lu-uq (G+). Doubtful.

ḫalqum "fugitive (slave)."

PN ḪAL = ḫal-<kum>? and PN ÚŠ (Kish 1930, 406 passim) compared with

PN A+ḪA and PN ÚŠ (MDP XXIV 384 passim).

ḫulluqum "to destroy."

mu-ḫa-li-iq ra-gi-im (YOS IX 62, Dêr).

ḫuluqqā᾿um "destruction," "loss."

ḫu-lu-ga-um (D 21 end).

ḪMD? ḫindum? (a container).

Akk. lw. in Ur III Sum.:

ḫi-in-tum (UET III 518; 662; 1498 rev. iv end). Cf. NB ^{KUŠ}ḫi-in-du.

ḪMDR.

Sarg. PN:

Ḫa-ma-da-ru-um (G).

ḪMR.

Ur III Amorite PN:

Ḫu-um-ra-nu-um MAR.TU (SO IX/1 No. 58).

ḪMṢ.

Sarg. and Ur III PN's:

Ḫu-mi-zum (FM)

Ḫu-ma-za (D; YOS IV 53, U)

Ḫu-um-zum (CT XXXII 20 iv; 21 v, U).

ḪMṢR? ḫunṣīrum? "mouse."

Ur III PN:

Ḫu-un-zé-ri (TCL II 5508 ii). Or Ḫun-zeri, cf. under ḪNN.

ḪMŠ ḫanšā "fifty."

Ur III PN:

⌈Ì⌉-lí-Ḫa-an-ša, number "fifty" deified (UET III 1080 iii).

ḪMṬ ḫumṭum, ḫunṭum "heat."

Ur III MN:

ITI Ḫu-um-tum (RA XIII 134) comparable with

EZEN Ḫu-un-ti (CT XXXII 4 xi, CM).

ḪN᾿$_x$ ḫanītum.

Sarg. MN:

Ḫa-ni-it and Ḫa-ni-i (MAD I p. 234).

ḪNB ḫunnubum "luxuriant."

Ur III PN:

Ḫu-nu-bí-a (AAA I Pl. XXXI rev.).

ḪNN ḫanantum "merciful?"

Sarg. PN:

Ḫa-na-an-tum, f.n. (NBC, unnumbered).

ḫunnum "mercy?"

Ur III PN's:

Some PN's below sound Akk., such as Ḫunnum; others are clearly non-Akk. and non-Sum.

Ḫu-un-da-aḫ-še-ir (A 3004)

Ḫu-un-du-du (BIN V 109:7)

Ḫu-un-gi$_4$-la-a[k] (Jacobsen, CTC 13)

Ḫu-un-gi-[la-ak]? (Jean, ŠA LXXI ii 8)

Ḫu-un-gu-úr-bi (A 3252)

Ḫu-un-ḫa-ab-ri (Fish, CST p. 11, translit. only)

Ḫu-un-ḫa-ab-ur (De Genouillac, TD 86+)

Ḫu-un-ḫa-ad (CT XXXII 34 i)

Ḫu-un-ḫa-al-bi-it (Fish, CST p. 11)

Ḫu-un-ḫi-li (Boson, TCS 140)

Ḫu-un-ki-ib-ri (TCL II 5508 ii)

Ḫu-un-ná-a (Orient. XLVII 249:59)

Ḫu-un-na-zi (A 5477)

Ḫu-na-zi (Orient. XLVII 126:4, in broken context)

Ḫu-un-NI-NI = Ḫu-un-ì-lí? (ZA VI 161)

Ḫu-un-nu-um (U 1562+)

Ḫu-nu-um (Fish, CST p. 11; MDP XXVIII 424)

Ḫu-un-um (Legrain, TRU 25)

Ḫu-un-ša$_6$-ša$_6$ (TCL V 5674 ii+). Cf. Ḫu-un-za-za in MDP XXII 76, OB

Ḫu-un-^{d}Šul-gi (U 1558+)

Ḫu-un-tu-úḫ?-li (UET III 1437)

Ḫu-un-zé-ri (TCL II 5508 ii). Cf. ḪMṢR?

Ḫu-un-zu-lu (ITT IV p. 57, 7529)

Cf. also Ḫu-un-da-aḫ-la in MDP XXIII 230 and Ḫu-un-na-al-zi-áš in 291 rev. and 296, OB.

ḪNṢR, see ḪMṢR? ḫunṣīrum?

ḪNŠ naḫnušum "to submit?"

in si-ip-rí ^{d}Innin GA.LUL-ma /kaluma?/ ki-ib-ra-tu[m] ar-ba-um iš-ti-ni-iš i-ḫa-ni-su$_4$-ma im-ḫu-ru-nim "by the command of Innin .... the four quarters together were subsued? and faced me," i.e. "submissively faced me" (PBS V 36 rev. x+ii, NS.). The expected form of IV Pret. is iḫḫanšā, but for the -ū suffix in Fem. cf. MAD II 209.

ḫanīšum "submission."

DN Ḫaniš. Cf. Gelb in AOr XVIII 1/2 189ff.

^{d}Ḫa-ni-iš (Gelb op. cit. p. 189, Šulgi; UET III 1504 vii, U; TCL V 6053 iv, U, reading after Lambert RA XLV 92).

Sarg. and Ur III PN's:

En-bí-iq-^{d}Ḫa-ni-iš (UCP IX p. 205 iii)

Ri-im-Ḫa-ni-iš (RTC 122; ITT I p. 23, 1371)

Šu-Ḫa-ni-iš (ZA XII 335)

....-^{d}Ḫa-ni-iš (UET III 1504 vii, U).

Since $^{(d)}$BE stands for Ḫaniš (see Gelb, loc. cit.) also the foll. PN's may belong here:

Be-lí-BE (D)

Ì-lí-BE (D+)

Ì-lum-BE (YOS IX 2, PSarg.)

Iš-dup-BE (MO)

Su-BE (G)

Šu-BE (D)

Šu-^{d}BE (U 699; A 5143+, U).

ḪNT?, see ḪMD? ḫindum.

ḪNZB, see ḪṢB.

ḪP? ḫuppum (an object of bronze).

Akk. lw. in Ur III Sum.:

3 ^{URUDU}ḫu-bu-um KI.LAL.BI 10 1/2 MA.NA 5 GÍN (ITT III 6546; similarly in TCL V 6037 vii; Reisner, TUT 124 ix; UET III 437; 752 rev. i; Lau, OBTR 42)

1 ^{URUDU}ḫu-bu-um GIŠ.IG ŠU.DU$_{7}$.A! KI.LAL.BI 1/2 MA.NA 7 GÍN (Nikolski, Dok. II 424)

2 ^{URUDU}ḫu-bu-um UMBIN KI.LAL.BI 4 MA.NA LAL 2 GÍN (Orient. XLVII 339)

1 ḫu-bu-um GIŠ.GIGIR .... KI.LAL.BI 1/2 MA.NA (RA XLIX 93 No. 38).

Cf. 1 ḫu-bu-um MAR.GÍD.DA in BE VI/2 137:8, OB

1 ^{URUDU}ḫu-pù-um KI.LAL.BI 2 MA.NA 15 GÍN (UET III 326).

ḪP'$_{6}$? ḫapāwum? "to break," "to smash."

ša ALAM i-ḫa?-pu? (Morgan, MSP IV 158, Lullubum).

ḫipîtum "breech."

Ur III PN:

Ḫi-bi-tum (A 2790 iii).

ḪPŠŠ ḫupšašûm (a vessel).

ḫúp-sa-šum (FM 41:7, school text?).

ḪR'$_{x}$ ḫurium (a plant).

Akk. lw. in Sum.:

x QA ḫu-rí-um (Pinches, AT No. 69 passim; Reisner, TUT 121 xi; ITT II 892 iv; V 10011 ii; RTC 307 iv; Barton, HLC III Pl. 112 vi).

In all the above cases from Ur III ḫu-rí-um occurs with ŠE zi-bí-tum, ZAG.ḪI.LI, etc. In Boson, TCS 364 ^{Ú}ḫu-rí-a-núm occurs with ŠE zi-bí-tum, ZAG.ḪI.LI, etc. Therefore ḫu-rí-um = ḫu-rí-a-núm, denoting a plant to judge from the det. Ú [ḫu-r]í-um (MDP XIV 22). With [ŠE zi-b]í-tum.

ḪR'$_x$ ḫuriānum (a plant). See ḪR'$_x$ ḫurium.

Akk. lw. in Ur III Sum.:

^{Ú}ḫu-rí-a-núm (Boson, TCS 364)

^{Ú}ḫu-ri-a-nu-um (RA XVIII 59 vi, Voc. prat.).

ḪR'$_x$ ḫirîtum (a metal object).

Akk. lw. in Ur III Sum.:

1 ḫi-rí-a-tum KUG.GI ḪUŠ.A É.BA.AN KI.LAL.BI 2 2/3 GÍN (UET III 703)

4 ḫi-rí-a-tum KUG.GI SI.SÁ (UET III 1498 ii)

1 ḫi-ri-tum ^{NA_4}ZA.GÌN GAR.RA (YOS IV 296:19).

ḫirîtum "ditch."

Ur III GN:

Ḫi-rí-tum (ZA LI Pl. II after p. 74 iii 14, 15).

ḪR'$_x$ ḫarûm, see KR kirrum.

ḪRB? ḫarūbum "carob."

Sarg. PN:

Ḫa-ru-ba (G).

ḪRM.

DN in Sarg. PN's:

DAM-^{d}Ḫa-ri-im (ITT V p. 39, 9451, 9452, 9453, translit. only; same as DAM-?Ḫa-rí-im-?A.ZU in RTC 96 rev. ii?)

^{d}⌈Ḫa⌉?-ri-im-be-lí (Kish 1930, 170c)

PÙ.ŠA-^{d}Ḫa-rí-im (ITT I 1287; ITT II/2 p. 22, 4388).

ḪRP ḫurup(p)um (a container).

Akk. lw. in Ur III Sum.:

ḫu-ru-bu-um UD.KA.BAR (RA XII 61). Cf. ḫu-ru-pa-a-te URUDU in TCL II l. 363, NA.

ḪRR ḫarrānum "road," "trip," "expedition."

Written syllabically or logographically as KASKAL.

ḫa-ra-nam a-ḫu-z[a-a]m "I have taken the road" (FM 53:8). Doubtful KASKAL KI.⌈UD⌉-su or KASKAL^{KI} ⌈UD⌉-su a i-si-ir "may not succeed" (ZA IV 406, Gutium). Cf. ḫa-ra-an ú-ma-ka-al in RA VIII 65 ii 7, OB

KASKAL^{KI} su$_4$-a .... ma-na-ma la i-lí-ik (UET I 274 ii, NS.).

Sarg. and Ur III PN's:

Ḫar-ra-ni (IAMN XII Pl. IV 8 iii)

Nin-ḫar-ra-ni (Jacobsen, CTC 54 iv, U).

A sort of oil:

2 QA A-ga-dè NI ḫar-ra-núm (BIN VIII 317 etc.)

2(QA) NI ŠIM ḫar-ra-núm (BIN VIII 295)

2 NI ḫar-ra-núm QA A-ga-dè[KI] (BRM III 103 twice).

ḪRR ḫurrum "hole," "mine."

a-ti-⌈ma⌉ ḫu-rí KUG "up to the silver mines" (M xxvi). Cf. ḫu-ur-ru-um ša KUG.[BABBAR] in TCL XXII 73:19, Mari.

ḪRR ḫarratum or ḫurratum (an object, probably a weapon).

Akk. lw. in Sum.:

ḪAR-ra-tum (Thureau-Dangin, SAKI p. 128 vii 15, Gudea).

ḪRS?

Ur III PN:

Ḫi-ir-zum (Univ. Illinois 147).

ḪRṢ ḫurāṣum "gold."

Occurrence of KUG.GI is rather rare in the Sarg. texts: HSS X 215:1f.; FM 33:61; 44:8; etc.

The relationship of gold to silver is 8:1 in ITT II/2 4647 and 7 1/2:1 in Louvre AO 8638.

Ur III PN:

Ḫu-ra-zi (CT XXXII 36 i).

ḪRṢ?, see ḪṢN ḫaṣinnum.

ḪRṢ?

Ur III PN:

ḪAR-za-an (Boson, TCS 313 rev.; MCS III 43 No. 12).

ḪRŠ ḫuršānum "mountain."

ḪUR.SAG Ba-ša-ar (RA IX 57 SA 3, U) compared with Ba-sa-ar KUR (RTC 124).

Sarg. PN's:

Ḫur-sa-núm (Porada, CPML No. 189)

Si-ḪUR.SAG (D+).

ḪRŠ ḫaršîtum (a type of sheep).

x UDU ŠE ḫa-ar-ši-tum (YOS IV 217 obv., U). A gentilic from Ḫaršum? or GN Ḫaršîtum?

1 SILA$_4$ ḫa-⌈ar⌉-<ši>?-tum (CT XXXII 50 rev. 9, U)

"àr-àr (= SISKUR) ḫa-ar-ši-tum" (ITT V p. 45, 9601, thus translit.).

Ur III GN:

ḪUR-ši-tum (ZA LI Pl. II after p. 74 iii 16, 17). Cf. above and/or ma-a-at Ḫu-ur-ši-tim in VAS I 115.

ḪRŠ?

Akk. lw. in Sum.?:

2 [...]..DA ḫa-ra-šu-tum (UET III 1498 rev. i).

ḪRŠB ḫuršubium.

Ur III MN:

Ḫur-šu-bi-um (MDP X 126; XXVIII 454). Cf. Langdon, BM p. 46.

ḪRZN?

Akk. lw. in Sum.:

ḪAR-zi-nu-um (RA XVIII 53 iii, Voc. prat.). Among fruits. Same in MDP XXVII 54.

ḪSP?

1 ḫa-za-pum among implements of UD.KA.BAR (Ist. Mus. Adab 241).

ḪSS ḫasāsum "to think," "to remember."

Sarg. and Ur III PN's:

Ḫu-zu-us-DINGIR (Kish 1930, 406 rev. ii)

Ḫu-zu-uz-za-ar-ra-ri-iš (Legrain, TRU 337, U, read thus against Ḫu-su-us-sà-ar-ri-iš of Stamm, ANG p. 368 top). Meaning of sarrārum unknown, since sarrārum "rebel," "liar" (cf. TCL XXIV 12:18, 24 and XXVI 81:18, both Mari) hardly fits

Ḫu-zu-uz-za-ra-ri-iš (UET III 1383, U; A 5326, U)

Iḫ-zu-zum (D+).

ḫassum "remembering," "wise," "thoughtful."

Ur III PN's:

dŠul-gi-ḫa-zi-is (U 920+)

dŠu-dEN.ZU-ḫa-zi-is (YOS IV 284:4).

ḫussusum "to remind."

ḫu-zu-zi-iš (HSS X 197:13).

ḪSS? or ḪSṢ.

Sarg. PN's:

Ḫu-za-zum (G)

Ḫu-zu-za (D).

ḪṢB ḫaṣbum.

Sarg. and Ur III PN:

Ḫa-za-ab-tum (Kish 1930, 151; Legrain, TRU 264, U)

Ḫa-an-za-ab-tum (A 3329, U).

ḪṢN? ḫaṣṣinnum "ax." Root unknown. For ḪRṢ cf. Furlani, Rassegna di studi etiopici VI 1-11 and Salonen, SO XVII/2 pp. 8f. Akk. word passed into Sum. in the form ḪA.ZI, ḪA.ZI.IN, and ḪA.ZI.NA.

1 ḫa-zi-núm šu 4 EME-su "four-bladed ax" (MDP IV Pl. 2 iii). Cf. 1 ḪA.ZI.IN EME 2 (Fish, MCS I 37 H. 7836, U)

1 ḫa?-zi-[núm]? (D 50)

1 ḪA.ZI UD.KA.BAR (RTC 22 ii, PSarg.)

41 GIŠ ḪA.ZI (De Genouillac, TSA 26 iv, PSarg.). Made of wood!

1 ḪA.ZI UD.KA.BAR, 3 ḪA.ZI IŠ.RA (ITT V Pl. 76, 9249, PSarg.)

6 URUDU ḪA.ZI UD.KA.BAR, NÍG.ŠÁM 1 GIŠ.TUKUL 5 GÍN KUG.BABBAR (MO C

viii, and similarly C iii, vii, xiii, xiv)

1 ḪA.ZI UD.KA.BAR URUDU KI.LAL.PI 3 1/2 MA.NA (PBS IX 33)

6 ḪA.ZI UD.KA.BAR KI.LAL.BI 4 1/2 MA.NA 4 GÍN (ITT III 6244, U)

13 ḪA.ZI UD.KA.BAR KI.LAL.BI 9 MA.NA LAL 3 GÍN (ITT III 6366, U)

8? URUDU ḪA.ZI KI.LAL.BI 8 1/3 MA.NA 5 GÍN (ibid.)

1 ḪA.ZI UD.KA.[BAR] KI.LAL.BI 1 MA.NA 10 GÍN (ITT V 6853 ii)

5 URUDU ḪA.ZI NAGAR (ITT V 9264)

x URUDU ḪA.ZI.IN (ITT II 6380, U; Reisner, TUT 126 ii 12; viii 1, U; PDTI 380, U)

3 URUDU ḪA.ZI.IN 1 1/2 MA.NA TA (ITT V 6789, U)

6 ḪA.ZI.IN UD.KA.BAR.ḪI.A (Reisner, TUT 126 i 29, U)

14 URUDU ḪA.ZI.IN KI.LAL.BI 13 1/2 MA.NA (Univ. Illinois 14, U)

5? URUDU ḪA.ZI.IN UD.KA.BAR KI.LAL.BI 9 2/3 MA.NA (BIN V 2:32, U)

1 ḪA.ZI.IN UD.KA.BAR KI.LAL.BI 3 GÍN (TCL V 6044 i, U)

ḪA.ZI.IN of URUDU or UD.KA.BAR (UET III p. 101 passim, U)

2 GIŠ ḪA.ZI.NA (ITT V 9283 rev.).

ḪṢṢ?, see ḪSS?

ḪŠ'ₓ ḫašûm "thyme."

1 GÚ ḫa-su-ù (MDP XIV 8). Also šakirûm plant in the same text.

ḪŠ'ₓ ḫašiānum, ḫašuānum (a plant).

Akk. lw. in Ur III Sum.:

20(QA) ḫa-ši-a-núm (Reisner, TUT 113:6)

Úḫa-šu-an-nu-um (TMH n.F. I/II 358:12)

Úḫa-šu-an-um (Amer. Journal of Pharmacy 1947 p. 425)

x ḫa-šu-a-núm (UET III 1021).

ḪŠḪ ḫašāḫum "to desire."

⌈i⌉-li-ik-šu-nu la iḫ-ši-ḫu (CT XXXII 2 v, CM)

Ur III PN:

Ḫa-áš-ḫa-me-ir PA.TE.SI Iš-ku-un-dEN KI.ZU (CT XXI 6, 89126, Ur-Nammu).

ḪŠḪR ḫašḫurum "apple-tree."

Ur III GN:

GIŠ.SAR-ḫa-aš-ḫu-ri KI (UET III 1087).

ḪŠL ḫašālum "to grind."

ÁŠ a-na ḫa-ša-lim (HSS X 132:2, 12). Cf. ŠL 191.

ḪŠM.

Ur III Amorite PN:

Ḫa-aš-ma-nu-um MAR.TU (A 4648).

ḪŠR ḫašurrum (a tree).

Lw. from Sum. or vice versa:

ḪA.ŠU.ÚR (Thureau-Dangin, SAKI p. 108 xix 6, 112 xxii 3, Gudea).

Name of mountain.

ḪŠṬ?

A gentilic formation in Ur III:

2 TÚG ḫa-ši-ti-um SU.A (Fish, CST 599, U). Among garments

18 KUŠ UDU ḫa-ši-ti-um (Fish, MCS I 51 H. 7944, U).

ḪTR, see ḪDR?

ḪṬ ḫaṭṭum "scepter," "rule."

Written logographically or syllabically.

The examples below show the word is of fem. gender.

[PA] ⌈a⌉-na [^{d}E]n-líl [....] (PBS V 36 rev. iv, NS.)

PA a-na ^{d}EN-líl .... a u-gi-il (UET I 276 ii, NS.).

Ur III PN's:

Da-bur-PA-tum (De Genouillac, TD 87; PDTI 454)

^{d}Šu-^{d}EN.ZU-li-la-bi-ir-ḫa-da-am (CT XXXII 12 i)

Tu-ki-in-PA-mi-ig-ri-ša (RLA II 146 No. 111, date)

Wa-at-ra-at-ḫa-tum (Nikolski, Dok. II 457)

Wa-at-ra-at-PA (AnOr VII 16).

ḪZB, see ḪṢB.

ḪZN ḫazānum (a title). Root ḪZʾ$_{7}$ impossible. Cf. also ZZK zazakkum.

Akk. lw. in Ur III Sum.:

PN ḫa-za-núm (ITT II/1 p. 40, 896; 2643; III 5047; 5607; 6548; Chiera, STA 10 v; Moortgat, VARS No. 265; Barton, HLC III Pl. 130, 310; Yondorf a; Orient. VI 60 No. 11, read thus against ḫa-a-lum of translit.; ZA XXV 206; CT VII 36 a; Reisner, TUT 160 viii)

PN ḫa-za-a-núm (ITT IV p. 11, 7107)

PN ḫa-za-núm Nak-su^{KI}-gé (TCL V 6163 rev. 3+, also ḫ. of DUL$_{6}$-GIŠ.AB.BA)

PN ḫa-za-núm Lu-lu-bu^{KI} (ITT III 5367 rev.).

Sarg. PN:

Ḫa-za-núm (RTC 249 i).

ḪZR ḫuzīrum "pig."

Sarg. and Ur III PN's:

Ḫu-zi-ra (G+)

Ḫu-zi-ri (RA IX 57 SA 12 rev., U; Oppenheim, CCTE p. 188, U).

K

K ki "as," "when," "like."

Conjunction with verb:

ki DN .... i-ti-nam-ma (UET I 275 iii, NS.)

ki .... ⌈i⌉?-mu-tu (MCS IV 13 rev.). Also ki?-ma in the same text

ki GURUŠ.GURUŠ u-wa-ga-mu "when the workers will ...." (JRAS 1932 p.

296:16)

a-na-lim ki a-la-kam "and when I will come to the city" (ibid. l. 34).

Preposition with noun:

ki ma-ì, ki na-ri-im, ki gal-bi-im, ki me-ra-ni-im "like water," etc. (3 NT 30, U, cf. ṣabātum).

PSarg., Sarg., and Ur III PN's:

Dan-ki-ì-lí (HSS IV 88, U)

ì-lí-ki-a-bi (ITT II p. 32, 853, U)

I-sar-ki-dUTU (Jean, ŠA CXIII rev., U). Cf. I-sar-ki-ma-dUTU in OECT IV 155 ii 39, OB, and NḪD?

Li-bur-ki-dEn-líl (BIN VIII 203+)

Ma?-ki-be-lí (CT VII 4, 22451, PSarg.)

Ma-an-ki-be-lí (U 2238)

Ma-nu-um-ki-dAMAR-dEN.ZU (UET V 690:22, U)

Ma-an-núm-ki-dŠul-gi (PDTI 550 rev., U)

Sar-ru-ki-dUTU (Fish, CST 6; 17)

Ša-ki-be-lí (AOF VIII 258 Abb. 6a). Or ŠQʾ$_7$?

Ša-ki-DINGIR (E+). Or ŠQʾ$_7$?

kima "as," "when."

ki-ma PN il-li-kam-ma (MDP XIV p. 12 v).

Kʾ$_x$?

ki-um (D 274, school text?; FM 43:12, school text?).

Ur III PN:

Ki-um-ì-lí (HSS IV 61). Miscopied for En-um-ì-lí?

Kʾ$_6$B? kûbum? "foetus."

Ur III PN's:

Gu-ub-dEN.ZU (RTC 387)

Gu-ub-dUTU (Arnold, ABTR 10 rev.; 17 rev.).

Kʾ$_6$L kullum "to hold," "to hold back."

ti-a-am-dam a-lí-dam ù [sa]-bil-dam ù sa-tu-e ga-la-su-nu-ma a-na dEn-líl u-ga-al (R xxv)

GÁN GN PN u-ga-al (BIN VIII 291)

sá-bi-NI-a-me u-ga-al "I? hold back my assualters?" (Ist. Mus. Lagash 11001)

DUMU.DUMU A-ga-dèKI PA.TE.SI-gu-a-(a-)tim u-ga-lú "the sons of A. are holding governorships" (S iv, ix)

PA a-na dEn-líl sar-ru-dam a-na dInnin a u-gi-il "may he not hold the scepter for Enlil and the kingship for Innin" (UET I 276 ii, NS.)

ŠE .... PN u-gi-ìl (HSS X 94:11)

[.... t]u-gi-ìl (FM 9:24)

u-ki-il-ši-im-ma (CT XXXII 2 iv, CM, in difficult context).

K'_xM? kîmtum? "family."

Sarg. and Ur III PN:

DINGIR-gi-ma-at (E+). Cf. Ì-lí-ki-im-ti in Stamm, ANG p. 299

DINGIR-ki-ma-at (TCL II 5520, U; PDTI 355, U).

K'_6N kuānum "to be firm."

Written syllabically.

PSarg., Sarg., and Ur III PN's:

Da-ku-um-ma-tum (UET III p. 9, U)

Da-ku-ma-tum (BE III 116 rev., U)

I-gu-^{d}Ma-lik (G+)

I-gu-núm (D+; ITT IV p. 92, 8109, U)

I-kun_x(KUM)-núm (BE I Pl. VII iii)

I-ku-nu-um (U 1609+)

I-ku-núm (U 1610+)

I-gu-Sá-lim (G; JCS X 26 vi)

I-gu-ì-lí (Walters Art Gall. 41.107 vi, PSarg.)

I-ku-É-a (MO)

I-ku-⌈Il⌉ (CT V 3 iv, PSarg.). Cf. also CT XXXII 8 ii A i, PSarg.

I-ku-La-im? (CT XXXII 8 iv A, PSarg.)

I-ku-me-sar (ITT II/1 p. 52, 966, U)

I-ku-mi-sar (U 1608+)

I-ku-bu-sa (OIP XIV 150)

I-ku-un-sar-su (MDP XVIII 73, U)

Ku-na-ma-tum (TCL II 4681+, U).

kînum "established," "regular," "firm," "well."

Written logographically or syllabically.

3 GURUŠ za-bi-ù gi-nu-tum (Kish 1930, 559a)

iš-bi-gi gi-nu-tim "the regular grain-accumulations," Acc. Pl. (JRAS 1932 p. 296:39).

Sarg. and Ur III PN's:

A-ba-GI (G+)

A-ba-GI_4 (Pinches, AT p. 15)

A-bí-iš-ki-in MAR.TU (TCL II 5508 i)

A-bìl-GI (MO+)

A-bìl-ki-in (A 5646, U)

A-ḫu-ki-in (Yondorf b, U)

Be-lí-GI (D+)

Pù-GI (BE I Pl. VI ii+)

Pù-su-GI (D+)

KA-su-GI (BIN VIII 143)
DINGIR-GI (FM+)
Gi-núm-u-ba-at (D)
Gi-nu-mu-bí (BIN VIII 144 rev. iv)
Gi-nu-ba (E)
Gi-núm-BALA (D)
Gi-núm-ba-la (D)
Gi-núm-ni-.... (Ist. Mus. Adab 280)
Gi-nu-mu-si = Kînum-uššī? (A 2736; YOS IV 53, U)
Ḫa-bil-ki-in (Gutian king)
I-dur-GI (D+)
Iq-bí-GI (D+)
I-sar-ki-in (Nikolski, Dok. II 519, U+)
I-su-GI (FM+)
Iš-lam-GI (BE I Pl. VI vi+). See note under ŠLM
Li-da-at-GI (D)
Nin-líl-iš-gi-in (FM)
Pù-uš-ki-in (PDTI 529 x, U)
Sar-gi-in (ZA XII 335, translit. only)
Sar-gi-NI (ibid.)
Sar-ru-GI (king)
Sar-um-GI (king)
Sar-ru-GIM (CT VII 25, 13164, U)
Su-mu-GI (MO+)
Su-ru-uš-GI (D+)
Su_4-ru-uš-GI (RA IX 76)
Šu-ru-uš-ki-in (U 2696+)
Su-ru-uš-GIM (ITT IV p. 9, 7090)
Šu-ru-uš-gi-in (A 2790 iii, U)
SUḪUŠ-GI (Porada, CPML No. 290, U)
SUḪUŠ-gi-in (U 2514+)
SUḪUŠ-ki-in (U 2515+)
Uš-šu-ki-in (U 1441)
Uš-si-gi-in (D)
Zi-gur-GI (RTC 127 iii; ITT I 1472 ii).

Reading kin_x(GIM) or DÍM:
A-bí-DÍM (RTC 137 i)
A-bìl-DÍM (CT I 2 ii, U)
I-sar-DÍM (RTC 249 i).

Deified PN in Ur III:

dSar-ru-gi(n)-in (PDTI 605).

Deified PN in Sarg. and Ur III PN's:

Sar-ru-GI-ì-lí (MO)

| Ur-dSar-ru-GIM (Orient. XLVII 41:5, U; Nies, UDT 93, U)
| Ur-Sar-ru-GIM (Orient. IV p. 59, U; Oppenheim, CCTE C 1 iv, U; PDTI 126, U)
| Ur-dSar-ru-gin (RA IX 56 SA 241, U, translit. only).

kunnum "to establish."

PN's šu-ut PN u-ga-nu (Ist. Mus. Adab 280 twice)

offerings ú-gi-in-šum (MDP IV Pl. 2 ii)

u!-gi-i[n-....] (Böhl, MAW Letterkunde 76B No. 9 p. 12 and photo).

Sarg. and Ur III PN's:

| Gi-nu-uš-sa-am "make firm the foundation" (G). Cf. Ki-nam-iš-ti (OIP XLIII 153 Nos. 42f., OB)
| Gi-in-uš-sa-am (ZA XII 333+)

Ki-in-dŠul-gi (UET III 1498 rev. iii twice, U)

⌈Ki⌉?-nam-Da-ba-an (D). Cf. Ki-nam-ì-lí (Stamm, ANG p. 176)

Tu-ki-in-PA-mi-ig-ri-ša (RLA II 146, date, U)

U-gi-in-Ul-maš (AO XVII/XVIII No. 229).

kittum "justice."

da-ia-an ki-na-tim (YOS IX 62, Dêr).

PSarg. PN:

Ba-la-ki/gi-na-ti-im (PSarg. king)

Ì-lí-ki-ti (ITT II/1 853, U)

Ša-ma-aš-ki-ti (PDTI 529 x, U)

[Interpret ki-za in Da-ti-ki-za (G etc.) not as kît-sa but as DN Ki-za with Schonevelt, BO IX 173].

kîniš "truly."

lu gi-ni-iš-ma (R xxiii, xxvi; RA VIII 136, R.; RA VII 105, Mi.; M xxvii).

K'$_x$Ṣ? kâṣum "comb."

Akk. lw. in Sum.?:

Occurs only in Sum. GIŠ.GA.ZUM, for which cf. Oppenheim, CCTE p. 66; also 5 GA.ZUM in ITT II/2 p. 32, 4570 and KAM.GA.ZUM in ITT I 1243 and p. 18, 1285. For the root cf. GA.ZUM = ka-a-ṣu in Izi V 167.

KBB kabābum (a weapon). "Sling" according to Thureau-Dangin, RA XXXVI 57ff.

Akk. lw. in Sum.:

GIŠga-ba-bu-um MAR.TU (RA XVIII 71, Voc. prat.)

Cf. also ga-ba-bu-um made of leather in BIN IX 14, 85, etc., OB.

KBB? kabbum? (a tree or object of wood).

Akk. lw. in Ur III Sum.:

x kab-bu-um (De Genouillac, FT II Pl. XLIX AO 12177)

x GIŠ kab-bu x+6 KÙŠ TA (TCL V 6037 iv)

Cf. GIŠ kab-bu-um in MDP XXVII 188 iii.

KBR kibrum.

Ur III PN's:

DINGIR-ki-ib-<ri> (Orient. XLVII 366)

DINGIR-ki-bi-rí (AnOr I 112 rev.)

Il-ki-ib-ri (Chiera, STA 10 v)

Ì-lí-ki-ib-rí (Oppenheim, CCTE p. 188)

Ḫu-un-ki-ib-ri (U 1561)

Ìr-ra-ki-ib-rí (UET III 33).

kibrātum "(world's) quarters" (or the like).

PN LUGAL ki-ib-ra-tim ar-ba-im (NS.; Enridawizir; Š., BS., ŠS.)

NS. .... LUGAL ^{d}UB 4.BA (PBS XV 81)

[....] LUGAL ki-ib-ra-[tim] ar-ba-im (PBS XV 18, unknown king)

DN LUGAL [ki]-ib-ra-tim! ar-ba-im (OIP XLIII 143, Diyala, U)

ki-ib-ra-tim ar-ba-im [....] (MDP X Pl. 3, 1a)

in ki-ib-ra-tim ar-ba-im (BE I 120 ii, NS.)

[ki-ib]-ra-tum [ar-ba]-um and ki-ib-[ra-tim] a[r-ba-im] (Böhl, MAW Letterkunde 76B No. 9 p. 12, NS.?)

ki-ib-ra-tum ar-ba-um (IAMN XII Pl. IV, NS.; PBS V 36 rev. x+ii, NS.).

KBR? kabrum? "thick."

so much silver PN íl-gi-ma a-na ga-bar-tim i-ti-in (D 282). To be interpr. perhaps as f.n. Ga-bar-tim.

KBR?

Ur III Amorite PN:

Gu-ba-ru-um MAR.TU (Univ. Illinois 265).

KBS kabāsum "to tread," "to bleach."

x (ŠE) a-na TÚG.ŠÀ.GA.DÙ ga-ba-zi-im "so much barley for bleaching a garment" (D 258).

Ur III PN's:

Ik?-bu-zi-na-at (TCL II 5484)

Ku-bu-us (BE III 94). Formation like Naplis, Ṣuruḫ.

KBT kubbutum "heavy."

Sarg. and Ur III PN's:

Gú-bu-da (BE III 44, U)

Gu(d)-bu-da (TMH n.F. I/II 316:8, U)

Ku-bu-tum (D+)

| Gu(d)-bu-tum (AnOr I 177, U, translit. only).

KBT?

Ur III PN:

| Gu-ba-tum (UET III 1357 rev.). Cf. [f]Ku-ub-ba-tu(m) etc. quoted in NPN p. 323a

| Ku-ba-tum, f.n. (APAW 1936 Phil.-hist. Kl. Nr. 13 p. 23; BO IX 173:15; misread in both cases). Also in PDTI 431; 583+.

KBT? kibtum?, see NKP? nikiptum.

KD?

[m]a-am-ma-an [la iz-z]i-za-am [la ka-d]a-a-am (CT XXXII 1 ii) = ma-am-man la iz-zi-za la ka-da-a (RA VII 180 ii) in CM.

KD?

iš-tum BÀD ga-da?-im a-na BÀD da-ni-im (UET I 275 vff., NS.).

KD?

various people be-lu ga-da-tim (MDP XIV 71 ii).

KD?

Ur III PN:

DINGIR-ki-da (Barton, HLC II Pl. 84, 83 i; CT III 9 i; cf. also Delaporte, CCL II A 277).

KD?, see QD?

KDN, see $G^{\supset}{}_7D$?

KDN kudānum "mule."

PSarg. and Ur III PN's:

| Gu-da-nú̱m (HSS IV 88 rev., U)

| Ku-da-núm (Reisner, TUT 214 i, U)

| Gu-da-nú(m)-um (ITT IV p. 92, 8111, U)

Gu-da-ni (OIP XIV 51 rev. v, PSarg.)

Cf. Ku-da-nu-um in Ranke, EBPN p. 117.

KK kakkum "weapon."

Normally written logographically as GIŠ.TUKUL, once syllabically.

DN GIŠ.TUKUL-su li-iš-bir$_5$ (S ix, xi; PBS V 34 x, Lugalzagesi)

DN GIŠ.TUKUL-kam a el-bi-ma (UET I 276 ii, NS.). Interpr. unknown

GIŠ.TUKUL-gi-su in ti-a-am-tim Ì.LAḪ (S ii, vii, viii)

in GIŠ.TUKUL-ki DN (UET I 275 i, NS.).

Sarg. PN's:

Gak-ku-um DUMU É-a-da-me-iq (Delaporte, CCL II A 87)

GIŠ.TUKUL-ga-su-al-si-in (MO)

I-da-GIŠ.TUKUL-ki (ITT V 9275).

KKB kakkabum "star."

Sarg. GN:

KUR Ga-ga-ba-an^{KI} (Iraq VII p. 66 F 1153 rev.).

KKL kakkultum (a container).

Ur III GN:

Gag-gu-la-tum^{KI} (CT XXXII 19:6).

KKN?

Akk. lw. in Sum.?:

1 KU.KU.NA 1 GÚ ḫa-su-ù ("thyme") (MDP XIV 8)

Cf. ŠL 318, 173 and Orient. V 43, who reads x sa ú-durun-durun-na in DP 368f. and translates "x Bündel Heu." Cf. also GAR ku-ku-na in Nikolski, Dok. I 140 ii, iii; 141 i, ii; 143 i; etc.

KKR kakkartum "loaf of bread?"

Akk. lw. in Ur III Sum.:

20 GAR ga-ga-ar-tum 2 QA GABA (TCL II 5520)

Cf. GAR ga-ga-ar-tum in RA XVIII 59 vi, Voc. prat. = MDP XXVII 54 iii and examples quoted in SLB I (2) p. 44.

KKR kukurum, kukrum (a resinous plant).

Akk. lw. in Sum.:

1 PISAN+GI ŠIM gúk-ru-um (ITT I p. 13, 1214)

x QA ŠIM gúk-ru-um (ITT I p. 21, 1330; II/2 4461 rev.; 4587; 5766 rev.; V 9293)

ŠIM ku-ku-ru-um (BIN VIII 300; 319)

x QA gu(d)-ku-ru (TCL II 5680 ii, U; Reisner, TUT 122 vii, U; Nikolski, Dok. II 445 rev., U)

gu(d)-ku-ru-BI (TCL II 6042 i, rev. i, U)

x QA gu(d)-ku-<ru>-um (TMH n.F. I/II 307, U).

KKR? kikurum?

Akk. lw. in Ur III Sum.:

Among woods or objects of wood. Interpret perhaps as gigurrum?

3 ki-ku-ru-um (BE III 76 rev. 23; 78:7)

5 ^{GIŠ}ki?!-ku-ru (BE III 77:2).

KKS?

Akk. lw. in Sum.:

quantities of gu-gu-zum among fruits and legumes (ITT II/2 p. 36, 4658, translit. only). For k cf. PN Ku-ku-zum in Kh. 1935, 110, OB.

Sarg. and Ur III PN's:

Ku-gu-za-na (HSS IV 49 i, U; ITT IV p. 34, 7302+)

| Gu-gu-za-núm (FM)

| Gu(d)-ku-za-núm (UE X 410, U).

KL kalum "all" (noun).

The word appears as ga-lí- in Gen., ga-la- in Acc., and perhaps ga-lu(l)- in Nom.

a-na ga-lí É GEMÉ (D 290:8)

su-lum É ga-lí-su (D 290 rev. x+3)

NS. sa-bi-ir KIŠ MI ḪI KALAM NIM^{KI} ga-lí-sa-ma (UET I 274 i)

[....] ga-la-ma i-ti-šum (R xxv)

sa-tu-e ga-la-su-nu-ma .... u-ga-al (R xxv)

i-nu NS. da-nim in si-ip-rí ^{d}Innin GA.LUL-ma ki-ib-ra-tu[m] ar-ba-um iš-ti-ni-iš i-ḫa-ni-su$_4$-ma "at the time of NS., by the command of I. all? (= ga-lu(l)-ma) the four quarters together were subdued" (PBS V 36 rev. x+ii, NS.). Cf. ^{d}Ša-^{d}UTU-ka-lu-ma in Iraq VII 41, Chagar Bazar; also ARMT XV 208.

Sarg. PN's:

| Bi-in-ga-lí-LUGAL-rí (RA IX 82+)
| Bi-ga-lí-LUGAL-rí (RTC 94)

DINGIR-ga-lí "God is my all" (MO)

Ga-lí (G+)

Ga-lí-^{d}EN.[ZU]? (D)

Ga-lí-ì-li (MO)

Sar-ga-lí-LUGAL-rí and ^{d}Sar-ga-lí-LUGAL-rí (Sarg. king)

A-ŠI-ga-la (G+). Doubtful.

<u>kališ</u> "all" (adverb).

Sarg. PN's:

Gal-iš?-DINGIR (AnOr VII 372 iii, Sarg.?!)

| Ga-li-iš-DÙG (G+)
| Ga-lí-iš-DÙG (FM)
| Gal-iš-DÙG (D+)

Gal-iš-i-sar (ITT II/2 5885 ii). Cf. I-sar-ka-li-iš in OECT IV 155 ii 34, OB.

KL$^{\prime}_{x}$ <u>kuluʾum</u> "male prostitute?"

8 PN's, two of which are ŠEŠ.SAL PN, ku-lu-ù (FM 30:11).

KL$^{\prime}_{x}$?

Akk. lw. in Ur III Sum.:

1 ga-NI-tum KUG.GI SI.SÁ KI.LAL.BI 1/2 GÍN (UET III 452; 1498 rev. ii)

1 ga-[....] UD.KA.BAR [....] (UET III 315)

GIŠ.KU ga-a-NI-tum (UET III 560)

1 GIŠ.KU ga-NI-tum (UET III 1498 iv). Wood? Cf. 1 GIŠ.KU si-iq-tum (ibid.)

1 GIŠ.KU ga-NI-a-tum (UET III 670)

1 GIŠ.KU mi-na-tum ga-NI-a-tum (UET III 677)

2/3 MA.NA KUG.BABBAR MÁŠ ga-NI-tum GAR (Fish, CST p. 134 No. 542).

KLʾ$_x$?

Sarg. PN:

Ga-lí-tim, Gen. (D+).

KLB kalibum, kalbum "dog."

I seized him ki gal-bi-im ì-na ki-ša-ti-šu, ki me-ra-ni-im ì-na pi-ir-ti-šu (3 NT 30, U, cf. ṣabātum)

1 gal-pum UD.KA.BAR (OIP XIV 103). Here a figurine in form of a dog.

PSarg. and Sarg. PN's:

Ga-la-ab-É-a (MO)

Gal-pum (BIN VIII 11 i and v, PSarg.+; FM+)

Ga-lí-bu-um (PSarg. king).

KLL šuklulum "to complete."

Ur III PN:

Ú-šà-ak-li-il (U 1138; Fish, CST p. 159 iii end). For the formation cf. Ušagšim under GŠM?

Ú-ša-ak-lí-il (UET III 754 iii; 1048:3+).

kullum "totality," "all."

Sarg. and Ur III PN's:

In some cases interpr. as Sum. KU.LI ibrum "friend" also possible.

DINGIR-gu-l[í] (G)

DINGIR-ku-lí (D)

EN-ku-li (G+; Oppenheim, CCTE p. 125 P 2, U)

Gu-lí-DINGIR (G+)

Ku-lí-DINGIR (E)

Ku-lí-lum (G)

Gu-lí-sar (ITT I 1372)

LUGAL-ku-li (MO).

kullatum "totality."

Sarg. PN:

I-zi-ir-gul-la-zi-in (MO).

KLL kallatum "bride," "daughter-in-law."

Written syllabically and logographically as É.GI.A or É.GI$_4$.A.

⌈a⌉-na ^{d}A-a kal-la-tim (CT XXXII 1 i twice, 4 xi twice = RA VII 180) in CM.

Sarg. and Ur III PN:

Gal-la-tim, Gen. (E)

Gal-la-tum (D). Perhaps not a PN

Ga-la-túm (TCL V 6039 ii, U)

É.GI.A (FM)

É.GI_4.A (D+).

KLL <u>kilīlum</u> **"wreath" (or the like).**

1 ki-li-lum KUG.BABBAR (MO B i, iv; C vii)

3 ki-li-lu KUG.BABBAR KI.LAL.BI 1 MA.NA KUG.BABBAR (MO C viii)

1 ki-li-lum KUG.BABBAR KI.LAL.BI 1/3 ŠA KUG.BABBAR (MO C ix, xi; D iiif., here 15 GÍN KUG.BABBAR)

2 ki-li-lum KUG.BABBAR (MO D viii).

Akk. lw. in Ur III Sum.:

ki-lí-lum UD.SAR (UET III 687).

Ur III PN:

DINGIR-ki-lí-lí (CT III 36 iii; BIN V 55:7). Read thus against Anum-ki-ì-lí (BIN V p. 5) and cf. Ìr-ra-ki-li-li (TCL I 189:15, OB).

KLL?, see GLL?

KLM <u>kullumum</u> "to show."

LÚ-lam na-ga-ra-am u-gal-la-mu-ma "(whoever) shows (the statue) to another person" (UET I 276 i, NS.)

^{d}En-líl u-gal-lim (S xii, xv; R xxiii, [xxvi] = RA VIII 136 rev. i; BE I 1 i, Škš.). In all cases the sentence forms a complete unit, seemingly without connection with what precedes or follows. Perhaps an idiom with the meaning "Enlil brought it about," "Enlil volente"

10 QA NI.DUN .... Lu-lu ú-ga-lim (BIN VIII 144 ii). The meaning "to show" does not fit here since the 10 QA NI.DUN are listed again in the total: ŠU.NIGÍN .... 10 QA NI.[DUN] šu 5 ENGAR LUGAL Lu-lu iš-lu-[ul] (ibid. iii).

KLM <u>kalmatum</u> (a worm).

Sarg. PN:

Gal-ma-tum (D).

KLM <u>kalūmum</u> "young animal" (of small cattle).

ga-lu-ma-sa (Kish 1930, 143 rev.).

PSarg. PN:

Ga-lu-mu-um (PSarg. king). Cf. Ka-lu-mu-um in YOS VIII p. 14, OB.

KM <u>kimtum</u>, see $K^{\text{ʾ}}_xM$.

$KM^{\text{ʾ}}_7$ <u>kamājum</u> "to bind," "to capture."

Always with persons as object.

sar-rí-su-nu 3 i-ik-mi-ma (YOS I 10, NS.)

x LÚ in KAS+X i-ik-mi (PBS V 36 x+iii, NS.)

ì-nu .... su_4-ma da-li na-ra-ab-ti-su i-ik-mi-ù-su_4? "when .... he bound him at the door jambs? of his entrance" (UET I 275 iii, NS.)

ki .... ak-mi-[ù] (ibid.)

na-ak-ru-uz-zu ik-me (MDP XIV p. 10 i)

sar-rí-si-in .... ik-mi (Böhl, MAW Letterkunde 76B No. 9 p. 12, unknown king)

in 1 MU NS. .... PN ik-mi-ù (var. ik-mi-ME) (D 217, date; 220, date)

in 1 MU Škš. .... PN ik-mi-ù (RTC 130, date).

Ur III PN:

Ik-me-DINGIR (U 1703).

kamjum "bound," "tied."

sar-rí-si-in in ga-mi-e u-sá-rí-ib "he brought their kings in fetters" (CT XXXII 5, 98917, unknown king). The form is evidently in kamî from *in kamij, Indeterm. St. of kamjum.

Sarg. PN's:

Ga-mi-um (ITT V 9271+)

Ga-mi-a-tum (D).

KMKM kamkammatum "ring" (or the like).

Akk. lw. in Ur III Sum.:

1 kam-kam-ma-tum of KUG.BABBAR and KUG.GI ḪUŠ.A (UET III p. 110 passim)

1 kam-kam-ma-tum 6 GÍN (TA 1931, 237).

KML, see GML.

KMM kamamtum (a vegetable). Cf. kamantu in Thompson, DAB p. 380.

Akk. lw. in Ur III Sum.:

x QA ga-ma-am-tum (RTC 307 iv; ITT II 892 iv; ITT IV 10011)

x QA x GÍN ga-ma-àm-tum (Nikolski, Dok. II 341)

x QA ^Ú ga-ma-àm-tum (Chiera, STA 11 ii; Fish, CST 719)

ga!-ma!-àm-tum-BI x QA (Boson, TCS 364 end of obv.)

^Ú ga-ma-am-tum (RA XVIII 58, Voc. prat.).

KMN kamūnum "cumin."

Evidently Akk. lw. in Sum.:

1 DUG GA.MUN (BIN VIII 132 iii; 271). In both cases GA.MUN occurs with zibibiānum; cf. kamūnu and zibibianni at Nuzi in HSS XIII 353 = RA XXXVI 169.

KNK kanākum "to seal."

2 persons KÁ in na-ap-ḫa-rí-su-nu li-ik-nu-ku (Cop. 10055 rev.).

x ŠE.GUR La-ma i-ga-ni-ik (MDP XIV 45 rev.). Meaning?

KNK? kinkum?

Ur III MN:

^ITI Ki-in-kum (TA 1931, 423).

KNN kannum (a vessel?).

Akk. lw. in Ur III Sum.:

x DUG ga-an-núm (ITT II/1 892 rev. iv; V p. 47, 9640; RTC 307 rev. iv)

[....] ga-an-nu-um MEŠ (UET III 1498 vi).

KNN kinūnum "hearth," "brazier."

Ur III PN:

Gi-nu-na (YOS IV 254 iii; PDTI 216).

KNN? kunnunum?

Sarg. PN:

Gu-nu-núm (Kish 1930, 406). Cf. Holma, Quttulu p. 85: qu, ku, or gu.

KNŠ kanāšum "bow down."

Ur III PN:

Ku-un-si-ma-tum (Jean, ŠA LVIII).

KNŠ kunāšum "emmer."

Written ÁŠ and ÁŠ.AN (passim)

ÁŠ.NUMUN-su (HSS X 36 iv)

[Á]Š.AN-su (BIN VIII 263 twice).

KNZL?

Ur III PN:

Ki-in-zu-lum (Oppenheim, CCTE p. 190).

KPL kuppulum "twisted?"

Sarg. PN:

Ku-bu-lum (D).

KPTR kapturrum (a container).

kap-dúr-ru ZÍD.ŠE (FM 43:4, school text?).

KR kârum "quai" (and similarly).

Apparently a lw. from Sum. KAR.

MÁ .... in ga-rí-im ši A-ga-dè^{KI} ìr-ku-us (S vi)

MÁ.MÁ .... in kar-rí-<im> ši A-ga-dè^{KI} ìr-gu-us (UET I 274 v, Mi.)

PN ⌈GIŠ?.GAG⌉ in ga-rí-im im-ḫa-zu, Subj. (BIN VIII 121 iv)

ŠE .... a-na karîm(-im) (thus translit. in ITT I p. 4, 1078).

KR?

Apparently an Akk. element occurs in the foll. PN's.

Connection between various writings cannot be proved.

Written GÀR:

A-za-GÀR (Louvre AO 8637)

Be-lí-GÀR (E+)

DINGIR-GÀR (D+)

DINGIR-šu-GÀR (MO+)

Il_x-su(d)-GÀR (BIN VIII 11 ii, PSarg.)

E-la-GÀR (HSS IX 86, U; Fish, CST p. 64, U)

^{d}EN.ZU-GÀR (D)
Eš$_4$-dar-GÀR (D+)
Gàr-ì-li (MDP XIV 76)
Gàr-ì-lí (JAOS LII 113)
Ì-lum-GÀR (DP 2 i, PSarg.)
^{d}Ìr-ra-GÀR (D)
Sar-ru-GÀR (G).

Written KÁR and kar:
DINGIR-KÁR (Kish 1930, 148)
^{d}EN.ZU-KÁR (RA IX 34 v, copy)
Iš-má-KÁR (E+)
LUGAL-KÁR (E)
LUGAL-kar-ri (TMH n.F. I/II 97, U). Clear
Šu-KÁR-rí (G+).

Written GÁR:
Iš-má-GÁR (D+).

Written GUR$_7$:
Be?-lí-GUR$_7$ (FM)
Eš$_4$-dar-GUR$_7$-šu (Oppenheim, CCTE p. 186, U, translit. only; read perhaps Eš$_4$-dar-il-šu).

KRʾ$_7$ <u>kurjum</u> "short."
Sarg. PN:
Gu-rí-tum (Kish 1930, 177g).

KRʾ$_x$ <u>kirium</u> "orchard."
Lw. from Sum. kiri written GIŠ.SAR.
ki-rí-šum tu-ur$_4$-da "hurry to the orchard!" (Kish 1930, 143)
ki-rí-iš ^{d}EN.ZU (ibid.).

KRʾ$_x$?
Sarg. and Ur III PN's:
DINGIR-ku-ri (Nikolski, Dok. II 329 ii, U)
Gu-ri?-^{d}En-líl (ITT V p. 39, 9447)
Il$_x$-ku-rí (TCL V 6039 iv, U)
Ku-ru-É-a (Prinz, Altorientalische Symbolik XII 15, U?)
Ku-ru-^{d}Gìr-ra (BE I Pl. VI v)
Ku-ru-um (Gutian king; U 1850).

KRB <u>karābum</u> "to pray."
ik-ru-ub-ma, ik-ri-bi-šu ^{d}KA.DI iš-me-ma (Speleers, RIAA 4 ii, Dêr).
Sarg. and Ur III PN's:
DINGIR-ku-ru-ub (De Genouillac, TD 61, U; YOS IV 254 iv, U)
DINGIR-guru$_5$(URU+GU)-ub (ITT III 6558, U)
E-la-ag-ku-ru-ba (AnOr XII 277 iii, U). Elag is a DN

E-la-gu-<ru>-ub (AnOr I 128, U)
Ì-la-ag-ku-r[u-ub] (D)
Ik-ru-ub-DINGIR (MO+)
Ik-ru-ub-É-a (MO+; UET III p. 17, U)
I-sar-kur-ba-aš (U 1650; U 1651?)
Ku-ru-ba (FM+)
Ku-ru-ub-ba-lìḫ (Ist. Mus. Adab 90)
Ku-ru-ub-DINGIR.DINGIR (D+)
Ku-ru-ub?-^{d}EN.ZU (D)
Ku-ru-ub-GI.AD (ITT IV p. 88, 8045, U). Ununderstandable
Ku-ru-ub-Ì-la-<ag> (D)
Ku!-ru-ub-Ì-la-ag (Kish 1930, 406 ii+)
Kur-ru-ub-E-lá-ag (BE III 110 ix 1, U)
Ku-ru-ub-bi-la-ag (ITT IV 7067, U; UET III 1034 i?, U)
Kur-bi-la-ag (U 1858+)
Kur-bi-lag (RA III 134 ii, U)
Kur-bi-la-gab-TA (AnOr I 175 rev., U, translit. only)
Ku-ru-ub-^{d}IM (SO IX/1 No. 24, U)
Ku-ru-ub-Ìr-ra (U 1853; AnOr VII p. 26, U)
Kur-ru-ub-Ìr-ra (Boson, TCS 257, U)
Ku-ru-ub-^{d}UTU (E; RT XIX 49, U)
Gu-ru$_{x}$(URU+X)-ub-^{d}UTU (Pinches, AT p. 122, U).

karābum "prayer."
Sarg. and Ur III PN's:
Ga-ra-bí (TCL V 6039 iii, U)
Ì-lí-kára-bí (FM). For KÁR = kára cf. Clay, PNCP p. 180 under KRB. Or read Ì-lí-kár-bí /Ilī-qarbī/ and cf. Ilī-maḫrī.

ikribū "prayer."
ik-ru-ub-ma ik-ri-bi-šu ^{d}KA.DI iš-me-ma (Speleers, RIAA 4 ii, Dêr)
DN ik-rí-bi-su iš-me-má (MDP XIV p. 12 v).

kirbānum.
Sarg. and Ur III PN:
Kir-ba-núm (D+)
Gìr-ba-núm MAR.TU (Langdon, TAD 38, U).

KRKR kurkurratum or kurkurrum, Pl. kurkurrātum (a container). Cf. Landsberger, AOF XII 138.
Akk. lw. in Ur III Sum.:
10 LAL 1 ^{DUG}kur-kur-ra-tum LÀL LÁL.BI 1(PI) 3 QA, i.e. 7 QA per 1 container (TCL II 5530 rev.). This word cannot be identified with ^{DUG}KUR.KU.RÚ/DÙ (ibid. l. 1 and ŠL 366, 97) because the latter

contains about 90 QA.

KRM kurummatum "victuals," "provisions."

lords ŠUK.^{d}INNIN-su maḫ-rí-[su] u-sa-rí-[bu] (UET I 274 ii, NS.).

KRN?

Ur III GN:

Ki-rí-LUM (ZA LI Pl. II after p. 74 iv 10, 11).

KRN?

Sarg. and Ur III PN's:

Ku-ru-na-tim, Gen. (D)

Ku-ru?-núm (Fish, CST p. 160 x 9, U).

KRN?

Ur III PN's:

Kur-ni-tum (TCL II 6039 iv)

Kur?-ni-da (Orient. II 62).

KRR kirrum (a vessel).

3 and 5 kir-ru (HSS X 170:2, 7). Listed among vessels copied and read as 1 ⌈ḫa⌉-ru NI.NUN (Pinches, AT p. 23). Since the expected form is uncontrasted ḫariu(m), reading ⌈kir⌉-ru may be preferred.

KRR? kirrum (a kind of sheep).

Akk. lw. in Ur III Sum.:

x UDU kir-ru-um (Barton, HLC II Pl. 75 iii, iv; UET III 106; RA VIII 157 AO 5653)

x UDU kir-ru-um ŠE (UET III 160)

x UDU kir-ru-um ŠE SIG_5 (UET III 103)

x UDU kir-ru-um ŠE NITAḪ and the like (UET III 1200)

x UDU.NITAḪ kir-ru-um (UET III 1232+)

x GANAM kir-ru-um (UET III 1232+)

x $SILA_4$ kir-ru-um (RA VIII 157 AO 5653).

KRŠ karāšum "camp," "destruction."

x GURUŠ.GURUŠ in URU^{KI}.URU^{KI} Šu-me-rí-im u-su-zi-am-ma a-na ga-ra-si-im iš-kun_x(KUM) (R xvii, xix, xxi twice).

KRŠ karāšum "leek."

Sum. GA.RAŠ or GA.RAŠ^{SAR} is evidently a lw. from Akk. karāšum. Cf. the Semitic etymologies in Thompson, DAB p. 52.

KRŠ?

Ur III PN:

Ga-ra-sum (Univ. Illinois 291, U).

KRŠ?

Ur III GN:

GIŠ.SAR Gàr-šum^{KI} (UCP IX p. 183, 34; ITT V 9515)

GIŠ.SAR GEŠTIN Gàr-šum^{KI} (Pinches, AT 54:3; Barton, HLC I Pl. 21, 102:4; III Pl. 125, 267 x+9)

GIŠ.SAR Gàr-šum (ITT V 6925 rev.).

KRŠ? kiršum?

Akk. lw. in Ur III Sum.:

1 kir-šu-um KUG.BABBAR (UET III 730 ii)

1 kir-<šu>-um UD.KA.BAR (UET III 738).

KRŠ?

Ur III PN's:

Kur-ša-an (3 NT 796 ii)

Kur-ša-núm (U 1862; UET III p. 19+)

Cf. Kur-ša-nu-um (Kh. 1935, 16 and 51, OB).

KSʾ$_7$ kusîtum (a garment).

Akk. lw. in Sum. GU.ZI.DA.

1 ^{TÚG}gu-zi-tum ŠÁM 1 GÍN KUG.BABBAR (BM 54309 ii)

28 ^{TÚG}gu-zi-a-tum ša-at URU-SAG.PA.KAB.DU^{KI} ŠÁM 7 GÍN KUG.BABBAR (col. iiif.)

^{TÚG}gu-zi-ti-[im]? (FM 48:13). See also under kussiʾum

1 TÚG.GU.ZI.DA (D 187)

1 TÚG.GU.ZI.DA GAL (FM 7:3)

TÚG.GU.ZI.DA SÍG? (FM 34:6).

KSʾ$_x$ kussiʾum "chair."

The normal Sum. form is GIŠ.GU.ZA, presupposing the existence of Akk. kussaʾum.

The Sum. form GU.ZÉ in É.GU.ZÉ (FM 8:18) besides É.GIŠ.GU.ZA (D 336:6) corresponds to Akk. kussiʾum.

30 gu-zi-ù TUR (MDP XIV 8)

2? PN's sa-ti-da g[u]-zi-[im]? (FM 49 rev. x+3). Or g[u]-zi-[ti-im]?

KSP kaspum "silver."

Written logographically as KUG.BABBAR, BABBAR.KUG, KUG or syllabically (in PN's only).

The logographic spelling makes it difficult to distinguish kaspum "silver" from kaspū "money," "price."

x MA.NA x GÍN KUG.BABBAR (HSS X 110 etc.)

a-na ŠÁM x KUG.BABBAR GÍN (HSS X 211; similarly 72 end)

so much KUG.BABBAR el-lum "purified" (D 303)

x GÍN KUG.BABBAR and x GÍN BABBAR.KUG (FM 5)

x GÍN KUG.BABBAR and x GÍN KUG (FM 35; RTC 101)

x GÍN KUG (ITT II 2, 2917; similarly BIN VIII 35; 43)

many objects (also x MA.NA KUG.LUḪ.ḪA) KUG.BI x MA.NA x GÍN x ŠE NÍG.ŠÁM GÁN.KAM (ITT I 1091)

KUG.BABBAR-am (JRAS 1932 p. 296:26, 35)

KUG.BABBAR-su "its price" (ITT II/2 5798; 5893; MO A ii etc.)

KUG.BABBAR-su-nu (MO C ii etc.)

KUG.BABBAR-si-in (MO C viii, xii)

KUG.BABBAR = NÍG.ŠÁM, as in 10 NI QA KUG.BABBAR-su 2 MA.NA KUG.BABBAR compared with 1 DUMU.SAL NÍG.ŠÁM-sa 15 GÍN KUG.BABBAR (MO C ix)

45! ŠE.GUR a-na KUG ("price") 1(GUR) 2(PI) 30(QA) GUR na-ti-in, KUG-su 1/2 MA.NA (Kish 1930, 138)

KUG.BABBAR-su and KUG.BABBAR-su-nu "its/their silver" (in weight) (MDP XIV 86 passim)

a-ti-ma .... KUR.KUR KUG "silver mountains" (S vi)

a-ti-⌈ma⌉ ḫu-rí KUG "silver mines" (M xxvi).

Sarg. and Ur III PN's:

A-ḫa-KUG.BABBAR-sa (FM). Doubtful

A-li-KUG.BABBAR-si (D)

KUG.BABBAR-sa (FM+)

KUG-sa (A 751)

Gas-bu-ša (U 580+; YOS IV 217, U; Nies, UDT 92, U). Cf. Ka-áš-pu-ša, Grant in Haverford Symposium on Archaeology p. 8, OB

Gas-bu-ša$_4$(DU) (PBS XI/3 52, perhaps older than Ur III)

KUG-šu-na (Jacobsen, CTC 54 iv, U; ITT IV p. 60, 7559, U+).

KSP <u>kusiptum</u> "cake?" (or the like).

Akk. lw. in Ur III Sum.:

60 MA.NA gu-zé-ba-tum 5 MA.NA TA, KUG.BI IGI.5.GÁL 6 ŠE (Reisner, TUT 121 xii).

KSRK <u>kusarikkum</u> (an ox-like animal).

x+5 gu(d)-za-rí-ku?!(wr. ŠÈ) 2 la-aḫ-ma-an KUG.GI iš-mu-tu ù ik-ba-ri? ìr-ku-zu "they plucked down? (melted?) x+5 kusarikkum(-figurines) and 2 laḫmum(-figurines) of gold and tied (in their place?) ikbarum" (PBS IX 30). Spelling with GUD suggests an ox-like animal, as proposed by Landsberger, Fauna pp. 92f. Cf. also kusarikkum and laḫmum together in the Agum-kakrime inscription (V R 33 iv 50f.).

KṢʾ$_x$? <u>kiṣʾum</u>? "morning?"

1 UDU in ki-zi-im 1 UDU in me-ḫi?-im ù-mi-sá-am ú-gi-in-šum "1 sheep in the morning?, 1 sheep in the evening?, daily he established" (MDP IV Pl. 2 ii). The occurrences of 1 UDU ŠE a-na ki-iz-zi-im ("chapel") šà ^{d}INNIN.ERIN (MDP X 11 and similarly in 34, 45, 46, 47, etc.) may be different.

KṢR kāṣirum "walker," "bleacher."

PN ù ga-zi-ru [M]a-má-tim (FM 51 rev. x+9).

kiṣrū "hire."

ad-da ARÁD da-sa-am-ma a-na-gu 6 MU ki-iṣ-ri-su [....] "you shall buy the slave and I [shall pay]? his hire for 6 years" (BM 54318 rev.).

kaṣṣārum "walker," "bleacher."

30 GURUŠ ga-za-ru (HSS X 71:6).

Sarg. and Ur III PN:

| Ga-za-ru (G)
| Ga-za-ru-um (2 NT 634, U).

KŠʾ$_6$? kašāwum?

x MÁŠ (šu-ut PN$_1$ ši PN$_2$) PN$_3$ ik-su-am (D 235).

KŠʾ$_x$?, see TKŠ? takšium.

KŠD kašādum "to reach," "to arrive," "to conquer."

in 1 MU NS. 2 rivers ik-su-tu (D 231; 236, date).

Sarg. and Ur III PN's:

Ga-si-id-^{d}A-ba$_4$ (RTC 95+)
| ^{d}EN.ZU-ga-si-id (Porada, CPML No. 284, U)
| ^{d}EN.ZU-ga-ši-id (A 5281, U)

| Ik-su-tum (E+)
| Ik-šu-tum (U 1706+)

Ik-su-zi-na-at (MO). "He (the new-born boy) has arrived for them (sisters)"

Ì-lu-ga-sa-ad (RA VIII 158 AO 5659).

kišādum "neck."

I seized him ki gal-bi-im ì-na ki-ša-ti-šu, ki me-ra-ni-im ì-na pi-ir-ti-šu (3 NT 30, U, cf. ṣabātum).

KŠKT? kiškattûm (class of working people).

Lw. from Sum. GIŠ.KIN.TI.

Ur III GN:

Ki-iš-ga-ti^{KI} (CT XXXII 20 i; 22 v).

Ur III PN:

Giš-ga-ti (HSS IV 67 rev.).

KŠP.

Ur III PN:

Ki-iš-bu-bi-ru (Orient. XLVII 54). Meaning unknown.

KŠR, see GŠR.

KŠZP kišzappum "threshing board."

40 GIŠ.KA ki-iš-za-bi (FM 33:17)

80 si-na-at ki-iš-za-bi (ibid. l. 31)

40 GIŠ ki-iš-za-bi (ibid. l. 36).

KT'$_7$ taktijum.

DUB dak-ti GÁN ù É ù NI.DU.DU (D 155). Ununderstandable.

KTL?

Sarg. GN:

Ku-tu-la-at (G).

KTM naktamtum "cover."

na-ak-da-ma-at ap-tim "covers for the window" (FM 41:1).

KTM?

Ur III Amorite PN:

Ga-at-ma-nu-um MAR.TU (A 5158).

KTN kutānum (a garment).

TÚG gu-da-núm (HSS X 217 x+7)

4 TÚG gu-da-nu (MDP XXVIII 524)

2 TÚG gu-da-na-an (ibid.).

KTN kutnum (cloth).

gu-ut-nu-um with its measurements (FM 11:13).

KZL, see GZL.

KZZ, see GZZ.

L

L lu- with verb forming a Precative "may ...."

Written lu, occasionally lú in PN's.

li-sa-me-id-ma, li-ti-in, li-zu-ur-ma, li-zu-ru, li-zi-ib (HSS X 5)

li-zu-ur (HSS X 6:4)

li-se$_{11}$-rí-am (HSS X 6 rev. x+2)

li-li-am (HSS X 7:6)

li-iš-bu (HSS X 10)

li-se$_{11}$-bi-lam (HSS X 10; 11)

[l]i-iṣ-ba-at (HSS X 11:12)

lu tu-mu-at "may thou be conjured" (RA XXIII 25)

lu ti-da "may thou know" (JRAS 1932 p. 296:41). Or "truly you know"

lu tal-gu-ut (RA XXXIV 173f., Mari)

a-na-ku-ú lu GEMÉ (Yondorf a, U)

25? UD li-im-la-ma "when 25? days pass" (Cop. 10055).

Sarg. and Ur III PN's:

DINGIR-lu-ba-ni (TMH n.F. I/II p. 18+, U)

I-sar-lu-ba-lí-iṭ (UET III 28, U)

I-šar-lú-ba-lí-⌈iṭ⌉ (UET III 49, U)

Lú-ba-lí-iṭ! (Arnold, ABTR 8 rev., U)

Lu?(wr. KU)-ba-lí-iṭ (UET III 264, U)

Lú-ba-na (G)

L[u]-ba-na (FM)

Lú-be-lu (G+)

Lu-da-mi-iq (TCL II 5484, U)

Lu-da-na-at (MO)

Lu-da-rí (ITT IV p. 11, 7105, U)

Lu-šá-lim (E+)

Lú-ša-lim (U 2043+). Not Awīl-ša-lim.

lū "verily."

ù-má .... in ra-ma-ni-ga lu da-na-da-nu "I swear that verily yourself shall give" (JRAS 1932 p. 296:33)

ú-má lu a-ga-ma-lu-su$_4$ "I swear that verily I shall spare him" (Ist. Mus. Lagash 11001 rev.)

DN's ú-má la zu-ra-tim lu gi-ni-iš-ma "by DN's I swear: 'they are not lies, verily, it is true'" (R xxiii; RA VIII 136; M xxvii; RA VII 105)

ni?-is-ku-su a-na? GN lu it-tal-ku "his nisqū verily went to GN" (Ist. Mus. Lagash 11001 rev.).

ûlū "or," < û+lū "or verily."

su-tu-uḫ-ḫa-tim ù-lu ki-sa-ma-ri te-ir-rí-iš (FM 52 rev.). Ununderstandable.

L'$_1$ lâ "not."

Written la.

Before a noun:

la ba-ti-tum "unopened," "virgin" (MDP XIV 90)

la ḫa-bi-el a-wi-lim "the non-oppressor of man" (YOS IX 62, Dêr)

la zu-ra-tim "not lies" (R xxiii; xxvi; RA VIII 136; M xxvii)

la zu-ra-tum (RA VII 105, Mi.)

la-ga-ma-al (an object; see under GML)

Sarg. and Ur III PN's:

La-á-ra-ab (FM)

La-'à-ra-ab (D+)

La-'à-ra-bu-um (Gutian king)

La-ra-bu-um (AnOr VII 42 rev., U)

La-ba-a'-šum (Gadd, EDSA Pl. 3)

La-da-bu-um MAR.TU (PDTI 335, U)

La-gi-pum (MO+)

La-gi-bu-um (RTC 249 ii; U 1892)
La-gi-bu (TMH n.F. I/II p. 21, U)
La-gi-ip (U 1893+)
La-gi$_4$-ip (UET III p. 19, U)
La-ì-ni-iš (JCS X 30 No. 10 rev., U)
La-ma-ḫa-ar (U 1899+)
La-te-ni-iš (UET III 1215 vi, U)
La-te-in-iš(-E) (TCL V 6163, U).

Before a verb in Subj., in subordinate clause:
lu tu-mu-at .... la da-mu-ru .... la da-la-ʾà-mu .... la dag-ru-s[a]?-am .... la tu-sa-bu (RA XXIII 25:12ff.)
he swore la a-ra-ga-mu (RA XXXII 190, U)
ì-nu .... la i-ti-nu-šum (PBS V 36 rev. x+iii)
ma-na-ma la i-mu-ru (PBS V 36 rev. x+ii)
a-ti PA.TE.SI la ù-wa-e-ru-uš (HSS X 12:11)
Sargon šu ^{d}En-líl ma-ḫi-ra la i-ti-nu-šum (S iv; viii; ix).

Perhaps also in the following cases, where verbs in Indic. may represent second and third forms in subordinate clauses:
^{d}Innin ma-ḫi-ra la it-ti-šum (UET I 274 ii, NS.)
[....] ma-ḫi-ra la da-at-ti-in-šum-ma (RA VIII 34 i, NS.?)
ma-na-ma .... la ib-ni (R xxvii). Lâ after indefinite pronoun
ma-na-ma la i-lí-ik (UET I 274 ii, NS.)
mim-ma-su la ti-su (FM 8:15).

In interr. sentences:
mi-nu-um aš-da-na-ba-ra-ma la du-ša-ba-lam "how is it that I write to you continuously and you do not send me (the silver)?" (NBC 5378, U, soon to be publ. by Sollberger)
á-tum mi-nim la è/i-e-sa-ru (D 290 rev.). Doubtful.

After šumma:
šum-ma .... ŠE la i-ma-ḫa-ru (HSS X 5:12).

ulâ < u+lâ "not."

Written ù-la, once ú-la in the 2nd example.

Before a verb:
ma-ma-na ba-ni-su ù-la u-ba-al "he does not give pardon to anybody" (S xii; xv)
e-ri-ib-su ú-la ip-ru-us (MDP IV Pl. 2 iv)
ZÍD.BA-ṣu ù-la e-bí-iš "his flour ration he will not make" (FM 53 rev.)
a-na a-mu-te ù-la e-bí-iš? (MDP II p. 63 ii; XIV p. 20 ii)
GÁN-lam ù-la a-ru-uš (JRAS 1932 p. 296:9)

x silver .... ù-la a-ḫu-uz (BM 54309 i)
a-na-gu mim-ma ù-la a-ga-bi (ibid. l. 25)
ad-da MÁŠ.ANŠE ù-la da-na-za-ar (ibid. l. 37)
a-na 10 ŠE.GUR ù-la da-ki-ba-an-ni (EK III Pl. XI W. 1929, 160).

Before a verbal phrase:
mi-núm ù-la a-bí ad-da "why are you not my father?" (ibid.)
in DUB-su ù-la ḫu-bu-ut (BIN VIII 141)
ù-la KUG.BABBAR ù-la URUDU DÙL-su "his statue is not of silver (and) is not of copper" (MDP II p. 63 ii; XIV p. 20 ii).

Ur III PN's:
Ú-la-ì-ni-iš (U 1128+; CT XXXII 23 i; 26 ii; TCL II 5484 rev.; Nies, UDT 115)
Ú-li-ì-ni-iš (Nies, UDT 97:11)
Ú-la-e-ni-iš (Univ. Illinois 147)
Ú-la-ni-iš (PDTI 579 rev.).

Lʾ$_{x}$?
li-tum GUR (FM 41:4, school text?).

Lʾ$_{3\text{-}5}$ʾ$_{7}$ la'ājum "to be strong," "to prevail."
Sarg. and Ur III PN's:
íl-e-da-núm (RTC 203+)
íl-e-^{d}EN.ZU (D)
íl-[e]?-ma-al-[kum]? (D)
íl-e-mu-bí (Iraq Mus. 43612)
íl-e-sar (ITT II/2 p. 6, 2914+)
íl-e-um (Kish 1930, 406 rev. i+)
íl-te-um (Kish 1930, 144a rev. iii)
Ì-lí-ši-na-at (Nikolski, Dok. II 361, U). Cf. I-li-šu-nu-ti (Delaporte, CCL II A 536, OB)
Ì-lí-si-na-at (RTC 429, U).

Lʾ$_{3\text{-}5}$ʾ$_{7}$? la'ium, le'ûm "strong?"
Ur III PN's:
I-sar-la-e (TMH I/II 7:12)
I-sar-la-ì (YOS IV 224)
I-sar-li-i (PDTI 186)
La-i-um (Porada, CPML No. 553 E). Cf. La-ú-um, La-i-im, etc. in ARMT XV 151, Mari.

lîtum "strength." See also ʾ$_{7}$D idum.
Ur III PN:
^{d}Šul-gi-li-ti(-ti)? (HSS IV 47 rev.).

Lʾ$_{6}$ʾ$_{3}$ lî'um "(stone) tablet."

Akk. lw. in Sum.:

li-um (Thureau-Dangin, SAKI p. 94 v 3; vi 4, Gudea). Cf. also li-um-ma gur-ru-dè/dam in OB inscriptions pertaining to Narâm-Sin and Lugalannimundu (Güterbock, ZA XLII 26:20 and 40:5)

60 li-um GAG (RTC 221 v)

1 li-im GAG (RTC 225 i). Doubtful.

Lʾ$_6$B?

Sarg. PN's:

La-wi-ib-tum (FM)

Lá-wi-ib-tum (FM)

La-wi-pu⌈m⌉ (D).

Lʾ$_x$B?

Sarg. PN:

La-e-pum (D+).

Lʾ$_3$M <u>laʾāmum</u> "to taste."

GAR KAŠ la da-la-ʾà-mu "(you are conjured) that you may not taste bread (and) beer" (RA XXIII 25:13).

Lʾ$_x$M?

DN? in PSarg. PN:

I-ku-La-im? (CT XXXII 8 iv A).

Lʾ$_x$M.

Sarg. and Ur III PN's:

La-mu-sa (MO+)

La-mu-ša (HSS IV p. 32+, U)

La-muš-ša (A 5169, U). Cf. Ur-La-muš-ša in JRAS 1937 p. 472 No. 4, U

La-mu-  (G+)

La-muš (Reisner, TUT 105 i, U)

La-mu-um (MO+).

Lʾ$_x$N.

Ur III Amorite PN:

La-a-mu-um MAR.TU (De Genouillac, TD 25 iii).

LBʾ$_x$ <u>labʾum</u> or <u>labwum</u> or <u>labûm</u> "lion."

See discussion in MAD II 190f.

Sarg. and Ur III PN's:

A-mur-la-ba (RTC 197; 198)

Be-lí-la-ba (D+)

Da-a-ga-la-ba (SO IX/1 No. 36:10, U)

DINGIR-la-ba (G+)

DINGIR-su-la-ba (MO)

Eš$_4$-dar-la-ba (D)

^{d}ÍD-la-ba (A 4853+)

I-nin-la-ba (G; KAH II 1:3, U)

It-be-la-ba (Kish 1930, 144a; 170d, collated)

KA-la-⌈ba⌉? (D)

La-ba-DINGIR (ZA XII 332)

La-ba-Ù (BE I Pl. V ii+). Ù is a DN

Sar-ru-la-ba (RTC 112+)

Si-la-ba (D)

Šu-la-pi (BE I Pl. VI i)

Ur III GN:

Sar-ru-la-ba (ZA LI Pl. II after p. 74 iii 18, 19).

labâtum "lioness."

Sarg. PN:

Si-la-ba-at (D+).

LB'$_x$?

ù šum-ma PN_1 ù PN_2 la?-ba-a (HSS X 11:10).

LBB libbum? "heart."

[ŠÀ.BA (HSS X 38 iii x+2) corresponds to Akk. in kir-bí-su].

Sarg. PN:

Tu-da-LUGAL-li-bí-iš (D+). Interpr. unknown

Tu-da-sar-li-bí-iš (D+).

LBK?

various objects?, including na-al-ba-na-tum, šu-ut la-ba-ak (NAGAR) (FM 43:7, school text?).

LBN labānum "to make bricks."

Mi. la-bi-in SIG_4 la ma-ni-tim (CT XXXII 1 i = RA VIII 180) in CM.

libittum "brick."

Normally written logographically as SIG_4; see above and passim.

nalbattum "brick mould."

various objects?, including na-al-ba-na-tum, šu-ut la-ba-ak (NAGAR) (FM 43:6, school text?).

LBN.

DN in Ur III PN:

Šu-La-ba-an (Barton, HLC II Pl. 97, 122 rev.).

LBR lubburum "to make old," "to make live long."

Ur III PN:

^{d}Šu-^{d}EN.ZU-li-la-bi-ir-ḫa-da-am "may ŠS. make old the rule" (CT XXXII 12 i).

labirum "old."

LIBIR-ù (HSS X 134:3; 208:6). Interpr. unknown.

Ur III PN:

La-bi-ru-um (Barton, HLC III p. 41+).

LBŠ lubuštum (a garment).

1 TÚG lu-bu-uš-<tum> (MDP XXVIII 526, U?).

LG, see LKʾ$_x$ lakjum.

LḪḪ laḫḫum.

Ur III MN:

^{ITI}La-ḫu-um (MDP XXVIII 467; Oppenheim, CCTE No. 25* rev.). Cf. MN La-aḫ-ḫu-um in Susa texts (Langdon, BM p. 46) and La-ḫi-im at Mari (Studia Mariana p. 48 n. 13).

Ur III PN:

La-ḫi-^{d}En-líl (PDTI 563 ii).

LḪM laḫmum (an ox-like animal).

x+5 gu(d)-za-rí-ku?!(wr. ŠÈ) 2 la-aḫ-ma-an KUG.GI "x+5 kusarikkum(-figurines) and 2 laḫmum(-figurines) of gold" (PBS IX 30). For the animal cf. Landsberger, Fauna p. 55. Cf. also kusarikkum and laḫmum together in the Agum-kakrime inscription (V R 33 iv 50f.)

Cf. also la-ḫa-ma (Thureau-Dangin, SAKI p. 116 xxiv 27, Gudea), ^{d}Laḫma/u (Deimel, PB No. 1816), and ^{d}La-ḫa-ma, ^{d}La-ḫa-mu, ^{d}La-ḫa-mun (ibid. Nos. 1795ff.).

DN in Ur III PN:

Dan-La-aḫ-[ma-at] (De Genouillac, TD 62 rev.). Cf. MDP XXVIII 546:5, OB

Dan-La-ma-at (MCS VI 85 AO 10342 rev.).

LKʾ$_x$? lakjum "small" (or the like).

Sarg. PN:

La-gi-tum (FM 40:9). Cf. ^{f}Lakîtum in Stamm, ANG p. 267.

LL? lillum?

Sarg. and Ur III PN's:

Li-li (FM; D)

Li-lum (RTC 91 iii+; PDTI 517, U).

LL?

Ur III PN:

Lu-li (PDTI 103).

LLʾ$_x$ lalāʾum "desire?," "fullness."

Sarg. and Ur III PN's:

AMA-la-lum (RA XIX 42 No. LX, U)

DINGIR-la-la (D)

La-la (U 1894+)

La-a-la-a (Jean, ŠA LXVIII rev. i, U)

La-la-a (MAD II 76, U)

La-la-MU (ibid.)

La-lí-a (ibid.)

La-lí-MU (ibid.)

La-lí (Porada, CPML No. 239; U 1902+)

La-lí-ša (TCL V 6039 rev. iii, U)

La-a-lum (CT III 35 i, U)

Tab-la-la-ki "good is your fullness" (A 3026, U).

LLM lulumtum (a garment).

Akk. lw. in Ur III Sum.:

10 TÚG lu-lu-um-tum ŠU.NIR KI.LAL.BI 4 2/3 MA.NA (PDTI 540)

Cf. luluntum = naḫlaptu tâḫazi in CT XVIII 18:82, Synonym list, and a royal lulumtum in RA XXXV 2 ii 8, Mari ritual.

LIŠ liliššum (a musical instrument). Corresponds to later lilissum.

1 URUDU li-li-iš KI.LAL.BI 2 MA.NA (TCL V 6055 ii, U). Cf. Sum. LI.LI.ÈŠ (ŠL II 59, 22) and LI.LI.EŠ (JCS III 7).

LMG?

PSarg. and Sarg. PN's:

LAM-gi-um (MO)

LAM+KUR-gi-um (ITT II/2 p. 27, 4482)

LAM-gi$_4$-Ma-rí (RA XXXI 140, PSarg.).

LMN lamnum, limnum "bad."

DN's ar-ra-dam [l]a?-mu-ut-dam-li-ru-ru-uš (PBS V 36 rev. iv, NS.)

DN's ar-ra-dam la-mu-dam li-ru-ru-uš (UET I 276 ii, NS.)

DN's ir-ra-dam li-mu-dam li-ru-ru-uš (Morgan, MSP IV 161 ii, Lullubum)

LÚ-lam? lam-nam (MDP XIV 90 rev.).

LMS lamassum (a demon).

Ur III PN's:

La-ma-zi (U 1898)

La-ma-zum (Oppenheim, CCTE p. 191)

La-ma-sá (U 1897)

La-ma-ša (U 1900; UET III 1000). Here a figurine.

lamass(a)tum (a demon).

3 ^{d}LAMA-tum$_x$ KUG.GI (UET III 686, U). Here a figurine.

Sarg. and Ur III PN's:

La-ma-as?-tum (FM)

La-ma-za-tum (UET III 1357, U).

LMŠ?

Sarg. GN:

La-ma-šum (G).

LP luppum (a leather container).

Akk. luppum is lw. from Sum.?:

x ^{KUŠ}LU.ÚB of flour (BIN VIII 132; 260; 280)

x LU.ÚB of flour (BIN VIII 276)

84 ^{KUŠ}LU.ÚB (RTC 239 rev. i, U).

LPP?

Sarg. PN:

La-bi-pum (D).

LPT šulputum "to ravage."

ma-na-ma GN_1 ù GN_2 la u-sa-al-bí-tu (UET I 275 i, NS.).

liptum "touch" (or the like).

Sarg. and Ur III PN's:

Li-bí-it-ì-li (YOS I 10)

^{d}Šu-^{d}EN.ZU-li-bi-it-É-a (UET III 1357, U).

LPT? liptum?

36 GÁN [šu]? li-ip-tim (D 332:10).

$LQ^{\text{ʾ}}_3$ laqāʾum "to take."

KUG.BABBAR PN íl-gi-ma (D 282:6)

e-nu PN šu-ut PN íl-gi-am-ma it-ba-lu (FM 7:23).

LQP, see $Q^{\text{ʾ}}_7$P.

LQT laqātum "to tear out."

Written syllabically only.

DN SUḪUŠ-su li-zu-uḫ ù ŠE.NUMUN-su li-il-gu-ut (S iv)

⌈....⌉ a-ti-⌈ma⌉ ḫu-rí KUG íl-gu-ut (M xxvi)

^{d}Innin ŠE.NUMUN-šu lu tal-gu-ut (RA XXXIV 173f., Mari)

2 DN's SUḪUŠ-su li-zu-ḫa ù ŠE.NUMUN-su li-il-gu-da (PBS V 34 x, Lugalzagesi; RA XXI 66 and 71, S.; S ix, xi twice, xv; R xviii twice, xix, xx; xxi twice, xxiv, xxv, xxvi, xxvii; RA VIII 136; 139; Mi.; NS.; BE I 2, Škš.; MDP II p. 66; ZA IV 406, Gutium)

2 DN's .... li-il-gu-da(m) (RA VIII 200 end, NS.)

2 DN's MU-šu li-il-gu-da (RA IX Pl. 1, Urkiš and Nawar)

3! DN's SUḪUŠ-šu li-zu-ḫa ú ŠE.NUMUN-[š]u li-il-ku-da (AOF III 112, Mari)

DN's SUḪUŠ-su li-zu-ḫu ù ŠE.NUMUN-su li-il-gu-tu (BE I 120, NS.; BE 1, Škš.; MDP VI Pl. 2, 1 ii)

DN's ŠE.NUMU[N-su] li-i⌈l⌉-gu-[du] SUḪUŠ-[su] li-iš-ba-al-ki-du (MDP II p. 63 iii)

DN's SUḪUŠ-[su] li-zu(wr. su)-ḫu ù NUMUN-[su] li-il-[gu-du] (MDP IV Pl. 2 v)

DN's zé-ra-šu? li-il-ku-du (Morgan, MSP IV 161, Lullubum).

LQT?

PSarg. PN:

La-ga-tum (OIP XIV 51 ii).

LQT?

Sarg. PN's:

Lu-ga-tum (Kish 1930, 144a rev. ii). Cf. Lú-ga-tum in PBS VII 7:5, 22, OB

Lu?!-ga-ti-a (Porada, CPML No. 253).

LŠ lišānum "tongue," "blade."

1 ḫa-zi-núm šu 4 EME-su "1 ax with 4 blades" (MDP IV Pl. 2 iii). Construction with BÀD-si-in "their 'covers'" (ibid.) shows that lišānum is of fem. gender.

Sarg. and Ur III PN:

Li-sa-núm (MO)
Li-sá-núm (RA XIX 35, U)
Li-ša-núm (U 2225+).

LTK latākum.

1(PI) KAŠ.Ú.SA PN a-na la-da-ki-im (HSS X 160 iii x+8)

Cf. von Soden, Orient. n.s. XX 162ff.

LTM?

e-nam la-?tim-dam ....-dam E.SIG ZÉ (MDP XIV 90). Sign tim clear, but read perhaps mun? (LMN).

LZZ luzzuzum.

Sarg. PN:

Lú-zu-zum (G)
Lu-zu-zum (MO)

Cf. von Soden, Orient. n.s. XX 266f.

M

M miš = mi + iš "where?." See also MN.

Sarg. PN:

Mi-iš-da-ti "where is my beloved?" (E). Cf. DINGIR.MU me-e-eš at-ta "my god, where are you?" (Craig, Assyro-Babylonian Religious Texts II 7:7).

mišum = mi + iš + um "why?"

[m]i?-šum [á]š-tu-ru "as? I wrote" (FM 53:4).

Sarg. PN's:

Ì-lí-me-šum (G)
I-li(m)-me-šum (Carnegie, Catalogue of the Southesk Collection Qe 6).

This reading is more plausible than I-ši-me-dak-lí

I-nin-me-šum (MO)

Li-bur-me-šum (Kish 1930, 559c).

M -ma, ma "and." Cf. also adîma, appunama, enma, ištumma, kalama, kaluma?, mammana, manama, mimma, matîma, šuma, šumma.

Between verbs or sentences; -ma attached to a verb:

li-sa-me-id-ma li-ti-in "may he procure and give" (HSS X 5:7)

.... šu-ut PN íl-gi-am-ma it-ba-lu ".... which PN took and carried away" (FM 7:23)

PN íl-gi-ma a-na ga-bar-tim i-ti-in (D 282)

x GURUŠ.GURUŠ in URU^{KI}.URU^{KI} Šu-me-rí-im u-su-zi-am-ma a-na ga-ra-si-im iš-kùn (R xvii, xix, xxi twice)

ma-na-ma MU R. LUGAL KIŠ u-sa-za-ku-ma al DÙL R. MU-su i-sa-ga-nu-ma DÙL-mi-me i-ga-pi-ù (R xviii, xxiv, etc.)

ù ba-ni ENGAR.ENGAR li-zu-ur-ma e-ri-su-nu li-zu-ru da-ni-iš "and may he watch the faces? of the farmers and may they watch strongly their cultivation" (HSS X 5 rev.)

Cf. also ŠPR šapārum.

-ma attached to a verb in a final clause:

en-ma PN_1 a-na PN_2 ki-bí-ma "thus says PN_1, say to PN_2" (passim in letters)

in du!-a-rí-su GN na-ki-ir-ma SAG.GIŠ.RA "in his return he vanquished GN (which) had rebelled (against him)" (R xvii)

ib-ba-al-gi-it-ma "if he transgresses, then ...." (Louvre AO 8959)

.... zu-si-ib-ma "settle ...." (JRAS 1932 p. 296:13)

ti-bu-dam li-se_{11}-ù-ni-kum-ma "may (the workers) help you" (ibid. l. 19).

Attached to a noun:

a-bu-na-ma Gu-ti-um-ma-me GÁN-lam ù-la a-ru-uš a daq-bí "do not say: 'the Gutian is (here) in large numbers?, and (therefore) I could not plough the field'" (JRAS 1932 p. 296:7)

a-na-lim-ma ki a-la-kam "when I shall come to the city" (ibid. l. 34).

Sarg. and Ur III PN's:

Á-bí-lum-ma (U 76+)

| A-ḫu-ma (G; U 140+)

| A-ḫu-um-ma (U 139+)

Be-lí-ma (TMH n.F. I/II 138, U)

Dan-ma-lum (Nikolski, Dok. II 48 rev.)

DINGIR-ma (Iraq Mus. 43612). Same PN in Kh. 1935, 79 and 101, OB

DINGIR-ma-a-bí? (A 4979, U)

ì-lí-mi-la-at /Ilī-ma-Illat/ (3 NT 796 iii, U)

ì-lum-ma (TCL V 6165 rev. twice, U)

KA-ma-DINGIR (ITT I 1365+)

Sar-ma-ì-lum (OIP LIII 147 No. 5, PSarg.). Cf. Ass. king Šar-ma-^{d}Adad and Sar-ru-um-ma-DINGIR quoted in Gemser, BPN p. 178 n. 3

Za-ak-lum-ma (YOS IV 212 ii, U).

Unattached particle:

mi-núm ù-la a-bi ad-da (beg. of line:) ma a-na 10 ŠE.GUR ù-la da-ki-ba-an-ni "how is it that you behave like not my father and did not trust me with 10 GUR of barley" (EK III Pl. XI W. 1929, 160)

DN_1 .... ti-a-am-dam a-lí-dam i-ki-iš-šum (beg. of line:) ma in GIŠ.TUKUL-ki DN_2 .... NS. GN's en-ar "DN_1 .... presented to him the Upper Sea, and with the weapon of DN_2 NS. conquered GN's" (UET I 275 i, NS.).

M <u>-me</u>. Cf. also annime.

A particle indicating direct speech or quotation.

DÙL-mi-me i-ga-pi-ù "(whoever) says: '(this is) my statue'" (R xviii, xxiv)

DÙL-mi-me i-ga-bi-ù (UET I 276 i, NS.)

MU-su-me bí-si$_4$-iṭ-ma MU-mi su-gu-u[n] i-ga-bi-⌈ù⌉ "(whoever) says: 'erase his name and put my name'" (UET I 276 i, NS.)

MU-mi-me su-gu-un i-ga-pi-ù (PBS V 36 rev. x+iv, NS.)

a-bu-na-ma Gu-ti-um-ma-me GÁN-lam ù-la a-ru-uš a daq-bí "do not say: '(here) is the Gutian in large numbers?, and (therefore) I could not plough the field'" (JRAS 1932 p. 296:7)

uš-bi-ma MÁŠ.ANŠE-me Gu-ti-ù it-ru-ù ù a-na-gu mim-ma ù-la a-ga-bi (ibid. l. 22). Interpr. difficult

en-ma PN_1 a-na PN's a-zé-ḫa-me da-ni-iš da-ni-iš "thus says PN_1 to PN's: 'I laughed very heartily'" (D 298:6, 15)

en-ma a-na-gu-ma sá-bi-NI(-)a-me u-ga-al (Ist. Mus. Lagash 11001). Interpr. difficult

li-iš-ru-ga-me ù .... li-li-kam?-me (Kish 1930, 170c). Interpr. difficult.

$Mʾ_1$ <u>miʾatum</u>? "hundred."

 MÁ ᴅ mi-at D EL.ŠUM.KI (Iraq IV 185, A 381 and A 393).

M_7 <u>maʾū</u> "water."

aṣ-ba-zu ki ma-ì, áp-ru-uk-šu ki na-ri-im "I seized him like water, I closed him in like a river" (3 NT 30, U). Cf. ṣabātum.

A form meʾū may exist in the following RN.

Ur III RN:

^{fD}Me-^{d}En-líl-lá, Gen. (De Genouillac, Kich II D 60 rev.)

Me-EN-ì-lí (ZA LI Pl. I after p. 74 ii 2, 4, IV iv 1, 2)

Cf. also PN's under $M^{\supset}_{x}$ mûm, MBRK? meburkum, ^{fD}Me-e-Ku-bi (VAS XIII 87:5, OB), A.MEŠ-^{d}En-líl (II R 52, No. 2c 62), and the discussion by Kraus in ZA LI 71 and 73.

$M^{\supset}_{x}$ mûm?

Reading ME may be preferred to IŠIB if Me-e-Ku-bi (MDP XXVIII 401:16, OB) can be identified with Me-Ku-bi (MDP II p. 80, OB).

PSarg., Sarg., and Ur III PN's:

⌈ME⌉-^{d}AB+ḪA (D)

ME-DINGIR (D)

ME-^{d}En-líl, f.n. (UET I 51, U)

ME-^{d}IM (JCS X 26 i)

ME-Ìr-ra (FM)

ME?-Iš?-ḫa-ra (D)

ME-Ki-dè (FM)

ME-^{d}NI[N.X] (D)

ME-^{d}Nisaba (D)

| ME-Sá-lim (MO+)

| ME-SILIM (PSarg. king)

ME-ŠEŠ.ŠEŠ (MO)

ME-^{d}Tišpak (D)

Cf. also Ur III RN under $M^{\supset}_{7}$ ma$^{\supset}$ū.

$M^{\supset}_{1}$D ma$^{\supset}$ādum "to be plentiful."

Sarg. and Ur III PN's:

En-ni-ma-ad (UET III p. 13+, U). Or Enni-ma-abī

I-dur-ma-ad (MO). Or I-dur-ma-at

| Im-ti-dam (U 1739+)

| Im-ti-da (RTC 325 rev., U)

| I-ti-dam (ITT V 6887 rev., U)

Ma-ad-na-ḫu-um (FM). Cf. Ma-ad-nu-ru-u[m] in UET V 554:44, OB

Ma-da-am-en-nam (UET III 1052; 1449 rev. i, U).

$M^{\supset}_{x}$L, see $N^{\supset}_{7}$L majjaltum.

$M^{\supset}_{2}$R mûrum (a young animal). Cf. Arabic muhr "poulain"; "premier petit d'une bête."

⌈mur-ni-is⌉-ku, see under NSQ nisqum

mu-ra-áš "her mûrum" (Kish 1930, 143 rev.).

Ur III Amorite PN:

Mu-ra-nu-um MAR.TU (U 2298).

$M^{\supset}_{6}$T muātum "to die."

ki na-tu-ni-a? in bu-bu-tim ("in hunger") ⌈i⌉?-mu-tu (MCS IV 13 rev.).

Sarg. and Ur III PN:

I-mu-tum (D+)

Ì-a-mu-tum MAR.TU (U 2407).

<u>mîtum</u> "dead."

Ur III PN:

^{d}Ìr-ra-il-mi-ti (SO IX/1 No. 31 rev. 1). Doubtful.

<u>mûtum</u> "death."

Ur III PN:

Ù-bi-mu-ú-tum (YOS IV 2). Cf. Ú-KA-ma-tum under Mʾ$_{x}$T. Very doubtful.

Mʾ$_{x}$T <u>mâtum</u> "land," "country."

Although Semitic etymology is unknown, the Sum. form MA.DA is apparently a lw. from Akk. or another Sem. language.

Written logographically MA.DA or KALAM or syllabically.

MA.DA (Thureau-Dangin, SAKI p. 104 xiv 8, Gudea)

a-na MA.DA PN u-bìl (MDP XIV 8 rev.)

PN .... GÌR.NITAḪ MA.DA NIM (RA XXIII 18 No. 2, U)

ARAD-^{d}ŠEŠ.KI PA.TE.SI Sa-bu-um^{KI} ù ma-da Gu-te-bu-um^{KI}-ma .... GÌR.NITAḪ LÚ.SU ù ma-da Kar-da-ka (Thureau-Dangin, SAKI p. 180, ŠS.)

MU BÀD MA.DA^{KI} BA.DÙ (RLA II 142, date of Š. 38)

Various compounds in MA.DA GN^{KI} (UET III p. 44, U)

Sargon LUGAL KALAM.MA^{KI} (S ii, iii, vii, ix)

KALAM^{KI}-zu .... SAG.GIŠ.RA (S viii) = KALAM.MA^{KI}-zu (S ii)

ma-dam a-lí-dam i-ti-šum (S vi, xiv)

a-na ba-la-ti-šu [ù] ba-la-a[ṭ]! [ma]-ti-⌈šu⌉ (Speleers, RIAA 4 ii, Dêr)

Škš. da-núm DINGIR ma-ti X^{KI} (Pope, SPA I 281)

PN GÌR.NITAḪ ma-ti GN (MDP II p. 58, p. 63, etc. in texts from Elam)

ŠU.NIGÍN ma-[ta-tim] (CT XXXII 1 ii, CM)

Ki-maš^{KI} ù ma-at^{KI} Ḫu-úr-tim^{KI} (MDP XIV p. 10 i). Not sure

LUGAL ma-at Wa-ri-im (OIP XLIII 143f., Diyala)

KA.LUM TAR.TAR ma-tim (MDP XIV 34). Interpr. unknown.

Sarg. and Ur III DN's:

^{d}LUGAL-ma-tim (Syria XXI 162f., Mari)

^{d}Nin-ma-da (A 644; Thureau-Dangin, SAKI p. 124 iv 2, Gudea) comparable with Nin-ma-a-túm (RTC 400 iii i, U).

Sarg. and Ur III PN's:

Da-ku-um-ma-tum (UET III p. 9, U)

Da-ku-ma-tum (BE III 116 rev., U)

Da-rí-iš-ma-tum (U 795)

[I]-sar-ma-ti-iš-su (E)

I-dur-ma-at (MO). Or I-dur-ma-ad

Ku-na-ma-tum (Nikolski, Dok. II 450, U; TCL II 4681, U)

Ku-un-si-ma-tum (Jean, ŠA LVIII, U)

MA.DA-ì-lí (BE III 11:14, U)

MA.DA-mu-gi (AnOr VII 295 iii, U). Sum. PN

MA.DA-mu-gi_4 (U 2245; Fish, CST p. 160 vii, U)

^{m}Šu-^{d}EN.ZU-nu-úr-ma-ti-iš-zu (PBS XIII 13 seal, U)

Ú-KA-ma-tum (D). Cf. Ù-bi-mu-ú-tum under $M^{\prime}{}_{6}T$.

$M^{\prime}{}_{x}Ṭ$ mi'ṭum, see MṬ? miṭṭum.

MB?, mu-bí, cf. $^{\prime}{}_{6}P^{\prime}{}_{x}$ mûpium and $NB^{\prime}{}_{x}$ mubbi'um.

MBRK? meburkum (a plant).

Akk. lw. in Ur III Sum.:

x ^{TÚG}da-ki-ru-um me-bur-ku-um LUGAL (UET III 1705 rev. iii, iv), compared with ^{Ú}KI.KAL (a plant) da-ak-ki-ru-um (TMH n.F. I/II 240, U). This plant appears as (el-pi-tum) me-e bur-ki in later periods (CT XIV 40 Rm. 11 41:10).

MD?

Ur III Amorite PN:

Mi-da-nu-um MAR.TU (U 2312).

MD? mudum? (a garment) = muttum? (head covering?).

Akk. lw. in Sum.:

x ^{TÚG}mu-du_8-um SIG_5 (RTC 197; 198; 270, U)

x ^{TÚG}mu-du_8-um (RTC 219; ITT IV p. 45, 7396; p. 50, 7466; p. 56, 7522; 7527; p. 57, 7531; 7533; V 6812; p. 35, 9348; p. 50, 9695, U; 9699, U).

MDD madādum "to measure out."

so much ŠE PN im_x(DU)-tu-ud "he measured out (= sold)" (HSS X 41:4)

so much ÁŠ PN im-tu-ud (CT I 1b twice)

[....] im-[d]u-ud (FM 9:21)

[....] im-tu-ud (D 158)

^{d}EN.KI ÍD-[su a-na] za-ki-ki-im li-im-tu-ud "may E. turn? his river to slime" (CT XXXII 4 xii, CM)

^{d}En-líl ÍD?-su? A li-im-tu-ud "may E. measure out water? (= flood?) for his river?" (UET I 276 ii, NS.)

i-ma-da-ad (RT XIX 57, U, without context).

MDL mudulum (meat-meal).

Akk. lw. in Ur III Sum.:

x UDU.ŠE mu-du-lum (RA IX 57 SA 17; Nikolski, Dok. II 467; sim.

Legrain, TRU 116; 117; Nesbit, SRD 24)

x UDU.ŠE mu-du-lum-MA (YOS IV 207:158)

animal offerings mu-du-lu-ŠÈ (Legrain, TRU 356)

animals mu-du-lum É.KIŠIB.BA.ŠÈ (PDTI 102).

MDL? <u>madalum</u>?

Akk. lw. in Ur III Sum.:

x ^{GIŠ}DIM$_4$ ma-da-lum (TCL V 6044 rev. i, ii)

x URUDU má-da-lum (UET III 740; 752 ii)

Cf. GI.DIM$_4$.ME MÁ.DA.LAL in Salonen, SO VIII/4 p. 119 and x ^{GIŠ}MÁ.
DA.LAL in UET III 272 iii, vi.

MDL? (a bronze or wooden object?).

Akk. lw. in Ur III Sum.:

2 URUDU ma-UD-lum KI.LAL.BI 3 1/2 MA.NA 8 GÍN (UET III 327). Or 2
URUDU.MA UD.LUM (bronze ornaments in form of figs?)

6 URUDU ma-UD-lum KI.LAL.BI 12 MA.NA 4 GÍN (ibid.)

1 GIŠ ma-UD-lum (UET III 835). But cf. x+1 ^{GIŠ}MA nu-zu-ḫum (ibid.).

MDLʾ$_6$, see DLʾ$_6$.

MG? (an object).

4 ma-gi KUG.BABBAR (MDP IV Pl. 2 iii).

MGL? (a boat).

Akk. lw. in Sum.:

má-gi$_4$-lum (Thureau-Dangin, SAKI p. 118 xxvi 13, Gudea).

MGL?

2 ma-ki-lum (HSS X 170:8). Among containers.

MGI?

Ur III FN:

A.ŠÀ Me-gi-il-tum (UET III 1372).

MGN?

Ur III Amorite PN:

Ma-ga-nu-um MAR.TU (Legrain, TRU 295).

MGR?

Ur III PN:

Ma-ga-ru-um (UET III 46).

MGR, see GRN magrattum.

MGR <u>migrum</u> "favorite."

PN mi-kir ^{d}KA.DI (CT XXI 1c, Dêr; YOS IX 62, Dêr; OIP XLIII 155 No.
55, Dêr).

Sarg. and Ur III PN's:

Me-kir-DINGIR.DINGIR (D)

Tu-ki-in-PA-mi-ig-ri-ša (RLA II 146, date, U)

⌈Su⌉?-mi-ig-rí (BIN VIII 121 i)

^{d}Šu-^{d}EN.ZU-mi-kir-^{d}En-líl (Nakahara, ST 47, U)

^{d}Šu-^{d}EN.ZU-mi-kir-Eš$_{4}$-dar (BIN V 29, U; JCS X 30 No. 9, U).

MḪ? maḫatum (an object of reed).

Akk. lw. in Ur III Sum.:

2 ^{GI}ma-ḫa-tum (BE III 76:20).

MḪ?

Sarg. PN:

Me-ḫa-tum (E+).

MḪʾ$_{x}$? miḫʾum? "evening?"

1 UDU in ki-zi-im 1 UDU in me-ḫi?-im ù-mi-sá-am ú-gi-in-šum "1 sheep in the morning?, 1 sheep in the evening?, daily he established" (MDP IV Pl. 2 ii). The sign ḪI looks like ḪI plus a vertical wedge

NS. sa-bi-ir /šāpir/ or /šābir/ KIŠ MI ḪI KALAM NIM^{KI} (UET I 274 i). Sign ḪI plus a vertical wedge. Ununderstandable.

MḪʾ$_{x}$ tamḫiʾum "evening."

ur-rí tam-ḫi-e "mornings and evenings" (MDP IV Pl. 2 ii).

MḪʾ$_{x}$ maḫḫûm (a profession).

A lw. from Sum.:

a-na ^{LÚ}MAḪ-im ša ^{d}Innin ša Gír-zu^{KI} (RA XXIV 44, U, copied ZU, transliterated SU).

MḪʾ$_{x}$? muḫḫûtum (a fem. profession).

ir-e-mu ú-da-bi-bu-si-ma ù iš-ku-nu-⌈si⌉? a-na mu-ḫu-tim "the irʾemū have ....ed her and placed her ...." (Kish 1930, 143 rev.). Cf. LÚ muḫḫûm and SAL muḫḫûtum at Mari (von Soden, WO I 400; also TCL XXVII 45).

MḪḪ muḫḫum "top."

SÁ.DUG$_{4}$ a-na mu-úḫ SÁ.DUG$_{4}$ lu u-ra-ad-di (CT XXXII 1 iii, CM).

MḪR maḫārum "to receive."

Object: grain, silver, bronze, garments, flour, animals, skins:

i-ma-ḫa-ru (HSS X 5 rev.; Kish 1930, 152 rev.)

àm-ḫur (A 748)

dam-ḫur, Fem. (D 119; 187 ii; BIN VIII 124; BE I Pl. VII v; Louvre AO 7983 rev.; 8961)

im-ḫur (HSS X 45 rev.; 47 rev.; 48 rev.; 58 rev.; 59; 63 rev.; 65 rev.; 66; 75; 76; 83 twice; 92; 105; 107; 108 rev.; 120 rev.; 126; 132; 136 twice; 144; 160 iv; 185 vi; 190 rev.; D 18 rev. twice; 45 x+ii; 51 x+i; 128; 150 rev.; 157; 168 x+iii; 179; 187; 200; 201; 292 rev.; 316; 321 rev.; 334; FM 3; RTC 108 rev.; 117 rev.; 202 rev.; ITT I 1296; MDP XIV 7; 12; 13; 21; 45; 48; 76; OIP XIV 165;

188; CT I 1c rev.; JCS I 348a rev.; b obv., rev.; PBS IX 122 rev.; BIN VIII passim)

im_x(DU)-ḫur (Kish 1930, 141)

ím-ḫu-ur (CT XXXII 2 iv, CM)

im-ḫu-ru, Subj. (HSS X 41 rev.; 81 rev.; 132)

im-ḫu-ru, Pl. (HSS X 60 rev.; 187 v; D 58; 80; 168 x+ii; 328 rev.; PBS IX 119)

im-ḫur-ru, Pl. (HSS X 103 rev., wr. im-ḪI-ru); 123 rev.; BE I Pl. VI vii, VIII; Kish 1930, 138

im-ḫu-ra, Du. (HSS X 42 rev.; 77; 82 rev.; 136; 185 v; D 51 x+ii; 67 x+ii; 269 rev.; 328)

im-ḫur-ra, Du. (BE I Pl. VIII iv; Louvre AO 8960 rev.).

barley, silver ana šîmē X maḫārum "to receive barley, silver for the price of X," i.e. "to sell":

barley PN_1 [a-n]a ŠÁM PN_2 [i]š-dè PN_3 [i]m-ḫur (HSS X 99 rev.)

barley a-na ŠÁM DUN PN im-ḫur (HSS X 107 rev.)

silver a-na ŠÁM PN_1 PN_2 im-ḫur (D 33 twice)

silver a-na ŠÁM-me ŠIM PN im-ḫur (D 2 rev.; 279 rev.; 300 rev.)

silver a-na ŠÁM-me PN_1 PN's KUG.BABBAR im-ḫu-ru (Iraq Mus. 43612)

silver a-na ŠÁM-me ⌈SÍG⌉ PN_1 PN_2 [im-ḫ]u-ra (D 162)

15 KUG.BABBAR GÍN a-na NÍG.ŠÁM 2 KUG.GI GÍN PN_1 iš-dè PN_2 im-ḫur (Louvre AO 8638).

x GÁN šîmūšu x KUG.BABBAR and/or x ŠE PN imḫur "PN sold x field for the price of x silver and/or barley":

x GÁN NÍG.ŠÁM-su x KUG.BABBAR .... PN im-ḫur (BE I Pls. VIff. passim)

x GÁN ŠÁM-su x KUG.BABBAR and/or x ŠE PN im-ḫur (D 45; 48; 50; 51; 52; 67; 74; 111; 119; 128; 168). In most cases value in silver, payment in barley.

ana ḫubullim maḫārum "to receive on loan," i.e. "to borrow":

silver and barley a-na ḫu-bu-lim PN im-ḫur (D 291)

barley šu PN ḫu-bu-lam im-ḫu-ru (D 11).

Meaning "to be in front of somebody," "to come to somebody," "to confront."

With Dat.:

ki-ib-ra-tu[m] ar-ba-um iš-ti-ni-iš i-ḫa-ni-su_4-ma im-ḫu-ru-nim "the four quarters together were subdued? and faced me," i.e. "submissively face me" (PBS V 36 rev. x+ii, NS.)

ki-ib-[ra-tum] a[r-ba-um ....] i[š-ti]-ni-i[š] im_x(DU)-ḫu-r[u]-ni-su_4-ma .... "the four quarters together faced him and ...." (Böhl, MAW Letterkunde 76B No. 9 p. 12).

With Acc.:

su$_4$ li-im-ḫu-ra-an-ni "may he come to me" (Ist. Mus. Lagash 11001 rev. twice).

Sarg. and Ur III PN's:

Dam-ḫur-^{d}UTU, f.n. (NBC, unnumbered)

La-ma-ḫa-ar (U 1899+; De Genouillac, TD 60, U)

Mi-da-ḫar (ITT II/1 p. 26, 783, U). Cf. Mittallik under MLK

^{d}Šu-^{d}EN.ZU-la-ma-ḫa-ar (U 900+).

<u>māḫirum</u> "recipient."

PN's ma-ḫi-ru KUG.BABBAR (D 303:13; BE I Pl. VII ix)

ma-ḫi-ru (MCS IV 13 rev.)

(2 women) ma-ḫi-ir-da KUG.BABBAR (Univ. Michigan 509).

<u>māḫirum</u> "the one who is in front," "an adversary."

Sargon šu ^{d}En-líl ma-ḫi-ra la i-ti-nu-šum (S iv; viii; x)

Sargon šu ^{d}En-líl ma-ḫi-ra la i-ti-<nu>-šum (S vi)

Rîmuš šu ^{d}[En-líl] ma-[ḫi-ra] l[a i-ti-nu-šum] (R xxii)

^{d}Innin ma-ḫi-ra la it-ti-šum, Subj. (UET I 274 ii, NS.)

[....] ma-ḫi-ra la da-at-ti-in-šum-ma (RA VIII 34 i, NS.?)

ma-ḫir ⌈....⌉ (MDP XIV p. 12 v).

Sarg. and Ur III PN's:

Ma-ma-ḫir /Man-māḫir/ (G+; YOS IV 246 ii, U; PDTI 341, U)

Ma-ma-ḫir-su (MO+).

<u>maḫar</u> "before."

This preposition is to be considered a Constr. St. of maḫrum "front."

Written logographically as IGI, IGI.ME or syllabically.

IGI PN's tamāʾum (MDP XIV 44)

IGI.ME ^{d}En-líl i-za-az = igi ^{d}En-líl-la-šè ì-gub (R xxviif.) = maḫriš, q.v. For the logogram cf. maḫrijum

in GN$_1$ IGI GN$_2$ (HSS X 201:7; ITT I 1096; 1439; BIN VIII 141). Cf. in GN$_1$ URU^{KI} GN$_2$ (OIP XIV 117 rev.). For constr. cf. e.g. KAV 183:14, etc.

in IGI GN (HSS X 177:5, 7)

ma-ḫa-ar ^{d}EN.ZU (UET I 275 iv, NS.)

ma-ḫar-su (S vi)

ma-ḫa-ar-su (MDP IV Pl. 2 ii)

ma-ḫa-ar-šu-nu (FM 8:16; 12:16; Oppenheim, CCTE p. 139, U)

ma-ḫ[a?-ar-su-nu]? (D 135).

Sarg. and Ur III PN:

ì-lí-maḫ-rí (D+; Nies, UDT 91 iv, U).

<u>maḫrijum</u> "first," "earlier."

Sarg. MN:

Ba-ḫi-ir IGI.ME (PBS IX 119 rev.) = Ba-ḫi-ir IGI [?] (OIP XIV 92 rev.) = Ba-ḫi-ir ma-<aḫ-rí>? (D 154).

maḫriš "before," "in front."

maḫ-rí-iš DN (PBS V 34 x, Lugalzagesi; S ix, xi; YOS I 10, NS.; Böhl, MAW Letterkunde 76B No. 9 p. 12)

maḫ-rí-iš ì-lí-su (R xviii, xxiv; UET I 274 iv, NS.; UET I 276 ii, NS.)

maḫ-rí-iš Šar-ru-GI = igi Šar-um-GI (S iv, ix).

maḫri "before," "in front."

maḫ-ri PN (Cop. 10055 rev.).

In the following examples the word may be maḫri or maḫriš plus pron. suffixes:

^{d}U.MES á-lí-ik maḫ-rí-su (R xviii twice)

maḫ-rí-[su] u-sa-rí-[bu] (UET I 274 ii, NS.)

ma-aḫ-ri-šu-nu iq-bí (MDP XXVIII 424 rev., U).

maḫrānum.

Ur III Amorite PN:

[M]a-aḫ-ra-nu-um MAR.TU (A 5994).

meḫrum.

me-eḫ-ru DUB [....] LUGAL "copy of a tablet"? (D 210 end)

in m[i]-iḫ-rí URU-Gi-tim "(fields) in front of the city Kite" (FM 25:9).

miḫurum.

Akk. lw. in Ur III Sum.:

x GÍN NI.GIŠ mi-ḫu-ru-um-ŠÈ (TA 1931, 222).

mitḫariš "correspondingly."

Ur III PN:

Mi-it-ḫar-iš (Nikolski, Dok. II 464 rev.; Boson, TCS 326).

muḫurrā'um "receipt" (received things).

6 ŠE.GUR mu-ḫur-ra-um in GN (D 275:2)

NI.NUN to different persons mu-ḫu-ra-um (D 323:14)

KUŠ.DÙG.GAN mu-ḫu-ra-um (D 268).

namḫārum (a container).

x KUŠ MÁŠ nam-ḫa-ru ZÍD.ŠE "x goat-skins, containers for barley flour" (FM 34:2).

tamḫarum "battle."

Akk. lw. in Sum. DAM.ḪA.RA (Thureau-Dangin, SAKI p. 38 i 26, Entemena).

MḪṢ maḫāṣum "to beat," "to strike," "to beat in," "to drive."

ma-ḫi-iṣ ga-ga-ad um-ma-an GN's (CT XXI 1c, Dêr)

(ì-nu ....) ga-ga-ad um-ma-nim si-a-ti im-ḫa-zu-na (Speleers, RIAA 4 ii, Dêr)

ŠU.NIGÍN 15 AB+ÁŠ su-ut PN ⌈GIŠ.GAG⌉ in ga-rí-im im-ḫa-zu a-na na-si LUGAL (BIN VIII 121)

.... GIŠ.GAG [a]-na DI!.TI.LA Na-ra-am-^{d}EN.ZU ma!-aḫ!-za-at (UCP IX p. 205, 83 iv).

mitḫuṣum "to fight (with each other)."

in GN uš?-da?-lí?-sa-ma im_{x}!(DU)-da-aḫ-za-ma "for the third time? they fought" (S vii, collated).

MḪṢ miḫṣum.

4 KÙŠ ù si-ir-i me-eḫ-zum (HSS X 156 x+3, 6). A spatial term, opposite of rupšum.

MḪŠ?

DN in Ur III PN:

Ur-^{d}Má-ḫa-šu-um-MA (TCL V 6047 ii). Perhaps Sum.
Ur-^{d}Ma-ḫa-šum? (TCL V 6038 rev. ii)

See below.

MḪŠ?

DN in Ur III PN:

Ur-^{d}Maḫ-sá-an-ka (RA VIII 185f. No. 4 twice, U). Probably Sum.
Ur-^{d}Maḫ-ša-an-ka (AnOr XIX No. 306, translit. only)

See above.

MḪŠ? namḫašum, see PR$^{\prime}{}_{5}$Š pirḫašum.

MḪZ, see Ḫ$^{\prime}{}_{6}$Z maḫâzum.

MK$^{\prime}{}_{x}$?

Ur III PN:

Ma-ki-a-nu-um (TA 1931, 237).

MKL, see MGL.

ML, see MN$^{\prime}{}_{7}$ menjum.

ML$^{\prime}{}_{1}$ malā'um "to be full."

25? UD li-im-la-ma "when 25? days pass" (Cop. 10055).

šumlu'um "to fill."

ba-áš-da-dam u-sa-am-la-su_{4}-ma in šum-lu-ì-su i-na-za-ar "with b. he will fill it (the skin) up; in filling it up he will watch" (MDP XIV 90 rev.).

mala'.

various objects ma-la-su a-na MA.DA PN u-bìl (MDP XIV 8). Meaning "all of it?." Hardly a PN.

tamlī'um "filling."

Sarg. and Ur III PN's:

Dam-li-um (ITT II/2 p. 38, 4683+)

UD-li-šu-na (RA XIX 41 No. L rev., U).

MLḪ malāḫum "sailor."

Lw. from Sum.

barley šu MÁ.LAḪ$_4$-e (MDP XIV 26)

PN MÁ.LAḪ$_4$ (FM 12:3; ITT I 1436; MO B iv)

10 MÁ.LAḪ$_4$ (HSS X 202:2)

MÁ.LAḪ$_4$.ME (MDP XIV 20)

PN MÁ.LAḪ$_4$.GAL (ITT I p. 16, 1252; II/2 5722).

Ur III PN:

Ma-la-ḫu-um (U 2249; Nies, UDT 91 vii).

MLK malākum "to counsel."

Sarg. and Ur III PN's:

Am-da-lí-ik (CT X 46, 18964 rev., U)

Im-lik-É-a (U 1736; CT XXXII 12 iv)

Dam-da-lik (D+)

Dam-lik (MDP XIV 66)

Im$_x$(DU)-da-lik (D+)

Mi-da-lik (PBS IX 121). Cf. Mitaḫḫar under MḪR

Me-da-lik (Kish 1930, 406 rev. ii+)

Mi-it!-lik (MO C xvi).

malkum, malikum "counsellor" (or "prince"?).

ma-al-ku[m] (D 172, in broken context).

PSarg., Sarg., and Ur III PN's:

^{d}AMAR-^{d}EN.ZU-ma-lik (UET III p. 10, U, misread as -ma-ma; UET V 690:15, U)

É-a-ma-lí-ik (HSS IV 58 rev.+, U)

É-a-ma-lik (2 NT 624, U)

Íl-[e]?-ma-al-[kum]? (D)

Ì-lí-ma-al-ki (Fish, CST p. 12, U)

Ma-li-kum MAR.TU (A 5508, U)

Su$_4$-ma-ma-lik (CT XXXII 8 iii A, PSarg.).

DN (or deified GN) Malkum in Ur III:

animal offerings ^{d}Ma-al-ku-um-ŠÈ (Schneider, Biblica XVIII 399)

Ma-al-kum-ŠÈ (Legrain, TRU 350; Lutz, UCP IX p. 244, 52)

Ma-al-ku-um-ŠÈ (UET III 883)

Cf. also M⌈a-al⌉-ku-um in BIN IX 440 rev., OB.

DN Malik in PSarg. and Sarg. PN's:

PÙ.ŠA-^{d}Ma-lik (Ist. Mus. Adab 280)

I-gu-^{d}Ma-lik (G+)

Il-su-Ma-lik (UET II Pl. XXXVI 308, PSarg.)
Ìr-am-^{d}Ma-lik (MO+)
Ìr-e-^{d}Ma-lik (MO)
^{d}Ma-lik-zi-in-su (MO)
Šum-Ma-lik (BE I Pl. VII vi)
Šum-^{d}Ma-lik (RTC 163+)
U-zé-^{d}Ma-lik (De Sarzec, DC II p. LVII).

malkatum "princess."
Sarg. PN:
Eš$_4$-dar-ma-al-ga-at (D).

milkum.
Ur III Amorite PN:
Mi-il-ga-nu-um MAR.TU (PDTI 335).

MLŠ mullušum "a person with pulled out hair."
Sarg. and Ur III PN's:
Mu-lu-šum (E+)
Mu-lu-uš-tum (D)
Mu-lu-uš (U 2295).

MM?
Sarg. PN:
Ma-ma-tum (G+)
[M]a-má-tim, Gen. (FM).

MN, see also M miš, mišum.

MN man, manum "who?"
PSarg., Sarg., and Ur III PN's:
Ma-an-ba-lum-^{d}Da-gan (Ist. Mus. Adab 111)
Ma-ba-lum-^{d}Da-gan (BM 54318)
Ma-an-gi-ìr (CT XXXII 34 ii 17, U)
Ma-an-iš-tu-su (Sarg. king). For other forms see under ʾ$_6$ŠT
Ma-an-ki-be-lí (U 2238)
Ma?-ki-be-lí (CT VII 4, 22451, PSarg.)
Ma-an-ki-im-lu-uš (D)
Ma-an-sa-ki-su (MO)
Ma-an-sa-nin-su (D+)
Ma-ma-ḫir (G+; YOS IV 246 ii, U; PDTI 341, U)
Ma-ma-ḫir-su (MO+)
Ma-nu-a (JAOS LII 113)
Ma-núm-a-ḫi (BIN VIII 151)
Ma-núm-ki-^{d}Šul-gi (YOS IV 63 rev., U; Legrain, TRU 367, U)
Ma-nú(m)-um-ki-^{d}Šul-<gi> (Legrain, TRU 367 seal, U)

Ma-an-núm-ki-^{d}Šul-gi (PDTI 550 rev., U)

Ma-nu-um-ki-^{d}AMAR-^{d}EN.ZU (UET V 690:22, U)

Ma-nu-um-e-mu-uq (Fish, CST p. 160 ix, U).

mammana "whoever."

mammana < man(a)-mana with verb in Subj. = "whoever":

ma-ma-na DÙL su$_4$-a u-a-ḫa-ru (PBS V 34 x, Lugalzagesi; S ix, xi).

mammana with negation = "nobody":

ma-ma-na ba-ni-su ù-la u-ba-al "he does not give pardon to anybody" (S xii, xv)

[m]a-am-ma-an [la iz-z]i-za-am (CT XXXII Pl. 1 ii) = ma-am-man la iz-zi-za (RA VII 180 ii) in CM.

manama "whoever."

manama < mana-ma with verb in Subj. = "whoever":

ma-na-ma MU Rí-mu-uš LUGAL KIŠ u-sa-za-ku-ma (R xviii, xxiv)

ma-na-ma MU-mi .... u-sa-za-ku-ma (UET I 276 i, NS.).

manama with negation = "nobody":

ma-na-ma .... la ib-ni (R xxvii)

sar in sar-rí ma-na-ma la i-lí-ik (UET I 274 ii, NS.)

(ša) sar in sar-rí ma-na-ma .... la u-sa-al-bí-tu (UET I 275 i, NS.)

(ša) sar in [sar-rí] ma-na-ma la i-mu-ru (PBS V 36 rev. x+ii, NS.)

ma-na-ma MU-mi a?! u-sa-zi-iq (UET I 275 iv, NS.)

min, minum "what?" (probably adverbs and adverbial constructions).

mi-nam da-mu-ur-ma "how is it that you saw?" (HSS X 8:5)

á-tum mi-nim la è-e-sa-ru (D 290 rev. x+10). Ununderstandable

[á]-tum mi-nim (Ist. Mus. Lagash 11001, in difficult context)

[a]?-mi-nim iš?-da-na-ba-ra-am (D 126).

Sarg. and Ur III PN's:

Mi-na-ar-ni "what is my sin?" (Chiera, STA 29 vi, U)

Mi-su$_4$-a "what is it?" (MO+).

Interpr. of the foll. Sarg. and Ur III PN's is unknown:

Mi-na-a-mu (D)

Mi-na-mu (G+; Fish, CST p. 160 viii, U)

Mi-na-na (Fish, CST p. 160 viii, U)

Mi-na-ni-a (E)

Mi-na-num (ITT II/1 p. 16, 721, U).

minūm "why?"

mi-num da-ap-ru-us "why did you withhold?" (FM 52:5)

mi-núm ù-la a-bí ad-da "why are you not my father?" (EK III Pl. XI W. 1929, 160)

mi-nu-um aš-da-na-ba-ra-ma la du-ša-ba-lam "how is it that I write to you continuously and you do not send me (the silver)?" (NBC

5378, U, soon to be publ. by Sollberger).

mimma "anything."

a-ni-me mim-ma-su la ti-su "now? nothing of it thou hast" (FM 8:14)

a-na-gu mim-ma ù-la a-ga-bi (JRAS 1932 p. 296:25).

Sarg. PN:

Mim-ma-sa (D+).

mimmijum "anything," "all."

Ur III PN:

Mi-im-mi (TCL II 5481 rev.).

MN?

Akk. lw. in Ur III Sum.:

GIŠ.KU mi-na-tum ga-NI-a-tum (UET III 677).

MN'7 manājum "to love."

Ur III PN's:

Im-ni-dIM (Orient. XLVII 423). Or '7MN imnum

Ma-ni (U 2263+)

Ma-ni-DÙG (U 2264)

Ma-ni-DINGIR (PDTI 720)

Ma-ni-Il MAR.TU (Oppenheim, CCTE p. 196)

Ma-ni-lí (ITT II/2 p. 21, 4383; p. 37, 4675)

Ma-ni-dIM (U 2265)

Ma-ni-um MAR.TU (A 2996).

menjum "love."

Interpr. doubtful. Cf., however, mMe-ni-DINGIR in KAV 31:11.

Sarg. and Ur III PN's:

A?-bí-me-NI (D)

Eš4-dar-me-NI (D)

Sá-lim-me-NI (FM)

Sar-me-NI (D)

Šu-me-NI (Oppenheim, CCTE E 26, U)

U-zé-me-num (E)

E-zé-me-NI (UET III 1452, U)

E-zé-me-na (YOS IV 289, U)

A-da-me-na (U 106)

Me-ni-šu-na (Barton, HLC I Pl. 28, 248 i, U).

MN'7? manājum or manāwum "to measure."

Mi. la-bi-in SIG4 la ma-ni-tim (CT XXXII Pl. 1 i = RA VII 180) in CM.

MNG? mangum?

ma-an-ga nu-úr-ma (UET III p. 127+, U). Here an object or ornament.

MNGG? mangagum (part of date palm).

1 GÚ ma-an-ga-ga (Reisner, TUT 121 vi, U). With dates

12 KIR.GA ma-an-ga-ga (YOS IV 238, U). With dates.

Sarg. PN:

Ma-ga-ga (D+).

MNZ?

Sarg. DN

dMa-zi-a[t] (MDP XI p. 3 i 20, time of NS.)

Cf. discussion and references in Lewy, Orient. n.s. XV 401.

DN in Sarg. and Ur III PN:

| Da-núm-Ma-an-zi-at (ITT II 3782; V p. 61, 9965)

| Da-núm-Ma-an-zi-da (ITT V p. 57, 9879, U). If DA = id, then cf. fMa-an-zi-it-ú-tu-uk-ku? in MDP IV p. 191:7; on the other side cf. DUB Ma-an-zi-da in AJSL XXIX 135 No. 6, U.

MQT <u>šumqutum</u> "to smite," "to kill."

x GURUŠ.GURUŠ u-sa-am-gi$_4$-it (R xvii, xix, xxii)

x GURUŠ.GURUŠ u-sa-am-ki-it (R xx twice, xxi)

EN.EN-su-nu u-sa-am-[ki]-it (RA VII 104, Mi.)

su$_4$-ma u-sa-am-ki-it-zu (RA VIII 200 ii, NS., copy).

<u>miqittum</u> "killing," "killed (people)."

ŠU.NIGÍN x GURUŠ.GURUŠ a-ti mi-gi$_4$-tim a-ti LÚ+ŠU "total of x men, including killed and captive" (R xxiii).

MQT? <u>maqqātum</u>? (a profession?).

a-na 1/2? DA?.NA TA ma-ag-ga-ti zu-si-ib-ma (JRAS 1932 p. 296:12).

MR?

Form Me-ir in Sarg. and We-ir in Ur III.

Cf. dIlumer, dIluwer, dIlimer, dMermer, dMermeri, dWer under Adad in Deimel, PB No. 23 and dItûrmer No. 1459. Cf. also me-ir = IM = šá-a-rum in ŠL 399, 15. Discussion by Dossin in Syria 153ff.

Sarg. and Ur III PN's:

A-ḫu-We-ir (U 143+)

| È-lu-Me-ir (RTC 127 rev. vi+)

| I-lu-Me-ir (ITT V p. 36, 9377)

| dKA-Me-ir (G+). See also below

| KA-Me-ir (D+)

Ni-wa-ar-Me-ir (Syria XXI 153, Mari)

PÙ.ŠA-We-ir (Fish, CST p. 160 vii, U)

dUTU-lu-Me-ir (ITT II/2 p. 3, 2852). Misread for dKA-Me-ir?, see also above.

Form Me-ra in Sarg. and Ur III PN's:

Connection with Me-ir is not provable.

DINGIR-Me-ra (Reisner, TUT 214 rev., U)

Me-ra-DINGIR (A 5232; MDP XIV 72 ii; SO IX/1 No. 31, U+).

MRʾ$_1$ mar ʾum, mer ʾum "son," "boy."

Written logographically only.

Meaning "son":

PN_1 DUMU PN_2 (passim)

DUMU PN (HSS X 190:11; MDP XIV 82)

PN_1 DUMU ši PN_2 (D 128; UCP IX p. 210 No. 89)

PN_1 DUMU PN_2 DUMU PN_3 (D 161; HSS X 197; FM 9:4f.)

PN_1 DUMU PN_2 ù PN_3 (fem.?) (D 161)

PN DUMU-su (YOS I 10, NS.; HSS X 208:3)

PN ù 1 DUMU-sa (D 7 passim)

PN ⌈ù⌉ 3 DUMU-sa (D 7; similarly D 77)

1 PN ù 1 DAM-zu ù 2 DUMU-su (D 246)

PN_1 PN_2 2 DUMU-a PN_3 (FM 2:12)

PN_1 PN_2? DUMU-a PN_3 (D 150)

PN_1 PN_2 DUMU-a ši PN_3 (D 162; TA 1931 unnumbered frag.)

PN_1 PN_2 2(or 3 or 4, etc.) DUMU PN_3 (MO passim)

PN ù DUMU.DUMU (D 291 end).

In the writing DUMU.ARAD or DUMU.UŠ the meaning is "boy," parallel to DUMU.SAL:

(HSS X 103; 183; 184; 187; 188; 190; etc.).

The spelling DUMU.DUMU in MO does not mean "sons" but "grandsons," "descendants," and even "men belonging to a certain 'clan,'" as in:

PN_1 DUMU PN_2 DUMU.DUMU PN_3 ši PN_4 (MO C xi) compared with PN_2 DUMU PN_3 DUMU.DUMU PN_4 ši PN_5 (MO C ixf.)

PN_1 PN_2 2 DUMU PN_3 DUMU.DUMU PN_4 (A iv)

PN_1 PN_2 2 DUMU PN_3 DUMU.DUMU PN_4 PN_5 DUMU PN_6 DUMU.DUMU PN_7 3 DUMU. DUMU PN_7! (D iiiff.)

PN_1 LÚ.ÉŠ.GÍD .... DUMU.DUMU PN_2 (C xiv) = PN_1 LÚ.ÉŠ.GÍD .... DUMU. DUMU PN_3 (C xvii)

17 GURUŠ DUMU.DUMU PN (A v, viii, ix, etc.).

Meaning "citizen" (or the like):

190 GURUŠ DUMU.DUMU BÀD-^{d}EN.ZU^{KI} (MO A x and similarly B vii, C xix, D xv)

49 DUMU.DUMU A-ga-dè^{KI} AB+ÁŠ.AB+ÁŠ GÁN "witnesses" (MO A xvi etc.)

DUMU.DUMU A-ga-dè^{KI} iššiakkuātim ukâlū (S iv, ix).

mar ʾatum, mer ʾatum "daughter," "girl."

Meaning "daughter," parallel to DUMU:

PN_1 DUMU.SAL PN_2 (HSS X 137:4)

PN_1 DUMU PN_2 DUMU.SAL PN_3 (RA XXIV 96)

PN DUMU.SAL-zu (De Sarzec, DC II Pl. LVII = Pl. 26bis Fig. 2)

1 DAM DUMU.SAL PN (D 255 vi twice)

1 DAM 1 DUMU.SAL (D 255 iii)

Meaning "girl," parallel to DUMU.ARAD:

(HSS 103:10; 183 rev. x+3; 184; 188; 190; 196; 198; 200; etc.).

marânum, merânum "young animal," "whelp."

I seized him ki gal-bi-im ì-na ki-ša-ti-šu, ki me-ra-ni-im ì-na pi-ir-ti-šu (3 NT 30, U, cf. ṣabātum).

Sarg. and Ur III PN's:

Me-ra-núm (D+)

Mi-ra-num (ITT II/2 p. 17, 3145, translit. only). Cf. Me-ra-nu-um, Me-ra-nim (TCL XXII 115:5, 15, Mari)

A.ŠÀ Ma-ra-núm (Nies, UDT 66 iii, U; RTC 412 rev. iii, U).

MR'_1 marāʾum "to fatten?"

1(or 60) UDU.UŠ a-na ZAR-tim ma-ra-iš ("for fattening") nu-ru-am (D 159).

MR'_x mirîtum (a musical instrument).

Mirîtum may mean instrument from the country Mêr, Mâri

The word zamirîtum may be a compound of Sum. za(g).(mí) plus mirîtum.

Akk. lw. in Ur III Sum.:

mi-ri-tum (Thureau-Dangin, SAKI p. 130 x 11, Gudea). Cf. also ^{GIŠ}mi-rí-tum, clearly a musical instrument, in AJSL XXXIX 168:29, OB

x ^{GIŠ}za-mi-rí-tum (BE III 76:22). Cf. za-mi-rí-t[um] UD.KA.BAR in MDP XXVII 254:2

x za(g)-mi-rí-tum UD.KA.BAR (TCL II 5488; Oppenheim, CCTE p. 55 E 32). And KUG.BABBAR GAR.RA (2 NT 601)

2 MA.NA URUDU KI.LAL za(g)-mi-rí-tum 8.KAM (De Genouillac, TD 82)

^{GIŠ}za(g)-mi-rí-tum (UET III pp. 97+ and 189f.). Among them 1 ^{GIŠ}za(g)-mi-rí-tum li?-e-tum (No. 455)

1 za(g)-mi-rí-tum UD.KA.BAR GIŠ.BI KUG.BABBAR ŠUB.BA (Iraq Mus. 46306)

Cf. also ^{URUDU}za(g)-mi-rí-tum in BIN IX 338, OB, and za-mi-<rí>?-tum of KUG.GI in No. 38, OB.

MRḪ merḫum or meraḫum.

Ur III PN:

Me-ra-aḫ-^{d}Šul-gi (PDTI 529 x). Cf. ^{LÚ}merḫum in Syria XIX 111, Mari, and merḫūtum in TCL XXII 62 rev. 8, 11, Mari, also Gu-ri-me-ra-aḫ in MDP XXVIII 480:2 and Me-ra-aḫ-I-da-du in MDP X 10:2, both OB.

MRḪŠ marḫušum (a precious stone).

Lw. from Sum. or vice versa.

3 NA4BUR MAR.ḪU.ŠA (TCL II 5529 rev., U)

1 NA4ma-al-tum GÍD.DA MAR.ḪU.ŠA TUR (ibid.)

1 NA4DUG.KAM MAR.ḪU.ŠA (ibid.)

NA4BUR.ŠAKAN MAR.ḪU.ŠA! (UET III 693, U).

MRQ murruqum.

Sarg. PN:

[M]u-ru-kum (D).

MRQ? maruqtum?

Ur III PN:

Ma-ru-uq5-tum DUMU.LUGAL (UET III 1222). Doubtful.

MRR marratum (a tree).

Akk. lw. in Ur III Sum.:

x KIL GIŠ.RU ma-ra-tum (UET III 812; 1498 rev. i).

MRṢ marṣum "sick."

1 UDU kab-la-su ma-ar-za-ma ⌈iṭ-bu⌉-ḫu "1 sheep - its 2 hips (qablān) afflicted - they slaughtered" (D 178)

namrāṣum "powerful," "mighty."

Sarg.?! PN:

Nam-ra-za (AnOr VII 372 iv).

MRŠ? (kind of flour).

Akk. lw.? in Ur III Sum.:

30(QA) ZÍD mar-sa-šum (UET III 906). Or ZÍD.MAR.SA.ŠUM

1(PI) ZÍD mar-sa-šum (UET III 907).

MRT?

Ur III PN's, probably not Akk.:

Mu-úr-ti-ga-ba (Nikolski, Dok. II 476 i)

Mu-úr-di(n)-ga-ba (Legrain, TRU 256 rev.)

Mu-úr-di(n)-GABA (CT XXXII 36 ii).

MRZ, see RSN? marsattum?

MṢ'x? "to reach," "to arrive."

Sarg. and Ur III PN's:

Ma?-zi-am-Eš4-dar (Coll. De Clercq I 121). Cf. Ma-ṣí-am-ì-lí in Stamm, ANG p. 163, translated as "genug für mich, mein Gott!"

Ma-zé-da-rí (Barton, HLC II Pl. 67, 32 iii, U). Doubtful

Me-zé-ì-lum (MO).

MṢR? namṣarum? (a sword).

Akk. lw. in Ur III Sum.:

8 GÍR nam-za-[ru-um]? (TCL V 6044 i).

MŠ mašum "pair" (twin). Cf. also MŠD? mašdum?

Akk. lw. from Sum. MAŠ.

Sarg. and Ur III PN's:

Ma-šum (D+; U 2266+)
Ma-sum (SO IX/1 No. 11, U)
Maš-um (RTC 389 obv. and rev., U)
Ma-áš (UET III p. 24+, U)
Maš (Radau, EBH p. 404, U).

MŠ?

Akk. lw. in Sum.:

1 ma-šum GIŠ KI.LAL.PI 7 MA.NA (PBS IX 5 i, PSarg.). Mistake for URUDU?

1 ma-šum? URUDU KI.LAL.PI 7 MA.NA (PBS IX 6 i, PSarg.)

Cf. von Soden in BO XIII 33a: URUDU ma-šum of the Eshnunna Laws.

MŠ$^{\circ}{}_{7}$ <u>mušjum</u> "night."

i-na mu-ši-im (UET III 270 iv, post-Ur III).

MŠ$^{\circ}{}_{7}$?

Ur III DN:

BALA ^{d}Mu-si-tum Marad-da^{KI} (TCL II 5589). Cf. BALA SANGA Marad-da^{KI} (TCL II 5577) and Mu-ši-tum in Tallqvist, AGE p. 377.

MŠ$^{\circ}{}_{7}$?

Sarg. PN:

Me-si-tum (BIN VIII 227).

MŠ$^{\circ}{}_{x}$.

[a]?-na mu?-su?-tim iṭ-bu-ḫu (D 178). Ununderstandable.

MŠD? <u>mašdum?</u>

Sarg. and Ur III PN:

Ma-áš-tum (D+; UET III p. 24, U). Or fem. of Mašum?
Maš-tum (FM+).

MŠD <u>mušdum</u>.

Sarg. and Ur III PN's:

Mu-uš-tum (D)
Muš-da-núm (CT VII 7 ii, U; not Muš-da-lum as in Ungnad, MAS p. 83)
Muš-da-nu-um MAR.TU (A 4218 rev. i, U).

MŠD? <u>maššadum</u> (a weapon).

The first example below indicates the writing maššad/tum and a weapon. The RTC examples show this object to be of metal. Only the UET III examples may contain the word mašaddum (ŠDD) "shaft (of a wagon)" or a part of it.

3 ^{URUDU}maš-sa-tum UD.KA.BAR NÍG.ŠÁM 1 GIŠ.TUKUL (weapon) 5 GÍN KUG.BABBAR (MO C viii; D iv; viii).

Akk. lw. in Sum.:

x maš-sá-tum KUG.GI GAR.RA (RTC 222 iv; 223 rev. i; 224)

x maš-sá-tum KUG.BABBAR GAR.RA (RTC 222 iv)

x maš-sá-tum (RTC 224; 230)

x silver ma-sá-tum-MA GÁ.GÁ.DÈ (BIN V 148:2, U)

1 GIŠma-sá-tum (UET III 811, U). Cf. also BIN IX 461, OB

1 GIŠmaš-at (UET III 805, U).

Ur III GN:

Ma-sa-tumKI (an unpubl. Ur III tablet in private possession: šà nam-ra-ag Ḫa-ar-šiKI ù Ma-sa-tumKI). Cf. i-na Ma-ša-ad-diKI in Gordon, SCT 106:3, OB

Ma-ša-tumKI (A 5297).

MŠḪ mašḫum (a container).

Akk. lw. in Ur III Sum.:

1 URUDUmaš-ḫu-um KAŠ.Ú.SA (UET III 739). Cf. mašḫu at EA and Qatna and JAOS LXV 234.

MŠḪ?

Ur III PN:

MAŠ-ḫi-DINGIR (Legrain, TRU 278).

MŠK maškum "skin."

Written syllabically or logographically.

ma-sa-ak-sa ⌈u⌉?-uš-ba-la-ga-at-ma "her (of sheep) skin he will strip" (MDP XIV 90)

ma-sa-ak-su (ibid.)

Otherwise regularly written KUŠ. Cf. also:

KUŠ.GUD-su-nu (MDP XIV 86 ii; rev. i, ii)

KUŠ.MÁŠ-su-nu (ibid.).

MŠL mašalum "mirror."

[1 ma?-ša?-lu]m URUDU (FM 7:1). URUDU is unique

"ma-ša-lum de bronze" (ITT II/2 p. 2, 2839)

1 ma-ša-lum UD.KA.BAR (OIP XIV 100)

5 ma-ša-lum UD.KA.BAR GAL (OIP XIV 103)

10 ma-ša-lum UD.KA.BAR TUR (ibid.)

Akk. lw. in Ur III Sum.:

1 ma-ša-lum KUG.GI KI.LAL.BI IGI.3.GÁL [....] (ITT V 10009)

1/3 ŠA KUG.GI ḪUŠ.A ma-ša-lum-ŠÈ (UET III 503; similarly 335)

1 ma-ša-lum UD.KA.BAR (BIN V 2:30; Reisner, TUT 124 viii; 126 i; 129 iii; UET III 1498 rev. ii; etc.)

1 ma-ša-lum KI.LAL.BI 2/3 MA.NA (TCL V 6044 ii)

7 ma-ša-lum KUG.BABBAR (UET III 730)

1 ma-ša-lum SAG+DU ÁB.ZA.ZA NA_4.ZA.KUR (ibid. 415)

ma-ša-lum NA_4 ZA.KUR BA.AN.GAR (ibid. 795).

mušālum "mirror."

5 and 4 UD.KA.BAR mu-ša-lum (ITT V 9262; 9302)

3 mu-ša-lum (BIN VIII 145).

muššulum.

Sarg. PN:

Mu-šu-lum (ITT II/2 p. 27, 4492).

tamšīlum "image," "likeness."

dam-si-[lí] ab-ni (UET I 275 iii, NS.)

dam-ši-il-su ib-ni-ma (RA VIII 200 ii, NS.)

dam-si-il-su ib-ni-ma (RA IX 34 i, NS.).

Akk. lw. in Ur III Sum.:

dam-ši-lum-BI "its image" (PBS V 68 x+12).

tamšīlum (a garment).

Akk. lw. in Ur III Sum.:

1 GAD.DU dam-ši-lum (UET III 1554 iv; 1569).

MŠL? tamšilum? (a resinous plant).

Akk. lw. in Ur III Sum.:

x MA.NA dam-ši-lum (TMH n.F. I/II 307)

x MA.NA dam-še-lum (TCL V 5680 ii; 6037 iv; 6042 i, ii; Chiera, STA I ii; ŞO IX/1 p. 27)

x MA.NA ^{ŠIM}dam-ši-lum (UET III 944 rev.; 1777)

dam-še-lum-BI x MA.NA (TCL V 6042 i; Orient. XV 55). For making perfumes.

MŠR?

Sarg. PN:

Maš-ir-tum, f.n. (D+).

MŠT?, see $Š'_7N$ muštinnum.

MT mutum "mate," "husband."

[NS.]? mu-ut ^{d}Innin An-nu-ni-tim (RA IX 34 ii, copy).

PSarg., Sarg., and Ur III PN's:

A-bí-a-mu-ti MAR.TU (Legrain, TRU 267 twice, U)

$Eš_4$-dar-mu-ti (PSarg. king)

I-wi-mu-ti MAR.TU (A 5508, U)

Mu-ti-pi-lí (TMH V 29 rev. vi, PSarg.?)

Mu-tum-DINGIR (Fish, CST p. 159 i, U)

Su_4-ma-mu-tum (MO).

MT? (a food).

Akk. lw. in Sum.:

1 QA mu-tum (RTC 217 twice; 218; ITT IV 7100). Same as later Akk. mundu? Cf. also mun-tum used for making medicine in the Ur III medical text published by Haas in American Journal of Pharmacy 1947 p. 424 rev. ii.

MT mat, mati "when?"

Ur III PN's:

Ma-at-DINGIR (PDTI 525 ii)

Ma-at-ì-lí (U 2231+; UET III 885) and Ma-at-ti-ì-lí (ibid. on seal, also A 26349). Cf. Ma-ti-DINGIR in Stamm, ANG p. 162, OB

Ma-ti-ì-lí (CT XXXII 50 rev. 23; PDTI 556 rev.)

Ma-ti-lí (Pinches, AT p. 183 rev.)

^{d}Šul-gi-ma-ti (CT XXXII 15 rev.+).

matîma "ever," "always."

ma-ti-ma .... ug_5-gi_4 "(sacrifices) for ever .... I established" (CT XXXII 1 v, CM)

ma-ti-ma .... la i-ba-aš-šu-ú "(sacrifices) never .... exist" (ibid. vi).

adi-matum "until when?"

Ur III PN's:

A-ti-ma-tum (U 203; AnOr VII p. 19)

⌈A⌉-ti-ma-at (TMH n.F. I/II 338).

MTN? metēnum (object of wood).

Akk. lw. in Ur III Sum.:

x GIŠ me-te-núm (RA XVI 19 i, iv, ix, xi, xii). Among woods and objects of wood.

MTQ matqum "sweet" (or a plant: "sweet almond?").

Akk. lw. in Sum.:

1 DUG NI ma-at-kum (RTC 109 rev.).

MṬ? miṭṭum "battle-mace."

Akk. lw. in Sum.:

mi-tum (Thureau-Dangin, SAKI p. 128 vii 14, 24; 134 xiii 23, Gudea)

^{TUKUL}mi-tum SAG 50 (RTC 198 rev., date of Gudea?)

mi-ì-tum SAG 50 (RTC 197 rev.; 199 twice, date of Gudea?). Unusual spelling indicating double consonants as in li-i-ba, ki-i-ta-am in the Lipit-Ištar inscription (Gadd, EDSA Pl. III). For double consonants compare also the Ur III PN NI-x-mi-da-šu (RLA II 141 No. 35, date of Šulgi), interpreted questionably as (L)í-wir_x-mi-tá-šu by Sollberger in AOF XVII 22 n. 55. The form miṭṭašu like ummašu, tuppašu.

MZ'_7 namzîtum (a container).

na-am-zé-t[um]? (D 274:4, school text).

namzi'um, nemzi'um (a press).

Sarg. and Ur III GN:

Nam-zé-im^{KI}, Gen. (D 201)

Nam-zi-um (ZA LI Pl. II after p. 74 iii 20, 21, U)

Nim-zé-um^{KI} (JCS X 29 No. 7 rev., U)

Ne-im-zi-im, Gen. (ibid. No. 8 rev., U).

N

N'_x.

Sarg. and Ur III PN's:

Nu-um (FM)

Nu-um-e-ri-eš (TMH n.F. I/II 271 iii, U). Doubtful

Nu-ú-a (Fish, CST p. 160 ix, U).

$N'_3 '_7$ na'ājum "to turn." Root in accordance with Arabic NḤJ.

Kiš^{KI} a-ša-rí-su i-ni (ù) URU^{KI}-lam_x u-šá-ḫi-su-ni = Sum. Kiš^{KI} ki-bi bí-gi_4 uru-bi ki-gub e-na-ba "he restored Kiš to its place and caused them to settle the city" (S iv, ix). Since GI_4 = târum "to turn," the derivation from $N'_3 '_7$ seems preferable to that from $'_4N'_7$ in Ungnad, MAS p. 39

URU^{KI}-lam Si?-ku?-ma-núm^{KI} KI-su e-ni (UET I 275 v, NS.).

na'ê ertim "one who turns the chest," "an adversary."

ì-nu ^{d}En-líl .... na-e e-ir-tim la i-ti-nu-šum (PBS V 36 rev. x+iii, NS.)

na-e [i]r-tim (BE I 120 ii, NS.).

N'_xB?

Sarg. and Ur III PN's:

Da-na-ab-šum (ITT II/2 p. 27, 4490, translit. only). See also below

Da-ri-lu-na-ab (D)

La-na-ab (Legrain, TRU 129; TCL II 5568; Oppenheim, CCTE p. 191; YOS IV 106 seal, all U)

La-ni-bu (Chiera, STA 15 ii, U; Oppenheim, CCTE p. 77, U; AnOr I 292:33, U)

PÙ.ŠA-na-ab (3 NT 796 iii, U)

Tu-da-na-ab-šum (D+). Cf. also under watā'um and Tu-na-ab-šum (TA 1930, 166, OB). See also above.

N'_1D na'ādum "to praise."

Sarg. PN's:

LUGAL-na-da (Cop. 10083)

Na-id-mu-bí (ITT I p. 30, 1466).

Ur III PN's:

A-ba-na-da (YOS IV 14)

É-a!-na-da (TMH n.F. I/II 155 rev.)

En-in-na-da(n) (Jacobsen, CTC 54 v; Virolleaud, CC XXVIII)

In-na-da(n) (RA XIX 33)

En-ni-na-da(n) (Nies, UDT 57 i; CT VII 7 iii; X 43; 14333 rev.; Barton, HLC I Pl. 25 iv)

Ìr-ra-na-da (U 1765+)

Ìr-ra-na-da(n) (U 1766; AnOr VII 79:8; De Genouillac, TD 3; ITT IV p. 78, 7868)

^{d}Šul-gi-na-da (U 929+)

Cf. also n. on wadāʾum "to know."

Doubtful Ur III PN's:

KA-in-na-da(n) (RA XII 155 No. 10)

MUN-na-da(n) (TCL V 6053 iv)

AM-ni-na-da(n) (TMH n.F. I/II 155 rev.)

GÚ-ni-na-da(n) (TMH n.F. I/II 250 rev.).

<u>nuʾudum</u> "to praise."

Sarg. and Ur III PN's:

DINGIR-nu-id, Impv. (MO+)

Eš$_4$-dar-nu-id (D+)

Ì-la-ag-nu-id (D+)

I-la-ag-nu-id (E; UET III 885, U)

Ì-la-nu-id (Kish 1930, 139; 144a rev. iii)

E-la-ag-nu-id (U 1054; UET III p. 13, U)

DINGIR-la-ag-nu-[i]d (LB 1847)

Ìr-ra-nu-id (U 1767ff.)

Nu-id-Ì-la-ag (D+)

Nu-i-da (Orient. XVIII 6:2, 4, U+). Cf. also Nu-ni-da under NN?

Nʾ$_1$D <u>naʾdum</u> "waterskin."

Akk. lw. in Ur III Sum.:

2 ^{KUŠ}na-a-du-um (BE III 76:29; 78:2).

Nʾ$_6$Ḫ <u>nuāḫum</u> "to be restful."

Ur III PN's:

Ne-ḫi-lum (Barton, HLC I Pl. 25 iii)

Nu-úḫ-DINGIR (AnOr VII 295:55; Fish, CST p. 159 iii)

Nu-úḫ-ḫi-DINGIR (PDTI 542, translit. as ÙḪ)

Nu-ḫi-DINGIR (U 2405+)

Nu-ḫi-lum (U 2406; RTC 363 twice)

Nu-ḫa-lum (Pinches, AT p. 180)

Nu-ḫi-Eš$_4$-dar (UET III 1041).

munîḫum "one who gives rest."

Ur III PN:

Mu-ni-ḫu-um (Delaporte, CCL II A 245).

Nʾ$_6$Ḫ? nâḫum "rest."

Sarg. PN:

Ma-ad-na-ḫu-um (FM). Cf. Ma-ad-nu-ru-u[m] in UET V 554:44, OB.

Nʾ$_7$L majjaltum "bed" (or the like).

Written normally ma-a-al-tum in Sarg. and ma-al-tum in Ur III.

Akk. lw. in Sum.:

^{GIŠ}ma-a-al-tum (VAT 16442 ii, school text)

1 GIŠ ma-a-al-tum UD.KA.BAR GAR.RA ZU (RTC 221 iv)

1 GIŠ ma-a-al-tum TÚG (RTC 221 iv)

1 GIŠ ma-a-al-tum ḪA.LU.ÚB (RTC 221 v)

52 URUDU ḪAR.GÁL GIŠ ma-a-al-tum TÚG (RTC 239 rev. i)

5 ma-al-tum GIŠ.AM (BIN VIII 256). Exceptionally written. Collated

7 GIŠ ma-al-tum ḪA.LU.ÚB (HSS IV 5 iv, U)

1 ma-al-tum AN.BÍ (RTC 304 i, U)

x NA$_4$ BUR ma-al-tum (ibid.)

1 ma-al-tum NA$_4$ (A 2697, U). Note that it is made of stone

2 ma-al-tum NA$_4$ (BIN V 2:37, U)

4 NA$_4$ ma-al-tum (Reisner, TUT 126 ix, U)

1 NA$_4$ ma-al-tum GÍD.DA MAR.ḪU.ŠA TUR (TCL II 5529 rev., U)

1 NA$_4$ ma-al-tum GÍD.DA BUR TUR (ibid.)

2 GIŠ ma-al-tum ḪA.LU.ÚB UD.KA.BAR GAR.RA (Pinches, BTBC 89 ii, U)

4 GIŠ ma-al-tum ḪA.LU.ÚB TUR (ibid.)

1 GIŠ ma-al-tum MES TUR (ibid.)

8 GIŠ ma-al-tum TUR (ibid.)

1 [ma]?-al-tum UD.KA.BAR KI.LAL.BI 12 1/2 MA.NA 5 GÍN (UET III 289, U, and more on p. 127).

Sarg. PN:

Ma-al-tum-BALA (Nikolski, Dok. II 35 i). How to interpret this PN?

Nʾ$_6$Q$_7$ nuāqum "to lament."

Sarg. PN:

I-nin-a-na-aq (G+). Parallel to A-na-aḫ-ì-lí.

Nʾ$_2$R nârum "river."

Written logographically and syllabically (once).

aṣ-ba-zu ki ma-ì àp-ru-uk-šu ki na-ri-im "I seized him like water, I closed him in like a river" (3 NT 30, U, cf. ṣabātum) in ÍD kab!(wr. Á)-lí-tim (R xxiii, xxv)

^{d}EN.KI ÍD-[su a-na] za-ki-ki-im li-im-tu-ud (CT XXXII 4 xii, CM)

^{d}En-líl ÍD?-su? /nârišsu?/ A li-im-tu-ud "may Enlil measure out water? (flood?) for his river?" (UET I 276 ii, NS.).

DN Nârum (for which cf. Thureau-Dangin, RA XXXI 142) in Sarg. PN's:

^{d}ÍD-la-ba (A 4853+)

| I-ti-^{d}ÍD (D+)

| I-ti-ÍD (BE I Pl. VI viii)

Pù-su-^{d}ÍD (D)

Pù-ŠA-^{d}ÍD (D)

Šu-ÍD (Iraq VII p. 66 F 1159).

Ur III GN:

Bi-na-ra-tum^{KI} (TCL V 6041 i).

N$^{\text{ʾ}}_{3}$R na^{ʾ}ārum "to smite"; cf. Arabic NḪR "to strike," "to smite," "to pierce," also NḤR "to pierce" in Aramaic.

Written syllabically:

NS. GN_1 ù GN_2 en-ar (UET I 275 ii, NS.)

en-a-ru (HSS X 38 iii x+1, in difficult context)

PN_1 ù PN_2 en-a-ra (HSS X 206 x+4)

1 ARÁD LUGAL ZAG.U MÁ Da-kum en-a-ru (ibid. l. 7). "To mark in form of branding?" (piercing); cf. BÍ.U in 205

[in 1 MU ....] PN? en-a-[ru] (ITT V 9265, date, king unknown).

Written logographically SAG.GIŠ.RA:

S. GN SAG.GIŠ.RA = Sum. e-ḫul (S ii, vii)

S. SAG.GIŠ.RA GN (S xi; UET I 9, R.). Act. Part.

ì-nu GN SAG.GIŠ.RA-ni (RA XXI 66, S.; BE I 5, R.; UET I 10, R.; BE I 10, R.; M xxvi)

NS. SAG.GIŠ.RA GN (RA X 101 No. 1). Act. Part.

GN SAG.GIŠ.RA (MDP XIV p. 10 i)

GN's lu SAG.GIŠ.RA lu e-be-el (CT XXXII 1 ii = RA VII 180 i) in CM

GN na-ki-ir-ma SAG.GIŠ.RA (R xvii).

nîrum "smiting," "smiter."

DN nir_x ša-nin-ú-tim (RA IX Pl. 1 opp. p. 1, Urkiš and Nawar). The interpr. of GAZ+NIR as nir_x is not sure. The construction ni-ir GN (KAH I 17:4), ni-ir dap-nu-ti (KAH I 3:3; etc.), ni-e-ir dap-nu-ti (KAH II 35:3) looks like a Pass. Part. in form, but Act. Part in meaning. As Act. Part. nā^{ʾ}ir cannot develop to nêr (cf. e.g. da-iš in KAH I 17:6), the only possibility which seems to remain is to take nîr, nêr as a Constr. St. of a noun nîrum, nêrum "smiting," later probably also "smiter." Parallel to rîṣum "help," "helper," rîsum "smiting," "smiter." Cf. MAD II 205f.

N'$_6$R naw(i)rum, namrum "shining." Cf. also NNR?

Ur III PN's:

AD.DA-na-wi-ir (ITT V 6787 rev.)

AD.DA-na-bi-ir (U 232; BIN V 106:3)

AD.DA-na-PIRIG (CT VII 34, 18409 rev.; X 28 ii)

AD.DA-na-bìr (HSS IV 65)

^{d}EN.ZU-NAM-ri (Legrain, TRU 3)

Eš$_4$-dar-na-wi-ir (Delaporte, CCBN No. 68)

LUGAL-nam-mir (ITT II/2 p. 50, 5857, translit. only)

Na-me-ir-DINGIR (U 2349+)

Na-wi-ir-DINGIR (U 2359+; TCL II 5580)

Na-mi-rí-lum (Chiera, STA 3 iii)

Ù-zi-na-wi-ir (Nikolski, Dok. II 523 rev.).

ni(w)rum "shine."

Ur III PN:

Ni-wa-ar-Me-ir (Syria XXI 153, Mari). Cf. Capp. Ni-mar-ša-ra-ma-tí OIP XXVII p. 21 No. 2.

nûrum "light."

Sarg. and Ur III PN's:

Be-lí-nu-rí (D)

Eš$_4$-dar-nu-rí (D)

^{d}IM-nu-ri (UET III p. 9, U)

Nu-ra (MO)

Nu-ra-a (U 2403)

Nu-ra-a-ti (ITT IV p. 72, 7787, U)

Nu-úr-AD (Reisner, TUT 157 ii, U)

Nu-úr-ì-lí (ITT IV p. 92, 8111+, U)

Nu-rí-ì-lí (ITT IV p. 7822, U; HSS IV 84, U)

Nu-ru-um (D+; U 2404)

Nu-úr-Eš$_4$-dar (E+; U 2397+)

Nu-úr-^{d}IM (U 2390+)

Nu-úr-Da-ad (Chiera, STA 33, U)

Ša-lim-nu-ri (TCL V 6047 ii, U)

Šu-^{d}EN.ZU-nu-úr-ma-ti-iš-zu (PBS XIII 13 seal, U)

^{d}Šul-gi-nu-ri (Iraq V 176 No. 26, U)

Ù-zi-nu-ri (U 1126+)

Ú-zi-nu-ru-um (Delaporte, CCL II A 266, U).

namurrum "shining."

Sarg. PN:

Na-mu-ru-um (MO).

namurratum "shine."

PSarg., Sarg., and Ur III PN's:

Na-mu-ra-zu (U 2351; CT XXXII 34 i)

Na-mu-ra-[....] (DP 2 ii, PSarg.).

namrīrum "shine."

Sarg. PN:

[Na]m-ri-ru-um (Kish 1930, 170d, collated).

Nʾ$_7$R nîrum "yoke," "crosspiece."

10[+x GIŠ ni]?-ru (D 325:8)

x GIŠ ni-ru (A 675 twice)

In the Ur III texts "mat used as crosspiece," discussed fully by Goetze in JCS II 165ff. Cf. also Fish, MCS III 42-45.

Akk. lw. in Ur III Sum. Cf. e.g.:

7 GIŠ ni-ru-BI (ITT V 6668)

x GIŠ ni-ru SI.SÁ (RA XVI 20 ix, xi)

x GIŠ ni-ru AR.ḪA (ibid. and xii)

x GI.KID nir-ru-um (TCL V 6036 v, vi, vii, etc.)

x KID nir-ru-um (AnOr I 155; etc.)

x GI nir-ru-um (AnOr I 256)

x nir-um (Nikolski, Dok. II 225)

x KID nir-um (ITT V 8229)

x GI nir-um (Oppenheim, CCTE p. 99)

x GI nir-ru (ŠL II 85, 351).

Nʾ$_x$R.

⌈a⌉?-ni-ìr-kum (FM 53:6). Interpr. unknown.

Nʾ$_x$R nârum?, nuārum? "singer."

Akk. nârum can be taken as a loan word from Sum., but the existence of Akk. nuārum leads to a more likely assumption that Sum. nar is a loan from Semitic.

Written logographically only.

NAR-e .... ù-sá-az-me-ir (MDP IV Pl. 2 ii)

PN NAR (HSS X 20 rev. x+4; 130 rev. x+i; etc.)

PN NAR.GAL DN (ITT I 1412).

Nʾ$_x$R nûrum.

Akk. lw. in Sum.:

20 nu-ru-um ŠU 110 LAL 1 GI SA (ITT II/2 4430, complete).

Nʾ$_3$Š naʾāšum "to live" (or the like).

Sarg. PN:

Li-na-áš (D+).

naʾ(a)šum, nêšum "life."

Written syllabically or logographically as MU.

In ex-voto's for the life of a person, mainly king:

a-na na-ʾà-si NS. da-nim (MDP VI 6)

a-na na-ʾà-si ŠD. (Gadd, EDSA Pl. 3)

a-na-ʾà-si-su a-na-ʾà-si PN DUMU-su (Iraq I Pl. IXb)

a-na na-si-su! (YOS I 18, U)

a-na na-si PN (RA XXIV 81, U)

[a-na] ne-ši Šul-gi (PBS V 41, U). Doubtful.

Oath by the life of the king (and queen in one case):

na-ʾà-áš LUGA[L] it-má (D 135)

PN's ni-iš sar-ri-im ⌈it⌉-ma-ù (MDP XIV 44)

PN ni-iš LUGAL it-ma (Yondorf a, U)

ni-iš sar-ri-im at-ma (MDP XXVIII 424, U)

na-ʾà-áš LUGAL ù na-ʾà-áš NIN lu tu-mu-at (RA XXIII 25)

⌈e⌉?-ni na-ʾà-áš ᵈSar-ga-lí-LUGAL-rí ù-má "behold?, by the life of Škš. I swear" (JRAS 1932 p. 296:28)

na-ʾà-áš-su ù-ma (A 708, referring to [LUG]AL?)

PN's ni-iš LUGAL-im it-ma-ù (Oppenheim, CCTE TT 1, U)

na-áš LUGAL it-ma (Kish 1930, 170d rev.)

a-na na-si LUGAL (BIN VIII 121)

MU LUGAL-im PÀD (RA XXXII 190, U).

Sarg. PN:

Na-ʾà-šum (MO).

$N^{\text{ʾ}}{}_6$ŠḪ?, see NBŠḪ.

$N^{\text{ʾ}}{}_x$T? <u>nâtum</u>? "handle (of a knife)?"

Akk. lw. in Ur III Sum.:

2 GÍR.LU.BE UD.KA.BAR na?-tu-um KUG.BI SAG.BI (TCL II 5515 i 9). Cf. na-a-tu šá ni-gal-lim in LTBA I 17 i 46

na-tu-um ᵈInnin GIŠ.KU (De Genouillac, TD 77).

$NB^{\text{ʾ}}{}_1$ <u>nabāʾum</u> "to name."

MU-su i-bí (M xxviii).

PSarg., Sarg., and Ur III PN's:

I-bí-ba-na (ZA XII 333)

I-bí-DINGIR (D+; U 1585+)

I-bí-É-a (E+)

Ì-bí-ᵈEn-líl (Ist. Mus. Adab 280). Or Ni-bí-ᵈEn-líl

I-bí-ᵈEN.ZU (D+; U passim)

I-bi-ᵈEN.ZU (TMH n.F. I/II 149, U)

I-bí-ì-lum (MO)

I-pi-ì-lum (TMH V 11 iv, PSarg.?)

Ì-an-bí-ì-lum MAR.TU (TCL II 5508 i, U). Cf. Ia-ab-bi-^{d}Da-gan (TCL XXIV 52:9, Mari)

I-bí-^{d}KA.DI (PDTI 86, U)

I-bí-Lu-lu (TCL II 5542, U)

I-bí-^{d}Nanše (Kish 1930, 177n)

I-bí-^{d}URU$^{\ulcorner KI \urcorner}$ (G). Cf. also GN I-bí-URU^{KI} in MO A xv etc.

I-bí-^{d}UTU (DP 2 i, PSarg.)

I-bí-^{d}Za-ba$_4$-ba$_4$ (Kish 1930, 406)

I-bí-ZU (D+; U 1590)

I-bí-ZU.AB (MO)

Ì-lum-i-pi (TMH V 170 i, PSarg.?)

Na-bí-^{d}En-líl (U 2340+)

Na-bí-^{d}En-líl-lá (RA XIX 40 No. XX, U+)

Na-bí-^{d}EN.ZU (U 2341+)

Na-bí-^{d}Šul-gi (U 2340)

Na-bí-Ùl-maš (D+)

Na-bí-um (D+; HSS IV 49 i, U)

Su$_4$-i-bí (TMH V 38 ii, PSarg.?).

PN in Ur III GN:

É.A-I-bí-lum-ma (ZA LI Pl. I after p. 74 i 24, 25).

Interpr. of the following PN's is unknown:

Be-lí-BÍ (D+)

Eš$_4$-dar-BÍ (TA 1931, unnumbered frag.)

Ì-lí-BÍ (D+)

Sar-ru-BÍ (D)

Ú-bí-BÍ (OIP XIV 48 i, PSarg.).

<u>nibʾum</u>.

Sarg. PN's:

EN.TI-ni-bí (ITT II/2 4362)

Ni-bí-^{d}En-líl (Ist. Mus. Adab 280). Or Ì-bí-^{d}En-líl

Ni-bi-ì-lí-šu (MDP XXIII 286:24).

NBʾ$_1$? <u>mubbiʾum</u>?

mu-bi? lu ti-da "my instructions? (or order?) may you know" (JRAS 1932 p. 296:41). Copied and read as mu-duk, but duk is never used syllabically in the Sarg. period; for <u>bi</u> in mu-bi cf. a-ga-bi in l. 25. *Munbiʾum with m like mušpalum?

Sarg. PN:

Mu-pum-ba-lik (D), to be read as MU Pù-ba-lik?

Cf. also ʾ$_6$Pʾ$_x$ mûpium.

NBʾ$_x$? <u>nabaʾum</u> (an object for a boat).

Akk. lw. in Ur III Sum.:

8 É na-ba-um, GÍD 1 GAR 1 KÙŠ, DAGAL 5 KÙŠ TA, MÁ LUGAL-ŠÈ (PDTI 546).

NBD?, see NP? napatum?

NBḪ, see ʾ$_x$BḪ nâbiḫum, nêbaḫum and ḪBT? naḫbatum.

NBŠḪ nabašuḫum (a garment).

Akk. lw. in Ur III Sum.:

1 TÚG na-ba-šu-ḫu-um SIG$_5$ (UET III 1563 twice)

[x TÚG]? na-wa-šu-ḫu-um (BE III 166)

Cf. the namašuḫum garment in Cappadocian (CCT I 15a 5; 39a passim; etc.).

NDʾ$_x$ nadāum "to throw."

a-ti za-wa-ar-su ù za-wa-ar-ki (Kish 1930, 143 rev.). Meaning unknown.

Sarg. and Ur III PN's:

Na-ti (ITT II/2 5695 rev.)

Na-ti-um (Ward, SCWA No. 187a, U)

Na-di-^{d}EN.ZU (Boson, TCS 371:4, U)

nādîtum (a priestess).

Bu-la-la-tum DUMU.SAL Da-ti-na-LUM na-ti-it ^{d}KA.DI (Legrain, CCC No. 55).

Ur III PN:

Na-ti-tum (Fish, CST p. 160 viii).

nidjum, see ʾ$_7$D idum.

NDD? nuddudum?

Sarg. PN:

Nu-tu-tum (BIN VIII 291 rev.).

NDN nadānum "to give."

Written syllabically.

ša il?!-su i-na-da?-nu-šum? (UET I 275 iv, NS.)

ma-ḫi-ra la i-ti-nu-šum, Subj. (S iv, vi, viii, x; R xxii)

ma-ḫi-ra la it-ti-šum (UET I 274 ii, NS.)

ma-ḫi-ra la da-at-ti-in-šum-ma, Fem. (RA VIII 34 i, NS.)

ti-a-am-dam i-ti-nu-šum, Subj. (S iv, [viii])

ti-a-am-dam i-ti-šum (S xii)

ma-dam a-lí-dam i-ti-šum (S vi; xiv)

sar-ru$_x$-dam i-ti-nu-šum, Subj. (R xvi; xxiii)

2 DN's UŠ? [a] i-ti-na-šum (R xviii, xxiv)

2 DN's UŠ [?] ù [MU]-su [a i]-ti-na-šum (UET I 274 iv, NS.)

2 DN's UŠ ù MU [a] i-ti-na-šum (UET I 276 ii, NS.; BE I 120 iv, NS.)

ì-nu DN .... zi-ra-at ni-se$_{11}$ ga-ti-iš-su i-ti-nu ù na-e e-ir-tim la i-ti-nu-šum (PBS V 36 rev. x+iii, NS.)

[....] ga-la-ma i-ti-šum (R xxv)

GN's i-ti-šum (UET I 275 i, NS.)

ki DN GN's i-ti-nam-ma (UET I 275 iii)

ì-nu DN .... PN ga-ti-iš-su i-ti-nu-ma (UET I 275 iii)

in 1 MU DN .... ki-ib-ra-tim ar-ba-im [....] i-ti-nu-[šum] (MDP X Pl. 3, 1a and 1b)

x wool a-na PN li-ti-nu (Cop. 10055 rev.)

i-ti-iš-s[u?-um]? (D 172). Doubtful.

In economic documents and letters.

Object: silver, garments, flour, tablet, barley, fields, ship, woods, animals:

a-na-da-kum (JRAS 1932 p. 296:26)

a-na-da-nu-kum, Subj. (ibid. l. 35)

da-na-da-nu, Subj. (ibid. l. 33)

i-na-da-an (D 7791; A 5906 rev.)

⌈a⌉-ti-šum (FM 35 rev.)

a-ti-na, Subj. (FM 21 rev.)

DUB a-ti-nu-šum, Subj. (Kish 1930, 170c)

e da-ti-in "may thou not give" (D 315 rev.)

i-ti-in (HSS X 94 rev.; D 259; 282 rev.; Louvre AO 8961; FM 53 rev.; JCS X 26 iii)

i-ti-nam (FM 35 rev.)

a i-ti-in "may he not give" (HSS X 5 rev.)

li-ti-in (HSS X 5 obv. and rev.; BIN VIII 151)

i-ti-na, Subj. (FM 3 rev.)

šu PN i-ti-nu-šum (MCS IV 13)

i-din$_x$(DÍM) (FM 36; Iraq Mus. 28860 rev.)

da-ti-in, Fem. (MDP XXIV 342; BE I 11)

i-ti-in, Impv. (A 4746; RA XXIV 44, U)

PN na-da-ni-iš ga-bi "PN was told to give (silver)" (RA XIII 133, U)

PN na-da-nam iq-bí šum-ma i-ta-ti-in "PN told him to give; if he (then) gave (it)" (TMH n.F. I/II 7, U).

In some of the above examples nadānum may have the meaning "to sell" or "to buy," but the context does not allow of unequivocal translation.

In the cases below nadānum means "to sell" or "to buy":

PN's a-na ŠE at-ti-kum "I sold you PN's for barley" (FM 8 rev.)

PN$_1$ a-na ŠÁM 5 KUG.BABBAR GÍN a-na PN$_2$ PN$_3$ ⌈i⌉-ti-in "PN$_3$ sold PN$_1$

to PN_2 for 5 shekels of silver" (HSS X 211)

silver a-na ŠÁM X PN_1 a-na PN_2 i-ti-in "PN_1 bought X for silver" (FM 4)

silver, bronze, oil a-na ŠÁM É PN i-ti-in "PN bought a house for silver, bronze, oil" (MDP XIV 4 rev.)

45 ŠE.GUR a-na KUG 1(GUR) 2(PI) 30(QA) GUR na-ti-in KUG-su 1/2 MA.NA "45 GUR of barley was sold for the price of 450 QA (per 1 shekel of silver); its price is 1/2 mina" (Kish 1930, 138)

PN_1 ŠÁM.MA.NI 2 GÍN IGI.3.GÁL a-na PN_2 ga-ga-za ⌈a⌉-na ŠÁM i-ti-in "PN_1 sold herself to PN_2 for 2 1/3 shekels of silver" (Yondorf a, U).

Sarg. PN's:

NU.BANDA IGI A-i-ti-su /Aj-iddinšu/ (ITT I 1439 rev.). For NU.BANDA IGI cf. RTC 127 iii etc.

Da-ti-Gi-za (G)

Da-ti-Eš$_4$-dar (D+)

Da-ti-na-LUM (Legrain, CCC No. 55)

I-din-DINGIR (D+)

I-din-É-a (E)

I-din-Ìr-ra (E)

I-ti-Ìr-ra (MCS IV 13)

I-ti-^{d}Da-gan (D+)

I-ti-DINGIR (D+)

I-ti-LUM (D+)

I-ti-DINGIR.DINGIR (MO)

I-ti-É (CT I 1a)

I-ti-É-a (MO+)

I-ti-Eš$_4$-dar (MO+)

I-ti-^{d}ÍD (D+)

I-ti-ÍD (BE I Pl. VI viii)

I-ti-na-pum (BIN VIII 166)

I-ti-na-um (Ist. Mus. Nippur 2614). Ununderstandable; read I-ti-na-<bu>?-um /Iddin-abum/

I-ti-sa[r]? (ITT V 6670)

I-ti-sum (G+)

I-ti-šum (MO+)

I-ti-ZU (OIP XIV 6)

Sar-a-ti-gu-bi-si-in (RA IX 73+). "O king, I gave their laments." Doubtful.

Selected Ur III DN's:

Da-ti-Eš$_4$-dar (U 803; UET III 1733, f.n.)
Da-din-Eš$_4$-dar (U 806+, f.n.)
Da-din-Eš-dar (Chiera, STA 10 v, f.n.)
Da-ti-^{d}Innin (U 801)
Da-ti-in-^{d}Innin (U 802)
Da-ti-Ki-za (U 804; UET III p. 9+, f.n.)
Da-din-Ki-za (U 808)
I-ti-a-ḫu-um (Fish, CST p. 159 ii)
I-ti-in-a-ḫu-um (3 NT 796 i)
I-din-^{d}Da-gan (U 1679+)
I-ti-DINGIR (U 1669; RA XXXIV 13f., Mari; UET III p. 17)
I-din-DINGIR (U 1677)
I-ti-ì-lí (UET III p. 17)
I-din-ì-li (Nikolski, Dok. II 368)
I-ti-É-a (UET III p. 17+; instead of I-din-È-a in U 1682 read I-ta-è-a)
I-din-É-a (RA XIX 33)
I-ti-ne-a (Oppenheim, CCTE p. 188)
I-ti-^{d}EN.ZU (AnOr I p. 29; UET III p. 17)
I-din-^{d}EN.ZU (U 1681+)
I-ti-Eš$_4$-dar (U 1675+)
I-din-Eš$_4$-dar (RA XIX 33)
I-ti-DINGIR-su (UET III 157)
I-ti-^{d}IM (U 1670+; UET III p. 16)
I-din-^{d}IM (U 1678+; AnOr I p. 29)
I-ti-na-da-ad (Nikolski, Dok. II 386)
I-ti-ìr-ra (U 1674+; UET III p. 17)
I-ti-^{d}ìr-ra (U 1671)
I-din-ìr-ra (U 1684+)
I-ti-nir-ra (ITT IV p. 73, 7757)
I-din-I-šum (U 1683+)
I-ti-Lu-lu (ITT V p. 59, 9941)
I-ti-na-bu-um (Univ. Illinois unnumbered)
I-ti-^{d}UTU (Fish, CST p. 65; UET III p. 17).

<u>nidnum</u> "gift."

King of Dêr:

⌈^{d}Ni-id-nu-šal⌉ (YOS IX 62).

NG$^\circ{}_7$? <u>nigîtum</u>? (a resinous plant).

This plant is different from niqdum because both occur in TCL II 5680 iif.

Akk. lw. in Ur III Sum.:

x MA.NA ni-gi$_4$-tum (TCL V 5680 ii; Chiera, STA 1 iii 17; Nikolski, Dok. II 445 rev.; Orient. XV 55)

ni-gi$_4$-tum-BI (TCL V 6042 i)

x MA.NA GIŠ ni-ki-tum (ITT II/2 4573, Sarg.?)

x MA.NA ŠIM ni-ki?-tum (TMH n.F. I/II 307 rev.).

NGB? negibum (a metal object).

Akk. lw. in Ur III Sum.:

ne-gi-bu-um KUG.BABBAR "pale d'argent" (RA XVII 210)

x ne-gi-bu-um UD.KA.BAR (UET III 650; 723; 1498 iv; and others quoted on p. 135).

NḪB?

Sarg. PN:

Na-ḫa-ba (G+).

NḪD? naḫādum "to heed," "to attend."

Ur III PN:

I-ḫi-id-^{d}UTU (Boson, TCS 314). Read as I-šar-di-^{d}Babbar by Boson in Aegyptus X 265 (= /Išar-dîn-Šamaš/). Or Iḫîṭ-Šamaš on comparison with Ilī-ḫîṭanni in Stamm, ANG p. 167. Cf. also I-sar-ki-^{d}UTU.

NḪR.

Sarg. and Ur III PN:

Na-ḫa-ru-um (G+; Oppenheim, CCTE p. 197, U).

NḪR nuḫḫurum (a man with certain nasal characteristics).

Sarg. and Ur III PN:

Nu-ḫu-ra (ITT II/2 p. 23, 4426; IV p. 6, 7063, U). Cf. Nuḫḫurum in Stamm, ANG p. 12).

NḪS naḫāsum.

1(PI) ZÍD.ŠE a-na na-ḫa-zi GU (D 229 twice).

NḪŠ naḫšum "rich."

Sarg. and Ur III PN's:

Na-aḫ-šu-a (Jean, ŠA LXVII iii, U)

Na-aḫ-šum (E+)

Na-aḫ-šum-BALA (Kish 1930, 170g; U 2331; Chiera, STA 36, U; TCL II 5504 ii, U; RA IX 58 SA 36, U)

Na-ḫi-iš-tum (E+; Chiera, STA 3 iii, U)

Na-ḫi-áš-[t]um (Orient. XLVII 331, U). ÁŠ miscopied for ÉŠ?

Na-ḫi-éš-tum(-MA) (TCL V 6162 i, U)

PN DUB.SAR šu Na-ḫi-iš-tim (BM 54309 i).

nuḫšum "prosperity."

Sarg. PN's:

Eš$_4$-dar-nu-uḫ-si (D)
Ì-lí-nu-uḫ-si (D).

NKD?, see NQD?

NKP? nakāpum?

Sarg. PN:

Šu-na-ak-pum (FM+).

NKP? nakkaptum?

Na-ga-ab-tum and Na-kab-tum, sometimes misread as Na-da-tum, is a location in Ur III texts, often mentioned in connection with animals:

Na-ga-ab-tum (Nikolski, Dok. II 435; BIN V 132; 269; Fish, CST 611 rev.; 628; Contenau, CHÉU 5; TCL V 5669 ii, rev. i)

Na-kab-tum (Fish, CST 240; 241; 255; 272; 278; 283; 284; YOS IV 211 iv; 217:18; CT XXXII 12 iii; Legrain, TRU 5; 91; 93; TCL II 4691 seal; 5524 rev.; 5551 rev.; 5641; BIN V 237; De Genouillac, TD 24; RTC 306 rev. iii; etc.)

For more examples cf. Oppenheim, CCTE p. 23.

Sarg. RN:

Na-kab-tum ÍD (D).

NKP? nikiptum? (a resinous plant).

Akk. lw. in Sum.:

x MA.NA ŠIM ^{d}NIN.IB-tum (Reisner, TUT 122 v, U; ITT V 6736, U)

NI ("oil") ni(n)-ki-ip-tum (RTC 109 rev.)

[ŠI]M? ni(n)-ki-ip-[tum] (PBS XIII 26).

NKR nakārum "to be different," "to rebel," "to refuse."

ì-nu-me GN$_1$ ù GN$_2$ i-gi-ru-uš i-li-ik-ma na-ak-ru-uz-zu ik-me "when GN$_1$ and GN$_2$ rebelled against him, he went and captured his enemies" (MDP XIV p. 10 i)

in du!-a-rí-su GN na-ki-ir-ma SAG.GIŠ.RA "in his return he vanquished GN, (which) had rebelled (against him)" (R xvii)

šum-ma-sa da-na-kir "should she refuse" (D 282:10).

nakrum "enemy."

ì-nu-me GN$_1$ ù GN$_2$ i-gi-ru-uš i-li-ik-ma na-ak-ru-uz-zu ik-me "when GN$_1$ and GN$_2$ rebelled against him, he went and captured his enemies" (MDP XIV p. 10 i).

nakarum "another (person)."

LÚ-lam na-ga-ra-am u-gal-la-mu-ma "(whoever) shows (the statue) to another person" (UET I 276 i, NS.).

nukrānum.

Ur III Amorite PN:

Nu-uk-ra-nu-um MAR.TU (Univ. Illinois 133).

NKS nukkusum.

sheep PN u-na-ki-is (BIN VIII 141)

various things u-na?-ki?-[is]? (D 231 iv). Very doubtful.

NM?

Ur III PN:

Na-mu-tum (AnOr VII 147).

NMʾ$_x$ namaum (a container?).

na-ma-ù ŠE (FM 43:3, school text?). Cf. na-mu-ú among URUDU implements in LTBA I 33 vi 23.

NMR? namārum?, see ʾ$_x$MR?

NMR? namārum? (object of metal).

Akk. lw. in Ur III Sum.:

1 na-⌈ma⌉?-ru-um UD.KA.BAR (TCL II 5589). Cf. ^{KUŠ}na-ma-ru (weapon or the like) in Delitzsch, AHWB p. 91b. Or naʾmarum "mirror?"

NN? nannûm.

PSarg. and Sarg. PN's:

Na-ni (DP 2 i, PSarg.; D+)

Na-ni-a (G+)

Na-num (FM)

Na-núm (D).

DN in Ur III PN's:

I-bí-iq-Na-ni (ITT V p. 60, 9951)

I-bí-iq-Na-nu-um (A 2980)

For the DN cf. I-din-^{d}Na-ni in TCL I 237:30, OB, Wa-ti-ir-Na-nu-um, -Na-nim, -Na-nam in TCL XXIII 44, Mari, Ur-^{d}Na-nu-um in BE VI/2 13 seal, OB, Me-gir-Na-ni and Šu-Na-ni in TA 1931, 443, OB, Ki-iš-Na-ni in TA 1931, 463, OB.

NN?

Sarg. and Ur III PN's:

Na-na-tum (G+; MCS III 25, U)

Na-na-ti (Delaporte, CCL I T 160, U)

Na-na-ti-a (U 2356)

Na-na-tim, Gen. (MO D vii).

In Ur III DN:

^{d}Geštin-an-na-na-na-tum (Nikolski, Dok. II 236 ii).

NN?

Sarg. and Ur III PN's:

Nu-ni-a (Legrain, TRU 364:11, U)

Nu-ni-da (MO; U 2402+). Cf. also Nu-i-da under Nʾ$_1$D

Nu-ni-tum (D+).

NNG?

Ur III PN:

Nu-nu-ug-tum (U 2399; Fish, CST p. 160 viii).

NNR? nannarum? (< Nʾ$_6$R *nanwarum?).

Sarg. and Ur III PN's:

Na-nar(LUL) (U 2348+)

Na-na-ri (D).

NP? napatum? (part of a chariot).

1 na-ba-tum (FM 33:13).

Akk. lw. in Ur III Sum.:

62 ^{GIŠ}na-ba-tum LAM?! (BE III 77:3). Cf. also 30 ^{GIŠ}na-pa-at GIŠ. TÚG.ḪI.A of a forest in A 3533, OB.

NPL napālum "to tear out," "to mine."

sa-tu-e a-bur-ti ti-a-am-tim sa-bil-tim NA$_4$.NA$_4$-su-nu MI i-bu-l[am-ma] (UET I 274, Mi.)

in sa-tu-su-nu NA$_4$.NA$_4$ E.SIG-im? i-bu-lam-ma (MDP VI Pl. 1, 1, NS.).

NPL napālum.

Ur III Amorite PN's:

Ì-an-bu-li MAR.TU (TCL II 5508 i)

Na-ap-la-nu-um MAR.TU (U 2323+)

Na-ap-la-núm MAR.TU (U 2324+).

NPL?

Sarg. PN's:

Na-ba-li (BE I Pl. VI ii+)

Na-ba-lul (G+)

Na-ba-lí-im, Gen. (D).

NPQ? napāqum?. See also ʾ$_x$PQ ipqum.

Sarg. and Ur III PN's:

En-bí-iq-^{d}Ḫa-ni-iš (UCP IX p. 205 iii)

I-bí-iq-Ìr-ra (U 1588; ArOr VII p. 25, U)

I-bí-iq-Eš$_4$-dar (UET III p. 16, U)

I-bi-iq-La-az (UET III p. 16, U)

I-bí-iq-Na-ni (ITT V p. 60, 9951, U)

I-bí-iq-Na-nu-um (A 2980, U)

I-bi-iq-ri-e-ú MAR.TU (A 29365+, U)

Cf. Ib-bi-iq-Eš$_4$-dar (Kh. 1935, 11, OB).

NPQ?

Ur III? PN:

Na-bi-kum (Coll. De Clercq I 100). Cf. Na-bi-gu-um in UET V 569 rev., OB.

NPQ? <u>nuppuqum</u>.

Sarg. PN:

Be-lam-nu-bi-iq (A 725; 974).

NPŠ <u>napāšum</u> "to breathe."

Sarg. PN:

Li-bu-uš-ì-a-um "may mine (i.e. 'my child') breathe" (De Sarzec, DC II Pl. LII). Parallels: Lippuš-ilum and Luppuš-ilum "may he/I breathe, O god!," quoted in Stamm, ANG p. 172.

<u>napšum</u>.

Ur III Amorite PN:

| Na-ap-sa-nu-um MAR.TU (PDTI 335)
| Na-ap-ša-nu-um MAR.TU (U 2328).

<u>napaštum</u>, <u>napištum</u> "life" (or the like).

Sarg. and Ur III PN's:

Be-lí-na-ba-áš-ti (D+)

| ^{d}Šul-gi-na-piš-ti-?.... (A 2964, U)
| ^{d}Šul-gi-ZI.MU (U 918f.).

NPŠ?

Sarg. PN:

Tu-da-na-ap-šum (D+). Interpr. unknown. Cf. also N'$_{x}$B?

NQ'$_{7}$ <u>naqājum</u> "to libate."

Sarg. and Ur III PN's:

| I-ki-DINGIR (G). Interpr. doubtful
| I-ki-LUM (MO+). Doubtful.

<u>niqjum</u> "libation."

a-na ni-ki-im SÁ "for the complete? libation" (HSS X 5:22). Reading ni-ki-im-di by Meek, HSS X p. xix is impossible because the sign DI does not have the value di in Old Akk. On the other side, SÁ šalmum is not attested in the early periods.

NQB, see NKP?

NQD?

PN? i-la-ak li-sá-ki-id li-li-ik "PN? will go, may he go quickly?" (ITT V 6682).

NQD?

in ru-ùḫ-ti [x na]-ak-tim (Kish 1930, 143:5)

ru-ùḫ-ti [i]n? na-ak-tim (l. 10).

Ur III PN's:

A-ba-na-ak-tum (UET III 1394)

DINGIR-na-ak-túm (UET III 1046 seal)

Šu-nak-da (TCL II 5498 ii).

NQD nāqidum (and? naqqadum) "shepherd."

NA.GAD "shepherd" is a Semitic lw. in Sum. from the Fara period on. Cf. ŠL 70, 48.

Sarg. and Ur III PN's:

Na-ga-da (Louvre AO 11267)

Na-gi-da (ITT II 2737 seal, U)

^{d}EN.ZU-na-gi$_4$-id (UET III 1048, U).

Ur III FN:

A.ŠÀ Na-ga-da-tum (Barton, HLC I Pl. 44, 90).

NQD? niqdum (a plant). Cf. ni-IG-du in Thompson, DAB p. 65.

This plant is different from nigîtum because both occur in TCL II 5680 iiif.

Akk. lw. in Ur III Sum.:

x QA ZÍD.KAL ni-ik-tum (TCL II 5521 passim)

x QA ni-ik-tum (TCL V 5680 iii; 6037 rev. vi; ITT V 6996)

x QA ni-ik-tum al-la-ḫa-ru (TCL V 6037 rev. vi). Cf. x MA.NA a-al-la-ḫa-ru ni-ik-tum in BIN IX 83, OB.

NQM?

Ur III Amorite PN:

En-gi-mu-um MAR.TU (Legrain, TRU 29; SO IX/1 No. 21; PDTI 529 viii).

NRM? nurmûm "pomegranate."

A Semitic lw. in Sum.:

GIŠ.NU.ÚR.MA (UET III pp. 94 and 142, U)

1 GIŠ.LU(L).ÚR.MA (RTC 221 rev. i)

NU.ÚR.MAN (RA XVIII 53 iii, Voc. prat.).

NRR?

Sarg. PN:

Nir-ra-DINGIR (A 5232). Thus clear on tablet.

NSB?

a-na DN be-lí-su ni-is-ba-at ni-is-ba-at-ma e-ri-ib-su ú-la ip-ru-us (MDP IV Pl. 2 iv). Meaning unknown. Perhaps something like "whatever his wishes"; dialectal nizmat?

NSḪ nasāḫum "to tear out."

DN SUḪUŠ-su li-zu-uḫ ù ŠE.NUMUN-su li-il-gu-ut (S iv)

2 DN's SUḪUŠ-su li-zu-ḫa ù ŠE.NUMUN-su li-il-gu-da (PBS V 34 x, Lugalzagesi; RA XXI 66 and 71, S.; S ix, xi twice, xv; R xviii twice, xix, xx, xxi twice, xxiv, xxv, xxvi, xxvii; RA VIII 136; 139; Mi.; NS.; BE I 2, Škš.; MDP II p. 66; ZA IV 406, Gutium, 3 DN's)

DN's SUḪUŠ-su li-zu-ḫu ù ŠE.NUMUN-su li-il-gu-tu (BE I 120, NS.; BE I 1, Škš.; MDP VI Pl. 2, 1 ii)

DN's SUḪUŠ-[su] li-zu(wr. su)-ḫu ù NUMUN-[su] li-il-[gu-du] (MDP IV Pl. 2 v)

3 DN's SUḪUŠ-šu li-zu-ḫa ú ŠE.NUMUN-[š]u li-il-ku-da (AOF III 112, Mari)

SUḪUŠ GN_1 in UKÙ GN_2 i-zu-uḫ-ma (R [xxiii], xxv)

grain [ù]-la i-na?-zi?-iḫ šu Ku-ur-ma (HSS X 62:4). = innasiḫ?

animals a-na PN na-zi-iḫ in DUB-su ù-la ḫu-bu-ut (BIN VIII 141).

NSḪ nusḫum (a container).

Akk. lw. in Ur III Sum.:

1 ^{KUŠ}nu-us-ḫu (BE III 76)

Cf. also GI.PISAN nu-us-ḫu-um in BIN IX 361 and UET V p. 69, OB.

NSḪ nusuḫum (a wooden object).

Akk. lw. in Sum.:

^{GIŠ}nu-zu-ḫu-um (ITT V p. 46, 9624)

x ^{GIŠ}MA nu-zu-ḫum (UET III 835, U). Doubtful

[....] nu-zu-ḫu-um TUR SIR (UET III 733 i, U).

NSK, see NZK šuzzukum.

NSP nasappum (a container).

1 DUG na-za-bu NI.DUN, 1 [DUG] na-za-bu zi-bí-bí-a-núm, 1 DUG na-za-bu Ú.TIR (BIN VIII 267). Interpr. as na(n)ṣābum also possible.

NSQ nisqum (a profession; kind of slave, servant).

Akk. lw. in Sum.:

PN ni-is-ku (Fish, CST 9; Iraq Mus. 30350; OIP XIV 138; 194; A 979)

PN ni-is-ku-E (ITT V 9259)

ENGAR ni-is-ku (OIP XIV 93)

NU.BANDA ni-is-ku (OIP XIV 162)

PA ni-is-ku (ITT IV 7052 rev.)

51 ni-is-ku 20 NAR (OIP XIV 98)

9 ni-is-ku 27 ŠÀ.DÙG (A 695). Animals?

GÁ.DUB ni-is-ku BA.A+ḪA ni-is-ku BA.ÚŠ "fugitive and dead" (A 900)

ni-is-k[u] ù GÍN.[UŠ]? (A 1015)

1 1/2 MA.NA ni-is-ku (A 5240). PN?

"compte de NI.GIŠ.KU et de LÚ.URU" (ITT V p. 37, 9383)

PN_1 ni-is-kam ZAG.U PN_2 [li]-ḫu-$uš_x$(EŠ) (D 278). The nisqū's were marked!

ni?-is-ku-su a-na? UNUG^{KI} lu it-tal-ku (Ist. Mus. Lagash 11001 rev.)

(small cattle delivered? by) ni-is-ku-um LUGAL (A 4966; A 5686, both U) x GUD BA.ÚŠ ŠÀ ni-is-kum LUGAL?! (TCL II 5503, U)

⌈mur-ni-is⌉-ku (Thureau-Dangin, SAKI p. 94 vi 13, Gudea) and ni-is-ku (ibid. p. 104 xiv 25), explained as "magnificent or splendid donkey-colt" by Poebel, AS XIV 43ff., and similarly Falkenstein in ZA XLIX 328. Cf. also ANŠE ni-is-ku/kum in Barton, MBI 3 ii 7 and VAS X 198:26, and ni-is-kum in Orient. n. s. XXIII 50, all Sum.

NṢB? (an object of metal). See also NSP nasappum.

Akk. lw. in Ur III Sum.:

2 ša-za-ab-tum AN.NA KI.LAL.BI 5/6 GÍN (Jean, ŠA LXXVII x+6, rev. x+8). Among ornaments. It is tempting to correct ŠA to IN or AN, but the copy is against it.

NṢR naṣārum "to watch," "to guard."

ad-da MÁŠ.ANŠE ù-la da-na-za-ar (JRAS 1932 p. 296:5)

i-na-za-ar (MDP XIV 90 rev.)

li-zu-ur (HSS X 6:4)

li-zu-ur-ma (HSS X 5:17)

li-zu-ru (HSS X 5:19)

ù-zu-ur, Impv. (JRAS 1932 p. 296:37).

PSarg., Sarg., and Ur III PN's:

DINGIR-na-zi-ir (D+)

E-lu?-na-zé-ir (ITT IV p. 65, 7635, U)

E-zur-an-ni (Nikolski, Dok. I 18 rev. i, PSarg.)

I-zu-ur-ba-s[u] (FM)

I-zur-^{d}EN.ZU (U 1580)

I-zur-ì-lí (TMH n.F. I/II p. 20, U; U 1581+)

I-zu-ur-ì-lí (TMH n.F. I/II p. 20, U)

E-zur-ì-lí (U 1033+)

E-zu-rí-ì-lí (HSS IV 57 rev., U)

⌈In⌉-na-zé-ir (RTC 347 i)

Ì-na-zé-ir (ITT III 4926, U)

Na-aṣ-ru-um (D+)

Na-zi-ir-ì-li (FM+)

Ú-zu-ur-ba-su (D)

Ú-zur-ba-šu(m) (U 1125).

niṣrum.

Sarg. PN:

Ni-iz-ru-um (D). Doubtful.

maṣṣarum "guard."

Sarg. PN:

Ma-za-ar-su (FM). What meaning as a PN? Cf. perhaps Ì-lí-ma-za-ri in Ist. Mus. 31172, OB.

Ur III GN:

Ma-za-ru-um (ZA LI Pl. I after p. 74 ii 24, 27, 28, Pl. II iv 14).

maṣṣartum "watch(-tower?)."

dead sheep received in ma-za-ar-ti Ne-im-zi-im (= GN) (JCS X 29 No. 8 rev., U).

NŠ nišū "people."

Used in Pl. of Fem. gender.

ì-nu ^{d}En-líl .... zi-ra-at ni-se$_{11}$ ga-ti-iš-su i-ti-nu (PBS V 36 rev. x+iii, NS.)

iš-tum da-ar si-ki?-ti ni-se$_{11}$ (UET I 275 i, NS.)

ni-se$_{11}$ ša-at ^{d}Da-gan BÍL-iš i-ki-su-šum (UET I 275 ii, NS.)

SUḪUŠ GN$_1$ in UKÙ GN$_2$ i-zu-uḫ-ma (R [xxiii], xxv).

Sarg. PN's:

SIPA-ni-se$_{11}$ (G)

Si-tu-ul-ni-šè (ITT I 1062 rev.).

Sarg. GN:

Ši-tu-ul-ni-šè^{KI} (Kish 1930, 406 rev. iii).

NŠ.

Sarg. and Ur III PN's:

A-ḫu-ni-sa? (Kish 1930, 177n)

^{d}Ba-ú-ni-ša$_6$ (AnOr I p. 27, U). Probably Sum. ^{d}Ba-ú-ì-ša$_6$

É-a-ni-ša (CT XXXII 36 i, U; PDTI 99, U)

^{d}En-líl-ni-ša$_6$ (AnOr I p. 27, U). Probably Sum.

Eš$_4$-dar-ni-sa (D+)

I-šar-ni-si (BE III 46 rev., U). Cf. ^{d}Nin-líl-ni-ši in PBS XI/2 p. 132, OB

Ma-ma-ni-ša, f.n. (Delaporte, CCL I D 26, U).

NŠ -ni-šu, see ʾ$_7$Šʾ$_6$.

NŠʾ$_1$ našāʾum "to raise," "to carry."

ga-ti lu aš-ši (CT XXXII 2 iv, CM)

ti-bu-dam li-se$_{11}$-ù-ni-kum-ma "may (the workers) come to your help" (JRAS 1932 p. 296:19)

GIŠ.ÍL DN ì-lí-su na-se$_{11}$-<a>?-nim "(the people = nišū) bear? the corvée of DN, his god" (UET I 275 ii, NS.).

Ur III PN's:

Šu-mu-li-iš-ši (UET III 1305 seal). Unique

Na-si-bí-tum (Oppenheim, CCTE p. 197). Doubtful.

nišî (ênim) "favored."

Sarg. and Ur III PN's:

Ni-se$_{11}$-^{d}É (PBS XI/3 No. 55, U)

Ni-se_{11}-e-ni-sa, f.n. (RA XXIV 96+)
Ni-se_{11}-e-ni-su (D+).

NT?, see N'_xT?

NT?

Akk. lw. in Sum.?:

NI.TUM PN_1 DUMU PN_2 or NI.TUM PN_1 ši PN_2 or NI.TUM PN_1 ŠEŠ PN_2, and the like (D 241).

$NṬ'_6$ naṭāwum "to be suited."

šum-ma e-ra-si-iš na-tu "if (it) is suitable for plowing" (HSS X 5:23).

NZ?

Sarg. PN:

Na-zi-tim (MO).

NZ?

Ur III PN's:

Ni-za-at (Barton, HLC III Pl. 150 iv)
Ni-za-tum (Fish, CST p. 160 viii).

NZK šuzzukum or šussukum "to damage."

Von Soden in AOr XVII/2 366f. interprets this verb as NSK šussukum "flach hinwerfen lassen."

ša DUB su_4-a u-sa-za-ku-ni (PBS V 34 x, Lugalzagesi; S iv, ix, xi, with and without -ni; R xviii, xix, xx, xxi twice, xxiv, xxv, xxvi, xxvii; RA VIII 136; 139; Mi.; NS.; Škš.; ZA IV 406, Gutium)

šu DUB šu-a ù-sá-za-gu (MDP VI Pl. 2, 1 ii)

šu DUB šu-a ù-sa-za-gu (MDP X Pl. 3, 1a, 1b, 2). Read ù-sa!-za-gu in the inscription of Idadu-Šušinak in the post-Ur III period (MDP VI Pl. 5 end) against the questionable ù-šam-za-gu of Ungnad, MAS p. 72

[ša DUB su_4-a u-š]a-za-ku (AOF III 112, Mari)

ša DUB su_4-a u-sa-za-gu (RA XXXIV 173f., Mari)

su_4 DUB šu-a-ti ú-sá-za-ku (RA IX Pl. 1 opp. p. 1, Urkiš and Nawar)

ša za-al-mi-in an-ni-in ù DUB-ba-am ù-ša-za-ku (Morgan, MDP IV 161, Lullubum)

(šu) ú-sa-za-gu-ni (MDP II p. 63 ii = MDP XIV p. 20 ii)

[.... ú-s]a-za-gu (MDP II p. 66)

ma-na-ma MU Rí-mu-uš .... u-sa-za-ku-ma (R xviii, xxiv)

ma-na-ma MU-mi .... u-sa-za-ku-ma (UET I 276 i, NS.)

ma-na-ma MU-mi a?! u-sa-zi-iq (UET I 275 iv, NS.).

NZZ, see Z'_6Z.

P

P pum "mouth," "word."

Written syllabically or logographically. No evidence in Old Akk. whether the word has 1 or 2 consonants or whether the vowel is short or long. Constr. St. pu and (rarely) pi.

In many occurrences below the word for "word" must be considered a DN, presumably prototype of later Logos.

PSarg., Sarg., and Ur III PN's:

Bí-su-šè-ip-num (MO). Interpr. doubtful

DINGIR-BU (UET I 12, PSarg., and Jacobsen, AS XI 103)

E-te-al-pi$_{x}$(KA+KÁR)-^{d}Da-gan (Bab. VIII Pl. V 17:9+, U)

I-da-bí-ì-li (D+; FM). Cf. I-da-bí-DINGIR in BIN IX 316:24, OB

I-ku-pu-sa (OIP XIV 150)

I-zu-ur-ba-s[u] (FM)

K[A]-be-lí (FM)

KA-Da-ba-an (D)

^{d}KA-da-bi (Chiera, STA 16 rev., U; Oppenheim, CCTE p. 77, U)

KA-la-⌈ba⌉? (D)

KA-ma-DINGIR (ITT I 1365+). Parallel to Šar-ma-ì-lum. Cf. also ^{d}EN.ZU-ma-DINGIR in UE X 541, OB, or ì-lí-ma-DINGIR in BE VI/2 46, OB

KA-Ma-ma (OIP XIV 71 ii, PSarg.; G+)

KA-Me-ir (D+)

^{d}KA-Me-ir (G+). Interpr. as Anum-pu-Mer (for such names cf. Stamm, ANG p. 233) apparently impossible in Old Akk.

KA-su-GI (BIN VIII 143)

KA-su-su (D+)

LUGAL-pum (OIP XLVII 41)

LUGAL-KA (E+)

Pi-ì-lí (TMH V 16+)

Pù-^{d}AB (D)

Pù-AD NIN (Woolley, UE II Pl. 191 U 10939, PSarg.). Misread as Shubad and the like

Pù-A-bi (E)

Pù-^{d}A-bi (LB 972 ii)

Bu-BALA (E+)

Pù-ba-lik (D). Or Mu-pum-ba-lik

Pù-be-lí (MO)
Bu-be-lí (Delaporte, CCL II A II 154)
Pù-^{d}DA (G+)
Pù-^{d}Da-gan (MO)
Pù-DINGIR (Louvre AO 8637; 8641)
Pù-^{d}E[N.ZU/LÍL] (D)
Pù-GI (BE I Pl. VI ii+)
Pù-ì-lí (D+)
Pù-^{d}Iš-ḫa-ra (D)
Pù-Na-na (G)
Pù-Nu-nu (PSBA XX Pl. I i, PSarg.)
Pù-sa-GAL (CT VII 4, 22451, PSarg.)
Pù-ša-ra-bí (HSS IV 86, U). Or Puzur-abī
Pù-su-DÙG (D+)
Pù-su-GI (D+; MDP XVIII 74, U)
Pù-šu-ki-in (UET III p. 8, U)
Bu-šu?(wr. si)-ki-in (Nies, UDT 94 rev., U)
Pù-su-^{d}ÍD (D)
Pù-su-lí (D)
Pù-uš-GAL (MO)
Pù-uš-ki-in (PDTI 529 x, U)
Pù-uš-sa, f.n. (BIN VIII 259)
Pù-sar (RTC 12 i+, PSarg.; Kish 1931, 122 rev. ii)
Pù-SU.KUR.RU (BIN VIII 11 iii, PSarg.)
Pù-^{d}Tišpak (D+)
Pù-^{d}UTU (D+)
Ú-zu-ur-ba-su (D)
Ú-zur-ba-šu(m) (RA VIII 194 No. 16, U)
Cf. also several Ur III PN's in U 1794ff.

Ur III GN:
Bi-na-ra-tum^{KI} (TCL V 6041 i).

Pʾ$_x$ pûtum "front." See also Pʾ$_x$D pûdum and Bʾ$_x$D bûdum.
a-ti-ma bu-ti ti-a-am-tim (S vi)
iš-tum-ma bu-ti UD.KIB.NUN ÍD (UET I 275 ii, NS.)
in bu-ti GN (RTC 130, date of Škš.).

Ur III GN's:
Bu-ut-tu-li-um^{KI} (RA IX 63 AM 14). Doubtful
Bu-ut-ša-dar^{KI} (CT XXXII 21 v). Doubtful.

Pʾ$_x$D? pûdum? "shoulder."
in bu-ti-su parallel to in ga-ti-su (Kish 1930, 143 rev.). See also

P'$_x$ pûtum.

P'$_6$Ḫ pûḫum "substitute."

Ur III GN:

Bu-úḫ-zi-gàr^{KI} (CT XXXII 19 iv; PDTI 448, read thus against translit.). Division of GN doubtful.

Ur III PN:

Bu-ḫi-lí-zi (Jean, ŠA LVIII rev.).

pûḫānum.

Sarg. PN:

Bu-ḫa-núm (Fish, CST 6). Cf. Bu-ḫa-nu-um (Frank, SKT Pl. XX/7, OB?).

P'$_x$Q?

ŠU.NIGÍN 3(PI) 10(QA) ŠE, ŠE-um bu-ku-um šu MÁ.LAḪ$_4$-e (MDP XIV 26).

PDN padānum "road."

Nergal ba-da-an NS. DA.NÚM ip-te-ma (UET I 275 i, NS.)

[pa]-da-an [m]i-sar-im [lu] ip-ti-a-am (CT XXXII 2 iv, CM).

DN in Sarg. and Ur III PN's:

ARÁD-ba-dan (A 3008, U)

E-na-ba-d[an]? (D)

Ì-lí-ba?-dan (Orient. XLVII 418:10, U)

I-sar-ba-dan (U 1645+)

I-sar-ba-da-an (Barton, HLC III Pl. 123, 263 rev., U)

I-sar-pa-da-an (AnOr I 228 i 10, U, translit. only). Cf. DN ^{d}I-sar-pàd-da = ^{d}I-sar-pa-da-an in RA XII 71, OB.

PSarg. DN:

^{d}Pa-dan (Deimel, PB No. 2954+).

PḪD puḫādum "lamb."

x bu-ḫa-du among small cattle (Louvre AO 11318).

Ur III PN:

Bu-ḫa-ti (U 526+; Fish, CST p. 159 iii).

PḪL? puḫḫulum.

Sarg. PN:

Bu-ḫu-lum (BE I Pl. VII v).

PḪR paḫārum "to come together."

GN$_1$ ù GN$_2$ .... a-na KAS+X ip-ḫu-ru-nim-ma (R xxii; RA VII 104, Mi.)

ip-ḫu-ru-[nim-ma] (MDP II p. 53, NS.).

Sarg. and Ur III PN's:

A-ḫu-ba-ḫír/ḫar (HSS IV 81 rev., U; Barton, HLC I Pl. 48, 361, U)

Dan-ip-ḫur (Nikolski, Dok. II 355, U)

Ip-ḫur (MDP XXVIII 526; U 1689; Barton, HLC II Pl. 97, 125, U+)

Ip-ḫur-Kiš^{KI} (D)

Ip-ḫu-ru-[um] (RTC 98).

puḫrum "assembly."

^{d}EN.KI be-al UKKIN (AOF III 112 twice, Mari).

napḫarum "total."

Written logographically and syllabically.

ŠU.NIGÍN (HSS X 15:11f. and passim)

in ŠU.NIGÍN-su-nu (PBS V 36 rev. iv, NS.; UET I 276 ii, NS.)

ŠU.NIGÍN.ŠU.NIGÍN "summa summarum" (RTC 101; 136; MDP XIV 45; MO A v; etc.)

2 PN's KÁ (object) in na-ap-ḫa-rí-su-nu li-ik-nu-ku (Cop. 10055 rev.).

tapḫurtum "gathering" or "totality."

4 persons in [GN$_1$] 2 persons i[n GN$_2$ ....] LÚ.A+ḪA.A.M[E] (space) d[a-a]p-ḫu-ur-tum (HSS X 204 rev., reading quite safe; text seems to refer to a collection of fugitives). Cf. DA.GA.AN.TUM.MA = ta-ap-ḫu-ur-tum (Landsberger, Ana ittišu p. 39) and DA.GAN (also DA.GA.AN) = kullatu (ŠL 335, 58).

PḪR paḫarum "potter."

Akk. word may be a lw. from Sum. BAḪAR.

PN PA.ḪAR (Pinches, AT p. 56 ii, U).

Sarg. and Ur III PN's:

Ba-ḫar (BIN VIII 273 ii; Barton, HLC II Pl. 89 ix 1, U)

Ba-ḫa-ru-um (D; ITT IV 7863, U).

PLʾ$_x$ palaʾum "period," "rule."

Akk. lw. from Sum. BALA.

Written syllabically or logographically.

Sarg. and Ur III PN's:

A-bu-BALA (Nikolski, Dok. II 35 ii)

Ba-la-ki-na-ti-im (PSarg. king)

Ba-la-zu (Barton, HLC I Pl. 47, 376 i, U)

Ba-lu-sa (D+)

Ba-lu-zu (D)

BALA-É-a (MO). Cf. Pa-la-^{d}Tišpak in Kh. 1935, 35, OB

BALA-ì-lum (BE I Pl. VI viii)

BALA-su (D+)

BALA-su-li-rí-ik (D)

Be-lí-BALA (RTC 127 rev. iv+)

DINGIR-BALA (D; MDP XVIII 72, U)

DINGIR-ba-la (U 294; Fish, CST p. 159 v, U)

Gi-núm-BALA (D)

Gi-núm-ba-la (D)

It-be-⌈bal⌉-la (Kish 1931, 122 ii) but It-be-la-ba (Kish 1930, 144a; 170d, collated)

Ma-al-tum-BALA (Nikolski, Dok. II 35 i)

Na-aḫ-šum-BALA (Kish 1930, 170g; U 2331+)

Bu-BALA (E+)

Šim-tum-BALA (Kish 1930, 406 rev. i)

Šu-ba-la (G+).

PLG palgum "canal."

ì-nu ba-la-ag Si-da-rí^{KI} ip-te-ù (MDP IV Pl. 2 ii)

x GÁN šu ba-la-ag Da-da(-?)rí-im (PSBA XX Pl. I i, PSarg.).

PLḪ palāḫum "to fear."

Ur III PN:

^{d}Šu-^{d}EN.ZU-i-ba-la-aḫ-^{d}En-líl (CT XXXII 43 iii)

^{d}Šu-^{d}EN.ZU-ì-ba-la-aḫ-^{d}En-líl (PDTI 563 iii).

palḫum "feared," "awe-inspiring."

Form paluḫ.

Sarg. and Ur III PN's:

Written syllabically or logographically.

Ba-luḫ-DINGIR (MDP XVIII 76, U)

TE.NA-DINGIR (D+)

Ba-luḫ-É (E)

Ba-lu-úḫ-É (E)

Ba-luḫ-É-a (Yondorf a, U).

Form paliḫ.

In some cases Paliḫ is clearly a DN.

Sarg. and Ur III PN's:

Written syllabically.

Be-lí-ba-lìḫ (D+)

Ku-ru-ub-ba-lìḫ (Ist. Mus. Adab 90)

Sar-ru-ba-lìḫ (G)

LU[GAL]-ba-lìḫ (ITT V 9259 rev.)

Šum-su-ba-lìḫ (RA IX 34 v). Cf. Šum-su-ì-šum

Ur-^{d}Ba-lìḫ (RA IX 59 SA 72 rev., U)

Cf. also PLQ palāqum.

PLL palālum. See also BLL balālum.

Sarg. and Ur III PN's:

Written syllabically or logographically.

DINGIR-IGI.D[U]? (D)

^{d}Ḫa-ni-IGI.DU (Orient. XIV 59 No. 12, U)

^{d}IM-pa-lí-il (AnOr I 201 rev., U)

^{d}ŠEŠ.KI-IGI.DU (U 977+)

^{d}Šul-gi-pa-lí-il (U 931+; CT XXXII 23 rev., U; TCL II 5500 ii, U)

^{d}UTU-IGI.DU (ZA XII 332)

[X-x]-ba-líl (D 70; cf. also ITT II/2 5885 rev., U, if not miscopied for -ba-lìḫ.

PLQ palāqum "to kill."

Interpretation of -ba-LIK as -pāliq is questionable; another possibility (without evidence) is to read -ba-liḫ$_x$(LIK) = -paliḫ.

PSarg., Sarg., and Ur III PN's:

A-ḫu-ba-lik (MO). Cf. A-ḫi-ša-gi-iš in Stamm, ANG p. 296

Be-lí-ba-lik (D+)

É-a?-ba-lik (Louvre AO 8638 rev.)

Eš$_4$-dar-ba-lik (D; f.n., PDTI 525, U)

Ì-lí-ba-lik (BIN VIII 249)

Ìr-ra-ba-lik (PBS XIV 255, U)

Mu-pum-ba-lik (D). To be read as MU Pù-ba-lik?

^{d}Nin-kilim-pa-lik (OIP LVIII 291 No. 7, PSarg.). Written in the order NIN.KILIM.AN.PA.UR. Possible interpr. is Ur-^{d}Nin-kilim ugula.

naplaqtum "battle-ax."

4 URUDU na-ap-la-ga-tum UD.KA.BAR, NÍG.ŠÁM 1 GIŠ.TUKUL 5 GÍN KUG. BABBAR (MO C viii)

1 URUDU na-ap-la-aq-tum UD.KA.BAR (MO C ix, xi).

PLS naplusum "to look."

in 1 MU DN ib-ba-al-su/zu-šum "in the year DN looked upon him" (MDP X Pl. 3, 1a).

Sarg. and Ur III PN's:

I-ba-lí-is (D+; U 1582; Jean, ŠA p. 79, U)

Na-ap-lí-is (Oppenheim, CCTE p. 196, U)

Na-ap-lí-is-DINGIR (YOS IV 254 i, U)

Na-ap-li-is-DINGIR (De Genouillac, TD 60:3, U)

Na-ap-lí-is-É-a (BIN V 29:15, U)

Na-ap-lí-zu-um (Delaporte, CCL II A 206, U).

pilsum.

Sarg. and Ur III PN:

Bìl-zum (G+)

Bil-zum (AnOr VII 372 iii, Sarg.?!)

Bi-il$_x$-zum (Nikolski, Dok. II 329 rev. i, U).

pullusum or bulluṣum.

Ur III PN:

Bu-lu-zu-um (U 530; YOS IV 246 i, v).

naplasum.

Ur III PN:

Na-ap-la-zum (Nikolski, Dok. II 487).

PN panû (plurale tantum) "face."

ma-ma-na ba-ni-su ù-la u-ba-al "he does not give pardon to anybody" (S xii; xv). For panî wabālum "to pardon" cf. Thureau-Dangin, RA XXI 12, and Landsberger, ZA XXXVIII 114

ba-ni ENGAR.ENGAR li-zu-ur-ma "may he watch the faces? of the farmers" (HSS X 5:19). Not sure.

PNQ?

Sarg. GN:

Ban-ga^{KI} (FM 33:46).

PNQ?

Ur III PN:

Bi-na-gu-um (Porada, CPML No. 281)

For the Sem. root PNQ cf. ZA XXXVIII 161.

PPS? pappasum? (a bird).

Sarg. PN:

Ba-ba-az (D+). Cf. Pap-pa-su in Stamm, ANG p. 257, and Ba-az-ba-zum in VAS VIII 14:15, OB.

Ur III GN:

Ba-ba-az^{KI} (Fish, CST p. 160 ix, x, xii; Iraq Mus. 10709).

Deified GN in Ur III PN:

| PÙ.ŠA-Ba-ba-az^{KI} (PDTI 542 rev.)
| PÙ.ŠA-Ba-ba-az (Fish, CST p. 160 vi, x).

PPS? pappūsum?

Sarg. PN:

Ba-pù-zum (FM). Cf. Pap-pu-zum in Chiera, PBS XI/1 No. 4 rev. v 12, OB.

PQD.

Sarg. PN:

Ba-aq-tum (G).

PQD?

Ur III PN's:

Ba-ga-ti-a (TMH n.F. I/II 106)

Ba-ga-tum (A 4584 rev.).

PQD?

Ur III PN's:

Bi-ga-ti (YOS IV 212 ii)

Bí-ga-tum (UET III p. 7).

PQD?

Ur III PN:

Bu-ga-ti (ZA XII 345).

PRʾ$_4$ pirtum "hair."

I seized him ki gal-bi-im ì-na ki-ša-ti-šu, ki me-ra-ni-im ì-na pi-ir-ti-šu (3 NT 30, U, cf. ṣabātum).

PRʾ$_x$ pirʾum "offspring."

bi-ri-šu ú šu-um-šu gods will destroy? (Morgan, MSP IV 158, Lullubum).

PRʾ$_5$Š pirḫašum "flea."

Sarg. and Ur III PN:

Bir$_5$-ḫa-šum (D+). Not Nam-ḫa-šum, as read there

Bir$_5$-ḫa-sum (OIP XIV 180)

Bir$_5$-ḫa-šu-um (CT IX 18 ii, U)

Bi-ir-ḫa-šum! (PDTI 566, U, translit. as Bi-ir-ḫa-ga-ni)

Cf. also Stamm, ANG p. 254: Piršaḫum.

PRK parākum "to set apart," "to assign," "to close in."

9 GÁN ŠE.BA SAL.ME ^{d}UTU a-na IGI.GUNU.NIM.BA.L[U] ip-ri-ka-am-ma (CT XXXII 1 iii, CM).

aṣ-ba-zu ki ma-ì áp-ru-uk-šu ki na-ri-im "I seized him like water, I closed him in like a river" (3 NT 30, U, cf. ṣabātum). Observe the form ipruk, not iprik.

Sarg. and Ur III PN's:

Bu-ru-uk (MCS IV 21 No. 18, U)

Ip-ru-uk (G).

PRS parāsum "to withhold."

e-ri-ib-su ú-la ip-ru-us (MDP IV Pl. 2 iv)

DN in ma-ti-su a-la-da-am li-ip-ru-us "may DN withhold child birth in his land" (CT XXXII 4 xii, CM)

mi-num da-ap-ru-us "(food?) why did you withhold?" (FM 52:5).

PRS parīsum.

Akk. PN:

Ba-r[i?-i]s?-tum (FM)

Ba-rí-za-tum (A 393; 394; 1070). All in difficult context.

PRS? pursîtum? (a container).

Sarg. GN:

Bur-zi-da-an^{KI} (Kish 1930, 147)

Cf. also QA.BUR.ZI and DUG.BUR.ZI discussed in Orient. IV 60.

PRS? pursum?

Akk. PN's:

Bur-zi-a (D+)

Bur-zum (MO).

PRṢ parṣum "sanctuary."

Sarg. GN:

Ba-ra-az-EDIN^KI (MO B vi; xiv).

PRŠG paršigum (a garment).

Lw. from Sum.

1 ba-ar-si-gu-um (MDP XXVIII 526+, U?)

In all other cases this word is written in Sum. as TÚG.BAR.SI, TÚG. BAR.SIG, BAR.SI, GAD.BAR.SI, and BAR.SI.GAD (garment made of wool or linen).

PRŠM puršumum (a temple official).

Sum. prototype of Akk. puršumum.

BUR.ŠU.MA (Deimel, Fara III 100 end).

PSL? pussulum?

Akk. lw. in Ur III Sum.:

1 ^URUDU^QA pù-KA-lum (Reisner, TUT 126 ii, U)

1 ^URUDU^A.LAL pù-KA-lum (ibid.). See also below.

PSN pussunum "veiled."

Sarg. and Ur III PN's:

| Pù-zu-nu-um (AnOr VII 321, U)
| Pù-zu-núm (U 424; YOS IV 224, U)
| Pù-KA-núm (Ist. Mus. Adab 187; 189; ITT IV 7055, U). See also above

Pù-KA-na-a (HSS IV 67; 68 rev., U).

PṢʾ₃ piṣʾum "white."

1 TÚG.NÍG.LÁM pi-ṣi-tum (CT XXXII 4 xi, CM).

PŠḪ pašāḫum "to become tranquil."

da-ba-ša-ḫi-ni (Kish 1930, 143 rev.). Doubtful.

Sarg. and Ur III PN's:

Ba-ša-aḫ (E)

| Ba-ša-aḫ-DINGIR (MO+)
| Ba-sa-aḫ-DINGIR (Iraq Mus. 43612)
| Bi-ša-aḫ-DINGIR (TCL II 4682:3+, U)
| Bí-ša-aḫ-DINGIR (Jean, ŠA CLXIV seal, U)
| Bí-sa-aḫ-DINGIR (Fish, CST p. 159 i, U)
| Bí-ša-ḫi-DINGIR (UET III 1582 rev. v, U)
| Bí-ša-ḫi-li (HSS IV 77 rev., U)
| Bí-ša-ḫi-lum (SO IX/1 No. 31 rev., U)

| Bí-ša-ḫa?(wr. za)-lum (U 559 = Orient. IV p. 59, translit. only)
| Pi_x(KA+KÁR)-ša-ḫa-lum (RTC 397 i, U), or PÙ.ŠA-ḫa-lum /Puzur-ḫâlum/
| Pi_x-ša-ḫa-li (Pinches, AT 61, U), or PÙ.ŠA-ḫa-li /Puzur-ḫâli/

Pi$_x$-ša-ḫa-lí (TCL II 5498 ii, U; Fish, CST p. 159 i, U).

Ur III FN:

A.ŠÀ Bí-ša-ḫu-um-MA (BE III 91:15).

PŠL pašallum (kind of gold).

x MA.NA (KUG.GI) ba-sa-lum (MDP XVIII 81 rev.).

PŠR pašārum (agricultural activity in connection with a) soil, b) grain; cf. Landsberger, Ana ittišu pp. 173ff., 187f.).

(GÁN)? šu ba-sa-rí-im (D 332 rev. x+5)

so much ŠE.GUR šu ba-sa-rí-im (D 2 rev. vii x+5).

PŠŠ pašāšum "to anoint."

Sarg. MN:

I-ba-ša-áš (OIP XIV 165 rev.).

PŠŠ pašīšum (a priest).

Apparently a lw. from Sum.

S. PAB.ŠEŠ AN (S ii, vii, ix)

PN PAB.ŠEŠ (BE I Pl. VI viii; VII iii; BIN VIII 131)

1 DUMU.SAL PAB.ŠEŠ (BIN VIII 143)

Mi. PA.ŠEŠ AN (CT XXXII 1 i = RA VII 180) in CM.

PŠT paštatum "flax?"

ba-áš-da-dam u-sa-am-la-su$_4$-ma "with flax? he will fill it (the skin) up" (MDP XIV 90 rev.). Also ba-áš-d[a?-nothing?]-tum or ba-áš-t[um? ....]-tum (ibid.). Interpr. doubtful. Cf. Hebrew pešet "flax" besides nomen unitatis pištā "flax plant."

PŠṬ pašāṭum "to erase."

MU-su-me bí-si$_4$-iṭ-ma, Impv. (UET I 276 i, NS.).

PŠṬ? puššuṭum?

PSarg. PN:

Pù-šu-tum (OIP XIV 48 ii+).

PTʾ$_3$ pataʾum "to open."

2 PN's KÁ ša ŠE li-ip-te-u-ma (Cop. 10055 rev.)

Nergal ba-da-an NS. DA.NÚM ip-te-ma (UET I 275 i, NS.)

ì-nu ba-la-ag Si-da-rí^{KI} ip-te-ù (MDP IV Pl. 2 ii)

[pa]-da-an [m]i-sar-im [lu] ip-ti-a-am (CT XXXII 2 iv, CM)

1 GANAM MI la ba-ti-tum "1 black ewe unopened," i.e. "virgin sheep" (MDP XIV 90).

Sarg. and Ur III PN's:

Ip-te-u-um (FM+)

Ip-ti-um (FM)

Ip-ti-DINGIR (D+; UET III p. 17, U).

PTʾ$_7$, see BṬʾ$_7$ baṭijum.

PTN *naptanum* "meal."

na-ap-ta-an ^{d}UTU (CT XXXII 1 iii; 2 v, vi, CM)

na-ap-ta-an UD.3.KAM (ibid.)

na-ap-ta-an ŠU.GI.NA (UET III 270 rev. i and ii, post-Ur III).

Akk. lw. in Sum.:

x QA GAR [n]a-ap-da-núm (MDP XIV 9 end)

2(GUR) 2(PI) 6 QA GAR GUR na-ap-da-núm ZI.GA Lú-gi-na (Pinches, BTBC 48)

4 GUR na-ap-da-núm Lú-^{d}[X] ŠU.BA.AN.TI (UET III 1126 rev. ii).

PTN?

Ur III PN:

Na-ap-da-núm (U 2322+). Cf. perhaps Na-ap-d[a-núm] in MDP XIV 37.

PTR? *pattarum* (a weapon) or PṬR *paṭarum* "dagger."

1 URUDU ba-da-ru-um UD.KA.BAR, NÍG.ŠÁM 1 GIŠ.TUKUL (weapon) 5 GÍN KUG.BABBAR (MO C ii)

Cf. perhaps 1 BA.DAR UD.KA.BAR (PBS IX 132).

PṬR *paṭārum* "to deduct."

[....] li-ip-du-ur (MDP XIV 32 ii)

3 GÍN KUG.BABBAR i-ba-ta-ar "he will deduct 3 shekels of silver" or "3 shekels of silver will be deducted" (TMH n.F. I/II 7, U).

ipṭirū, *ipṭirum* "redemption money."

Sarg. PN's:

Ip-ti-ru (D+)

Ip-ti-ru-um (D+).

PZR *puzrum* "shelter," "protection."

PSarg. and Sarg. PN's:

PÙ.ŠA-A-a (BE I Pl. VI iii)

PÙ.ŠA-^{d}A-bi (D)

PÙ.ŠA-A-bi (D; U 451+; UET III p. 8, U)

PÙ.ŠA-ra-bí (HSS IV 86, U). Or Puša-rabî

PÙ.ŠA-ra-a-bí (Reisner, TUT 204, U)

PÙ.ŠA-AD.DA (G+)

PÙ.ŠA-be-lí (ITT I 1156)

PÙ.ŠA-pi-lí (TMH V 3 i, PSarg.?)

PÙ.ŠA-DÙG (BE I Pl. VIII)

PÙ.ŠA-É-A (D+)

PÙ.ŠA-È-a (Nikolski, Dok. II 21+)

PÙ.ŠA-É.GAL (G+)

PÙ.ŠA-^{d}En-líl (BIN VIII 11 v+)

PÙ.ŠA-^{d}EN.ZU (G+)

PÙ.ŠA-Eš$_4$-dar (G+)
PÙ.Š[A-^{d}]Ḫa-rí-im (ITT I 1287)
PÙ.ŠA-^{d}ÍD (D)
PÙ.ŠA-ì-li (MO)
PÙ.ŠA-ì-lí (E)
PÙ.ŠA-Il-la (MO)
PÙ.ŠA-^{d}IM (MO+)
PÙ.ŠA-^{d}INNIN.ERIN (E)
PÙ.ŠA-INNIN.ZA (ITT V 5271)
PÙ.ŠA-Ìr-ra (D)
PÙ.ŠA-Keš (D)
PÙ.ŠA-Lu-lu (D+)
PÙ.ŠA-^{d}Ma-lik (Ist. Mus. Adab 280)
PÙ.ŠA-Ma-ma (D+)
PÙ.ŠA-MES (ITT II/2 p. 12, 3041)
[PÙ].ŠA-^{d}ME.SI (Kish 1930, 152)
PÙ.ŠA-^{d}MUŠ (PSarg. king)
PÙ.ŠA-^{d}Nu-muš-da (MO)
PÙ.ŠA-Nu-ni (MO)
PÙ.ŠA-PAB.PAB (MO)
PÙ.ŠA-^{d}Sa-mu-uš (D+)
PÙ.ŠA-ra-Ma-ma (TMH V 149 ii, PSarg.?)
PÙ.ŠA-ra-ra (CT V 3 v, PSarg.)
PÙ.ŠA-ru (BE I Pl. VII iii+)
⌈Pù⌉-uz-ru-ru (D)
PÙ.ŠA-ru-sa (G+). Cf. PÙ.ŠA-ša in BIN VII 2:5, OB
Pù-uz-ru-sa (D+)
PÙ.ŠA-ru-um (D+)
PÙ.ŠA-su (MO+)
PÙ.ŠA-zu (D)
PÙ.ŠA-su(d)-DÙG (CT XXXII 8 iii, PSarg.)
PÙ.ŠA-su-ni (D)
PÙ.ŠA-^{d}Za-ba$_4$-ba$_4$ (MO).

Selected Ur III PN's:

PÙ.ŠA-A-bi (cf. under Sarg.)
PÙ.ŠA-a-mi (U 453)
PÙ.ŠA-^{d}En-líl (U 467+)
PÙ.ŠA-Eš$_4$-dar (U 480+)
PÙ.ŠA-Eš-dar (Nies, UDT 90)
Pù-zur$_x$-Eš-dar (Pinches, AT 95). Written KA for SAG.GUNU

PÙ.ŠA-šu-ni (Oppenheim, CCTE p. 199; PDTI 534)

Ši-bu-uz-ri (Orient. XLVII 40:52)

Other PN's in U 452-489.

Ur III GN:

| É-)PÙ.ŠA-iš-^{d}Da-gan (RLA II 142, dates of Š. 40ff.)
| É-)PÙ.ŠA-^{d}Da-gan (ibid.).

PZR?

Sarg. and Ur III PN's:

Bu-zu-ru-um (MDP XVIII 31)

Pù-KA-ra (Reisner, TUT 194, U)

Pù-za-ra-a (YOS IV 224, U).

Q

$Q^{\supset}_{x}$, see $G^{\supset}_{x}$ and $K^{\supset}_{x}$.

$Q^{\supset}_{6}{}^{\supset}_{7}$ qu$^{\supset}$ûm "to wait."

KAS+X u-ga-e "he waited for the battle" (PBS V 36 x+iv, NS.).

$Q^{\supset}_{7}$P qiāpum "to trust."

a-na 10 ŠE.GUR ù-la da-ki-ba-an-ni "with 10 GUR barley you did not trust me" (EK III Pl. XI W. 1929, 160).

Sarg. and Ur III PN's:

Gi-ba-DINGIR (D)

| Gi-bu-tum (RTC 127 rev. vi)
| Ki-bu-tum (D+)

| Ki-bu (E)
| Ki-pum (D)

| La-gi-pum (MO+)
| La-gi-bu-um (RTC 249 ii; U 1892)
| La-gi-bu (TMH n.F. I/II p. 21, U)
| La-gi-ip (U 1893+)
| La-gi_4-ip (UET III p. 19, U).

muqîpum "guarantor" (or the like).

PN_1 ù PN_2 DUMU.NI mu-gi-bu (Yondorf a, U). In a slave-sale contract. Cf. LÚ.GI.NA = muqippu in ŠL 85, 159.

$Q^{\supset}_{7}$Š qiāšum "to donate," "to present."

Written syllabically.

[....] a-na PN's a-ki-iš-su_4-ni-si-im (MDP XIV 78)

foods and objects a-na GN's lu a-ki-iš (CT XXXII 4 xi twice, CM)

ti-a-am-dam a-lí-dam i-ki-iš-šum (UET I 275 i, NS.)

ni-se_{11} ša-at DN BÍL-iš i-ki-su-šum (UET I 275 ii, NS.)

[....] i-ki-iš (MDP XIV 44; 78).

Ur III PN:

ì-lí-i-ki-ša-am (Boson, TCS 371).

The Sumerogram A.MU.RU (UET I 10; BE I 6; etc.) or A.MU.NA.RU (MDP X 1-3; YOS I 17; 18, U; etc.) = Akk. iqîš is used from the Sarg. Period on, replacing SAG.KAB.DU = išruk of the PSarg. Period.

qîšum "gift."

Sarg. PN:

Gi-šum (D+).

qîštum "gift."

šu .... ki-iš-da-su i-ti-ru "whoever .... takes away his gift" (MDP IV Pl. 2 iv)

it-ti ìr-bi ù ⌈ki-š⌉a-a-tim (CT XXXII 1 ii) = it-ti ir-bi ù ki-ša-a-ti (RA VII 180) in CM.

$Q^{\supset}{}_{x}$T? qâtum "hand."

Written syllabically only.

ì-nu ^dEn-líl .... zi-ra-at ni-se$_{11}$ ga-ti-iš-su i-ti-nu (PBS V 36 rev. x+iii, NS.)

ì-nu .... ga-ti-iš-su i-ti-nu-ma (UET I 275 iii, NS.)

ga-ti lu aš-ši (CT XXXII 2 iv, CM)

in ga-ti-su (Kish 1930, 143 rev.)

ŠE.NUMUN ù GUD in ga-ti-ku-ni (Cop. 10055).

Sarg. and Ur III PN's:

Ga-zu-a-lum (D+)

Ga-zu-^dMES (Oppenheim, CCTE UU 16 rev., U)

U-bìl-ga-zu (MO+)

Za-ba-at-ga-zu (D).

Ur III PN's, all doubtful:

DINGIR-ga-tum (Nies, UDT 91 vii)

Ga-ti-li (UET III 1046; 1182; also ZA XII 333, Sarg.). Cf. Ga-ti-DINGIR in Kh. 1935, 121:30, OB

Ga-tum-.... (UET III 1107)

Šu-ga-tum (U 2674f.; AnOr I p. 35).

$QB^{\supset}{}_{7}$ qabājum "to say."

DÙL-mi-me i-ga-pi-ù "(whoever) says: 'this is my statue'" (R xviii, xxiv)

DÙL-mi-me i-ga-bi-ù (UET I 276 i, NS.)

MU-mi su-gu-u[n] i-ga-bi-⌈ù⌉ (UET I 276 i, NS.)

MU-mi-me su-gu-un i-ga-pi-ù (PBS V 36 rev. x+iv, NS.)

en-ma PN$_1$ a-na PN$_2$ ki-bí-ma "thus (says) PN$_1$, say to PN$_2$" (passim in letters)

a-la-kam (Inf.) aq-bí-si-im (D 315:13)

en-ma PN_1 a-na PN_2 be-lí ù a-bí ki-bí-ma (D 191)

en-ma PN a-na IŠ ki-bí (JCS I 348a)

en-ma PN_1 a-na PN_2 è-ga-bi (BM 54318 rev.)

a daq-bí (JRAS 1932 p. 296:10)

a-na-gu mim-ma ù-la a-ga-bi (JRAS 1932 p. 296:25)

PN na-da-ni-iš ga-bi (RA XIII 133, U)

na-da-nam iq-bí (TMH n.F. I/II 7, U)

um-ma sar-ru-um-ma a-na PN ki-bí-ma (RA XXIV 44, U)

ma-aḫ-ri-šu-nu iq-bí (MDP XXVIII 424 rev., U).

Sarg. and Ur III PN's:

Iq-bí-a-ni (D+)

Iq-bí-DINGIR (D+; U 1700+)

Iq-bí-GI (D+)

Iq-bí-SIG_5 (D)

Ki-bí-^{d}EN.ZU (RA XXIV 96).

qabijum.

Written syllabically or logographically as DUG_4.GA.

A-bi-DUG_4.GA (BIN V 130, U). Cf. A-bi-ga-bi (Wiseman, Alalakh p. 125) and ŠEŠ-qa-bi (Johns, ADD 425:8, 12)

Da-da-ga-bi (Fish, CST p. 159 iii 3, U)

Ga-bi-um (ITT II/2 p. 30, 4548).

qubājum? "lament."

Sarg. PN:

Sar-a-ti-gu-bi-si-in (RA IX 73+). "O king, I gave their (sisters') laments." Doubtful.

QBL qablum "hip" (see also n. on DNN?).

1 UDU qab-la-su ma-ar-za-ma ⌈iṭ-bu⌉-ḫu "1 sheep - its 2 hips (or loins) afflicted - they slaughtered" (D 178).

qablijum "middle."

in ÍD á-lí-tim or kab-lí-tim (R xxiii, xxv).

"middle," said of quality.

Akk. lw. in Sum.:

12 KAŠ kab-lí-um DUG (RTC 111)

1 DUG KAŠ kab-lí-um (ITT II/2 p. 25, 4452; similarly p. 14, 3085 and p. 26, 4474)

120 ŠIM ga-ab-lí-um 3 QA GABA and 50 ŠIM ga-ab-lí-um 6 QA GABA (Univ. Illinois 286, U).

QBL?

Sarg. and Ur III PN's:

Ga-ba-la (D)

Ga-ba-lum (U 563+).

QBL?

Sarg. PN:

Gu-ba-lum (G).

QD?

Ur III PN's:

For the root with Q cf. A-bi-qa-ad quoted below.

AB.BA-ga-da (Oppenheim, CCTE p. 181). Cf. A-bi-qa-ad in VAS VIII 14:43, OB, and A-bi-ga-ad in TA 1930, 237, OB

AD.DA-ga-da (U 227+)

Na-na-ga-da (2 NT 642)

Ri-ba-ga-da (UET III p. 27+; YOS IV 289)

Ri-⌈ba⌉-ga-du (CT XXXII 10 i)

^{d}Šul-gi-dan-ga-da (U 924; RTC 392 rev.)

^{d}Šul-gi-da-an-ga-da (Pinches, AT 119 twice; 120).

QDD quddudum "to subject."

GN's ù-ga-ti-id a-na DU-su "he subjected GN's to his feet" (MDP XIV p. 12 v).

QDD? qaddatum?

Sarg. MN:

Ga-da-ad (D).

QDD? qudādum "baby" (or the like).

Ur III PN's:

Gu-da-ti (YOS IV 300). Cf. qudādu = šerru "baby" in Delitzsch, AHWB p. 580b

Gu-da-da (UET III 1037)

Gú-da-tum (UET III 283). Doubtful.

QDŠ quddušum "to purify?"

gu-du-si-iš (FM 47:11, in difficult context).

Ur III PN:

Gu-du-ši (Iraq V 176 No. 26).

qudāšum.

Sarg. and Ur III PN:

Gú-d[a]-šum (HSS X 118 x+2, read as Gú-d[a]-mi-šum^{KI} ibid. p. XLII)

Ku-da-šum (Genava 1954 p. 241, U).

QMʾ$_3$ *qamʾum "flour."

Written ZÍD (passim). Cf. also:

ZÍD.BA-su (FM 53:14)

ZÍD.GU-su (BIN VIII 263)

ZÍD.SAG-su (ibid.)

ZÍD.ŠE-su (ibid.).

QNB? qunnabum? (a plant).

PSarg. PN:

Ku-na-bi, f.n. (Lenormant, CTC 2).

QNN? qinnum?

Akk. lw. in Ur III Sum.:

a garment UB.BI 8 (KUŠ), ki-in-nu-um-BI 2 (KUŠ) (TMH n.F. I/II 222). For parallels in Sum. cf. ITT II 909 i, U. Apparently an expression contrasting with UB = kibrātum, tubqātum. Any connection with qinnû "mountain" discussed by Meissner, AS I 26?

QQD qaqqadum "head."

ma-ḫi-iṣ ga-ga-ad um-ma-an GN's (CT XXI 1c, Dêr)

(ì-nu ....) ga-ga-ad um-ma-nim si-a-ti im-ḫa-zu-na (Speleers, RIAA 4 ii, Dêr)

PN_1 (f.n.) .... ga-ga-za ⌈a⌉-na ŠÁM i-ti-in "PN_1 sold herself" (Yondorf a, U). Used as a reflexive pronoun.

Sarg. PN:

Ga-ga-da (D+).

qaqqadānum "person with a large head."

Sarg. PN:

Ga-ga-da-núm (G+).

QQR qaqqarum "ground."

iš-tum ga-ga-rí-im a-na SAG BÀD (UET I 275 v, NS.)

ga-ga-ra-am lu u-ka?-ru-ú (CT XXXII 1 iii, CM).

Ur III PN:

Ga-ga-ri (ITT IV p. 78, 7871).

QRB qirbum "middle." Cf. also KRB.

in kir-bí-su "from it(s midst)" (HSS X 5:13; MDP XIV 12; BIN VIII 143; JCS I 348b. Corresponds to Sum. ŠÀ.BA (HSS X 38 iii x+2)

⌈ÍD⌉ in kir-bí-su u-su-zi (PBS V 36 x+iii, NS.).

QRB? qirbātum "midst."

ŠU.NIGÍN x GÁN šu kir-ba-ti GN (D 168).

QRD qardum "strong."

Sarg. PN:

Gàr-tum (G).

qarrādum "strong."

Ur III PN's:

DINGIR-gàr-ad (YOS IV 156)

E-la-ga-ra-ad (Pinches, BTBC p. 93 rev. 6)

Ga-ra-túm (Nikolski, Dok. II 32:9; TCL V 6039 i).

Ur III DN:

^{d}Kar-ra-túm (TCL V 5672 iii; BRM III 44:30; 45:25).

qurādum "strong."

ku-ra-tum (D 192).

PSarg., Sarg., and Ur III PN's:

Be-lí-ku-ra-ad (YOS IV 239, U)

Gu-ra-tum (BM 54318)

Gur-ra-túm (Jacobsen, CTC 54 x, U)

Ku-ra-túm (JCS X 26 i, iii, L.E.)

Ì1-šu-gur-ad (ITT IV p. 67, 7673, U)

Il-šu-ku-ra-ad (RA X 66 No. 99 vi, U)

Ì-lum-gur-ad (UET II Pl. XLVII 19, PSarg.)

^{d}Ìr-ra-gú-ra-ad (YOS IV 31 rev., U)

Ìr-ra-ku-ra-ad (BE III 116+, U)

Ku-ra-ad-ì-lí (U 1848+; TCL II 5528 rev., U)

Ku-ra-ti-ì-lí (Coll. De Clercq I 105)

Ku-ra-zu (U 1849).

qurdum "power."

Sarg. and Ur III PN's:

A-ŠI-gu-ru-ud (MO). Interpr. unknown

Kur-ti-^{d}Ba-za (TCL II 5484 rev., U; RA XVII 209, U). Doubtful

Kur-ti-lum (U 1864; AnOr I p. 30, U; CT XXXII 37 iii, U)

Ku-ru-da (D). Probably Gurruda

Ku-ru-za (D; YOS IV 254 i, U). Cf. Ku-ru-ud-za in PBS XI/3 77 rev. 4, OB

Ku-ru-zu (D).

QTN qatnum "thin."

Sarg. PN:

Ga-at-núm (D+).

QTP? qatāpum? "to pluck."

Ur III PN:

Ga-da-bi (TCL II 5500 i).

quttupum?

Sarg. and Ur III PN's:

Gu-du-ba (TCL V 5663, U)

Gu-du-bi (TCL II 5575, U)

KUM-du-pum (PBS V 34 xii, xvi).

R

R'$_4$ <u>ru'um</u> "companion."

a-na na-'à-si NS. da-nim ru-ì-su! (MDP VI 6).

R'$_4$'$_7$ <u>ra'ājum</u> "to pasture," "to provide with food?"

Sarg. and Ur III PN's:

ìr-e-^{d}EN.TI (G+)

Ir$_{11}$-e-GÍN.LAL (Orient. VI 59 No. 10, U, thus translit.)

ìr-e-^{d}Ma-lik (MO)

ìr-e-um (D+)

ìr-e-^{d}UTU (G+)

I-rí-DINGIR (G)

ìr-rí-^{d}Da-gan (ZA XII 334)

ìr-uš-DINGIR (De Genouillac, FT II Pl. 137, 1). Meaning?

<u>rē'ijum</u> "shepherd."

Written logographically or syllabically.

PN ri URU? ip-šum "the wise? shepherd? of the city?" (RA IX Pl. 1 opp. p. 1, Urkiš and Nawar). Cf. possibly Rí-a-li(m)-zu, for Rê-âliššu, below.

x GÁN šu ba-la-ag (palgum) Da-da(-?)rí-im (PSBA XX Pl. I i, PSarg.)

The logogram SIPA occurs as SIPA ÁB (D 152; 72); SIPA ANŠE (ITT I 1363; 1463; etc.); SIPA DUN (D 42); SIPA UDU (FM 16:6); SIPA ÙZ (A 3399); and simply SIPA (passim).

PSarg., Sarg., and Ur III PN's:

Be-lí-SIPA (D+)

^{d}Da-gan-rí-ì-su (D+)

DINGIR-SIPA (D)

^{d}EN.ZU-SIPA (G+)

I-bi-iq-ri-e-ú MAR.TU (A 29365+, U)

Ra-ì-lum (RTC 75 iii, PSarg.)

Rí-a-li(m)-zu (ITT I 1370). Sign ZU for SU? Cf. also Ri-i-a-li-šu in MDP XVIII 203 = XXI 50:42 and Ri-e-a-li-šu in MDP XXIV 380:20, OB

SIPA-da-rí (RTC 234)

SIPA-ì-lí (Delaporte, CCL I T 159, U)

SIPA-ni-se$_{11}$ (G)

SIPA-si-in (D+)

SIPA-še-in (AnOr VII 331:8, U)

Ri-ši-in (U 2573+)
Ri-ì-si-in (A 2908, U)
Su_4-ma-SIPA (MO).

rē'ītum "shepherdess."

Sarg. and Ur III PN's:

SIPA-ì-tum (FM)
SIPA!-tum (FM)
Ri-⌈ì⌉-tum (FM)
Ri-i-tum (TA 1931, 237, U).

R'$_3$B ra'abum (a vessel).

1 GAR DA.NAGAR 1 KAŠ ra-á-pum "1 receptacle for bread, 1 vessel for beer" (MDP XIV 7 rev. twice). This is the word that appears as rîbum in later periods; cf. AOB I 134f. n. 13.

R'$_3$B? riābum "to compensate."

'$_3$, instead of '$_7$, is assumed in the root because of spellings Ir'ib, ru'ubbā'um, below.

[....] ir_{11}-ti-ab (ITT I 1103). In difficult context. Spelling with IR_{11}(=ARAD+KUR) unique in the Sarg. Period.

PSarg., Sarg., and Ur III PN's:

Da-rí-bu, f.n. (Speleers, CIMC p. 116 No. 594; Reisner, TUT 159 iv, U)

Dar-ti-bu (G)

I-ri-ib (U 1660+; Oppenheim, CCTE p. 188, U)
Ìr-e-ib (YOS IV 264 ii, U+)
Ir_{11}(ARAD+KUR)-e-ib (Orient. XLVII 172, U). Unique spelling
Ìr-ri-ib (Orient. XLVII 343, U; U 1770+)
Ìr-ib MAR.TU (ITT II p. 10, 644, U)
Ìr-e-íb (Oppenheim, CCTE p. 190, U)
I-ri-íb (PDTI 529 iii, U)
Ìr-ri-íb (PDTI 484, U)

Ìr-íb-il-šu (Legrain, TRU 266 rev., U)

Ìr-e-pum (D+)
Ìr-e-KA (Kish 1930, 144a)
Ìr-rí-pum (G)
Ìr-ri-bu-um (Porada, CPML No. 275, U)
Ìr-ì-pum (OIP XIV 48 iv, PSarg.)
I-ri-bu-um (U 1658+).

rîbum "compensation."

Sarg. PN's:

Ri-bí (E+)

Rí-bi-iš (G)

Rí-pum (MO).

rîbatum "compensation."

Sarg. and Ur III PN's:

Ri-ba-tum (D)

Rí-ba-tim, Gen. (UCP IX p. 204, 83 iii)

Si-ri-ba-at (OIP XXXVII 50, U).

ruʾubbāʾum "compensation?"

2 animals iš-dè PN ru-ù-ba-um (HSS X 175 iii). The interpr. as a title rubājum, rubāʾum (as ibid. p. xxvii) does not fit because of the spelling ru-ù- and because a Gen. is required. Parallelism with 2 PN's ru-ku-ma-um /rugummāʾum/, on the one side, and with 1 animal iš-dè PN ḫu-bu-da-tum, on the other, favors the interpr. here given.

Rʾ$_7$Ḫ rîḫatum "rest."

Ur III PN:

Ri-ḫa-tum (TMH V 34 rev. v).

Rʾ$_x$Ḫ? rûḫtum?

in ru-ùḫ-ti [x na]?-ak-tim (Kish 1930, 143:5)

ru-ùḫ-ti [i]n? na-ak-tim (l. 10).

Rʾ$_1$M raʾāmum "to love."

DN ir-e-ma-am è-ra-a-am-su "DN loves the irʾemum" (Kish 1930, 143).

Sarg. and Ur III PN's:

I-la-ag-ra-am (UET III 1064, U)

Ìr-am-^{d}Da-gan (D+)

Ìr-ra-am-^{d}Da-gan (ITT II/2 p. 39, 4700)

I-ra-am-^{d}Da-gan (Legrain, TRU 126:8, U)

Ìr-am-D[INGIR] (G)

Ìr-am-^{d}Ma-lik (MO+)

Ìr-a-mu (MO; PBS XIV 126)

Ìr-a-mu-um (Iraq Mus. 30350)

I-sar-ra-ma (A 2965:4, U)

I-sar-ra-ma-aš (U 1654+)

Ra-im-^{d}En-líl (ITT I 1437)

^{d}Šul-gi-ra-ma (U 935+).

raʾūmum "beloved."

Sarg. PN:

Ra-um-tum (D).

narâmum "beloved."

PN na-ra-am DN (MDP IV p. 8, ŠS.; CT XXI 1c; YOS IX 62; OIP XLIII

155 No. 55, all Dêr; OIP XLIII 135, 144f., Diyala).

Sarg. and Ur III PN's:

Na-ra-me-a (ITT II/1 p. 13, 686, U)

Na-ra-am-É-a (U 2361+)

Na-ra-am-È-a (A 26349, U; RTC 377, U)

Na-ra-am-^{d}En-líl-lá (ITT V p. 61, 9971, U)

Na-ra-am-^{d}EN.ZU and ^{d}Na-ra-am-^{d}EN.ZU (Sarg. king; U 2360)

Na-ra-am-ì-lí (U 2362+)

Na-ra-àm-ì-lí (BIN V 93:8, U)

Na-ra-me-ì-li (RTC 127 rev. iv)

Na-ra-am-LUGAL (Oppenheim, CCTE p. 197, U)

^{d}Šu-^{d}EN.ZU-na-ra-am-^{d}En-líl (UET III 1357 twice, U; JCS X 30 No. 9 rev., U).

Ur III RN:

ÍD Na-ra-am-ša (UET III 1357).

<u>narâmtum</u> "beloved."

Tu-da-šar-li-bí-iš [na]?-ra?-ma?-at [x? L]UGAL (RTC 161). Thureau-Dangin, SAKI p. 164e reads without question marks: [ ]-ra-ma-at [ ] šarrim.

Ur III PN:

Na-ra-am-tum (ITT II/1 p. 44, 918).

<u>rîmum</u> "love."

For other possibilities, such as rîmum "Geschenk" or "Wildstier," cf. Stamm, ANG p. 259.

Sarg. and Ur III PN's:

^{d}IM-ri-mi (BMQ VIII Pl. IX e, U)

Ri-im-^{d}EN.ZU (Oppenheim, CCTE p. 199, U)

Ri-im-Ḫa-ni-iš (ITT I p. 23, 1371+)

Ri-mi-DINGIR (UET III p. 27+, U)

Rí-mu-uš (Sarg. king)

DN in Sarg. PN:

Ì-lí-Rí-mu-uš (ITT I 1096).

<u>rîntum</u> "love."

Ur III PN:

Rí-in-da-ni, m.n. (ITT II/1 920).

Rʾ$_{x}$N?

Akk. lw. in Ur III Sum.:

5 GIŠ rí-a-núm MÁ (UET III 805)

Cf. skins for GIŠ rí-a-núm MÁ in BIN IX 200 and 267, OB.

Rʾ$_{3}$Q <u>ruʾuqum</u> "to keep far," "to keep away."

Mu-ri-iq-Ti-id-ni-im (the name of a fortress in the date of ŠS. 4).

Variant Û-ri-iq-Da-at-na-am in Yondorf b.

<u>rûqum</u> "far (place)."

a-ḫu-uš$_x$(EŠ) ba-ki ša ru-ga-tim (Kish 1930, 143:12)

Cf. a-ru-gi-ma, possibly for ar-rûqimma "in the future," discussed under rašājum.

R'$_x$S, see R'$_x$Š ra'āšum.

R'$_6$Ṣ <u>rîṣum</u> "help," "helper."

PSarg., Sarg., and Ur III PN's:

Eš$_4$-dar-rí-⌈zi⌉ (D)

Ri-iṣ-DINGIR (PSBA XX Pl. I ii+, PSarg.; UET III 1654, U; JCS X 31 No. 11, U)

Ri-zé-DINGIR (UET III 920, copied as Ḫu-; 1647, U)

Ri-zi-DINGIR (U 2565)

Ri-zé-lum (YOS IV 152, U).

<u>rûṣum</u>.

Ur III PN:

Ru-zé-lum (ITT II/1 p. 9, 639).

R'$_1$Š <u>ra'šum</u> "head," "front," "width."

Written logographically as SAG or syllabically.

[....] SAG.GIŠ.RA SAG GN$_1$ ù GN$_2$ (UET I 6)

x ^{TÚG}bar-ru šu-ut SAG "head" (FM 7:7)

a-na ra-si-im "in the front," opposite of a-na ur-ki-im "in the back" (FM 11:12)

SAG "width," opposite of UŠ "length" (HSS X 13; 16; 20; 24; 26)

1)7 GÍN KUG.BABBAR 2)I-lul-DINGIR 3)a-na SAG 4)SAG ù-la a-ḫu-uz (BM 54309 i). Meaning unknown

13)šum-ma (referring to KUG.BABBAR) ⌈a-na⌉ SAG 14)[S]AG lu-sa-[bí?-la]?-kum (EK III Pl. XI W. 1929, 160).

Sarg. PN:

SAG-zu-ni (RA XIII Pl. I 5 opp. p. 8).

R'$_4$Š <u>ra'āšum</u> "to rejoice."

PSarg., Sarg., and Ur III PN's:

Da-rí-iš-ma-tum (U 795)

Ì-rí-iš (TMH V 56 iii+, PSarg.?)

I-rí-iš (TMH V 79 iii, PSarg.?)

I-rí-iš-be-lí (MO)

I-rí-iš$_x$(LAM+KUR)-^{d}En-líl (BIN VIII 123; 128)

Ta-ri-ša-àm, f.n. (UET III 15, U).

<u>rîšum</u> "rejoicing."

Sarg. and Ur III PN's:

Ri-iš-be-lí (U 2567)

Rí-iš!-^{d}IM (UET I 275 iii, NS.).

rîštum "rejoicing."

Ur III PN:

Ri-iš-tum (UET III 1041 i).

R'_{x}Š ra'āšum, ra'āsum "to smite."

ni-se_{11} ša-at ^{d}Da-gan BÍL-iš i-ki-su-šum u-ra-iš-ma (UET I 275 ii, NS.).

rîsum "smiting," "smiter."

(PN) ri-is Ba-ra-aḫ-si-im^{KI} (CT XXI 1c, Dêr)

Cf. SAG.GIŠ.RA = ri-e-su and ri-e-šu (also ni-e-rum) in CT XII 43 iv 16ff. Cf. note on N'_{3}R na'ārum.

R'_{x}Š rîšūtum.

1 ga-nu-núm a-na rí-su-ti 1 si-im-ti KÁ.GAL (PBS IX 21). Ununderstandable. Cf. GNN? ganūnum.

RB'_{7} šurbûm "to make great."

in GIŠ.TUKUL-ki ^{d}Da-gan mu-sa-ar-bí-ì sar-ru_{x}(URU)-ti-su "with the weapon of D., who makes great his kingship" (UET I 275 i, NS.)

rabjum "great," "elder."

Written syllabically or logographically.

ì-lu ra-bí-ù-tum (PBS V 36 rev. iv, NS.)

DINGIR ra-bí-ù-tum (UET I 276 ii, NS.)

i-lu ra-b[í-ù-tum] (Morgan, MSP IV 161 ii, Lullubum).

Elsewhere only GAL occurs either in the meaning "great" or "elder."

For the meaning "elder" cf.:

PN GAL opposite of PN TUR (HSS X 150:8ff.).

PSarg., Sarg., and selected Ur III PN's:

Be-lí-ra-bí (ITT II/2 p. 14, 3072)

DINGIR-ra-bí (D+; U 864+)

DINGIR-su-ra-bí (MO+)

DÙL-su-GAL (A 5906). Thus clearly on tablet

É-a-ra-bí (D+)

É-a-GAL (E)

$Eš_{4}$-dar-GAL? (FM)

$Eš_{4}$-dar-ra-bí-at (FM)

Ì-lí-GAL (FM+)

Ì-lum-ra-bí (BIN VIII 11 iv, vi, PSarg.)

Ì-lu-ra-bí (OIP XIV 61 i, PSarg.)

Pù-sa-GAL (CT VII 4, No. 26451, PSarg.)

Pù-ša-ra-bí (HSS IV 86, U). Or Puzur-abī

Pù-uš-GAL (MO)

Ra-bí (E+)

GAL-DINGIR (E)

Ra-bí-DINGIR (G+; U 2557)

Ra-bí-Il (OIP XIV 51 vii, PSarg.)

Ra-bí-ì-lum (CT XXXII 8 i A, PSarg.+)

Ra-bí-lum (Nikolski, Dok. II 48+)

Ra-bí-PI-li-ir (E)

^{d}UTU-ra-bí (RTC 133+).

Ur III GN:

Bí-tum-ra-bí-um^{KI} (date of BS. 7).

rubājum, see R'$_7$B ru'ubbā'um.

rubātum "princess."

Sarg. and Ur III PN's:

Ru-ba-tum (D+; A 5033, U; A 5648, U)

Ru-ba-at (Chiera, STA 14 i, U; 16 i, U).

RBB? rabbum? "light," "soft?"

2 TÚG ra-ba-tum (BE I 11). A kind of garment. Fem. rabbātum because of Du.?

5 ŠE.GUR.SAG.GÁL in GUR.UL LAL 2(QA) ša-ti 11 QA TA ra-ba-at PN$_1$ ⌈iš-dè⌉ PN$_2$ im-ḫur (Kish 1930, 170g). Interpr. unknown.

Sarg. and Ur III PN:

Ra-ba-tum (D; Nies, UDT 115, U).

RBṢ.

Sarg. PN:

Ra-bu-zum (G+).

RD'$_7$ ruddûm "to add."

lu u-ra-ad-di (CT XXXII 1 iii, etc., CM)

lu u-ra-at-ti (ibid. 2 v, etc.).

RD'$_x$?

x GURUŠ x GUD x ANŠE.LIBIR PN's [ŠIR].BUR.LA^{KI} [a?-n]a? ra-da-ni/ì LUGAL li-ru-ù-nim (ITT I 1057 rev.). Ununderstandable.

RDM?

Ur III Amorite PN:

Mar-da-mu-um MAR.TU (A 5508).

RGG raggum "bad," "evil."

mu-ḫa-li-iq ra-gi-im (YOS IX 62, Dêr).

RGM ragāmum "to claim."

[i]-ra-ga-mu (MDP XIV 44)

PN$_1$ MU LUGAL-im PÀD a-na PN$_2$ la a-ra-ga-mu (RA XXXII 190, U).

Ur III PN:

ARÁD-ir-gu-um (unpubl.).

rigmum "noise" (or the like).

Sarg. PN:

Rí-ig-mu-um (D+).

Ur III GN:

Rí-ig-mu-uš-dan (ZA LI Pl. II after p. 74 iii 8, 9).

rugummāʾum "claim."

2 PN's ru-ku-ma-um̃ (FM 49:5).

RGN, see RKN.

RḪʾ$_7$ raḫājum "to water," "to fertilize."

Sarg. RN:

Ra-ḫi-um (HSS X 1).

RḪṢ raḫāṣum "to inundate," "to flood."

^{d}IM li-ìr-ḫi-iṣ "may Adad flood" (CT XXXII 4 xii, CM).

RKB *rakkabum "messenger."

Sum. RÁ.GABA (ŠL 206, 65) and RA.GABA (ŠL 328, 39), from approximately the Ur III period on, is evidently a lw. from Semitic. RÁ.GABA is found also in Sarg. or older in Woolley, UE II Pl. 191 U 11990.

narkabtum "chariot."

Akk. lw. in Sum.:

^{GIŠ}na-ar-kab-tum (VAT 16442 ii, school text).

RKN?

Sarg. PN:

Ìr-gu-nu-um (A 959).

RKN?

Ur III PN:

Rí-ku-nu-um (U 2568 = Orient. XLVII 76:17). Doubtful.

RKS rakāsum "to tie."

MÁ of various countries in ga-rí-im ši A-ga-dè^{KI} ìr-ku-us (S vi, xiv)

MÁ.MÁ .... in kar-rí-<im> ši A-ga-dè^{KI} ìr-gu-us (UET I 274 v, NS.)

ik-ba-ri? ìr-ku-zu (PBS IX 30). Cf. KSRK kusarikkum.

RMK ramākum "to pour (water)," "to wash."

Ur III PN:

Ir-mu-uk-ìr-ra (TA 1931, 231). Meaning?

RMN? ramanum "self."

in ra-ma-ni-ga lu da-na-da-ru "yourself" (JRAS 1932 p. 296:32).

RPP, see RBB?

RPŠ rapšum "wide."

Sarg. and Ur III PN's:

Ra-ap-ši (Iraq V 173 No. 19, U)

Ra-ap-šum (D).

rupšum "width."

x KUŠ ru-up-šum (HSS X 156 x+1, 4). Opposite of miḫṣum.

RSN? marsattum?

1 mar-za-tum 1 na-ar-⌈tab⌉-tum (MDP XIV 8).

RŠʾ$_7$ rašājum "to get," "to own."

PN it-ma ^{12}šu-ma GEMÉ a-ru-gi-ma-<ni>? ^{13}ni-ir-da-si-ì ^{14}a-na-ku-ú lu GEMÉ "PN swore: if we got the servant-girl for claims, (then) truly I shall become a servant-girl" (Yondorf a, U). Or šu-ma GEMÉ a-ru-gi-ma /ar-rûqimma/ ni-ir-da-si-ì "if in the future we should get (back) the servant-girl."

Sarg. and Ur III PN's:

| A-ḫa-ar-ši (G+)
| A-ḫa-am-ar-si (Fish, CST p. 160 viii, U)

| Ar-ši-aḫ (RTC 249 rev. i; U 355+)
| Ar-ši-a-ḫa (G+)

| Ra-ši (U 2561+)
| Ra-si (MDP X 125, U).

RŠP.

DN Rašap in Sarg. PN:

I-zi-Ra-sa-ap! (MDP XIV 72 ii). Cf. Ia-aḫ-zu-^{d}Ra-sa-ap and A-bi-Ra-sa-ap from Mari cited by J. Lewy in Mélanges Dussaud I 275.

RTT?

Ur III Amorite PN:

Ra-ti-tum MAR.TU (Fish, CST 728 ii)

Cf. Ra-ti-ti in MDP XVIII 145; 173, OB.

RṬB narṭabtum (an irrigation machine).

1 na-ar-⌈tab⌉-tum (MDP XIV 8).

RṬB?

Ur III PN's:

| Mar-da-ba-an (ITT IV p. 4, 7031)
| Mar-da-ba-nu-um MAR.TU (A 2905).

S

Sʾ$_x$ sûtum "measure."

a-na 2(GUR) 40(QA) ŠE.GUR in zu-ti ANŠE (Louvre AO 8959).

Sʾ$_x$Ḫ? saḫum? (a container).

Akk. lw. in Sum.:

1 za-ḫu-um UD.KA.BAR KI.LAL.BI 1 MA.NA (BIN V 1 rev., U)

1 za-ḫum UD.KA.BAR KI.LAL.BI 1/2 MA.NA (BIN V 2 rev., U)

1 za-ḫum UD.KA.BAR KI.LAL.BI 1 MA.NA 1 5/6 GÍN (YOS IV 15, U)

1 za-ḫum UD.KA.BAR KI.LAL.BI 1 5/6 MA.NA 5 GÍN (YOS IV 296 rev., U)

1 za-ḫum KUB.BABBAR (De Genouillac, TD 86, U; YOS IV 15, U)

30 DUG za-ḫum NI (RTC 307 rev. iv, U; ITT II 892 rev. iii, U, copied GAG instead of NI)

1 za-ḫum TUR (RTC 223 ii)

1 za-ḫum TUR UD.KA.BAR (Reisner, TUT 126 i, U)

2 za-ḫu(m)-um URUDU (2 NT 644)

5 UD.KA.BAR za-ḫum (ITT V 6747; 9262)

3 URUDU UD.KA.BAR za-ḫum (BIN VIII 145)

1 GIŠ UR AN za-ḫum GIŠ.ŠINIG (ITT V 6854 ii, U). Doubtful

x za-ḫum among objects of UD.KA.BAR (ITT V 9302)

x za-ḫum UD.KA.BAR (RTC 203)

1 za-ḫum UD.KA.BAR Má-gan (OIP XIV 103).

S$^{\supset}_{x}$Ḫ sîḫum.

Akk. lw. in Ur III Sum.:

1 KUŠ.A.GÁ.LAL zi-ḫu-um (MDP XVIII 83).

S$^{\supset}_{x}$S sâsum "moth" (or the like).

Sarg. and Ur III PN's:

Za-zi (U 1461+)

Za-zum (G+; Fish, CST p. 159 iv, U)

Za-zu-um (G+).

sâsatum "moth."

Sarg. PN:

Za-za-tum (G+)

Cf. Za-za-tum in Ranke, EBPN p. 196.

SḪL saḫlijum "cress" (or the like).

Akk. saḫlûm is apparently a lw. from Sum. ZA(G).ḪI.LI, which in turn may be a lw. from Semitic š/ṯaḫlum. Note, however, that the sibilants do not correspond well, since the Sum. word should be written with a ŠA sign on the basis of Aram. taḥlê "cress." Cf. also note on SḪT *saḫatinnum.

NUMUN ZAG.ḪI.LI^{SAR} (ITT II 892 iv, U), NUMUN ZAG.ḪI.LI (ITT III 5926, U; Pinches, AT 69, U), NUMUN ZA.ḪI.LI^{SAR} (RA XVIII 59 vi, Voc. prat.), etc.

SḪR, see ṢḪR? ṣaḫartum.

SḪR? siḫrum? "rim (of a seal)," "mounting?"

Akk. lw. in Ur III Sum.:

13 GÍN 20 ŠE KUG.BABBAR KI.LAL sa-am-sa-tum 4 UD.SAR 2 zé-eḫ-ru-um 24 "so much silver, the weight of 4 sun disks, 2 sickles, 23 ...." (RA VIII 197 No. 22)

78? zé-eḫ-ru-um KUG.GI KI.LAL.BI 5 5/6 GÍN LAL 2 ŠE (A 5019). Also x UL KUG.GI and x še-ir-ḫu-núm KUG.GI.

SḪR? masḫarum? (an object of metal).

Also the reading maṣḫarum can be considered.

Akk. lw. in Ur III Sum.:

1 ma-az-ḫa-ru-um (UET III 765; 1498 i).

SḪT? *saḫatinnum (an onion).

Written ZA.ḪA.TI and ZA.ḪA.DIN from PSarg. on (ŠL 587, 130 and 132) with z, which cannot lead to Akk. šuḫa/utinnum. Cf. also SUM.ḪA.DIN in Oppenheim, CCTE p. 139, U, and note on SḪL saḫlijum.

SK, see ZKʾ$_7$?

SKK sakīkum "slime."

^{d}EN.KI ÍD-[su a-na] za-ki-ki-im li-im-tu-ud "may E. turn? his river to slime" (CT XXXII 4 xii, CM).

SKK sukkum "sanctuary" (or the like).

Mi. [e]-bi-iš [zu]-uk-ki-im ⌈a⌉-na ^{d}A-a (CT XXXII 1 i) = e-piš suk-ki an ^{d}A-a (RA VII 180) in CM.

SKK sukkukum "deaf."

Ur III PN:

Zu-ku-ku-um (Iraq Mus. 46306).

SKK, see SQQ.

SKL sikiltum "acquisition."

Ur III PN:

Zi-gi$_4$-il-ti (AnOr I 137:4). Cf. Zi-gi-il-da-nu-um in TCL XXII 103:5ff., Mari.

SKL?

Ur III PN's:

| Za-ak-li-li (RA XIX 192 No. 10)
| Za-ak-lí-lí (BIN V 5; A 4910)

Za-ak-lí-tum (Nikolski, Dok. II 329 ii)

Za-ak-lum-ma (YOS IV 212 ii).

SKL sukkallum (and šukkallum? before Ur III) "messenger" (or the like).

Written logographically and syllabically.

PN_1 DUMU PN_2 ši GAL SUKKAL-li (MO A xiii, xv)

PN SUKKAL-su (R xxii)

PN GAL.SUKKAL-su (ibid.).

PSarg., Sarg., and Ur III PN's:

DINGIR-SUKKAL (RTC 95; Fish, CST p. 159 iv, U)
ì-lí-SUKKAL (D+)

Zu-ga-li (PDTI 494, U)
Zu-ga-NI (UET III 15, U). Cf. Zu-ga-li in BIN IX 207:2, OB, and Zu-ka-li in CT VIII 47a 23, OB
KA-ga-NI (TMH V p. 16, PSarg.; ZA XII 332; U 839+)
KA-ga-li (U 838+)

Zu-ga-LUM (AnOr VII 285 rev. iii, U)
KA-ga-LUM (Nies, UDT 91 vii, U).

SKR sikkūrum "bolt (of a door)."

Akk. lw. in Ur III Sum.:

6 ^{GIŠ}zi-ku-ru-um (UET III 805)
16 ^{GIŠ}zi-gur$_8$-ru-um 1 1/2 KÙŠ TA (YOS IV 256:5)
13 ^{GIŠ}zi-gur$_8$-ru-um 2 KÙŠ TA (ibid. l. 44).

Same? word deified in Sarg. and Ur III PN's:

Cf. deified Šigar under ŠGR.

Zi-gur (BIN VIII 286 rev.+)
Zi-gur-GI (RTC 127 iii; ITT I 1472 ii)
Zi-gur-mu-bí (MO)

Zi-kur-ì-lí (Fish, CST p. 17+, U)
Zi-gur-ì-lí (2 NT 596, U).

sikkurtum.

Ur III PN:

Zi-gur$_8$-da (CT X 17 iii 24).

SL'$_x$ sullûm "to pray."

Ur III PN:

^{d}EN.ZU-u-zi-li (Boson, TCS 371). Cf. the names in Stamm, ANG p. 201.

SLMḪ silammaḫum (a garment).

Akk. lw. in Ur III Sum.:

1 TÚG zi-la-ma-ḫu-um (UET III 1727; 1756). Cf. si-lam-ma-ḫu among garments in CT XVIII 13 iii 38.

SMD simdum (kind of flour).

Akk. lw. in Ur III Sum.:

20(QA) ŠE zi-im-tum (AnOr I 64 rev.).

SMK?

PSarg. PN:

Za-muk (PSarg. king). Cf. Sa-mu-uk in Kh. 1935, 80, OB.

SMK?

su/zu-mu-uk-tum (FM 41:15, school text?).

SMM summatum "pigeon."

Ur III PN:

Zum-ma-tum, f.n. (UET III 24; 28). Cf. [I]Su-ma-tum in TCL XVIII 129:8, 14, OB.

SNKT sankuttum (a receptacle).

Goetze, JCS II 81 translates "allotment."

Possibly a lw. from Sum.

Ur III PN:

Za-an-gú-da (Jacobsen, CTC 54 viii).

SNQ.

Ur III PN:

Za-na-kum (Fish, CST p. 159 v).

SPL supālum, sapālum (a resinous tree).

There is no reason to take za-ba-lum to be different from supālum.

Akk. lw. in Sum.:

1 [GIŠ]zu(wr. ba)-ba-lum GÍD.BI 3 KÙŠ 1 ŠU.BAD (ITT II/2 4573)

x GÚ x MA.NA [ŠIM]zú-ba-lum (ITT II/2 4587 rev.; V 6669; 6736 rev.)

x GÚ za-ba-lum (YOS IV 295, U)

[ŠIM][zú]-ba-lum (MDP XIV 89:3, school text)

x MA.NA za-ba-lum (TCL V 5680 rev. i, U; 6037 iv; BIN V 292, U)

x MA.NA [GIŠ]za-ba-lum (UET III 944; 1777, U). Cf. also n. on ḪBN? ḫabānum?

[GIŠ]za-ba-lum (Thureau-Dangin, SAKI p. 102 xii 5; 106 xv 30, Gudea; RA XVIII 53 ii, Voc. prat. = MDP XXVII 55 rev.)

x za-ba-lum MA.NA (BIN VIII 300 among ŠIM; 319).

SPN? suppinnum (an implement).

⌈zu/su⌉?-bí-nu (FM 43:2).

SPR siparrum "bronze."

Written logographically only.

UD.KA.BAR-su-nu (MDP XIV 86 ii, iii, rev. ii)

objects of UD.KA.BAR (passim).

SQQ?

Ur III PN's:

Zu-ga-ga (U 1485+)

Zu/Su-ga-kum (AnOr VII 295:11). Cf. Ranke, EBPN p. 166.

SRD, see ZRD?

SRD sirdum (a tree).

Akk. lw. in Sum.:

x DUG GAL 15 QA NI zi-ir-tum (RTC 216)

1 GIŠ.NAD GIŠ.GURUN UMBIN.ŠÁL.LA zi-ir-tum (BIN VIII 260).

SRD'$_x$ sirdijum. See also Š'$_x$R? šêrtum.

Akk. lw. in Sum.:

^{GIŠ}zi-ir-ti-um GIŠ.BAN (RA XVIII 65 x, Voc. prat.).

SRQ, see ZRQ.

SRR sarrum "sinful," "lying."

URU^{KI}.URU^{KI} za-ar-ru-ti[m] (S xiii).

Ur III PN:

| Za-ar-ru-um (TCL II 5497). Cf. Sa-ar-rum in BA VI/5 109, OB
| Za-ar-um (BE III 166 ii).

surrum "lie."

la zu-ra-tim "they are not lies" (R xxiii, xxvi; RA VIII 136, R.; M xxvii)

la zu-ra-tum (RA VII 105, Mi.).

SRR sarrārum, see n. on ḪSS ḫasāsum.

SRŠ, see ŠRŠ.

SSK?

Sarg. and Ur III PN's:

Zu-zu-gu-ni (Iraq V 176 No. 26, U)

Zu-zu-ki (E).

SSL sussulum "basket" (or the like).

2 ^{GIŠ}zu-zu-la-an (FM 7:19).

Sarg. PN:

Zu-zu-ul (D).

SSN sasannum, see ZNZN?

Ṣ

Ṣ'$_7$Ḫ ṣiāḫum "to laugh."

en-ma PN$_1$ a-na PN's a-zé-ḫa-me da-ni-iš da-ni-iš "thus says PN$_1$ to PN's: 'I laughed (or I rejoiced?) very heartily'" (D 298:6, 15).

Ṣ'$_1$N ṣa'num "small cattle."

2 persons za-nam li-ig-zu-zu "may they shear the small cattle (and x wool may they give to PN)" (Cop. 10055 rev.).

Ṣ'$_4$N ṣa'ānum "to load." See also Z'$_x$N?

NA$_4$.NA$_4$-su-nu MI i-bu-l[am-ma] in MÁ.MÁ i-za-na-ma "he mined their black stones and loaded (them) on ships" (M xxvi).

Ṣ'$_2$R, see Z'$_7$R?

ṢB, see ZB?

ṢB'$_1$ ṣabi'um "worker," "soldier."

Written syllabically and logographically as ERIN (passim).

sheep a-na za-bi-im (JCS X 29 No. 8 rev., U) = ERIN.E (ibid. No. 7, U)

3 GURUŠ za-bi-ù gi-nu-tum (Kish 1930, 559a).

Sarg. and Ur III PN's:

Za-a-bi (Jean, ŠA CXXXIV, U)

Za-be-DINGIR (D+)

Za-bí-e, Gen. (D).

ṢB'$_x$?

so many za-bí-um, so many TUM(=íb?)-rí-um (ITT V 9261). Also so many DUR.GI.BÀD, DUR.GI.ÙR, DUR.GI.TUR.TUR, SIG$_4$.ZIKUM.MA.

ṢBT ṣabātum "to seize."

[1]aṣ-ba-zu ki ma-ì [2]áp-ru-uk-šu ki na-ri-im [3]ki gal-bi-im [4]ì-na ki-ša-ti-šu [5]ki me-ra-ni-im ì-na pi-ir-ti-šu "I seized him like water, I closed him in like a river, like a dog by his neck, like a whelp by his hair" (3 NT 30, U, inc.)

PN_1 DU PN_2 iṣ-ba-at (MDP XIV p. 12 v)

.... [l]i-iṣ-ba-at (HSS X 11:12)

persons za-ab-t[i]-su-⌈ni?-ti⌉?, Impv. (Kish 1930, 768).

Sarg. PN:

Za-ba-at-ga-zu (D).

ṣubātum "(wool-)cloth."

Written logographically as TÚG.

Of masc. gender, as deduced from ŠU.NIGÍN x TÚG.ḪI.A šu-ut .... (BE I 11).

ṢBT?

Sarg. PN:

Za-ab-tim, Gen. (D).

ṢḪR ṣaḫrum "small."

Sarg. PN:

ŠEŠ-za-ḫír/ḫar (G).

ṢḪR? ṣaḫartum (part of a door).

1 1/2 ga-nu-nu a-na za-ḫa-ar-tim (PBS IX 20). Cf. 2 ga-nu-nu a-na TUR.TUR (No. 21).

ṢḪR? ṣuḫārum "servant-boy."

Sarg. PN:

Zu?-ḫa-ar (ITT II/2 p. 48, 5819, translit. Su-ḫa-ar).

ṢḪR? ṣuḫartum "servant-girl."

Ur III PN:

Zu?-ḫar-tum (TCL V 6039 rev. ii, copied Su-ḫar-tum).

ṢḪR?, see also SḪR masḫarum, siḫrum.

ṢḪT ṣaḫtum.

Ur III PN:

Za-aḫ-ti-a (Oppenheim, CCTE p. 140).

ṣāḫitum? "oil-presser."

GEMÉ za?-ḫi-da-tum (MDP XIV 71 iii). Translit. as a-ḫi-da-tum, but ZA possible on photo. Cf. ṣāḫitāte in Pl. in TCL IX 67:12, 24, MA.

ṣaḫḫutum, ṣuḫḫutum.

Ur III PN's:

Za-ḫu-tum (MDP XXVIII 526, U?)

Zu-ḫu-tum (MDP XXVIII 526, U?)

Zu-ḫu-ti (Reisner, TUT 227 i).

ṢLL ṣaliltum.

Sarg. MN at Gasur and Lagaš:

Za-líl-tum (D p. 234).

ṢLL ṣalūlum.

Sarg. MN:

Za-lul (G).

ṢLL ṣillum "shade," "protection."

Da-da-ì-lum ZÉ? LIM dZU.EN (UET I 11, PSarg.); translated as "D. im Schutze (= ṣi-lum) des Sin" by Landsberger in OLZ XXXIV 127, but very doubtful since one would not expect to find LIM with the value lúm side by side with LUM = lum. Read perhaps ZÉ ši DN and cf. below.

Sarg. and Ur III PN's:

Written syllabically or logographically as MI and at least thrice apparently as ZÉ.

A-ḫi-MI-lum (Pinches, AT 77, U)

A-ḫu-MI-lum (AnOr I 97, U). Or Aḫum-ilum

Eš$_4$-dar-MI (FM+)

Ì-lí-zi-lí (UET III 11, U+)

Ìr-ra-zi-lum (RA XIX 42 LXXXV, U)

MI-lá-⌈a-bi⌉? (AOF III 112 end, Mari)

MI-la-su (D+)

MI-la-šu (Orient. XLVII 350:10, U)

Zi-la-šu (CIP XXXVII 50, U)

Zé-la-šu (U 2549+)

MI-Eš$_4$-dar (Oppenheim, CCTE p. 200, U)

MI-lí-tum (RTC 218+)

Zé-lí-tum (Kish 1930, 559e)

MI-lu-sa (D+)

MI-lu-uš-sa (MDP XVIII 82)

MI-lu-su (E)

Ša-lim-MI (U 2598+; HSS IV p. 39+, U)

Zé-li-^{d}IM (TCL II 5504 ii, rev. ii, U)

Zé-la-da-ad (RA XIX 41 XLII rev., U)

Zé-la-^{d}IM (UET III 1272; 1285, U). Same as

ZÉ-^{d}IM (ibid.; also RA XIX 40 XXXV, U, and ITT II/1 638, U). Another possibility is to interpret this form as Ṣijj-Adad < Ṣill-Adad

Zé-lu-uš-^{d}Da-gan (U 2550+)

Zé-lu-uš-DÙG!(wr. KAM) (RA IX 45 SA 42). Cf. Zé-lu-uš-DÙG (TA 1931, 463, OB)

Zé-lu-uš-^{d}Šul-gi (U 2551+).

ṣilūlum "shade."

Ur III PN's:

DINGIR-zé-lu-lí (Iraq V 173)

^{d}Šul-gi-zé-lu-ul (TCL V 6047 rev. iv end; PDTI 68).

ṢLL?

Ur III PN:

Za-la-LUM (BE III 92:11).

ṢLL?

Ur III PN's:

Za-al-lum (U 1449+)

Za-a-LUM (U 1445+)

Za-LUM (UET III 1414). Cf. also ZNN?

ṢLL? ṣulālum?

Ur III PN's:

Zu-la-la (UET III 272 i)

Zu-la-lum (U 1494+)

Zu(m)-la-lum (Oppenheim, CCTE p. 20).

ṢLL ṣillum, see ZK? zikum?

ṢLM ṣalmum "statue."

Written syllabically and logographically as ALAM and DÙL or ^{d}DÙL.

za-la-am-šu ù za-lam ^{d}Innin .... uš-zi-iz and ša za-al-mi-in an-ni-in ù-ša-za-ku (Morgan, MSP IV 161, Lullubum)

ša ALAM i-ḫa?-bu? and ALAM uš-zi-iz (Morgan, MSP IV 161, Lullubum)

ma-ma-na DÙL su_4-a u-a-ḫa-ru (PBS V 34 x, Lugalzagesi; S ix, xi)

al DÙL Rí-mu-uš (R xviii, xxiv; similarly UET I 276 i, NS.)

DÙL-mi-me i-ga-pi-ù "who says 'this is my statue'" (R xviii, xxiv)

DÙL-mi-me i-ga-bi-ù (UET I 276 i, NS.)

DN be-al DÙL su_4-a (R xviii, xxiv; UET I 274 iv, NS.; 276 i, NS.)

DÙL-mi ma-ḫa-ar ^{d}EN.ZU li-zi-iz?(wr. it) (UET I 275 iv, NS.)

DÙL-su ib-ni-ma (R xviii; UET I 275 iii, NS.)

DÙL-su ša KUG.AN ib-ni-ma = alan-na-ni an-na-kam ì-dím (R xxviif.)

DÙL-su ib-ni (UET I 274 v, Mi.; MDP VI Pl. 1, 1, NS.)

DÙL KUG.GI (RA IX 34 i, NS.?)

DÙL-su A.MU.RU (MDP VI 6, NS.)

dDÙL-su A.MU.RU (RA XXXIV 173f., Mari)

dDÙL-šu .... (RA XXXIV 175, Mari)

dDÙL-x SAG.KAB.DU (OIP LVIII p. 291 No. 4, PSarg.)

ù-la KUG.BABBAR ù la URUDU DÙL-su! (MDP II p. 63 ii; XIV p. 20 ii)

DÙL-su .... uš-zi-iz (MDP IV Pl. 2 ii)

DÙL-su(d) SAG.KAB.DU (CT V 2, 2146, PSarg.; RA XXXI 140, PSarg.)

DÙL SAG.KAB.DU (RA XXXI 143, PSarg.).

Sarg. PN:

DÙL-su-GAL (A 5906). Clearly sign DÙL not KA or PÙ.

ṣalmum "black."

Sarg. and Ur III PN:

Za-lim-tum (D; CT XXXII 34 ii, U).

In all other cases written logographically:

NA_4.NA_4-su-nu MI (M xxvi). Refers to dolerite

KAŠ MI (ITT I 1195; 1303; RTC 116)

GANAM MI (MDP XIV 90)

UDU MI (A 5233)

TÚG.BAR.TÚG MI (MDP XXVIII 525)

SÍG MI (CT XXXII 7 R.S., PSarg.; OIP XIV 166).

ṢMD ṣimdum "team"; "head band?"

ŠU.NIGÍN 210+[x] GURUŠ zi-me-id [....] (Kish 1930, 17a end)

1 TÚGzi-im-tum (FM 35:9).

ṢP, see ZB?

ṢRʾ$_3$.

Sarg. GN:

Za-ar-ʾà-númKI (Iraq VII 66). Cf. É-Za-ar-ḫa-anKI in the Mari texts (TCL XXIV 5:46 and ARMT III pp. 16 and 113, refs. from Dr. Kupper) and Za-ar-ḫa-nu-um, Za-ar-ḫa-nam in a date of Samsu-iluna 23 (RLA II 184).

ṢRḪ?

Ur III PN:

Zu-ru-úḫ (U 1497; Oppenheim, CCTE p. 209; CT XXXII 25 rev.).

ṢRM? ṣarmum.

Sum. DN of Akk. origin?:

dZa-ar-mu (Thureau-Dangin, SAKI p. 132 xi 10, Gudea). Cf. below.

ṢRM? ṣurmum.

Sum. DN of Akk. origin?:

^{d}KA-úr-mu to be read as ^{d}Zú-úr-mu (Thureau-Dangin, SAKI p. 132 xi 9, Gudea). Cf. ^{d}Zu-úr-mu ^{d}Za-ri-mu in TCL VI 54:16, NB.

ṢRN, see ZRN.

ṢRP ṣarpānum "silverly."

Ur III PN:

Za-ar-ba-na (ITT IV p. 42, 7368). Cf. later ^{d}Ṣarpānîtum.

ṢRR ṣirrātum "reins."

ì-nu ^{d}En-líl .... zi-ra-at ni-se$_{11}$ ga-ti-iš-su i-ti-nu "when Enlil .... placed the reins of the people into his hand" (PBS V 36 rev. x+iii, NS.).

ṢRR *ṣarrum (part of a wagon).

GIŠ.ZA.RA of GIŠ.MAR.GÍD.DA (RTC 239 ii; BIN VIII 127). Apparently a lw. from Akk. or another Sem. language. Cf. ŠL 586, 79, and von Soden, Orient. n.s. XXIII 342.

ṢRR'$_{x}$ ṣurārîtum (a lizard).

Sarg. PN?:

Zu-ra-rí-tim, Gen. (E).

ṢRṢR ṣaṣṣarum "cricket" (or the like).

Sarg. PN:

Za-za-ru-um (D). Cf. Zazzari and note in NPN p. 324.

Sum. DN of Akk. origin?:

^{d}Za-za-ru$_{x}$(URU) (Thureau-Dangin, SAKI p. 44 g ii 10, Urukagina)
^{d}Za-za-ru (ibid. p. 130 xi 4, Gudea)
Cf. also ^{d}Zar-za-ru-um (MVAG XXI 33 rev. 16, OB).

ṢTR, see ZTR? ziturum?

Š

Š šu, ši, *šunu, *šina "he," "she," "they"; "this," "these."

Personal Pronoun = Demonstrative Pronoun used as an Adjective. The distinction is not formal but functional.

1. Personal Pronoun šu "he."

Sg. Masc. Nom.:

su$_{4}$ li-im-ḫu-ra-an-ni "may he receive me" (Ist. Mus. Lagash 11001 rev.).

Sarg. GN:

Su$_{4}$-a-áš-da-gal^{KI} (G+).

PSarg., Sarg., and Ur III PN's:

Su$_{4}$-i-bí (TMH V 38 ii, PSarg.)

⌈Su⌉?-mi-ig-rí (BIN VIII 121 i)
Šu-BÀD (FM)
Šu-ba-la (G+)
| Su$_4$-be-la (G+)
| Šu-be-la (G+)
| Šu-be-lí (U 692)
| Su$_4$-be-lí (D+)
| Su-EN-lí (D)
| Šu?-EN-lum (G)
| Su?-pi-lum (Nikolski, Dok. II 31)
| Šu?-be-lum (Iraq VII 66 F 1159)
Šu-da-da (G+)
Šu-da-ti (MO)
Šu-la-pi (BE I Pl. VI i)
Šu-na-ak-pum (FM+). Doubtful
| Šu-TAB.BA (D)
| Šu-da-ba (ITT IV p. 81, 7925, U). Or Šu-ṭâba?
Šu-da-pi (UCP IX p. 210, 89)
Šu-TI.LA (G).

Personal Pronoun ši "she."

Sg. Fem. Nom.:

PSarg., Sarg., and Ur III PN's:
Si-a-sa-at (D)
Si-be-la (D)
Si-be-lí (HSS IV 68, U)
Si-da-ba (D+)
Si-da-da (E+)
| Si-da-na-at (E+)
| Ši-da-na-at (UET III p. 17, U)
Si-ḪUR.SAG (D+)
| Si-la-ba (D)
| Si-la-ba-at (D+)
Si-ri-ba-at (OIP XXXVII 50, U)
| Si-um-me (Nikolski, Dok. I p. 104, PSarg.)
| Si-um-mi (D)
| Si-wa-ra (D+)
| Si-wa-ra-at (G)
Ši-bu-uz-ri (Orient. XLVII 40:52, U)
Ši-e-lí (UET III 1041 ii, U)
Ši-sar-ra-at (U 2714+)

Ši-tu-ri (U 2716).

Personal Pronoun šuma "he himself."

50 PA.TE.SI ù LUGAL su_4-ma ŠU.DU_8.A "50 ensi's and the king he himself captured" (S vii; similarly S x)

ì-nu .... su_4-ma .... i-ik-mi-ù-su_4? "when .... he himself .... captured him" (UET I 275 iii, NS.)

(ì-nu ....) su_4-ma u-sa-am-ki-it-zu (RA VIII 200 ii, NS.).

PSarg. and Sarg. PN's:

Su_4-ma-ba-ni (MO)

Su_4-ma-DINGIR (G+)

Su_4-ma-ma-lik (CT XXXII 8 iiiA, PSarg.)

Su_4-ma-mu-tum (MO)

Su_4-ma-SIPA (MO)

Su_4-ma-UDU (MO). Perhaps incomplete SIPA.

Personal Pronoun šuatum, šuati "he."

Sarg. PN's:

Su_4-a-tum-mu-da (MO+)

Šu-a-ti (ITT II/2 p. 45, 5765)

Šu-a-tum (FM). Cf. Šuātu in Tallqvist, NBN p. 203.

2. Demonstr. Pronoun.

Sg. Masc. Gen.:

DN be-al DÙL su_4-a (R xviii; UET I 274 iv, NS.; 276 i, NS.).

Sarg. PN:

Mi-su_4-a "what is it?" (MO+). Doubtful.

Sg. Masc. Acc.:

ša DUB su_4-a u-sa-za-ku-ni (PBS V 34 x, Lugalzagesi; S iv, ix, xi twice; R xviii, xix, xx, xxi twice, xxiv, xxv, xxvi, xxvii; RA VIII 136; 139; Mi.; NS.; Škš.; ZA IV 406, Gutium)

ma-ma-na DÙL su_4-a u-a-ḫa-ru (PBS V 34 x, Lugalzagesi; S ix, xi twice)

šu DUB šu-a ù-sá-za-gu (MDP VI Pl. 2, 1 ii)

šu DUB šu-a ù-sa-za-gu (MDP X Pl. 3, 1a, 1b, 2)

ša DUB su_4-a u-sa-za-gu (RA XXXIV 173f., Mari)

su_4 DUB šu-a-ti ú-sá-za-ku (RA IX Pl. 1 opp. p. 1, Urkiš and Nawar).

Sg. Fem. Gen.:

in 1 MU si-a-ti (HSS X 72 iv 9)

ga-ga-ad um-ma-nim si-a-ti (Speleers, RIAA 4 ii, Dêr).

Sg. Fem. Acc.:

$KASKAL^{KI}$ su_4-a .... i-lí-ik (UET I 274 ii, NS.). Is KASKAL Masc. or Fem.? Cf. KASKAL .... a i-si-ir (ZA IV 206, Gutium)

SAL.ME su_4-a-ti (CT XXXII 2 iv, CM)

GÁN su_4-a-ti (ibid.)

GÁN su_4-a-tu (ibid.).

Pl. Masc. Acc.:

iš-tum KAS+X.KAS+X su_4-nu-ti $iš_x$(LAM+KUR)-ar-ru (YOS I 10, NS.; MDP VI Pl. 1, 1 i, NS.).

Š šu, šat, šūt šāt "he of," "of," "who," "whoever," etc.

Determinative Pronoun = Relative Pronoun used as an Adjective = Indefinite Pronoun. The distinction is not formal but functional.

1. Determin. Pronoun.

Sg. Masc. Nom.:

ŠE šu DN (HSS X 82:7)

x ŠE šu PN (HSS X 109+)

x ŠE šu GN (HSS X 111+; RTC 117)

x ŠE šu NÍG.ḪAR.RA (HSS X 111:9)

ŠE-um šu MÁ.$LAḪ_4$-e (MDP XIV 26)

ŠE šu KAT_5.RI.A (HSS X 36 iv; etc.)

x ŠE šu x MU (D 3; 204; 275; 326)

x ŠE šu GÁN 1 SAR (HSS X 35+)

x ŠE PN šu ZÍD.ŠE.MUN_x (HSS X 38 iii)

x ŠE šu GUR_7 BÍL, x ŠE šu ar-i-im (D 327)

x ŠE šu ba-sa-rí-im and šu ši-ib-ši-im (D 2 rev. vii)

x KUB.BABBAR x ŠE šu 1 LÚ (D 303)

ŠE.BA šu x MU (D 49; 322)

x ŠE.BA šu PN (BIN VIII 249)

x GÁN šu PN (HSS X 25)

x GÁN šu li-ip-tim, pù-ru-im, ba-sa-rí-im (D 332)

x GÁN šu kir-ba-ti GN (D 168)

x GÁN šu ba-la-ag (palgum) Da-da(-?)rí-im (PSBA XX Pl. I i, PSarg.)

É šu GN (FM 31:5)

ik-zum šu GUR_7 wa-ar-ki-im (D 270)

x ŠE ḫu-bu-lum šu PN_1 ši PN_2 (D 280)

1 GURUŠ šu PN (D 255 iii, iv, v)

1 (man) šu ANŠE (MDP XIV 71 ii)

PN DUB.SAR šu Na-ḫi-iš-tim (BM 54309 i)

PN šu GUD (HSS X 153 vii 8)

PN šu ANŠE (D 163 x)

PN_1 šu PN_2 (OIP XIV 48, PSarg.; passim in Diyala texts, Gasur texts, MO, and BE I Pls. VI-VIII). On the basis of comparison of Šu-ì-lí-su DUMU Mu-mu (3 times) with Šu-ì-lí-su šu Mu-mu (once) Meek,

HSS X p. xv drew the conclusion that both DUMU and šu mean "son (of)." Same conclusion might be drawn from Ì-lu-lu DUMU ME-DINGIR = Ì-lu-lu šu ⌈ME-DINGIR⌉ (both at D). Careful consideration of DUMU and šu in texts which use both terms makes Meek's conclusion unacceptable, and it might be suggested that the two cases in favor of the identification of DUMU with šu are due to a scribal confusion. The following texts suggest that šu means "grandson"

PN_1 DUMU PN_2 šu PN_3 ši PN_4 (MO A iii) =
PN_2 DUMU PN_3 ši PN_4 (MO A ii)

PN_1 DUMU PN_2 ši PN_3 (MO A iv) =
PN_2 DUMU PN_3 (ibid.)

PN_1 PN_2 PN_3 3 DUMU PN_4 ši PN_5 (MO A x) =
PN_4 DUMU PN_5 (MO A vii)

PN_1 DUMU PN_2 šu PA.TE.SI (BE I Pl. VII vii) =
PN_1 šu PA.TE.SI (ibid. v).

Further evidence can be drawn from D 335 listing barley assigned to Zu-na-núm and 4 other persons, all of whom are listed as šu-ut Zu-na-núm, evidently a different person from the other Zu-na-núm. Cf. also the text D 319 listing 14 persons with their paternity and ending with šu Zi-lu-lum.

Several occurrences of PN_1 šu (Nom.) PN_2 and PN_3 DUMU PN_4 ši (Gen.) PN_5 are found in JCS X 26.

Cf. also with professions:

PN_1 APIN.LAL šu PN_2 (OIP XIV 176)

PN šu GIŠ.KU LUGAL (HSS X 81 x+4)

PN SAG.ZUG$_x$ ⌈šu⌉? GN (HSS X 175 iv 6)

PN_1 GURUŠ.A.AN šu PN_2 (HSS X 205:14)

PN_1 AB šu PN_2 (ITT I 1291).

Other constructions are:

iš-dè PN_1 ši PN_2 (Kish 1930, 170e)

PN_1 DUMU PN_2 šu KUG.DÍM (MO C xviii)

PN_1 DUMU PN_2 ši PN_3 (FM 4; MO A ii; D 51; 254)

PN_1 DUMU ši PN_2 (D 128; 216; 232; 254; UCP IX p. 210, 89)

PN_1 PN_2 DUMU-a ši PN_3 (D 162) =
PN_1 šu PN_3 (D 179)

PN_1 šu PN_2 ši PN_3 (D 280:11f.)

PN_1 DUMU PN_2 ši PN_3 and later PN_4 DUMU PN_5, all of whom are DUMU.DUMU "descendants of" PN_3 (MO A viiif.). Here ši = DUMU.DUMU "descendant"

PN_1 PN_2 2 DUMU PN_3 ši PN_4 (MO A xi)

PN_1 PN_2 PN_3 PN_4 4 DUMU.DUMU ši PN_5 (MO B ii)
PN_1 PN_2 2 DUMU PN_3 DUMU.DUMU PN_4 ši PN_5 (MO C v)
PN_1 PN_2 2 DUMU PN_3 ši PN_4 DUMU.DUMU PN_5 ši PN_6 (MO C xiif.)

Occurrences of such expressions as IGI.DUB (MO A iiff.), TE.LAL.GAL (A xiif.), NAR (ibid.), PAB.ŠEŠ (ibid.), GAL SUKKAL-li (A xiii, xv), PA.RIM$_4$.GI$_4$ (A xiv), NIMGIR (C xii), PA.ḪI (C xiii), KUG.DÍM (C xviii), DÉ.DÉ (D xi) ^{d}Nin-kar (D xii), SAL.ANŠE (D xiii), ŠU.I (ibid.), ^{d}EN.KI (D xiv) after šu and ši make it likely that these two terms denote not only direct family relationship but also some clan organization.

PSarg., Sarg., and Ur III PN's:

Šu-An-tum (D+)
Šu-A-núm (G+)
Šu-Á-nu-um (G)
Šu-A-wa-al^{KI} (G)
Šu-Ba-ba (BE I Pl. VII vi)
Šu-^{d}Da-gan (MO; U 701+)
Šu-Dur-ùl (D+)
Šu-É-a (OIP XIV 23, PSarg.; U 715+)
Šu-È-a (wr. za in Fish, CST 5; Orient. XVIII 32:26, U)
Šu-e-li (RTC 143+). Cf. Šu-ì-lí
Šu-e-lum (G)
Šu-^{d}En-líl (Kish 1930, 177h)
Šu-^{d}EN.ZU (ITT II/2 p. 33, 4596+; U 713+)
Šu-Eš$_4$-dar (D+; U 724)
Šu-Ḫa-ni-iš (ZA XII 335)
Šu-ÍD (Iraq VII p. 66 F 1159)
Šu-^{d}IGI+UM.LA? (D)
Šu-ì-lí (ITT II/2 p. 5, 2899; U 719+). Cf. Šu-e-li
Šu-ì-li (MO+; PBS XIII 28, U)
^{d}Šu-ì-lí-a (OIP XLIII 143f., U). Deified ruler; there seems to be no reason to read Ilu-šu-ì-lí-a, as proposed there. See next name
Šu-ì-lí-su (D+; U 720)
Šu-^{d}IM (G+; U 696+)
Šu-^{d}Iš-ḫa-ra (D+; U 706; U 725)
Šu-Ma-ma (D+; U 728+)
Su-Ma-ma (BIN VIII 121 rev. iii)
Šu-Ma-na (G)
Šu-Na-na (D+)
Šu-Nu-nu (MO+)

Šu$_4$?-Nu-nu (E)

Šu-Ti-bar (D+)

Šu-Ti-ru-um (D; U 2700)

Šu-^{d}UTU (E+; U 698+)

Šu-^{d}Za-ba$_4$-ba$_4$ (Kish 1930, 177g)

Cf. also PN's under Du. Nom.

Sg. Masc. Gen.:

in ga-rí-im ši A-ga-dè^{KI} (S vi, xiv)

in kar-rí-<im> ši A-ga-dè^{KI} (UET I 274 v, Mi.)

a-na LÚ.MAḪ-im ša DN ša GN (RA XXIV 44, U)

a-na APIN.BÍL ši PN (D 157)

DUB ḫu-bu-lim ši GN$_1$ ù GN$_2$ (D 148)

x ŠE šu sa-bu-ul-ti Š[E]? ší PN (D 292)

DUB ŠE ši GN (D 173)

x MÁŠ šu-ut PN ši GN (D 235)

iš-dè PN$_1$ ši PN$_2$ (RTC 121:7)

x ŠE in ši 40(QA) šu ÉŠ.GÍD (HSS X 116). Cf. x ŠE in 30(QA) LUGAL or DINGIR (HSS X 72 ii, iii, and similarly in 107)

tab-ri-um IGI ŠABRA.É and tab-ri-um IGI AB+ÁŠ URU^{KI} (FM 44:6f.). Doubtful

a-na GÁN šu PN (BE I Pl. VII ii)

For constructions with PN's see šu above.

Sg. Masc. Acc. (strangely, mainly šu attested):

ŠE ša PN e-mu-ru (FM 6:10)

DÙL-su ša KUG.AN ib-ni-ma (R xxvii)

x ÁŠ šu GN PN im-ḫur (MDP XIV 21)

x ŠE šu GN (MDP XIV 21)

ŠE šu KAT$_5$.RI.A (HSS X 38 iii, iv; etc.)

ŠE šu GÁN.A (HSS X 48:8)

x ŠE šu x ITI (BIN VIII 130; 247; D 316)

x ŠE šu sa-bu-ul-ti Š[E]? ši PN (D 292)

ŠE.BA šu x ITI (HSS X 77:2; 108:26; 190:8, 10)

x ŠE si-tum šu ŠE.BA (HSS X 63:3)

ZÍD.ŠE šu iš-dè-su (HSS X 6:3)

1 ḫa-zi-núm šu 4 EME-su (MDP IV Pl. 2 iii)

GÁN ša-a PN$_1$ in GN$_1$ ŠU.DU$_8$, x GÁN šu PN$_2$ in GN$_2$ ŠU.DU$_8$ (MDP XIV 33 rev. i)

DUB ša-a Ú-gul-la-ni-su LÚ.GIŠGAL li-iš-ru-ga-me (Kish 1930, 170c).

Sg. Fem. Nom.:

x(GÁN) GÁN.SAR.A ša-at A-za-la (HSS X 1). Cf. other examples under eqlum

[Z]u?-zu ša-at GN (D 311). Doubtful, but cf. D 250 iii 21f.

1 ....-tum ša-at e-nim (MDP XIV 7 rev.)

PN_1 SAL.Ú.ḪÚB ša-at PN_2 (Ward, SCWA No. 217)

1 MÁ ša-at 30(GUR) TA (BIN VIII 151)

A.ŠÀ ša-at ᵈŠu-ᵈEN.ZU (TMH n.F. I/II 171 rev., U)

Da-bí-bí šu Bí-za dam-ḫur (BE I Pl. VII v). Instead of ša-at?

Sarg. and Ur III PN's:

Ša-at-É-a, f.n. (U 2581+)

Ša-at-ᵈEN.ZU, f.n. (U 2580+)

Ša-at-Ìr-ra, f.n. (U 2582+)

Ša-at-Ma-x-an (D)

Ša-at-Ma-mi, f.n. (U 2583+)

Ša-at-ᵈŠul-gi, f.n. (U 2579+)

Ša-at-ᵈTišpak (D)

Ša-at-Tu-tu (UET I 17).

<u>Sg. Fem. Gen.</u>:

in GUR.UL LAL 2(QA) ša-ti 11 QA TA (Kish 1930, 170g).

<u>Sg. Fem. Acc.</u>:

ÁŠ (or ZÍD) ša-at ÙR (HSS X 81 x+8).

<u>Pl. Masc. Nom.</u>:

x ᵀᵁᴳbar-ru šu-ut SAG (FM 7:7)

x si-na-at ki-iš-za-bi šu-ut PN (FM 33:32)

x UDU šu-ut É.MAR.URU_5 (MDP XIV 14)

trees šu-ut GN's (D 272)

x GIŠ.GIGIR x ANŠE.LIBIR šu-ut PN (HSS X 206:11)

skins šu-ut ENGAR.ENGAR (HSS X 162 rev. x+5)

provisions šu-ut GIŠ.Ú (HSS X 159 iv x+4)

animals? šu-ut GN (HSS X 176:8)

x DUMU.ARAD šu-ut 3 (or 2) GAR TA (HSS X 192:2, 3)

GIŠ.APIN.LAL šu-ut GN (HSS X 36 iv x+5)

12 Su-ba-rí-ù šu-ut PN (D 149)

workers šu-ut GN (HSS X 151 end; 152 end; 153 end)

workers šu-ut PN (ITT I 1465; HSS X 205:10)

PN's šu-ut PN (D 46; 335)

PN's šu-ut GN (A 4185).

In the foll. cases šu is used for šu-ut:

24 people A-gaz-ùᴷᴵ šu PN (HSS X 198:6)

30 ḪA.BA.ÙḪ šu PN (BIN VIII 280 iv)

x animals šu 1 (or 2) GIŠ.APIN (D 47; 136)

x PN's šu É.GAL.ME (MDP XIV 30 iii)

2 ÙZ šu PN (D 250 iv)

PN's AB+ÁŠ.AB+ÁŠ šu URU^{KI}.URU^{KI} (BE I Pl. VII iii).

Pl. Masc. Gen.:

a-na ŠE.BA ARÁD šu-ti A-ga-dè^{KI} (D 334:8).

Pl. Masc. Acc.:

x MÁŠ šu-ut PN (D 235)

x TÚG.ḪI.A šu-ut É.MUN (BE I 11)

x KUŠ šu-ut GN (D 201)

x GIŠ.GU.ZA šu-ut PN (D 336:7)

sar-rí-si-in šu-ut .... (Böhl, MAW Letterkunde 76B No. 9 p. 12).

Pl. Fem. Nom.:

16 ÁB ša-at PN (BIN VIII 273)

25 ÁB šu-ut PN (ibid.). Probably a mistake for ša-at

persons ša-at PN (D 7 x+ii)

persons ša-at TÚG.NI (D 163 ii)

28 gu-zi-a-tum ša-at GN (BM 54309 iii).

Du. Nom.:

2 PN's ša PN (D 16 twice; 280; 326 twice; 335:16; ITT I 1062)

2 (men) ša ANŠE (MDP XIV 71 ii).

Sarg. and Ur III PN's:

Perhaps in all cases a secondary form of šu.

Ša-DINGIR (D+)

Ša-ì-lí (RA XIX 36+, U)

Ša-^{d}IM (ITT II/1 p. 9, 638, U)

Ša-ki-be-lí (AOF VIII 258 Abb. 6a). Or ŠQ'$_{7}$

Ša-ki-DINGIR (E+). Or ŠQ'$_{7}$.

2. Relative Pronoun (construed always with the Subj.).

Sg. Masc. Nom.:

ḫu-bu-lum šu al PN i-ba-šè-ù (HSS X 109:22; 110:6)

Sargon šu ^{d}En-líl ma-ḫi-ra la i-ti-nu-šum (S vi, x; R xxii).

Sg. Masc. Gen.:

in É ši uš-da-a-bí-la (FM 10:8).

Sg. Masc. Acc.:

ŠE šu PN i-ti-nu-šum (MCS IV 13)

ŠE šu a-na ŠE.BA a-si-tu (HSS X 5:4)

x ŠE šu PN .... im-ḫu-ru (D 110:2)

x flour šu a-na PN a-ti-na (FM 21:5)

ŠE.ḪAR.AN .... šu PN .... ik-su$_{4}$-ra (FM 36:7).

Sg. Fem. Gen.:

in sa-an-tim sa-lí-iš-tim ša-ti ^{d}En-líl sar-ru_x-dam i-ti-nu-šum (R xxiii).

Pl. Masc. Nom.:

x AB+ÁŠ-bu-tum šu-ut en-ma PN_1 a-na PN_2 (FM 9:13)

x AB+ÁŠ šu-ut [en-ma] PN_1 [a-na] PN_2 (FM 11:5)

x AB+ÁŠ šu-ut ma-ḫa-ar-šu-nu [an-ma] PN_1 [a-na] PN_2 (FM 12:16)

[x AB+ÁŠ] šu-ut ma-ḫ[a-ar-su-nu] PN's na-ʾà-áš LUGA[L] it-má-[ù]? (D 135)

x AB+ÁŠ su-ut PN .... im-ḫa-zu (BIN VIII 121)

PN's šu-<ut> AB+ÁŠ-bu-ut si-da-t[im] i-mu-ru (D 336 end)

PN's šu-ut ma-ḫa-ar-šu-nu ni-iš LUGAL-im it-ma-ù (Oppenheim, CCTE TT 1, U).

Pl. Masc. Acc.:

PN's šu-ut PN u-ga-nu (Ist. Mus. Adab 280)

e-nu PN_1 šu-ut PN_1 .... it-ba-lu (FM 7:22).

Pl. Fem. Acc.:

ni-se_{11} ša-at DN BÍL-iš i-ki-su-šum (UET I 275 ii, NS.).

3. Indefinite Pronoun (construed always with the Subj.).

Sg. Masc. Nom.:

šu DI.TAR-su uš-ba-la-ga-du (MDP IV Pl. 2 iv)

šu DUB šu-a ù-sá-za-gu (MDP VI Pl. 2, 1 ii)

šu DUB šu-a ù-sa-za-gu (MDP X Pl. 3, 1a, 1b, 2)

su_4 DUB šu-a-ti ú-sá-za-ku (RA IX Pl. 1 opp. p. 1, Urkiš and Nawar)

ša DUB su_4-a u-sa-za-ku-ni (PBS V 34 x, Lugalzagesi; S iv, xi twice; R xviii, xix, xx, xxi bis, xxiv, xxv, xxvi, xxvii; RA VIII 136; 139; Mi.; NS.; Škš.; ZA IV 406, Gutium)

ša .... ù-ša-za-ku (Morgan, MSP IV 161, Lullubum)

ša ALAM i-ḫa?-pu? (ibid. p. 158, Lullubum)

ša DUB su_4-a u-sa-za-gu (RA XXXIV 173f., Mari).

Š šumma "if."

Cf. Rundgren, Über Bildungen mit (ˇ)s- und n-t-Demonstrativen im Semitischen pp. 148ff. with discussion of literature on the subject.

šum-ma Si-mu-ur_4-rí-ù^{KI} .... ŠE la i-ma-ḫa-ru (HSS X 5:9)

šum-ma e-ra-si-iš na-tu (ibid. l. 22)

šum-ma PN_1 ù PN_2 la?-ba-a (HSS X 11:7)

šum-ma-sa da-na-kir "if she should deny" (D 282:9f.). Doubtful

šum-ma MÁŠ.ANŠE Gu-ti-ù it-ru-ù (JRAS 1932 p. 296:30)

šum-ma KUG.BABBAR è-rí-šu!-ga "if they request silver from you" (EK III Pl. XI W. 1929, 160)

su-ma e-la-ga-x "if they (2 men) come" (Kish 1930, 768)

šum-ma i-ta-ti-in (TMH n.F. I/II 7 rev., U)

šu-ma GEMÉ a-ru-gi-ma-<ni>? ni-ir-da-si-ì (Yondorf a, U). Cf. under rašājum.

Sarg. PN:

Šum-ma-sa PA.TE.SI (FM 11:14).

Šʾ$_x$ <u>šeʾum</u> "barley," "grain" (in general).

Apparently a lw. from Sum.

DUB ŠE ši A-ga-d[è^{KI}] šu-ut PN (D 173, tag). ŠE is Masc.

ŠU.NIGÍN x QA ŠE, ŠE-um pu-ku-um šu MÁ.LAḪ$_4$-e (MDP XIV 26)

ŠE-su = ŠE.BA-su (MDP XIV 72 passim). Rations

ŠE.BA-su-nu (HSS X 65:19; 103:12, U; 113 x+5). Rations

ŠE is not only "barley," but also "grain" par excellence, as it includes ŠE, ÁŠ, BAPPIR, NÍG.ḪAR.RA, ŠE.BULÙG (BIN VIII 131), ŠE, ZÍD.ŠE, BULÙG.GAZ (BIN VIII 144), ŠE, ÁŠ (MDP XIV 21), etc.

Šʾ$_x$ <u>šuʾum</u> "lord?"

Sarg. and Ur III PN's:

Šu-um (FM+). Or šuʾum "sheep?"

<u>šuʾatum</u> "lady?"

Sarg. PN:

Ma-ma-šu-at (D+). Cf. šu-e-tum/tú ^{d}Ma-ma/mi in Craig, Assyrian and Babylonian Religious Texts I p. 52:44.

Šʾ$_x$ <u>šaʾum</u>.

šá-ù (FM 42:2, school text?).

Šʾ$_4$ʾ$_7$ <u>šaʾājum</u> "to look for," "to search."

Sarg. PN:

I-iš-e-si-na-at (HSS X 119:4)

Iš$_x$(LAM+KUR)-e-si-na-at (Kish 1930, 175c rev.)

Cf. Iš-i-DINGIR (TA 1930, 237, OB).

Šʾ$_x$ʾ$_x$?

Akk. lw. in Sum.:

2 si-a-um MA.NA (Nikolski, Dok. II 89). Doubtful.

Šʾ$_7$B <u>šîbum</u> "old man," "elder," "witness."

Written AB+ÁŠ, often with phonetic indicators allowing the reading šîbum, pl. šîbūtum.

Meaning "witness":

PN's ŠU.NIGÍN 8 AB+ÁŠ-bu-ut PN$_1$ É a-na PN$_2$ iš-du-da (FM 1:9)

PN's AB+ÁŠ PN (FM 2:16)

PN's AB+ÁŠ 1(PI) ŠE PN$_1$ a-na PN$_2$ i-ti-na (FM 3:7)

PN's AB+ÁŠ-bu-ut ⌈gu⌉?-su-ra-im (FM 4:14)

PN's 7 AB+ÁŠ-bu-ut gu-su[r-r]a-i[m] (D 179 end)

PN's AB+ÁŠ.AB+ÁŠ gu-su$_4$-ra-im (Louvre AO 8638 end)

PN's AB+ÁŠ .... (FM 5:11)

PN's ŠU.NIGÍN 6 AB+ÁŠ-bu-ut ŠE GA.KÚ ŠE ša PN e-mu-ru (FM 6:7)

PN's [x] AB+ÁŠ PN (FM 7:31)

PN's AB+ÁŠ en-ma PN$_1$ a-na PN$_2$ (FM 8:8)

PN's ŠU.NIGÍN 5 AB+ÁŠ-bu-tum šu-ut en-ma PN$_1$ a-na PN$_2$ (FM 9:12)

PN's AB+ÁŠ en-ma PN$_1$ a-na PN$_2$ (FM 10:5)

PN's [ŠU.NIGÍN x] AB+ÁŠ šu-ut [en-ma] PN$_1$ [a-na P]N$_2$ (FM 11:5)

PN's ŠU.NIGÍN 8 AB+ÁŠ šu-ut ma-ḫa-ar-šu-nu [en-ma] PN$_1$ [a-na P]N$_2$ (FM 12:15)

PN's 3 AB+ÁŠ (FM 13:6)

PN ù AB+ÁŠ-bu-zu (FM 14:11)

PN's ŠU.NIGÍN 15 AB+ÁŠ su-ut PN .... im-ḫa-zu (BIN VIII 121)

PN's ŠU.NIGÍN 7 AB+ÁŠ (Iraq Mus. 43612)

PN's ŠU.NIGÍN x AB+ÁŠ.AB+ÁŠ (HSS X 210:15; 212 rev. x+7)

PN's x AB+ÁŠ.AB+ÁŠ (HSS X 211:17)

PN's AB+ÁŠ.AB+ÁŠ ti-ir-ḫa-ti PN$_1$ a-na PN$_2$ u-ub-lu (D 169 iii)

PN's AB+ÁŠ-bu-tum (D 269 end)

PN's šu AB+ÁŠ-bu-ut si-da-ti[m] i-mu-ru (D 336 end)

[a-na]? AB+ÁŠ-bu-tim (D 282:12)

ŠU.NIGÍN x DUMU.DUMU GN AB+ÁŠ.AB+ÁŠ GÁN (MO A xvi, etc.)

PN's AB+ÁŠ.AB+ÁŠ a-na GÁN šu PN (BE I Pl. VII ii)

PN's AB+ÁŠ.AB+ÁŠ šu URU^{KI}.URU^{KI} ša É DN a-na GÁN PN (ibid. iii)

PN's AB+ÁŠ.AB+ÁŠ GÁN X (ibid. v, vi)

[19] or [18] AB+ÁŠ.AB+ÁŠ in É PN GAR KÚ (JCS X 26 vi).

Written AB+ÁŠ URU or AB+ÁŠ URU^{KI}; Akk. equivalent unknown. Cf., however, abu âlim "elder of a city."

Meaning "elder of a city":

PN AB+ÁŠ URU^{KI} (HSS X 49:3; 132:3, 14; 139 x+11; 142:3; 153 v 31; 161:10; 162:3; 167:4; D 144; D 207; D 227)

2 AB+ÁŠ URU^{KI}.ME (MDP XIV 19)

PN AB+ÁŠ GN (HSS X 210:4; MO A vi, vii)

PN AB+ÁŠ URU (MO C xiv)

PN AB+ÁŠ URU^{KI}-lim (RA IX 34 rev. v, NS.)

tab-ri-um IGI AB+ÁŠ URU^{KI} (FM 44:7). Ununderstandable.

Written AB+ÁŠ; possibly identical with AB+ÁŠ URU^{KI}:

PN AB+ÁŠ (HSS X 34:6; 115 x+7; 143 rev. x+5; 153 iii 27; iv 25, 27, ix 3; 154 iv x+1; 155 iii x+5; 158 ii 16, iii 5, iv 1; 159 iv x+2)

AB+ÁŠ.AB+ÁŠ (MDP XIV 9). Among professions

3 AB+ÁŠ (MDP XIV 18). Among professions

PN NU.BANDA AB+ÁŠ.AB+ÁŠ (MO A xv).

Sarg. and Ur III PN's:

AB+ÁŠ (D; FM)

AB+ÁŠ URU[KI] (FM 7:29; 17:16; 19:16). Perhaps not a PN

KI-Si-bu-um-ŠÈ (Legrain, TRU 380, U). This reading is more plausible than Ki-si-bu-um-ŠÈ.

<u>šîbtum</u> "old (woman)."

Ur III PN's:

Ši-ba-at-É.KUR (Legrain, TRU 77, PDTI 157)

Ši-ib-tum (UET III 1505 ix and perhaps 1504 vii end)

Cf. also si-ib-te-[....] in difficult context (FM 40:10).

Š'$_1$L <u>ša'ālum</u> "to ask."

Sarg. and Ur III PN's:

Iš-a-lum (MO)

Sa-a-NI-iš (FM)

Ša-il$_x$-tum MAR.TU.SAL (HSS IV 51 rev.; 53 rev., U)

For Muš-da-LUM see MŠD.

Š'$_4$LB <u>šâlibum</u>, <u>šêlibum</u>, <u>šâlabum</u>, <u>tâlabum</u> "fox."

Sarg. PN:

Ša-li-ba (Kish 1930, 406 i).

Ur III PN's:

Ša-lí-bi (RA XIX 36)

Še-li-bu-um PA.TE.SI Sa-bu-um[KI] (ITT V 6987+)

Ta-la-bu PA.TE.SI Sa-bu-um-MA (AnOr I 299 rev., translit. only)

"Šalabu patési d'Anshan" (thus translit. in De Genouillac, TD p. 12)

<Še>-li-bu-um PA.TE.SI An-ša-an[KI] (RTC 328)

Še-li-bu-tum (Jean, ŠA LXXVII rev.)

Ša-li-bu-tum (ibid. VI; PDTI 527 rev.)

Še-li-ib (Orient. XLVII 280:24; CT VII 7 iii)

Še-li-bí-a (TCL V 6167 rev.)

Cf. also Sum. names LUL.A and LUL.A.MU (U 2205ff.+).

Š'$_1$M <u>ša'āmum</u> "to buy."

The Akk. and South Arabic root Š'$_1$M evidently connected with Sum. ŠÁM (written NINDÁ+ŠE in older writing).

x SAR É, ŠÁM.NÍG(sic) x GÍN KUG.BABBAR, i-ti PN$_1$ PN$_2$ i-ša-am (Yondorf b, U)

ad-da ARÁD da-sa-am-ma "you shall buy the slave" (BM 54318 rev.)

x GÁN PN Ì.ŠÁM (MO passim)

PN$_1$ KI PN$_2$ PN$_3$ IN.ŠÁM "PN$_3$ bought PN$_1$ from PN$_2$" (Oppenheim, CCTE p. 139, Ur III text written in Akk.).

Sarg. PN:

Sa-a-mi-iš (FM). Cf. Šà-a-mu-um in MDP XVIII 171:21, OB.

šîmū "price," originally "equivalent?"

Written logographically as ŠÁM or NÍG.ŠÁM, or with syllabic indicators showing the Akk. word to be a plurale tantum šiʾmū or šîmū.

x GÁN ŠÁM-su(d) x KUG.BABBAR (CT V 3, PSarg.)

x GÁN ŠÁM-su(d) x ŠE (CT XXXII 7f., PSarg.)

x GÁN NÍG.ŠÁM-su x ŠE KUG.BABBAR-su x KUG.BABBAR NÍG.ŠÁM GÁN (MO passim); value in silver, payment in barley

1 URUDUba-da-ru-um UD.KA.BAR NÍG.ŠÁM 1 GIŠ.TUKUL 5 GÍN KUG.BABBAR KUG.BABBAR-su-nu 1 MA.NA KUG.BABBAR LAL 5 GÍN (MO C ii and similarly in C viiif., xii); šîmū(ŠÁM) = kaspū(KUG.BABBAR) "price"

NÍG.ŠÁM-sa (MO C ix)

ŠÁM 1 KUG.BABBAR GÍN ŠE 1(GUR) 2(PI) 30(QA) GUR (HSS X 72 iv)

ŠÁM 1 GÍN KUG.BABBAR ŠE "barley for 1 shekel of silver" (D 158 rev.)

(things) ŠÁM x KUG.BABBAR (D 43; 328)

x GÁN ŠÁM-su KUG.BABBAR x (D 195)

x sheep ŠÁM-su-nu x ŠE (Louvre AO 11254)

x ŠE a-na ŠÁM DUN (HSS X 105 i; 106)

x KUG.BABBAR a-na ŠÁM PN (D 225)

x ŠE a-na ŠÁM-me PN (D 140)

KUG.GI ŠÁM-mu-su "gold is its price" (FM 33 end)

ŠÁM-me lu-uš-ku-ul-kum "may I weigh out the price" (FM 10:9).

barley, silver ana šîmē X maḫārum "to sell X for barley, silver":

a-na ŠÁM X maḫārum (HSS X 99; 107 rev.; D 33 twice; 300)

a-na ŠÁM-me X maḫārum (D 37; 162; 279; Iraq Mus. 43612)

15 KUG.BABBAR GÍN a-na NÍG.ŠÁM 2 KUG.GI GÍN PN_1 iš-dè PN_2 im-ḫur (Louvre AO 8638).

x GÁN, šîmūšu x KUG.BABBAR and/or x ŠE, PN imḫur "PN sold x field for the price of x silver and/or barley":

x GÁN NÍG.ŠÁM-su x KUG.BABBAR .... PN im-ḫur (BE I Pl. VIff. passim)

x GÁN ŠÁM-su x KUG.BABBAR and/or x ŠE PN im-ḫur (D 45; 48; 50; 51; 52; 67; 74; 111; 119; 128; 168). In most cases the value of the fields is given in silver, the payment is in barley.

Meaning "to sell" or "to buy":

silver a-na ŠÁM X PN_1 a-na PN_2 i-ti-in "PN_1 bought X from PN_2 for silver" (FM 4)

silver, bronze, oil a-na ŠÁM É PN i-ti-in "PN bought a house for silver, bronze, oil" (MDP XIV 4 rev.)

PN_1 (object) a-na ŠÁM x KUG.BABBAR a-na PN_2 PN_3 ⌈i⌉-ti-in "PN_3 sold

PN_1 to PN_2 for silver" (HSS X 211)

a-na ŠÁM ŠE 1 É.GU.ZÉ PN_1 a-na PN_2 iš-du-ud (FM 8 rev.)

x KUG.BABBAR 1 GANAM BAR.GÁL.LA ŠÁM-su PN Ì.LAL (Oppenheim, CCTE p. 139, U)

x É ŠÁM-su-mu x KUG.BABBAR iš-dè PN_1 ù PN_2 PN_3 i-ḫu-uz (JCS X 26 i)

PN_1 KUG.BABBAR ŠÁM.MA.NI 2 GÍN IGI.3.GÁL a-na PN_2 ga-ga-za ⌈a⌉-na ŠÁM i-ti-in "PN_1 sold herself to PN_2 for 2 1/3 shekels of silver" (Yondorf a, U).

Š ʾ$_6$M <u>šûmum</u> "onion" or "garlic."

Sum. SUM, really ŠÚM, is evidently a lw. from Akk.; cf. Arab. ṯawm. Written logographically.

1 GIŠ.GIGIR SUM (D 302:5; RTC 119:2)

x GUR SUM (RTC 106; ITT I 1079)

1 bi-ra-ḫu SUM (D 313:5). "String of onions."

The occurrences of ^{ŠIM}ŠU.ME or ŠU.ME, used for making perfumes, may possibly represent the same word:

1 GÚ 2 MA.NA ^{ŠIM}ŠU.ME (ITT II/2 4587; 5766; V 6669; etc.)

10 1/2 MA.NA ŠU.ME (Pinches, AT 8).

Š ʾ$_7$M <u>šiāmum</u> "to fix," "to determine."

Sarg. and Ur III PN's:

Ì-lí-li(m)-šim (PBS XI/3 No. 55, U). Cf. Lišîm-ilum in Stamm, ANG p. 166

I-si-im-DINGIR (MO)

I-šim-É-a (Kish 1930, 170b).

Ur III GN:

I-šim-^{d}Šul-gi^{KI} (CT XXXII 19 i; RSO IX 473; RSO XI 97; De Genouillac, TD 26).

<u>šîmtum</u> "destiny."

Sarg. PN's:

Si-im-ti (D+)

Si-ma-zu (D)

Šim-tum-BALA (Kish 1930, 406 rev. i).

Sarg. and Ur III GN's:

GÁN Si-im-tum (MO D ix)

ÍD Ši-ma-at-^{d}Ìr-ra (ZA LI Pl. II after p. 74 iv 25 and perhaps iii 23, U).

Š ʾ$_7$M? <u>šîmtum?</u>

1 ga-nu-núm a-na rí-su-ti 1 si-im-ti KÁ.GAL (PBS IX 21). Ununderstandable.

Š ʾ$_7$M? <u>šîmtum?</u>

KAŠ? šu? si-[im]-tim ù? PA.TE.SI šu si-im-tim (FM 46:1ff., school text?)

KUG.BABBAR ù? si-im-tim (ibid. l. 9).

$Š^{\prime}{}_{7}M$? <u>šîmtum?</u>

Sarg. and Ur III PN:

| Šu-mu-ši-in-ti, f.n. (UET III 1040 iv twice, U)
| ⌈Su⌉-mu-ši-t⌈i⌉ (MCS IV 12 No. 2).

$Š^{\prime}{}_{7}N$ <u>šînātum?</u> "urine."

a-ḫu-$uš_x$(EŠ) ur_4-ki ša ši-na-tim "I gave the .... of urine?" (Kish 1930, 143:16). Because of spelling ši (not si) meaning "urine" more plausible than "teeth."

<u>muštinnum?</u> "urethra."

1 NUM ù mu-uš-ti-num (FM 40:6).

$Š^{\prime}{}_{x}P$ <u>šêpum</u> "foot," "leg."

Written syllabically and possibly logographically as DU. For the logographic spelling cf. Kraus, JCS IV 148 No. 32. Cf. also $^{\prime}{}_{x}ŠD$ išdum and ŠRŠ šuršum.

GN's ù-ga-ti-id a-na DU-su "he subjected GN's to his feet" (MDP XIV p. 12 v)

PN_1 DU PN_2 iṣ-ba-at (ibid.).

Sarg. and Ur III PN:

DU-DINGIR (E+). = Šuruš-kîn?

Še-ip-^{d}UTU (Boson, TCS 371, U).

$Š^{\prime}{}_{4-5}R$ <u>šârum</u> "wind," "breath."

Ur III PN's:

Ba-al-tu!-ša-ru-um (ITT II/1 p. 26, 779). Cf. Balṭu-šâru and Balṭu-šâr in NPN p. 315

| DÙG-ša-ri (U 2732+). Cf. Ṭâb-šâr-Šamaš in NPN p. 315
| Tab-ša-a-ri (Boson, TCS 340 rev. i)

Ša-ar-ì-lí (ITT IV p. 96, 8195+). Cf. Šâr-Adad in NPN p. 315.

$Š^{\prime}{}_{6}R$ <u>šûrum</u> "bull."

Sarg. and Ur III PN's:

Ì-lí-su-ur (ITT II/2 p. 45, 5769)

Šu-ur-^{d}EN.Z[U] (SO IX/1 No. 31:3, U). Cf. Šu-ur-^{d}IM in NPN p. 315.

$Š^{\prime}{}_{6}R$ <u>šawārum.</u> Cf. also $^{\prime}{}_{4}BR$.

Sarg. and Ur III PN's:

Sa-wi-ru-um (D). Cf. Sa-wi-ra-tum in UET V 378:5, OB

Mu-ša-wi-ir (Oppenheim, CCTE Pl. II TT 4 rev., U)

Mu-sa-ìr-su-nu (MO+). Doubtful.

$Š^{\prime}{}_{x}R$ <u>ša'ārum</u> "to battle," "to vanquish."

Written syllabically only. For the value iš$_x$ of LAM+KUR see MAD II.

in KAS+X GN iš$_x$(LAM+KUR)-ar = Sum. lú GN-da ^{GIŠ}tukul e-da-sìg TÙN.KÁR e-ni-sím (S ii, vii; R passim)

34 KAS+X iš$_x$-ar (S vi)

in GN KAS+X iš-ni-a-ma iš-gu-na-ma iš$_x$-ar in GN uš?-da?-lí?-sa-ma im$_x$!(DU)-da-aḫ-za-ma iš$_x$?-ar (S vii)

30 PA.TE.SI iš$_x$-ar (S xii)

GN's iš$_x$-ar (RA VII 104, Mi.)

NS. ša-ir 10 LAL 1 KAS+X (YOS I 10; MDP VI Pl. 1, 1 i)

iš-tum KAS+X.KAS+X iš$_x$-ar-ru (ibid.; MDP VI Pl. 1, 1 i)

in 1 MU (KAS+)X GN iš$_x$-a-ru (passim in dates of NS. in D 217; 220; 231; 236 wr. èš-a-ru; and of Škš. in D 268; RTC 130; ITT I 1115; cf. also ITT V 9265 rev.).

PSarg. PN:

Ì-lum-sa(g)-ir /šāʾir?/ (EK IV Pl. XL).

Šʾ$_x$R? šîrum (a garment).

Akk. lw. in Ur III Sum.:

1 TÚG ši-ru-um 4 (KÙŠ) UŠ (TMH n.F. I/II 242 rev.).

Šʾ$_x$R? šêrtum?. See also SRDʾ$_x$ sirdijum.

Akk. lw. in Ur III Sum.:

18 ^{TÚG}še-er-ti GIŠ.BAN KI.LAL.BI 2 MA.NA (UET III 789)

9 ^{TÚG}še-er-ti GIŠ.BAN KI.LAL.BI 5/6 MA.NA (ibid.).

Šʾ$_x$R šîrtum.

Sarg. PN's:

Si-ir-tum (G)

Si-ra-at-^{d}EN.ZU (D). Cf. Še-ri-it-^{d}Tišpak (Holma, Zehn altbab. Tontafeln 5:7f.), Amur-šerissa, Šerissa-amur (Stamm, ANG pp. 80f., 184).

Šʾ$_7$T šiātum "to leave."

ŠE šu a-na ŠE.BA a-si-tu "barley which I left for rations" (HSS X 5:4).

šîtum "rest," "remnant."

ŠE.GIŠ.NI si-tum (HSS X 3; and similarly 48:7; 50 iii x+4; 51 iv 2; iii 2; 52 iii 2; 55:16; 63:2; 96:3; D 105; D 267; A 910; A 5423)

ši-[nothing]?-tum al-[nothing]?-su i-ba-se$_{11}$ (FM 9:27)

a-na si-tim (FM 10:9)

si-tum "(as for) the rest" (FM 53:7).

The Akk. word occurs as lw. in Ur III Sum. texts in the form SI.TUM and SI.Ì.TUM. Cf. ŠL 112, 122, and 125, reading si-íb and si-ni-íb; Oppenheim, CCTE p. 124, reading si-íb and si-ì-íb; Jacobsen, CTC

p. 17, reading si-ì-tum and explaining it as a probable lw. from Akk. sîtum (rather šîtum). Cf. also the Ur III examples in UET III p. 151.

ŠB'$_4$, see ŠP'$_x$.

ŠB'$_4$ <u>šibî</u> (or <u>šebê</u>?) "seven."

Deified numeral in PSarg. PN's:

SA-^{d}Ši-bí (De Genouillac, TSA 11 vii; Nikolski, Dok. I 1 vii; 6 viii; etc.)

É-^{d}Ši-bí (TSA 12 viii). For SA = É cf. MAD II 62

Ur-^{d}Ši-bí (TSA 10 vi)

Cf. also Deimel, PB No. 2892 and MI.NI-^{d}Ši-bi in VAS VII 133:4, OB.

ŠB'$_x$? <u>šabîtum</u> (a musical instrument).

Perhaps an instrument from the country Šabum (later Sabum).

Akk. lw. in Ur III Sum.:

1 ^{GIŠ}sa-bí-tum (Pinches, BTBC 89 iii)

x GAG sá-bí-tum TUR (UET III 827)

sá-bí-tum TUR (UET III 821)

^{GIŠ}sá-bí-tu[m] (JCS X 30 No. 9)

Cf. also ^{GIŠ}sa-bi-tum, clearly a musical instrument, in the OB Sum. text AJSL XXXIX 168:29 and ^{GIŠ}sá-bí-tum in BIN IX 253; 334, OB.

ŠBL, see ŠPL.

ŠBN, see ŠPN.

ŠBR <u>šabārum</u> "to break." See also ŠPR šapārum.

(^{d}En-líl) GIŠ.TUKUL-su li-iš-bir$_5$ "may DN break his weapon" (S ix; xi).

ŠBŠ <u>šibšum</u> (a type of tax or payment for the usufruct of a field).

x ŠE.GUR šu ši-ib-ši-im (D 2 rev. vii x+7)

x ŠE.GUR so much ŠE.GUR si-ib-su-um (D 35)

ŠE .... si-ib-šum šu PN (Louvre AO 8637; AO 8643 rev.).

ŠBŠ?

Ur III PN:

Ša?-ab-ša-nu (Nakahara, ST 23 rev. 1).

ŠD'$_6$ <u>šadwum</u> "mountain."

The Akk. word appears in the form SA.TU as a lw. in Sum., as in Thureau-Dangin, SAKI p. 112 xxii 3, Gudea.

The spelling SA.TU may be considered a pseudo-logogram in Akk., as in the Cappadocian texts. We should perhaps write SA.TU-e etc. in the following examples.

The word is written syllabically or logographically as KUR.

sa-tu-e ga-la-su-nu-ma, Acc. (R xxv)

sa-tu-e a-bar-ti ti-a-am-tim sa-bil-tim (M xxvi)

in sa-tu-su-nu (MDP VI Pl. 1, 1 ii, NS.)

a-[....] Si-dur-[....] sa-tu-ì Lu-lu-bi-im ip-ḫu-ru-[nim-ma] (MDP II p. 53, NS.)

A-ma-nam sa-tu GIŠ.ERIN (UET I 275 i, ii, NS.)

SUKUD sa-tu-im "hill" (UET I 275 ivff., NS.)

i-na ša-du-im Ba-ti-ir uš-zi-iz (Morgan, MSP IV 161, Lullubum)

in Ba-sa-ar KUR (RTC 124, date of Škš.) compared with ḪUR.SAG Ba-ša-ar (RA IX 57 SA 3, U) on the one side, and with i-na A-bi-iḫ ša-du-im (ZA XLIII 115 i, Ilušuma) or ul-tu ^{KUR}Ḫa-a-ni KUR-e (Sumer II 51:2, Sennacherib) on the other

Ti-ba-ar sa-tu-im "on the mountain Dibar" (RA VIII 200 ii, NS., copy)

ù KAS+X sa-tu-a-tim [in]? Ḫa-si-ma-ar KUR [iš$_x$]-a-ru (ITT V 9265, date, king unknown). Is šaduātum another Pl. of šadwum?

a-ti-ma .... KUR.KUR KUG "up to .... the Silver Mountains" (S vi)

KUR Ga-ga-ba-an^{KI} (Iraq IV 66 F. 1153 rev.).

Sarg. and Ur III PN's:

A-bí-KUR (E)

A-bí-sa-tu (D+; UET III 936, U)

A-pù-sa-tu (D+)

A-bu-um-sa-ad (ITT V p. 53, 9787, U)

Be-lí-sa-tu (G+)

É-a-sa-tu (Iraq Mus. 43612)

Eš$_4$-dar-sa-tu (FM)

Ì-lí-sa-tu (Orient. XLVII 40:36, U)

<d>?IM-sa-tu (D)

I-nin-sa-tu (D+)

I-nu-sa-tu (BIN VIII 298 rev.)

Ma-ma-sa-tu (D)

Mu-mu-sa-tu (Iraq Mus. 30350). Cf. Mummu discussed by Heidel in JNES VII 98ff.

Sa-tu (RTC 80)

Sa-tu-DINGIR (G+)

Sa-tu-na (BE I Pl. VI iii)

Sa-tu-ni (MO)

Ša-du-a (CT XXXII 34 ii, U)

^{d}Šul-gi-sa-tu (PDTI 604, U)

^{d}UTU-sa-tu (G+).

ŠD'$_7$ šadijum? "east(ern)."

^{IM}sa-ti-um and ^{IM}MAR.TU (DP 2 ii, PSarg.). Elsewhere this word appears as ^{IM}KUR.

Akk. lw. in Ur III Sum.:

á ^{IM}sa(g)-ti-um-ma-bi (ZA LI Pl. I after p. 74 i 6, ii 3, Pl. II iv 18; PBS XV 37; cf. also discussion by Kraus in ZA LI 52 and 67).

Sarg. and Ur III PN:

Sa-ti-um (OIP XIV 193+)

Sa(g)-ti-um (Pinches, BTBC 24, U; Barton, HLC III Pl. 139, 367 ii, U). Not Reš-ti-um as in von Soden, AS p. 87.

ŠDD šadādum "to pull," "to drag," "to measure," "to measure out (with the intention to sell)," "to muster (troops)." See also MŠD.

Cf. discussion in FM pp. 188ff.

ŠU.NIGÍN 8 AB+ÁŠ-bu-ut PN_1 É a-na PN_2 iš-du-da (FM 1:12)

1 1/2 GIŠ.IŠ.DÈ É PN_1 a-na PN_2 iš-du-ud (FM 2:4)

1 É.GU.ZÉ PN_1 a-na PN_2 iš-du-ud (FM 8:21)

2? PN's sa-ti-da g[u]-zi-[im]? (FM 49 rev. x+3). Or g[u]-zi-[ti?-im]?

ŠU.NIGÍN 4 É.GIŠ.GU.ZA šu-ut PN's iš-du-du (D 336:12)

iš-du-du (DP 2 i twice, PSarg.). Text written in Akk. but interpr. v. doubtful

ba-rí-ti GN_1 ù GN_2 iš-tu-ud-ma KAS+X u-ga-e "he mustered (the troops) between GN_1 and GN_2 and waited for the battle" (PBS V 36 iv, NS.; cf. also col. iii).

šiddum or šiddatum "measure."

6 persons šu-<ut> AB+ÁŠ-bu-ut si-da-ti[m] (Sg. or Pl.?) i-mu-ru (D 336:19).

ŠDR, see ŠṬR.

ŠG? šagatum, šaggatum, or the like (a garment).

TÚG.ŠÀ.GA.DÙ (a wool garment) and GAD.ŠÀ.GA.DÙ (a linen garment) occur frequently in Sum. texts and as Sumerograms in Akk. texts (OIP XIV 145; 146; 181; MAD I 258:5; RTC 102; 197; 198; 203; FM 7:6; 34:10; ITT II/2 p. 5, 2889; 5804; III 6576 ii, U; IV p. 60, 7560, U; Nikolski, Dok. II 86; Reisner, TUT 126 iii, U, TÚG and GAD; ITT IV p. 64, 7629, U, translit. as "kid-sag-ga-rú"; etc.). On the basis of TÚG.ŠÀ.GA.TUM, used as Sumerogram in cun. Hittite, and Ass. sa-ga-tu and ^{TÚG}sa-ga-te (cf. Goetze in Festschrift Ferdinand Sommer pp. 54f.) it may be suggested that the Sum. word is a lw. from a Semitic language. x URUDU ŠA.GA.RU (RTC 221 v; UET III 327, U) represents a different word.

ŠGG, see ŠKK?

ŠGL, see ŠKL šakullum.

ŠGL$^{\supset}{}_x$ šugalla$^{\supset}$um (a profession).

Lw. from Sum. ŠU.GALLA.

PN ŠU.TE.LAL-um (RTC 80 rev.; 127 ii; ITT I 1427)

ŠU.TE.LAL-um (Nikolski, Dok. II 83; Frank, SKT 43)

PN ŠU.LAL.TE (D 179 rev.; ITT II/2 5709; OIP XIV 123).

ŠGR šigārum "yoke," "neck-stock." Cf. also ŠG?

PN (Acc.) in si-ga(r)-rìm a-na KÁ ^{d}En-líl u-ru-uš (S ii, vii)

in si-gar-im maḫ-rí-iš ^{d}En-líl a-bí-su [....]-su-ud (Böhl, MAW Letterkunde 76B No. 9 p. 12).

Apparently an Akk. lw. in Sum.:

x ^{GIŠ}SI.GAR ŠE.ḪI "of ŠE.ḪI-wood" (ITT V 6666)

Many examples in UET III p. 150, U.

DN in Ur III PN's:

Cf. deified Sikkūr under SKR.

Ur-Ši-gar (U 1395+)

Lú-Ši-gar (U 2001 = Contenau, CHÉU 69:3).

ŠGŠ šigūšum (a plant). Cf. Thompson, DAB p. 384.

Sarg. PN:

Ši-ku-sum (Louvre AO 8642).

ŠḪ$^{\supset}{}_x$, see $^{\supset}{}_1$ḪZ aḫāzum.

ŠḪR šaḫūrum (part of a temple).

PN DÍM sa-ḫu-rí (Syria XXI 159, Mari).

ŠḪR, see ṢḪR.

ŠḪT šuḫatinnum, see SḪT? *saḫatinnum.

ŠḪṬ šaḫāṭum "to jump."

a-áš-ḫi-iṭ ki-rí-iš ^{d}EN.ZU "I jumped to the garden of S." (Kish 1930, 143:17).

ŠK$^{\supset}{}_x$ šuka$^{\supset}$um? (door post?).

Is this word identical with šukûm, šugûm (from Sum. SUKU) discussed by Speiser, JCS II 225ff.?

DA.NAGAR šu-ga-e (FM 43 rev.). "Box for the door posts?"

ŠK$^{\supset}{}_x$N šuka$^{\supset}$unum "to bow (down)," "to prostrate oneself."

S. a-na ^{d}Da-gan uš-ga-en (S vi).

muška$^{\supset}$inum "serf."

The Akk. Part. muška$^{\supset}$inum "one who prostrates himself," "serf" may appear as lw. in the Sum. writing MAŠ.EN.GAG, to be interpreted perhaps as Muš$_x$(MAŠ)-ga(g)-en. Jacobsen, AS XI 17f. interprets as Maš-dà(GAG)-en. Cf. also ERIM.MEŠ MAŠ.KI.EN in JCS VIII 11 No. 180:31 and p. 12 No. 182:29, Alalakh.

PN MAŠ.EN.GAG (De Genouillac, TD 25 rev. ii, U; TCL II 4682:3, U) animals níg-ga MAŠ.EN.GAG lú GN_1 ù GN_2-gé-ne (Legrain, TRU 144:11, U)

Cf. also LÚ.MAŠ.EN.GAG in OECT VII 12 iv, PSarg.

ŠKB?

Sarg. and Ur III PN's:

Šu-gu-pum (D+)

Šu-gu-bu-um (U 2677+)

Šu-ku-bu-um (U 2684+)

Šu-gu-ub (A 26346; RA XLIX 90 No. 21, U)

Šu-gu-ba_x(KA+KÁR)-núm (HSS IV 79 rev., U).

ŠKB? (Perhaps Sum.)

PSarg., Sarg., and Ur III PN's:

Sag-gu-bí (E)

Šà-gú-bi (TMH n.F. I/II p. 23+, U)

Šà-gú-bí (RTC 294, U)

Šà-gú-ba (Fara III 64 rev., PSarg.; OIP XIV 49 iv twice, v, PSarg.; MO).

ŠKK?

Ur III PN's:

Šu-ga-kum (U 2673+)

Šu-ga-ga (U 693 and 2672).

ŠKL <u>šakullum</u> (a tree) or <u>šaggullum</u> (an implement).

Sarg. and Ur III PN's:

Sa(g)-gul-lum (MO+)

Šà-gul-lum (UET III 1650 seal, U). Cf. BIN IX p. 32 twice, OB.

ŠKL <u>šukkallum</u>, see SKL sukkallum.

ŠKN <u>šakānum</u> "to place," "to impose."

Written syllabically.

(whoever) al DÙL Rí-mu-uš MU-su i-sa-ga-nu-ma (R xviii, xxiv; similarly UET I 276 i, NS.)

MU-mi-me su-gu-un (PBS V 36 rev. iv, NS.)

MU-mi su-gu-u[n] (UET I 276 i, NS.)

in GN KAS+X iš-ni-a-ma iš-gu-na-ma $iš_x$(LAM+KUR)-ar (S vii)

x GURUŠ.GURUŠ in URU^{KI}.URU^{KI} Šu-me-rí-im u-su-zi-am-ma a-na ga-ra-si-im iš-kun_x(kum) (R xvii, xix, xxi twice)

[iš]-gu-nu [iš]-gu-un (MDP IV Pl. 2 i)

objects iš-gu-un (ibid.)

barley and onions of PN_1 DI.TAR .... al PN_2 iš-ku-un "imposed" (RTC 119:6)

in 1 MU PN uš-se_{11} É .... iš-ku-nu (RTC 86; 106; 144, date NS.; RTC 118, date Škš.)

[i]n 1 MU Škš. KAS+X GN iš-ku-[nu] iš$_{x}$-a-[ru] (RTC 130, date)

I swear GIŠ.TUKUL da-me al-su la a?-sa-ga-nu (Ist. Mus. Lagash 11001 rev.)

ù iš-ku-nu-⌈si!⌉ a-na mu-ḫu-tim "they have placed (her) ...." (Kish 1930, 143 rev.)

.... iš-ku-un (BE I 120 iii, NS.; D 172)

ša-ki-in me-ša-ri-im (YOS IX 62, Dêr).

Sarg. and Ur III PN's:

Iš-gu-[núm] (D)

Iš-ku-na (G)

Iš-kun$_{x}$(KUM)-DINGIR (MO)

Iš-ku-un-^{d}Da-gan (ITT I 1316+)

Iš-ku-un-Da-gan (ITT I p. 11, 1167)

Iš-ku-un-É-a (UET III 719, U; ITT III 5255, U)

Iš-gu-un-É-a and Iš-ku-un-É-a (ITT II/1 976, U)

Iš-ku-un-Ìr-ra (UET III 1357 rev., U)

Iš-ku-Ìr-ra (ITT IV 7449)

Ma-an-sa-ki-su (MO). Doubtful.

Ur III GN:

Iš-ku-un-^{d}EN.ZU^{KI} (CT XXI 6, 89126).

šikittum "creation."

iš-tum da-ar si-ki?-ti ni-se$_{11}$ "since the time of the creation of people" (UET I 275 i, NS.).

šukānum (a metal object).

1 (sic) su-ga-nu KUG.BABBAR maš-ga-na-at KI.LAL.BI 15 GÍN KUG.BABBAR (MO A ii, iii, vi).

iškinū, Pl. tantum (amount of money paid in addition to the price of a field or house).

Written logographically NÍG.KI.GAR, in one text NÍG.KU.GAR, or syllabically.

The word corresponds evidently to NÍG.DIRIG occurring in the PSarg. contracts published in RA VI 148ff. and TMH V 71, 75, 78) and to SI.BI from OB on (cf. examples in San Nicolò, Schlussklauseln pp. 16ff.).

x GÁN, ŠÁM-su(d) x KUG.BABBAR, NÍG.KI.GAR x TÚG.A.SU x ŠE x NI(.DUN) x KUG.BABBAR (CT V 3, PSarg.)

x GÁN, ŠÁM-su(d) x ŠE, NÍG.KU.GAR x ŠE x NI x SÍG (CT XXXII 7f., PSarg.)

x GÁN, NÍG.ŠÁM-su x ŠE (=x KUG.BABBAR), x KUG.BABBAR NÍG.KI.GAR GÁN. NÍG.KI.GAR is 1/10 of ŠÁM (MO D, C) or 3/20 of ŠÁM (MO A) x GÁN, NÍG.ŠÁM-su x KUG.BABBAR, NÍG.KI.GAR x KUG.BABBAR x ŠE x TÚG x BAPPIR x NI (BE I Pls. VIff.). Not all the items after KUG. BABBAR are given in some cases; in rev. iv, viii only x KUG.BABBAR is given. NÍG.KI.GAR is 1/10+ of ŠÁM

a-na NÍG.KI.GAR É grain, oil, etc. a-na NI.ZAG PN i-ti-in (JCS X 26 ii)

x GÁN, ŠÁM-su x KUG.BABBAR (= x ŠE), iš-ki-nu-su x KUG.BABBAR x ŠE x SÍG.GAN x BA.AN (D 45; 50; 51; 52; 67; 168). NÍG.KI.GAR is 1/12+ of ŠÁM

x ŠE a-na iš-gi-ni GÁN (Kish 1930, 138).

maškanum (type of settlement).

PN in maš-ga-ni PA.TE.SI .... u-ša-ab (ITT I 1468)

1200 GURUŠ in maš-ga-ni PN .... NINDA Ì.KÚ (MO C xix).

Akk. lw. in Sum.:

ŠU.NIGÍN 444,505 1/4 GÁN, ŠU.NIGÍN 20 LAL 3 URU SAG, ŠU.NIGÍN 8 MAŠ.GA.NA SAG (De Sarzec, DC II p. LVII). A territory of 1,568,774,544 m^2 in area, or slightly less than 40 kilometers by 40 kilometers in size, contains 17 important cities and 8 important MAŠ.GA.NA's.

Sarg. and Ur III GN's:

Maš-gán^{KI} (HSS X Index; BIN V 277:57, 80, U; etc.)

Maš-gan^{KI} (UCP IX p. 204, 83 rev. iii)

Maš-ga-ni^{KI}, Gen. (TMH V 50:8; D 272)

Maš-gán-BÀD-Ib-la (HSS X)

Maš-gán^{KI}-BÍL (HSS X)

Maš-gán-GAL^{KI} (HSS X)

Maš-gán-TUR^{KI} and Maš-gán^{KI}-TUR (HSS X)

Maš-gán-a-bí^{KI} (CT XXXII 20 i; 21 vi; 22 vi, U)

Maš-gan?!-Ga-im (D 280)

Maš-gán-GA.RAŠ!$^{SAR\ KI}$ (De Genouillac, TD 54 rev. i, U)

Maš-gán-PA.AL^{KI} (TCL II 5506, U; AnOr XII 278 iv, U; PDTI 507 rev., U)

Maš-gán-sar-ru-um^{KI} (Legrain, TRU 144, U; BRM III 37, 38, U; etc.)

Maš-gán-Du-du^{KI} (TCL II 5506, U; AnOr XII 277 iii, U; PDTI 702, U)

Maš-gán-ú-šu-ri^{KI} (CT XXXII 20 iv, U).

maškattum.

1 (sic) su-ga-nu KUG.BABBAR maš-ga-na-at KI.LAL.BI 15 GÍN KUG.BABBAR (MO A ii, iii, vi). Meaning?

ŠKNK šakanakkum "viceroy" (and the like).

Written logographically or syllabically.

PN GÌR.NITAḪ GN (S xii, xvi; R xxii; and passim in the inscriptions from Dêr, Elam, and Mari; once at Assur in KAH II 2, U)

Mi. GÌR.NITAḪ ^{d}A-ba$_4$ (CT XXXII 1 i = RA VII 180) in CM

Ḫu-un-ì-lí PA.TE.SI Ki-maš^{KI} GÌR.NITAḪ Ma-at-qa^{KI} (Thureau-Dangin, SAKI p. 176 No. XVIII, U)

ARAD-^{d}ŠEŠ.KI SUKKAL.MAḪ PA.TE.SI ŠIR.BUR.LA^{KI} .... GÌR.NITAḪ Ú-za-ar-Gar-ša-na^{KI} etc. (ibid. pp. 148ff., ŠS.)

E-bir$_5$-mu-bí PA.TE.SI Su-sim$_x$(NAM)^{KI} (MDP XIV p. 5) and E-bir$_5$-mu-bí GÌR.NITAḪ ma-ti NIM^{KI} (p. 6)

PN GÌR.NITAḪ (MO A xi; A 1007 twice; A 2736 twice; D 179)

PN$_1$ DUMU PN$_2$ GÌR.NITAḪ LÚ.GIŠ.TI (MO A xii). "General of archers?"

PN$_1$ DUMU PN$_2$ GÌR.NITAḪ LÚ.GIŠ.GÍD.DA (ibid.). "General of lancers?"

GÌR.NITAḪ with NU.BANDA, DUB.SAR, DUMU PA.TE.SI, NAR, etc. (Frank, SKT 43)

GÌR.NITAḪ.[ME]? with DI.TAR.ME (ITT I 1472 ii).

Sarg. and Ur III PN's:

GÌR.NITAḪ (D 150)

Šà-ga-na-kum (A 2966 rev. 3, U; Jacobsen, CTC 11, U)

Šà-ga-na-DU (TCL II 5504 ii, U)

Ša-ga-na-ak (TA 1930, 243, U; 543, U; 656, U).

ŠKR šikarum "beer."

Written KAŠ (passim).

KAŠ.SIG$_5$-su (BIN VIII 263 rev.).

ŠKR'$_x$ šakirûm (a plant).

1 GÚ sa-ki-ru-u (MDP XIV 8 twice). Also ḫašûm "thyme" in the same text.

ŠL'$_4$? šulânum "leper?"

Ur III PN:

Šu-la-núm (UET III 1135; Contenau, CHÉU 93+)

Cf. Šu-la-nu-um, Šu-la-nu, Šu-la-a-nu quoted in NPN pp. 323f. and note by Holma, Kleine Beiträge zum ass. Lexikon pp. 21f.

ŠL'$_7$ mašlijum "skin-bucket."

Akk. lw. in Sum.:

3 KUŠ maš-li-a-tum (FM 7:10)

x KUŠ maš-lí-um (BIN VIII 132; 267; RA XVIII 59 vii, Voc. prat.; UET III p. 120+, U)

x KUŠ.UDU maš-lí-um (PDTI 218, U)

x KUŠ máš-lí-um (BIN VIII 280 twice; Louvre AO 12904; De Genouillac, FT II Pl. L AO 12994, U)

1 KUŠ maš-li-(l)um (A 905, sic)

KUŠ A.GÁ.LAL maš-lì-um (RTC 239 ii)

x KUŠ A.GÁ.LAL máš-lí-um (TCL V 6052 i, U).

ŠLḪ šalḫum.

Ur III PN:

Ša-al-ḫu-ni (RTC 327).

ŠLK, see ŠLQ.

ŠLL šalālum "to carry away?"

various things PN iš-lu-ul (BIN VIII 144 ii, iii twice).

PSarg. and Sarg. PN's:

Da-áš-lul (Louvre AO 11283?)

Da-áš-lul-tum (D+)

Iš-lul-DINGIR (D+)

Iš-lul-Il (TMH V 31 ii, PSarg.).

šullatum "despoilment?"

Ur III DN:

| dSu-ul-la-at (Gelb, AOr XVIII 1/2 189)
| dŠu-il-at (TCL V 6053 iv, reading after Lambert, RA XLV 92)
| dŠ[ul]-l[a]-at (UET III 1504 vii).

šallatum "spoil."

Written syllabically or logographically as NAM.RA.AG.

in sa-la-ti GN a-na DN A.MU.RU (KAH II 1, Ititi)

in NAM.RA.AG GN A.MU.RU (BE I 5, R.; UET I 10, R.)

BUR NAM.RA.AG GN (I R 3 vii, NS.).

ŠLL?

Ur III PN's:

Sal-li (UET III p. 27+)

Sál-la-AN (Barton, HLC II Pl. 89 viii)

Ša-la-LUM (ITT IV 7055)

Ša-la-NI (Reisner, TUT 154 ii; Jacobsen, CTC 54 iii)

Ša-lu(m)-um (RTC 362).

ŠLL?

Sarg. PN:

Se_{11}-la-tum (HSS X 194 rev.).

ŠLL? šallatum?

Akk. lw. in Ur III Sum.:

2 šà-lá-tum .... GIŠ.GIGIR É.KAS_4-ŠÈ (ITT II 869)

1 TÚG.DU_8.A šà-lá-tum GIŠ.GIGIR LUGAL É.BA.AN (UET III 1498 rev. iii; 1744)

2 šà-lá-tum KI.LAL.BI 4 2/3 MA.NA (Reisner, TUT 132)

2 TÚGšà-lá-tum, 6 TÚGŠÀ.RA šà-lá-tum (ibid. rev.)

2 TÚGšà-lá-tum KI.LAL.BI 5 5/6 MA.NA SÍG.GI (ibid.)

1 šà-lá-tu[m] (ITT V 6923).

ŠLL? šallatum?

Ur III DN:

^{d}Ša-la-tum (PDTI 488).

ŠLM šalāmum "to turn friendly toward somebody" (in the sense of later salāmum).

DÙL-⌈su⌉ ib-ni-ma a-na ^{d}En-líl sa-lí-mi-su A.MU.RU "he built his statue and offered it to Enlil, his friendly helper?" (R xviii).

šalāmum "to be well."

Sarg. PN:

Iš-lam-GI (BE I Pl. VI vi+). For the meaning of this PN cf. Iš-lim-ki-nu-um in Riftin, SVIAD 2:27 and Šalim-kînum in Stamm, ANG p. 296. Note the old form išlam (as in other Sem. languages) instead of later išlim. Also the Mari text TCL XXIII 40:6 has AB-lam, to be interpr. as ìs-lam "he made peace."

šullumum "to make good," "to pay?"

ŠU.NIGÍN x ŠE.GUR PN_1 a-na PN_2 u-sa-lim "total of x GUR of barley PN_1 to PN_2 made good" (Kish 1938, 138 rev.). For this meaning cf. ú-sa-lim < *uštallim in KAV 45 and elsewhere.

šalmum "safe," "sound."

PN šál-ma-at (D 185)

a-ḫa-da-ki sá-lim-da "your 2 sisters are well" (ibid.)

a-na ni-ki-im SÁ "for the complete? libation" (HSS X 5:22). Reading ni-ki-im-di by Meek, HSS X p. xix is impossible because the sign DI does not have the value di in Old Akk.; interpr. uncertain.

Sum. SILIM is evidently a lw. from Akk.

Sarg. and Ur III PN's:

Lu-sá-lim (E+)

Lú-ša-lim (U 2043+). Not Awīl-ša-lim

Ša-al-maḫ (U 2584+)

Sa-al-maḫ (unpubl., U)

Sal-maḫ (Barton, HLC I Pl. 29 iv, U)

Ša-lim-á-aš = Ša-lim-<ni>?-á-aš (TCL V 6039 rev. ii, U). See below

Sá-lim-a-ḫu (D+)

Ša-lim-a-ḫu-um (U 2596+)

Sá-lim-be-lí (G+)

Ša-lim-be-lí (U 2597+)

Sal-lim?(wr. ME)-be-lí (Arnold, ABTR 17, U)

Ša-lim-be-lí-ni (RTC 342, U; Langdon, TAD 39, U)

Sá-lim-NAR (E)

Sá-lim-me-ni (FM)

Ša-lim-MI (U 2598+; HSS IV p. 39+, U)

Ša-lim-ni-aš (U 2600; Oppenheim, CCTE p. 200, U). See above

Ša-lim-nu-ri (U 2599)

Ša-lim-^{d}Šul-gi (ITT V 6787 rev., U).

DN in PSarg. and Sarg. PN's:

I-gu-Sá-lim (G; JCS X 26 vi)

Ku-un-Sá-lim (Iraq VII p. 66 F 1159)

ME-Sá-lim (MO+)

ME-SILIM (PSarg. king).

šulmum "peace."

su-lum É ga-lí-su (D 290 rev. x+3)

su-lum-ki su-bí-lim, Fem. (D 185).

ŠLQ? šalāqum? "to cut off" (or the like).

For the root cf. Iš-liq-^{d}IM (Ranke, EBPN p. 110b), interpreted as Iš-ur-^{d}Adad by Stamm, ANG p. 63, n. 2.

Sarg. and Ur III PN:

Ì-lí-sa-liq (D+)

Ì-lí-sa-lí-iq (CT VII 27, 18376 rev. 11, U).

ŠLQ?

Ur III PN:

Ša-la-kum (YOS IV 254 i).

ŠLŠ šalšum "third."

in sa-an-tim sa-lí-iš-tim "in the third year" (R xxiii).

šalištum.

[ù]?-la a-na sa-li-iš-tim ni-e-ra?-[ab]? (D 126).

šullušum "to do (something) for the third time."

in GN uš?-da?-lí?-sa-ma im$_{x}$(DU)-da-aḫ-za-ma "they fought for the third? time" (S vii).

ŠM šumum "name," "(male) progeny."

Written logographically or syllabically.

Meaning "name":

ma-na-ma MU Rí-mu-uš LUGAL KIŠ u-sa-za-ku-ma (R xviii, xxiv)

al DÙL Rí-mu-uš MU-su i-sa-ga-nu-ma (R xviii, xxiv; similarly UET I 276 i, NS.)

MU-mi-me su-gu-un (PBS V 36 rev. iv, NS.)

MU-mi su-gu-un (UET I 276 i, NS.)

MU-su-me bí-si$_{4}$-iṭ-ma (UET I 276 i, NS.)

ma-na-ma MU-mi a?! u-sa-zi-iq (UET I 275 iv, NS.)

ma-na-ma MU-mi .... u-sa-za-ku-ma (UET I 276 i, NS.)

MU-su u-sa-mi-id = Sum. me-te-ni ì-ŠID (R xxvii; RA VIII 139, R.). Corresponding Sum. not clear

MU-su i-bí (M xxviii).

Meaning "(male) progeny":

^{d}En-líl MU-su li-a-ḫir$_{x}$? (PBS V 34 x, Lugalzagesi; S ix, xi)

2 DN's MU-šu li-il-gu-da (RA IX Pl. 1 opp. p. 1, Urkiš and Nawar)

UŠ [?] ù [MU]-su [a i]-ti-na-šum (UET I 274 iv, NS.)

UŠ ù MU [a] i-ti-na-šum (UET I 276 ii, NS.; BE I 120 iv?, NS.)

UŠ É Ù TA MU ú-.... (MDP VI Pl. 2, 1 ii). Ununderstandable

bi-ri-šu ú šu-um-šu gods will destroy? (Morgan, MSP IV 168, Lullubum).

PSarg., Sarg., and Ur III PN's:

In-su-mi-su-da-nu (MO)

Su-mi-su (MO+)

Su-mu-^{d}A-a (DP 2 i, PSarg.)

Su$_{4}$-mu-be-lí (A 1087)

| Su-mu-da-ar (D)
| Su-mu-tar (D+)

| Su-mu-É-a (MO)
| Su$_{4}$-mu-É-a (BE I Pl. VIII)

Su-mu-^{d}EN.ZU (MO)

Su-mu-GI (MO+)

| Šum-Ma-lik (BE I Pl. VII vi)
| Šum-^{d}Ma-lik (RTC 163+)

Šum-su (MDP XXIV 342 twice+)

Šum-su-ba-liḫ (RA IX 34 v)

Šum-su-Ì-šum (BIN VIII 265)

Šu-mu-li-iš-ši (UET III 1305 seal, U). Doubtful

| Šu-mu-ši-in-ti, f.n. (UET III 1040 iv twice; U)
| ⌈Su⌉-mu-ši-t⌈i⌉ (MCS IV 12 No. 2)

Šu-mu-zi-ga-ar (Coll. De Clercq I 100, U?).

ŠMʾ$_{4}$ <u>šamāʾum</u> "to hear."

áš-má-ma (Ist. Mus. Lagash 11001)

NS. iš-má-su$_{4}$ (PBS V 36 x+iv)

ik-ri-bi-šu DN iš-me-ma (Speleers, RIAA 4 ii, Dêr)

DN ik-rí-bi-su iš-me-má (MDP XIV p. 12 v)

[s]u$_{4}$-bí-ti [lu] iš-me (CT XXXII 2 iv, CM)

[...]. li-iš-me (EK III Pl. XI W. 1929, 160, in broken context)

be-lí ʾà-wa-a-ti li-[iš?-m]e? (A 708).

PSarg., Sarg., and Ur III PN's:

| E-li-iš-ma-ni (OIP XIV 102)

Ì-lí-iš-ma-ni (D+)
Ì-lí-iš-me-ni (ITT II/2 p. 5, 2899)
Iš-má-^{d}Da-gan (Syria XXI 162, Mari)
Iš-me-^{d}Da-gan of Mari (PDTI 594:11, U)
Iš-má-DINGIR (D+; MDP XVIII 72)
Iš-ma-DINGIR (Kish 1930, 177g, not collated, possibly Iš-má-DINGIR)
Iš-má-ì-lum (BE I Pl. VI i+)
Iš-me-ì-lum (Walters Art Gall. 41.107 passim, PSarg.)
Iš-me-lum (TMH V 9 rev. v+, PSarg.; ITT V 6987, U)
Ès-me-lum (Nikolski, Dok. II 44; UET III p. 5, U)
Iš-me-DINGIR (Ist. Mus. Adab 325; AO XVII No. 191, seal; U 1786+)
Iš-má-^{d}EN.ZU (D+)
Eš-me-^{d}EN.ZU (ITT IV 7066, U)
Iš-má-GÁR (D+)
Iš-má-KÁR (E+)
Iš-me-^{d}UTU (PSarg. king)
Iš-má!-a-ni (Kish 1930, 150). Collated
Iš-me-ni (U 1788+)
Iš-me-É-a (U 1787+)
Ša-mi-um (D). Cf. Sa-mi-um, OB king
Ši-me-a-ni (U 1718).

tašmaʾtum "hearing."

Sarg. PN:

Da-áš-má-tum (D+). But cf. Da-áš-lul-tum, Da-áš-gi-tum for the formation.

ŠMʾ$_7$ šamājū? "heavens."

i-lu ra-b[í-ù-tum šu-ut ir-zi-tim]? ù ša-m[a-i]? (Morgan, MSP IV 161 ii, Lullubum).

ŠMK? šamaktum?

ša-ma-ak-tum (FM 40:7, school text?).

ŠMK šamkānum.

Sarg. PN:

Ša-am-ga-núm (D).

ŠMLʾ$_x$? šamallûm?

20(QA) šu ša-ma-l[i-i]m (FM 24 x+3).

ŠMM šammum "plant."

1 BE LU (= ÚŠ UDU?) sa-am-me (D 178 rev.). Doubtful.

ŠMN šummunum "fat."

Sarg. PN:

Su-mu-núm (MO+).

ŠMN šamnum "red" (or the like).

1 TÚG.NÍG.LÁM sa-mu-tum (CT XXXII 4 xi, CM); parallel to 1 TÚG.NÍG.LÁM

pi-ṣi-tum "white." Connection with sâmum "red" cannot be grammatically defended, since the expected form would be sâmtum. In our interpr. šamuttum is from šamuntum, from a root ŠMN which underlies SA.MA.NA, the Sum. word for a sickness characterized by redness. Akk. samanû is derived in turn from Sum.

ŠMR.

Perhaps an Amorite PN in Ur III:

I-la-ša-ma-ar (A 2964:12); cf. A-bi-sa-mar (TCL XXII 1:3; 2:3, 7, L.E. 2, Mari) and other PN's from Mari composed of -sa-mar.

ŠMŠ <u>šamšum</u> "sun" (as applied to gods and persons).

Written logographically or syllabically.

Sarg. and Ur III PN's:

A-bi-^{d}UTU-ši (UET III 1034 rev. i, U)

Be-lí-^{d}UTU-si (D)

Sa-am-si (FM+)

^{d}Šul-gi-ša-àm-si (ITT II 728, U)

^{d}Šul-gi-ša-am-<si>? (AnOr I 248, U)

^{d}Šul-gi-^{d}UTU-si (TA 1931, 236, U)

^{d}Šul-gi-^{d}šam-ši (RT XIX 58, 330, translit. only). Since the ŠAM value is unknown in Ur III we may have to interpret this transliteration probably as ^{d}Šul-gi-^{d}UTU!-ši, as in ZA XII 343 and PDTI 336, U)

Tu-li-id-^{d}UTU-ši (Nikolski, Dok. II 464 rev., U; Boson, TCS p. 28, U). See also Tu-li-id-^{d}UTU below

^{d}UTU-ši-la-at /Šamšī-Illat/ (Lau, OBTR 22, U). Cf. also ^{d}UTU-il-la-at below.

DN in PSarg., Sarg., and selected Ur III PN's:

Written logographically and once syllabically.

A-mur-^{d}UTU (Kish 1930, 144a ii; U 173+)

Dam-ḫur-^{d}UTU, f.n. (Yale unnumbered)

I-bí-^{d}UTU (DP 2 i, PSarg.)

I-ku-^{d}UTU (CT V 2, 12146, PSarg.)

I-mi-^{d}UTU (RTC 246)

Ìr-e-^{d}UTU (G+)

I-sar-ki-^{d}UTU (Jean, ŠA CXIII rev., U). Cf. also NḪD?

Iš-me-^{d}UTU (PSarg. king)

Ku-rù-ub-^{d}UTU (E)

Gu-ru$_{x}$(URU+X)-ub-^{d}UTU (Pinches, AT p. 122, U)

Nu-úr-^{d}UTU (U 2391+)

PÙ.ŠA-^{d}Sa-mu-uš (D+)

PÙ.ŠA-^{d}UTU (U 464)

Pù-^{d}UTU (D+)

Sar-ru-ki-^{d}UTU (Fish, CST 6; 17)

Ša-ma-aš-ki-ti (PDTI 529 x, U)

Šu-^{d}UTU (E+; U 698+)

Tu-li-id-^{d}UTU (Fish, CST p. 16, U). See also Tu-li-id-^{d}UTU-ši above

Tu-li-^{d}UTU (MDP XIV 78)

Um-mi-^{d}UTU (D+)

^{d}UTU-ba-ni (U 879+)

^{d}UTU-É (D+)

^{d}UTU-SA (D+). For SA = É cf. MAD II 62

^{d}UTU-il-la-at (RTC 108). See also ^{d}UTU-ši-la-at above

^{d}UTU-ìl-[la?-at]? (D)

^{d}UTU-il-at (RTC 180)

^{d}UTU-lu-me-ir (ITT II/2 p. 3, 2852). Read perhaps ^{d}KA?-Me-ir

^{d}UTU-mu-da (Louvre AO 11272)

^{d}UTU-ra-bí (RTC 133+)

^{d}UTU-sa-tu (G+).

šamšatum "sun disk."

Akk. lw. in Ur III Sum.:

sa-am-sa-tum of silver (RA VIII 197 No. 22)

1 URUDU sa-am-sa-tum LUḪ.ḪA KI.LAL.BI 2/3 MA.NA 7 1/2 GÍN (RA XIV 181:8)

UD.SAR sa-am-sa-tum of gold (UET III 557; 613; 647 and other examples quoted ibid. p. 146).

ŠMṬ šamāṭum "to pluck (down)."

iš-mu-tu (PBS IX 30). For fuller context see KSRK kusarikkum.

ŠMṬ?

Ur III Amorite PN:

Sa-mi-tum MAR.TU (PDTI 621).

ŠN šantum "year."

Written logographically as MU or syllabically.

in sa-an-tim sa-lí-iš-tim "in the third year" (R xxiii)

animals x MU (D 6; 8)

animals MU x (D 236)

šu 1 MU "of 1 year" (D 3 end; 49; 275; 326)

šu 2 MU (D 322; 326)

in 1 MU si-a-ti "in that year" (HSS X 72 iv)

in 1 MU /in šanat/ DN ib-ba-al-zu?-šum (MDP X Pl. 3, 1a)

in 1 MU PN .... iš$_{x}$-a-ru (RTC 130 and passim in dates).

ŠN šenā "two."

[a-na] še-na [lu a]-zu-uz (CT XXXII 1 ii) = a-na še-na lu-u a-zu-uz (RA VII 180) in CM.

ŠN'$_7$ sanājum "to do (something) for the second time," "to repeat."
in GN KAS+X iš-ni-a-ma iš-gu-na-ma iš$_x$(LAM+KUR)-ar (S vii).

PSarg.? and Ur III PN:

Iš-ni-lum (TMH V 97 ii, PSarg.?)
Iš-ni-DINGIR (U 1789).

šanijum "second."

MN at Adab and Lagaš?:

Ša-ni-i (see MAD p. 234).

šanajum?

PN$_1$ DUMU PN$_2$ NU.BANDA ša-na-e (MO A xiv).

ŠN'$_7$? šinîtum.

A kind of cloth; cf. ŠL 579, 288.

Akk. lw. in Ur III Sum.:

x SÍG si-ni-tum (Orient. I 58 Wengler 40, misread for TÚG?)
x TÚG.UŠ.BAR si-ni-tum (RA IX 157).

Sarg. and Ur III PN's:

Si-ni-tum (MDP XXVIII 526)
Ši-ni-tum (G; UET III 1232, U)

Ši-ni-da (Barton, HLC III Pl. 134, 358, U)
Ši-ni-da-a (CT X 17 iii+, U).

ŠN'$_7$?

Sarg. and Ur III PN's:

Šu-NI-a (ITT II/1 p. 25, 771, U)
Su-NI-iš-da-gal (D)

Su-NI-um (D+)
Su$_4$-NI-um (BE I Pl. VII vi)

Su$_4$-NI-da (BE I Pl. VII ii)
Šu-NI-da (Louvre AO 11267)

Su-NI-tum (FM+)
Šu-NI-tum (FM+; Arnold, ABTR 13, U).

ŠN'$_x$.

Sarg. PN:

Si-ni-sa (D+).

ŠNB?

Ur III PN:

Šu-na-bu-um (Fish, CST p. 159 iii). Hardly Šu-Nabûm. Miscopied for Šu-gu-bu-um?; see ŠKB.

ŠNG'$_x$ sangûm "priest" (or the like).

Ur III PN?:

| Ša-an-gu (É) ^{d}Dumu-zi (Reisner, TUT 246; Virolleaud, CC p. 4 No. III)
| Ša-an-gu (ITT V p. 39, 9485; Virolleaud, CC p. 4 No. III).

ŠNN šanīnum "opponent."

DN nir_x ša-nin-ú-tim (RA IX Pl. 1 opp. p. 1, Urkiš and Nawar). The interpr. of GAZ+NIR as nir_x is not sure.

Sarg. PN:

Ma-an-sa-nin-su (D+).

ŠNN šinnum, Pl. šinnātum "tooth."

40 GIŠ.KA ki-iš-za-bi, compared with 80 si-na-at ki-iš-za-bi, compared with 40 GIŠ ki-iš-za-bi "teeths of threshing boards" (FM 33:17, 31, 36)

Cf. also n. on Š$^{\text{ʾ}}{}_7$N šînātum.

ŠNT, see Š$^{\text{ʾ}}{}_7$T šîtum and Š$^{\text{ʾ}}{}_7$M? šîmtum.

ŠP šaptum "lip."

X ù ti-bu-ut-tum sa-ap-da-su ".... and .... are his lips" (Kish 1930, 143:27). The form is in Du.

ŠP šapātum, Pl. tantum, "wool."

Written logographically.

x MA.NA SÍG (passim)

SÍG-su-nu (MDP XIV 86+)

30 ⌈SÍG⌉ MA.NA in NA_4 KUG.BABBAR PN wa-bíl-si-in "30 minas of ⌈wool⌉, (measured by) the stone of silver, PN is their porter" (FM 36:18). The suffix -si-in shows that the subject is šapātum in Pl. Fem. Same conclusion can be drawn from KUG.BABBAR-si-in referring to x GÚ SÍG in MO C viii.

Š$P^{\text{ʾ}}{}_6$ šapāwum "to be silent."

da-áš-da-b[u] "you were silent" (HSS X 8:9). Perhaps Š$B^{\text{ʾ}}{}_6$.

Š$P^{\text{ʾ}}{}_7$ šapājum "to ask," "to pray."

a-na É.GI_4.A áš-bi-NI(=ià?)-ma a-na GN a-la-kam aq-bi-si-im "I asked? PN and I told her to go to GN" (D 315 rev.). V. doubtful.

šupîtum "prayer."

[s]u_4-bí-ti [lu] iš-me (CT XXXII 2 iv, CM).

Sarg. PN:

Su_4-bí-tum (D).

Š$P^{\text{ʾ}}{}_x$? šapāum.

Ur III PN's:

| Iš-bi-Ìr-ra (UET III 1421). I cannot find any evidence in favor of taking Iš-bi- from Š$B^{\text{ʾ}}{}_4$ "to be satiated," as done by Stamm, ANG pp. 63 and 291. As against it, cf. possibly Iš-pi-^{d}IM and Iš-pi-ia

in YOS XII, OB, soon to be publ.
dIš-bi-dIr-ra of Mari (ZA XLIX 60f.)
dKAL-sá-bí (Barton, HLC II Pl. 66 i)
SUKKAL-sá-bí (Barton, HLC I Pl. 8 i; Pl. 26 i, ii)
dUTU-sá-bí (Reisner, TUT Pl. 134, 163:6; 2 NT 726)
Cf. also Ša-bi-DINGIR in TCL XXIII 79:13, Mari, and VAS XI 28:26, EA, and Ša-bi-Il in Iraq VII 41, Chagar Bazar.

ŠPK šapākum "to pour," "to pile up."
NE.RU-dam in a-ša-ar URU al-su-nu iš-bu-uk (R xxiii, xxv)
KI.GAL iš-bu-uk (BE I 120 iii, NS.).
išpikū, Pl. tantum, "grain accumulations."
x ŠE iš-bí-ku PN (BIN VIII 205; 226)
iš-bi-gi gi-nu-tim a-rí-iš-ga (JRAS 1932 p. 296:38).

ŠPL šaplum "lower."
ti-a-am-dam a-lí-dam ù sa-bil-dam (S iv, viii, xii; R xxv)
iš-tum-ma ti-a-am-tim sa-bil-tim (S iv, ix)
a-ti ti-a-am-tim sa-bil-tim (R xvii)
ti-a-am-tim sa-bil-tim (M xxvi twice)
⌈iš-tum⌉? ti-a-a[m-tim] sa-bil-ti[m] (PBS V 36 x+iv, NS.)
in [ti]-a-am-t[im] sa-bil-tim (PBS V 36 rev. x+iii, NS.)
ti-am-[tum]? e-li-t[um]? ù ša-b[il-tum]? (Morgan, MSP IV 161 ii, Lullubum).

ŠPL?
6 ŠE.GUR.SAG.GÁL šu sa-bu-ul-ti Š[E]? ši PN (D 292:13)
barley a-na ša-bu-u[l]?-t[i? ŠE]? (D 321 x+9).

ŠPL? šuppulum?
Sarg. PN:
Šu-pù-la (BE I Pl. VII iii).

ŠPL? šuppulum?
Ur III PN:
Šu-bu-ul-tum (UET III p. 28+)
Šu-pù-ul-tum (RA XIX 44, 118).

ŠPN? šapānum? "to assault?" This root accords with later ŠPN, besides the more common SPN.
en-ma a-na-gu-ma sá-bi-ni-a-me u-ga-al "thus I said: 'I hold back my assaulters'" (Ist. Mus. Lagash 11001). The letter speaks of blood revenge.

ŠPN? šipnum?
Sarg. PN:
Bí-su-šè-ip-num (MO).

ŠPN?

Ur III PN's:

Šab-ni-^{d}Šul-gi (RA IX 63 AM 14 = U 2607)

Šab?-ni?-$^{d?}$Ìr-ra (Orient. XLVII 145 = U 2606)

Cf. Ša-ab-ni-Eš$_{4}$-dar in A 7652, 7653, OB.

ŠPN? *šapannum.*

Sarg. PN:

Sa-ba-an-núm (E+).

ŠPN?

Sarg. and Ur III PN's:

Se$_{11}$-ba-núm (RTC 244)

Si?-ba-nu-um (Delaporte, CCL II A 245, U).

ŠPP *šappum* and *mašappum* (a container).

Sum. logograms are evidently all lw.'s from Akk.

x SÁ.AB NI.NUN (OIP XIV 178; similarly in ITT II/2 4646; Pinches, AT 9f.; Pinches, BTBC 8f.)

x NI.NUN ŠAB (ITT I 1068; 1225; for NI in ITT II/2 4422)

x MA.SÁ.AB ḪA.GAR.KI, for fish (RTC 213f.)

x MA.SÁ.AB (OIP XIV 150)

MA.SÁ.AB of KUG.BABBAR and URUDU and $^{(GI)}$MA.ŠAB (UET III p. 127, U).

ŠPR *šapārum* "to send a message," "to write."

iš?-da-na-ba-ra-am (D 126)

mi-nu-um aš-da-na-ba-ra-ma la du-ša-ba-lam "how is it that I write to you continuously and you do not send me (the silver)?" (NBC 5378, U, soon to be publ. by Sollberger).

šāpirum "commander."

NS. sa-bi-ir KIŠ MI ḪI KALAM NIM^{KI} (UET I 274 i). Possibly "commander of the totality of .... of the land of Elam."

šap(i)rum.

On the basis of comparison of Maš-gán-PA.AL^{KI} (TCL II 5506, U; AnOr XII 278 iv) with Ma-aš-ka-an-ša-bi-ir^{KI} (TCL XXIII 72:5, Mari) it may be assumed that Sum. PA.AL = šabra is a lw. from Semitic. Akk. šabrû would in turn be a lw. from Sum. Cf. also RA XLV 74:26.

šiprum "message," "command"; "messenger."

in si-ip-rí ^{d}Innin "by the command of Innin" (PBS V 36 rev. x+i?, ii, iii, NS.)

PN si-ip-rí li-da-ni-in "may PN execute my order" (BIN VIII 151)

PN si-bi-ir sar-ri-[im] "PN, the messenger of the king" (MDP XXVIII 424 rev., U).

našparum (a garment).

In Sum. texts, lw. from Akk.

[1] na-áš-ba-ru-um (D 169)

x TÚG na-áš-ba-ru-um (RTC 203; ITT I 1082; OIP XIV 118; BIN VIII 270; ITT II/2 p. 4, 2884; p. 7, 2936; IV p. 11, 7109; p. 41, 7358; p. 86, 8011; V 9297)

1 TÚG na-á[š-ba]-ru-u[m] KUG.BI 10 GÍN (OIP XIV 160)

3 GAD na-áš-ba-ru-um (Nikolski, Dok. II 86).

Sarg. PN:

⌈Na⌉-áš-ba-rí-i⌈š⌉ (E).

našpartum (a garment).

1 TÚG na-áš-ba-ar-tum (FM 35:8).

ŠPR? šapparum "wild goat" (or the like).

Ur III PN:

I-zu-sa-bar (PDTI 559 rev.; CT XXXII 50:13). = Issu-šappar. Interpr. doubtful.

ŠPR? šaburum.

Ur III GN:

Sa-bu-ru-um^{KI} (Jean, RA XIX 42 No. LX).

ŠPŠ, see ŠBŠ šibšum.

ŠQ$^{\supset}{}_{7}$? šaqjum? "exalted."

Sarg. PN's, all doubtful:

Ma-an-sa-ki-su (MO)

Ša-ki-be-lí (AOF VIII 258 Abb. 6a)

Ša-ki-DINGIR (E+)

Ti-ru-ša-ki (G). Cf. ^{d}Adad-ša-ki in NPN p. 316.

ŠQ$^{\supset}{}_{7}$ šaqājum "to give drink."

Sarg. PN:

Da-áš-gi-tum, f.n. (D+).

mašqijum.

Akk. lw. in Ur III Sum.:

MAR ma-áš-gi$_4$-um UD.KA.BAR (UET III 734).

ŠQD šiqdum "almond."

Akk. lw. in Sum.

Oil of almond:

1 NI ši-iq-tum ŠAKAN .... (RTC 109 rev.)

1 ŠAKAN NI ši-iq-tim DÙG.GA (RTC 215)

1 NI ši-iq-tum ŠAKAN (ITT V 6667)

3 QA NI ši-iq-tum (NBC 1939, unpubl.)

NI si-iq-tum (RA XVIII 53 ii, Voc. prat. = MDP XXVII 55 rev.).

Wood of almond tree:

2 PISAN ^{GIŠ}si-iq-tu[m] (RTC 304 iii, U)

1 (receptacle)? ^{GIŠ}si-iq-[tum] (UET III 379, U)

1/2 ^{GIŠ}si-iq-da (Bab. VIII Pl. IX Pupil 36 rev., U). Here a receptacle

GIŠ.TUKUL si-iq-tum (UET III p. 93+, U).

ŠQL <u>šaqālum</u> "to weigh out," "to pay."

[m]u-ba-al-ki-tum [KUG.BAB]BAR? 1 MA.NA [i]-sa?-gal "the one who transgresses will pay? 1 mina of silver?" (UCP IX p. 205, 83 iv)

ŠÁM-me lu-uš-ku-ul-kum "may I pay the price" (FM 10:10)

PN (Fem.?) da-áš-ku-ul (Kish 1930, 559c).

$ŠR'_4$ <u>šir'um</u> "furrow"; "ripeness?"

4 KÙŠ ù si-ir-i me-eḫ-zum (HSS X 156 x+3, 6). Measurements of doors. Here šir'um is a spatial term, of 0.50 to 0.75 meters according to Landsberger, Ana ittišu pp. 152ff.

Sarg. PN:

Ši-ìr-e-si-na (FM).

$ŠR'_7$ <u>šarājum</u>.

Sarg. PN's:

Iš-rí-DINGIR (RA XIII Pl. I opp. p. 8 No. 5 seal)

| Sa-rí-Il (D). Interpr. doubtful

| Ša-rí-DINGIR (G+). Interpr. doubtful

Ša-rí-DINGIR-ni (UET II Pl. XLVIII 33 i). Interpr. doubtful.

$ŠR'_x$? <u>šarûm</u>? (a profession).

a-na SAL.[....] PN sá-rí-i[m] (D 169 ii).

ŠRḪ <u>šarāḫum</u>.

Ur III FN:

A.ŠÀ ša-ra-ḫu-um-MA (Nikolski, Dok. II 155; 162 rev.; 237 rev.; TCL V 5675 iii+)

KI.SUR?.RA ša-ra-ḫu-um-MA (Orient. XIV p. 64, IB 36).

ŠRḪ.

Sarg. and Ur III PN:

| Si-ir-ḫa-núm (Kish 1930, 140)

| Si-ir-ḫa-nu-um (Delaporte, CCL II A 209, U)

| Še-ir-ḫa-núm (UET III p. 28, U)

| Še-ir-ḫa?-num (CT III 35 i, U)

| Še-ir-ḫa-an (Contenau, CHÉU 25 and 47, U; TCL V 6036 iv, U). Read thus against In-ḫa-an and In-ḫa-ni of U 1744f.

| Ši-ir-ḫa?-an (U 2711 = Orient. XLVII 500:66, U). Copied and read as Ši-ir-za-an

| Še-ir-ḫa?-nu-um (Oppenheim. CCTE C 1 iv, U). Read as á-in-a-nu-um

ibid. p. 22.

ŠRḪN *širḫunum* (an ornament).

Akk. lw. in Ur III Sum.:

x še-ir-ḫu-núm KUG.GI (A 5019+)

še-ir-ḫu-núm of KUG.GI or KUG.BABBAR (UET III p. 163 passim).

ŠRK *šarākum* "to donate (ex voto)."

Written syllabically and logographically.

dam-si-[lí] ab-ni a-[na] ^{d}EN.Z[U] áš(wr. iš)-ru-u[k] (UET I 275 iv, NS.)

DUB .... PN li-iš-ru-ga-me (Kish 1930, 170c).

Logogram SAG.KAB.DU = Sum. sa(g)-rig$_x$ = Akk. išruk occurs only in PSarg. From the Sarg. Period on it is replaced by A.MU.RU or A.MU.NA.RU.

PN DÙL-su(d) DN (Dat.) SAG.KAB.DU (CT V 2, 12146)

PN DÙL-su(d) a-na DN SAG.KAB.DU (RA XXXI 140)

PN [a]-na DN [SAG.KAB].DU (CT VII 4, 22451)

PN DN (Dat.) SAG.KAB.DU (RA XXXI 142; CT VII 3, 22452; CT XXXII 8, 60036)

DÙL PN (Gen.) DN (Dat.) SAG.KAB.DU (RA XXXI 143)

PN title SAG.KAB.DU (BE I 109)

Cf. also OIP LVIII 291 Nos. 4, 5, 6, 10, and 11.

šarrākum (a profession).

Cf. URU.SAG.PA.KAB.DU = URU-šar-ra-ak-e = URU-šar-ra-ki in MAOG I/2 p. 6 and ŠE.BA SAG.PA.KAB.DU.NE (MDP XIV 3 ii).

PSarg., Sarg., and Ur III GN:

URU.SAG.PA.KAB.DU^{KI} (ITT I 1287; D 285; TCL V 5676 rev. x, U; YOS IV 217, U; etc.)

URU.SAG.PA.SAL.KAB.DU^{KI} (Nikolski, Dok. II 197, U)

URU.SAG.SAL.KAB.DU^{KI} (TMH V 64 i 3, PSarg.; 110:8; 211 ii x+2)

URU.SAG.PA.SAL.KAB$^{⌈KI⌉}$ (Reisner, TUT 200 rev., U)

URU.SAG.PA.KAB^{KI} (RTC 113 rev.)

URU!.KAB.DU^{KI} (OIP XIV 51 iii, PSarg.)

URU.SAG.SAL.KAB^{KI} (ITT V 6799, U)

URU.SAG.KAB^{KI} (CT VII 46, 17774 rev. 3, U).

širkum "gift."

Sarg. PN's:

Si-ir-kum (D+)

Si-ir-ga-núm (Kish 1930, 406 ii).

ŠRK *šerkum* (a quality of figs and apples).

Akk. lw. in Sum.?:

x QA še-ir-gu GIŠ.MA (RTC 217; 218; 220; 245; UET III 68, U)

550 GIŠ.MA še-ir-gu TAB.BA KI.LAL.BI 45 GÚ 46 MA.NA (TCL II 5530 rev., U)

x QA GIŠ.MA še-ir-gu (UET III 76 i; 209; 273; 1051, U)

5(QA) GIŠ.MA še-ir-gu 5(QA) GIŠ.MA.GUNU še-ir-gu (Nakahara, ST 19, U)

GIŠ.MA še-ir-gu 3 2/3 KÙŠ (Orient. XV 56, U). Stringed? figs measured in cubits, for making perfume

GIŠ.MA še-ir-gu-BI 1/3 KÙŠ (TCL V 6042 rev. ii, U). As above.

ŠRK.

si-ir?-gu-a i-da-su (Kish 1930, 143 rev.).

ŠRM.

An Ur III gentilic like UDU ḫa-ar-ši-tum?:

1 GANAM ša-ru-mi-um (Fish, CST p. 32, 206; SO IX/1 No. 26)

1 UDU ša-ru-mi-um (SO IX/1 No. 26; PDTI 596)

1 SAL.ÁŠ.GÀR ša-ru-mi-um (Langdon, TAD 51; RA IX 56 SA 231)

UDU, GANAM, and $SILA_4$ ša-ru-mi-um (PDTI 345 rev.).

ŠRM.

Ur III GN:

Še-ri-im-tum (ZA LI Pl. IV after p. 74 iii 24, 25).

ŠRMN? <u>šurmānum</u>, <u>šurmēnum</u> "cypress."

Akk.? lw. in Sum.:

^{GIŠ}šu-úr-me (Thureau-Dangin, SAKI p. 102 xii 5; 106 xv 29, Gudea)

šu-úr-me-BI (TCL V 6042 i, U; Orient. XV p. 55, U). For making perfumes

x MA.NA ^{GIŠ}šu-úr-me NU.LUḪ.ḪA (UET III 1777, U)

^{GIŠ}šu-úr-man (RA XVIII 53 ii, Voc. prat. = MDP XXVII 55 rev.).

ŠRN <u>šarānum</u> (a tree or a plant).

Akk. lw. in Ur III Sum.:

1 ^{GIŠ}GU.ZA ŠÌR.DA ša-ra-núm URUDU GAR.RA, compared with 1 ^{GIŠ}GU.ZA ŠÌR.DA ḪA.LU.ÚB URUDU GAR.RA (HSS IV 5 iii bottom).

ŠRN? <u>šurānum</u> (an animal).

Ur III PN:

| Šu-ra-núm (UET III p. 29+)
| Šu-ra-nu-um (unpubl.).

ŠRN?

Ur III PN:

Šu-ru-LUM (RTC 391).

ŠRQ <u>šurqum</u> "theft."

1 ÁB ŠÁM 5 GÍN KUG.BABBAR, 10 GANAM.UDU ŠÁM 10 GÍN KUG.BABBAR ⌈a⌉-na su-ur-ki É-ti-su PN_1 iš-dè PN_2 [im-ḫur]? (Cop. 10090).

ŠRP? <u>šarpānum</u>?

Sarg. PN:

Ša-ar-ba-an (RTC 246). Interpr. as Ša-ar-ba-DINGIR does not make sense.

ŠRR šarrum "king."

Written logographically as LUGAL or syllabically.

PN LUGAL GN (passim)

DN LUGAL GN (RA IX Pl. 1 opp. p. 1, Urkiš and Nawar; Speleers, RIAA 4, Dêr)

DN LUGAL da-núm (OIP XLIII 143, U)

dŠu-dEN.ZU .... sar-ru-um dan-núm sar GN ù sar ki-ib-ra-tim ar-ba-im (MDP IV p. 8)

sar in sar-rí (UET I 274 ii, NS.; 275 i, NS.; PBS V 36 rev. x+ii, NS.)

LUGAL-um (HSS X 6:5)

sar-rí-su-nu 3 i-ik-mi-ma maḫ-rí-iš DN u-sa-rí-ib (YOS I 10, NS.)

sar-rí-si-in .... ik-mi (Böhl, MAW Letterkunde 76B No. 9 p. 12, unknown king)

sar-rí-si-in in ga-mi-e u-sá-rí-ib (CT XXXII 5, 98917, unknown king)

a-na na-ʾà-si NS. .... LUGAL-rí ki-ib-ra-tim ar-ba-im (MDP VI 6)

a-na na-ʾà-si ŠD. LUGAL-rí A-ga-dèKI (Gadd, EDSA Pl. 3)

a-na na-si LUGAL (BIN VIII 121)

na-ʾà-áš LUGA[L] (D 135)

na-ʾà-áš LUGAL ù na-ʾà-áš NIN (RA XXIII 25)

ni-iš sar-ri-im (MDP XIV 44; XXVIII 424, U)

ni-iš LUGAL-im (Oppenheim, CCTE TT 1, U)

MU LUGAL-im (RA XXXII 190, U)

um-ma sar-ru-um-ma (RA XXIV 44, U)

PN si-bi-ir sar-ri-[im] "PN, the messenger of the king" (MDP XXVIII 424 rev., U).

Sarg. and Ur III DN's:

dLUGAL-bar-ga-at (BE I Pl. VII rev. iv). Or PN. Ununderstandable

dLUGAL-ma-tim (Syria XXI 162f., Mari).

Ur III GN:

| Maš-gán-sar-ru-umKI (Legrain, TRU 144+)
| Maš-gán-sar-umKI (BRM III 37; 38).

PSarg. and Sarg. PN's:

| Bi-in-ga-lí-LUGAL-rí (RA IX 82+)
| Bi-ga-lí-LUGAL-rí (RTC 94)

DINGIR-sar (D)

É-a-sar (Kish 1930, 406 ii)

[En]-na-LUGAL (G)

En-bu-LUGAL (G+)

^{d}EN.ZU-sar (D+)

Gu-lí-sar (ITT I 1372)

Ib-ni-LUGAL (BIN VIII 151+)

ìl-e-sar (ITT II/2 p. 6, 2914+)

ì-lí-sar-ru (MO)

ì-lum-sar (BE I Pl. VII vii)

^{d}IM-sar (Kish 1930, 170d+)

I-mi-sar-ru (JCS X 26 iv)

I-sar-sar-rí (RTC 127 rev. iv)

I-ti-sa[r]? (ITT V 6670)

LUGAL-da-rí (ITT II/2 p. 17, 3136)

LUGAL-da-ti (D)

Sar-ru-da-ti (RTC 127 rev. ii)

LUGAL-É (Kish 1930, 138)

LUGAL-ku-li (MO)

LUGAL-na-da (Cop. 10083)

LUGAL-nam-mir (ITT II/2 p. 50, 5857). Unique

Pù-sar (RTC 12 i+, PSarg.; Kish 1931, 122 rev. ii)

Sar-a-ti-gu-bi-si-in (RA IX 73:11+). Translate perhaps: "O king, I gave their (sisters') laments"

Sar-ga-lí-LUGAL-rí and ^{d}Sar-ga-lí-LUGAL-rí (Sarg. king)

Sar-gi-in (ZA XII 335, translit. only)

Sar-gi-NI (ibid.)

Sar-ma-ì-lum (OIP LIII 147 No. 5, PSarg.). Formation parallel to KA-ma-DINGIR

Sar-rí-iš-da-gal (RTC 170+)

Sar-ru-al-si-in (D)

Sar-ru-BÀD (MO)

Sar-ru-tu-rí (OIP XIV 116)

Sar-ru-ba-lìḫ (G)

LU[GAL]-ba-lìḫ (ITT V 9259 rev.)

Sar-ru-ba-ni (ITT I 1372+)

Sar-ru-BÍ (D)

Sar-ru-dan (E+)

Sar-ru-DÙG (ITT I 1080+)

Sar-ru-du-gul (D)

Sar-ru-GAL.ZU (ZA XII 335)

Sar-ru-GÀR (G)

Sar-ru-GI (Sarg. king)

Sar-um-GI (Sarg. king)

Sar-ru-GÚ (BIN VIII 121 ii)

Sar-ru-ì-lí (MO+)

Sar-ru-DINGIR (DP 246 iv, PSarg.; Zapiski klass. Otd. Imp. Russkago Arkheol. Obshch. IV 242 i, PSarg.)

Sar-ru-i-sar (RTC 127 rev. v)

Sar-ru-ki-^{d}UTU (Fish, CST 6; 17)

Sar-ru-la-ba (RTC 112+)

Sar-ru-mu-da (Nikolski, Dok. II 35 ii+)

Sar-ru-ru (ZA XII 335)

Sar-ru-si-in (ZA XII 335)

Sar-ru-SIG$_5$ (E)

Sar-ru-UR.SAG (Orient. n.s. XXIII Pl. XXI 1)

U-bi-in-LUGAL-rí (MO+)

^{d}Ù-sar (AnOr VII 372 ii, Sarg.?!). Cf. Ù-ì-lí (A 632 i 3) and ^{d}U-ì-lí (AJSL XXI 172ff.)

Tu-da-LUGAL-li-bí-iš (D+). Interpr. unknown

Tu-da-sar-li-bí-iš (D+)

ZU.EN-LUGAL (YOS IX 1, PSarg.).

Sarg. GN:

LUGAL-^{d}EN.ZU^{KI} (CT I 1, 91-5-9, 588).

Selected Ur III PN's:

Al-la-sar (U 258)

Al-la-sar-um (AnOr I p. 25)

Al-la-sar-ru-um (UCP IX p. 191, 63)

Al-la-ša-ru-um (U 261+; UET III p. 5)

Be-lí-sar (BIN V p. 6+)

É-a-sar (UET III p. 13)

I-ku-un-sar-su (MDP XVIII 73)

Sar-ru-a (RA VIII 185 No. 4)

Sar-ru-ba-ni (U 2634+)

Sar-ru-um-ba-ni (UCP IX p. 246, 56)

Ša-ru-um-ba-ni (RTC 397 rev.; U 2637+)

Ša-ru-ba-ni (Reisner, TUT 205)

Sar-ru-dan (De Genouillac, TD 59)

Sar-ru-um-ì-lí (U 2638+)

Sar-ru-um-mi-ì-lí (BIN V p. 10)

Ša-ru-um-ì-lí (ITT V 6739+)

Sar-ru-ì-lí (ZA XII 345; AJA XLVI 362 Fig. 5).

Deified PN in Ur III:

^{d}Sar-ru-gi(n)-in (PDTI 605).

Deified PN in Sarg. and Ur III PN's:

Sar-ru-GI-ì-lì (MO)

Ur-^{d}Sar-ru-gin (RA IX 56 SA 241, U, translit. only)

Ur-Sar-ru-GIM (Orient. IV p. 59, U; Oppenheim, CCTE C 1 iv, U; PDTI 126, U)

Ur-^{d}Sar-ru-GIM (Orient. XLVII 41:5, U; Nies, UDT 93, U).

Ur III GN:

Sar-ru-la-ba (ZA LI Pl. II after p. 74 iii 18, 19).

šarratum "queen."

Written syllabically.

Sarg. and Ur III PN's:

Ma-ma-sa-ra-at (D+)

Ma-ma-sar-ra-at (U 2257; TMH n.F. I/II p. 22, U)

Ša-ra-túm (TCL V 6039 rev. i, U)

Ši-sar-ra-at (U 2714).

Sarg. and Ur III FN's:

(field) ša-at Sar-ra-tum^{KI} (BE I Pl. VII vii)

A.ŠÀ Ša-ra-at (UET III 1358; 1551, U).

šarrūtum "kingship."

in GIŠ.TUKUL-ki ^{d}Da-gan mu-sa-ar-bí-ì sar-ru$_{x}$(URU)-ti-su (UET I 275 ii, NS.)

sar-ru-dam a-na ^{d}Innin a u-gi-il (UET I 276 ii, NS.)

when sar-ru-dam ^{d}En-líl i-ti-nu-šum (R xxiii and similarly R xvi)

[s]ar-URU+A-uz-zù (D 172).

Ur III PN:

Sar-ru-zu-da-bàt (UET III 754 ii).

ŠRŠ šuršum "root."

Sum. logogram SUḪUŠ, Akk. šuršum and išdum, may be a variant form of *šuruš, which in turn may be a lw. from Akk. šuršum. Cf. also ʾ$_{x}$ŠD išdum and Šʾ$_{x}$P šêpum.

Sarg. and Ur III PN:

Su-ru-uš-GI (D+)

Su$_{4}$-ru-uš-GI (RA IX 76)

Su-ru-uš-GIM (ITT IV p. 9, 7090)

Šu-ru-uš-ki-in (U 2696+)

Šu-ru-uš-gi-in (A 2790 iii, U)

SUḪUŠ-GI (Porada, CPML No. 290, U)

SUḪUŠ-gi-in (U 2514+; RTC 374, U)

SUḪUŠ-ki-in (U 2515+).

ŠRŠ širašûm, sirašûm "brewer."

Sarg. and Ur III PN's:

Si-ra-šu-um RA.GABA (RA XIX 36, U, translit. only)

Zi-ra-si (E).

ŠRŠR šeršerrum.

Akk. lw. in Ur III Sum.:

sheep given for the še-ir-še-ir-ru-um of DN's (AnOr VII 63:5).

ŠRŠR šuršurrum "chain."

Akk. lw. in Ur III Sum.:

2 ^{URUDU}sur-sur-ru-um GÍR (UET III 721).

ŠS'$_7$ šasājum "to call."

Da-ni-a Se$_{11}$-li-il da-áš-zi "PN$_1$ called to court PN$_2$" (BIN VIII 121).

ŠŠḪ šišiḫum (a garment).

Akk. lw. in Ur III Sum.:

x TÚG se$_{11}$-se$_{11}$-ḫu-um (UET III 1702; 1745).

ŠŠN.

Ur III PN:

Šu-ša-nu-um (Langdon, TAD 59:11).

ŠŠR? šašurum (an object of reed).

Akk. lw. in Ur III Sum.:

1 GI ša-šu-ru-um (BE III 76:21).

ŠT?

PSarg. PN:

Su-tu-ì-lum (OIP XIV 51 v).

ŠTḪ? šutuḫḫātum?

su-tu-uḫ-ḫa-tim ù-lu ki-sa-ma-ri te-ir-rí-iš "you request .... or ...." (FM 52:6). Also reading ^{KUŠ}tu-uḫ-ḫa-tim or šud/t/ṭuḫ ḫaṭṭim is possible.

ŠTL? šitellum?, šitillum?

Value si$_x$ for SIG$_4$ not attested anywhere, but suggested by spellings SIG-te-lá-ni and Ši-te-lí quoted below. Form with double ll reconstructed on the basis of -lá-ni (like ummani, tuppani).

Ur III PN's:

SIG$_4$-dè-la (TCL II 5540 seal)

SIG$_4$-te-lá-ni (Legrain, TRU 292; TCL V 6162 i; 6163 twice; JCS X 31 No. 11). Cf. SIG$_4$-te-lá-ni and SIG-te-lá-ni in a school text PBS XI/3 No. 53

SIG$_4$-te-li (Legrain, TRU 344 rev.; TCL II 5491; CT XXXII 23 rev.)

SIG$_4$-te-lí (Langdon, TAD 62)

SIG$_4$-dè-li(-E) (Pinches, AT 61)

SIG$_4$-ti-li (Legrain, TRU 325)
Ši-te-lí (Gordon, The Living Past, seal 23 opp. p. 128; sign clearly TE not TA as read by Gordon).

ŠTL? <u>šitullum?</u>

Sarg. PN:

Si-tu-ul-ni-šè (ITT I 1062 rev.).

Sarg. GN:

Ši-tu-ul-ni-šè^{KI} (Kish 1930, 406 rev. iii)

Cf. Ši-tu-ul-lum^{KI} (King, The Letters and Inscriptions of Hammurabi I 23:7, OB) and Ši-tu-ul-li-im^{KI} (RA XXXV 110, Mari). Spelling with double l makes the derivation from Š'$_1$L šitûlum impossible.

ŠTR? <u>šeturum?</u> (a garment).

Akk. lw. in Ur III Sum.:

2 TÚG še-tu-ru-um (3 NT 21)

Cf. also TÚG ša-dur-ra-du/ti in Goetze, Festschrift F. Sommer pp. 48 and 58, Bog.

ŠṬP <u>šaṭāpum</u> "to preserve (life)."

PSarg., Sarg., and Ur III PN's:

Da-áš-dup-ba, f.n. (G+)
Iš-dup-ba (ITT II/2 p. 35, 4637; Nies, UDT 54, U)
Iš-dup-BE (MO)
Iš-dup-pum (G+)
Iš-dup-DINGIR (MO+; Syria XVII Pl. VII opp. p. 24, Mari)
Iš-dup-DINGIR.DINGIR (CT XXXII 8 i A, PSarg.)
Iš-dup-^{d}EN.ZU (MO+)
Iš-dup-Il (CT XXXII 8 iii, PSarg.; A 25412 i, PSarg.)
Iš-dup-Il?-at? (TMH V 5, PSarg.?)
Iš-dup-ir-pum? (BE I Pl. VII ix).

<u>šaṭpum.</u>

Sarg. PN's:

Ša-aṭ-pum (OIP XLVII 35+)
Ša-aṭ-be-DINGIR (D+)
Sa-aṭ-be-DINGIR (D+)
Sa-aṭ-pi-DINGIR (RTC 78).

ŠṬR <u>šaṭārum</u> "to write."

whoever GIŠ.TAG-su i-sa-da-ru (ZA IV 406, Gutium)
[i]n DUB li-iš-tu-ru-nim (D 290 rev. x+4)
[m]i?-šum [á]š-tu-ru "as? I wrote" (FM 53:5).

ŠṬR?

x ŠE.GUR, x ŠE.GUR si-da-ru (D 2 rev. v x+3, 6, [9]; viii x+1)
a-ti si-dar KI-šu (AOF III 112, Mari). At the end of a curse formula.

ŠZB?, see NṢB šazabtum.

T

T'$_6$? tawum? "(temple) chamber?"

da-iš ì-li MU-su u-sa-mi-id = Sum. NI.UL dingir-ri-ne-ka me-te-ni ì-ŠID "he set up his name in the (temple) chamber of gods" (R xxvii). Interpretation of da-iš follows von Soden, WO I 356ff. Doubtful.

T'$_x$?

Akk. lw. in Ur III Sum.:

É GIŠ.IG ti-um GÁ.RA (TCL V 6036 v)

ti-um É ŠU.TUM NU.TUR.ŠÈ (TCL V 6036 vi)

3 SA.GI ti-um É UŠ.BAR.ŠÈ (Univ. Illinois 33)

x SA.GI ti-um-MA (YOS IV 256 ii, iii)

1 SA.GI.BÍ GI ti-um-MA-ŠÈ (UET III 849).

T'$_x$L tiālum (a tree).

Akk. lw. in Ur III Sum.:

x GIŠ.RU ZUM ti-a-lum (TMH n.F. I/II 313)

x KIL GIŠ.RU ZUM ti-a-lum (UET III 812)

x GIŠ.NAG.BAL ZUM ti-a-lum (TMH n.F. I/II 313)

x GIŠ.ŠAG$_4$ BAL.ZI ti-a-lum (ITT IV 7820).

T'$_2$M ti'āmtum "sea."

Written syllabically or logographically as A.AB.BA.

a-ti-ma ti-a-am-tim (S ii)

in ti-a-am-tim Ì.LAḪ (S ii, vii, viii)

a-ti-ma ti-am-tim (S viii)

ti-a-am-dam a-lí-dam ù sa-bil-dam (S iv, viii, xii; R xxv)

iš-tum-ma ti-a-am-tim sa-bil-tim (S iv, ix)

a-ti-ma bu-ti ti-a-am-tim (S vi)

a-ti ti-a-am-tim sa-bil-tim (R xvii)

URU^{KI}.URU^{KI} a-bar-ti ti-a-am-tim (RA VII 104, Mi.)

ti-a-am-tim sa-bil-tim MÁ.MÁ GIŠ.LA-e u-sa-pi-ir (M xxvi)

sa-tu-e ti-a-am-tim sa-bil-tim (M xxvi)

⌈iš-tum⌉? ti-a-a[m-tim] sa-bil-ti[m] (PBS V 36 x+iv, NS.)

in [ti]-a-am-t[im] sa-bil-tim (PBS V 36 rev. x+iii, NS.)

ti-a-am-dam a-lí-dam (UET I 275 i, NS.; IAMN XII Pl. IV, NS.)

[ti-a⌉-am-⌈t⌉im [a-l]í-tim (CT XXXII 5, 98917, unknown king)

ti-am-[tum]? e-li-t[um]? ù ša-b[il-tum]? (Morgan, MSP IV 161 ii, Lullubum).

DN Ti'āmat in Ur III PN's:

A.AB.BA-zi-im-ti (U 18)

A.AB.BA-ba-áš-ti, f.n. (APAW 1936 Phil.-hist. Kl. Nr. 3 p. 23).

T'$_6$R <u>tuārum</u> "to return."

in du!(copied as ta)-a-rí-su GN na-ki-ir-ma (R xvii, collated)

ì-nu ma-at A-wa?-an ú-te-ra/ru (Morgan, MSP IV 158, Lullubum). Cf. i-nu-mi .... ma-dam .... ú-ti-ru-na "lorsque .... le pays .... annexa" in RA XXXV 47 No. 22, Mari

lu u-ta-ì[r] and lu u-te-ìr "(the field) I returned" (CT XXXII 2 iv, CM).

Sarg. and Ur III PN's:

I-dur-DINGIR (Fish, CST p. 159 iii, U)

I-dur-^{d}EN.ZU (D+)

I-dur-GI (D+)

I-dur-ma-ad (MO). Or I-dur-ma-at

⌈I⌉-dur-si-na-at (Geneva MAH 16229)

ì-lí-tu-ra-am (UET III 272 rev. ii, U)

I-tu-ri-a (U 1664+; TCL II 4691 rev., U)

I-tu-ru-um (U 1665; TCL II 5483, U)

La-tu-ra-ma (Nies, UDT 97:22, U)

Tu-ra-^{d}Da-gan (AOF III 112, Mari)

Tu-ra-am-^{d}Da-gan (U 2740+)

Tu-ra-am-ì-lí (U 2741+)

Tur-àm-ì-lí (U 2746; Bedale, STU 16, U)

Tur-am-ì-lí (U 2745)

Tur-àm-mi-ì-lí (A 26349, U)

Tu-ra-àm-ì-lí (RA XIX 43 No. 111, U)

Tu-ra-ì-lí (RA XIX 41 No. XLII rev., U)

Dur-ra-ì-lí (RTC 346+, U).

TB'$_1$ <u>tabā'um</u> "to come up."

Sarg. PN's:

It-be-la-ba (Kish 1930, 144a; 170d, collated)

It-be-⌈ba⌉-la (Kish 1931, 122 ii)

It-be-um (D+).

<u>tibûtum</u> "onset," here "help?"

ti-bu-dam li-se$_{11}$-ù-ni-kum-ma "may (the workers) come to your help" (JRAS 1932 p. 296:18).

TBL <u>tabālum</u> "to carry away." See also '$_6$BL wabālum.

barley PN it-ba-al (MDP XIV 63)

sheep PN it-ba-al (BIN VIII 139)

animals, grain PN it-ba-al (Kish 1930, 145)

silver PN it-ba-al (BM 54309 iv)

it-b[a?-al/lu] (HSS X 141 x+7)

e-nu PN_1 šu-ut PN_2 íl-gi-a-am-ma it-ba-lu "the utensils of PN_1 which PN_2 took and carried away" (FM 7:24).

TBL? tabiltum? (a container).

Akk. lw. in Ur III Sum.:

Cf. 3 ta-bi-la-ti in UET V 805:7, OB, among vessels.

x ^{DUG}da-bíl-tum (UET III 875; 883)

x ^{DUG}QA.GAL da-bíl-tum (ibid.)

x ^{DUG}da?(copied á)-bíl-tum (ITT II 892 rev. iii 17, text parallel to RTC 307 rev. iii bottom).

TBQ tubuqtum "corner" (of the house, or the like).

in dub-ga-ti É (MDP XIV 90).

Sarg. PN:

Dub-ga-zu-nu (HSS X 71:9). Reading suggested by von Soden, AS p. 45.

TBŠL?

Ur III PN's:

Tab-ša-la (U 2729+)

Tab?-ša-a-lum (Contenau, UDU 31).

TDN?

Akk. lw. in Sum.?:

1 DA.TI.NA (MDP XIV 7). An object

DA.TI.NA (PBS IX 114 in broken context). Perhaps a PN.

Sarg. and Ur III PN's:

Da-ti-na (G)

Da-ti-num (Iraq V 171 No. 15, U).

TDN?

Sarg. PN:

Ti-da-nu (MO). Cf. Di-da-a-nu, an OA king in JNES XIII 210.

Ur III GN's:

Mu-ri-iq-Ti-id-ni-im (the name of a fortress in date of ŠS. 4). Variant Ù-ri-iq-Da-at-na-am in Yondorf b

Ti-da-núm, mountain of MAR.TU (Thureau-Dangin, SAKI p. 70 vi 13, Gudea). Cf. Gesenius, $HWAT^{17}$ p. 156 under DDN, and Albright's article "Dedan" in Beitr. zur hist. Theol. XVI 1-12.

TG'_x tigûm (a musical instrument).

ti-kum (FM 41:14).

TGL tigālum, see DGL digālum.

TḪ? taḫḫum? (a garment), see BTBDḪ?

TḪ <u>taḫḫum</u> "substitute (worker)."

Ur III PN:

Daḫ-ḫu-um (ITT II/1 p. 12, 682).

TKL <u>takālum</u> "to trust."

Construed with Dat. or Acc.? or with ana.

PSarg., Sarg., and Ur III PN's:

^{d}A-ba$_{4}$-iš-da-gal (MO+)

A-da-gal (De Genouillac, TSA 18 v, PSarg.; D+; PDTI 95, U)

A-da-gal-sá (DP 116 vii+, PSarg.). Doubtful; cf. PN below on the one side, and ŠEŠ-da-gal-sá (ŠL 331, 33 passim, PSarg.) on the other

A-da-gal-su(d) (BIN VIII 11 iii, PSarg.)

A-da-gal-šum (U 102+)

A-da-ka-al-šu-[um]? (ITT V 6815 rev., U). Cf. A-ta-ka-al-šu in A 21920, OB

A-na!(wr. ba)-^{d}EN.ZU-dak-la-ku (UET III 1220 iii, U)

A-na-^{d}I-bí-<^{d}EN.ZU>?-da-ak-la-ak-šum (UET III 998, U)

Be-lí-iš-da-gal (D+)

^{d}DA-iš-da-gal (ITT II/2 p. 6, 2914)

Da-ki-il-^{d}En-líl (A 3138, U)

^{d}EN.ZU-iš-ti-gal (UET III p. 12+, U)

^{d}EN.ZU-iš-da-<gal> (Kish 1930, 406 rev. i)

Eš$_{4}$-dar-iš-da-gal (RTC 127 rev. ii, v)

Ì-lí-iš-da-gal (D+)

I-lí-iš-da-gal (BIN V 1:19, U)

Ì-lí-iš-ti-gal (U 1631)

I-sar-i[š-d]a-gal (G)

Ma-ma-iš-da-gal (D)

Sar-rí-iš-da-gal (RTC 170+)

Su-ni-iš-da-gal (D)

^{d}Šul-gi-iš-ti-gal (Barton, HLC III Pl. 132, 335 rev., U; TA 1931, 213, U)

Ta-ki-il-ì-lí-šu (De Genouillac, Kich II D 60 rev., U).

Sarg. GN:

Su$_{4}$-a-áš-da-gal^{KI} (G+).

<u>tukkulum</u> "to trust."

Sarg. and Ur III PN's:

Du-kil-^{d}En-líl (CT I 1c+)

Du-kil-^{d}EN.ZU (D)

Ú-ta-ak-ki-il (Oppenheim, CCTE E 25, U).

<u>tukultum</u> "trust."

Sarg. and Ur III PN's:

Be-lí-tu-gul-ti (ZA XII 332)

Du-gul-tum (D+)

Tu-gul-tim, Gen. (MO)

Eš$_4$-dar-du-gul-ti (D+)

ì-lí-tu-gul-ti (RTC 127 v; Fish, CST p. 159 iii, U, misread as -ti-gul-ti in U 1638)

ì-lí-du-gul-ti (Kish 1930, 139)

^{d}IM-tu!(wr. LI)-gul-ti (UET III 1041, U).

TKL? tuk(u)lum?

^{GIŠ}TU.GUL.BI of a ship (TCL V 5673; etc., U; UCP IX p. 234, 18, U). The word is translated as "Stevenverstärkung, -schutz?" by Salonen in SO VIII/4 p. 96. Possibly a lw. from Akk. TKL.

TKR takkirum (a garment).

Akk. lw. in Ur III Sum.:

x TÚG GÙ.È da-ki-ru-um (TMH n.F. I/II 230)

^{Ú}KI.KAL da-ak-ki-ru-um-ŠÈ (240). With TÚG

^{TÚG}da-ki-ru-um (UET III p. 172 passim)

[...]. da-ki-[ru]-um LUGAL (ITT II/2 6858 i). Among garments.

TKR?

Sarg. and Ur III PN's:

Dak-ra-tu (D+)

Du-uk-ra (U 827+)

Cf. possibly Tu-uk-ri in Moortgat, VARS No. 498, OB.

TKŠ? takšium (an object of wood).

Apparently a Sum. lw. in Akk.; cf. ^{GIŠ}DAG^{da}.SI = ŠU-u in RA XXI 140 ii 22.

All in Ur III:

x ^{GIŠ}DA.AG.SI MES É.BA.AN (Pinches, BTBC 89 ii)

x ^{GIŠ}DA.AG.SI GIŠ.KÍN? É.BA.AN (ibid.)

x ^{GIŠ}DA.AG.SI É.BA.AN (Nies, UDT 1 rev.)

PN UTUL ÁB DA.AG.SI (Fish, MCS I 37 H. 7836)

x da-ak-ši-um (BE III 76 rev.; 78 obv.).

TL tallum "door jambs?"

ì-nu .... su$_4$-ma da-li na-ra-ab-ti-su i-ik-mi-ù-su$_4$? "at the door jambs? of his entrance" (UET I 275 iii, NS.).

TL tillum "tell."

Sum. DUL$_6$ is probably a lw. from Semitic, not vice versa; cf. Hebrew and Aramaic etymologies.

Selected PSarg., Sarg., and Ur III GN's:

DUL$_6$-^{d}Bil-ga-mes (A 693)

DUL$_6$-Ku-ti-um-MA (ITT V 6864 iii twice, U)

DUL$_6$-sa-bar-ra^{KI} (TMH n.F. I/II p. 30 passim, U)

DUL$_6$-sír-ra^{KI} (ITT I p. 5, 1090; 1101; p. 8, 1135; p. 14, 1222; etc.; Reisner, TUT 160 viii, ix, U)

DUL$_6$-sír-ra (DP 578 vi; 579 vi, PSarg.; ITT I 1464 rev.).

TLʾ$_x$?

Ur III PN:

Ti-lí-a-tum (UET III 1390 ii).

TLʾ$_4$ tuliʾum, tulaʾum "breast."

Ur III GN's:

Bu-ut-tu-li-um^{KI} (RA IX 63 AM 14). = Pût-Tulium? Very doubtful

Tu-lá-um (ZA LI Pl. IV after p. 74 iv 33).

TLL, see DLL? dililum?

TLM talimum "twin brother."

Sarg. and Ur III PN's:

Da-lim (FM; JCS X 26 iii)

Da-a-lim (BE III 129:10; 130:5, U)

Da-lim-^{d}En-líl (A 5907, U; Oppenheim, CCTE p. 183, U, read thus, not Da-ti!-^{d}En-líl since copy has clearly Da-ŠI-^{d}En-líl).

TM, see ṬMʾ$_7$ ṭemitum.

TM, see DM? damtum?

TMʾ$_1$ tamāʾum "to swear." See also ʾ$_6$Mʾ$_1$ wamāʾum.

Written syllabically or logographically as PÀD.

Normally followed by Subjunctive.

PN KÁ ^{d}Tišpak it-ma (FM 7:26)

na-áš LUGAL it-ma (Kish 1930, 170d rev.)

[KÁ] ^{d}Tišpak [it]-má-ù (FM 51 rev. x+3)

na-ʾà-áš LUGA[L] it-má-[ù]? (D 135)

PN's ni-iš sar-ri-im ⌈it⌉-ma-ù [.... la i]-ra-ga-mu (MDP XIV 44)

ni-iš LUGAL-im it-ma-ù (Oppenheim, CCTE TT 1, U)

ni-iš LUGAL it-ma (Yondorf a, U)

ni-iš sar-ri-im at-ma (MDP XXVIII 424, U)

[....] it-ma-ù (AnOr VII 372 iv, Sarg.?!)

PN$_1$ MU LUGAL-im PÀD a-na PN$_2$ la a-ra-ga-mu (RA XXXII 190, U).

tummuʾum "to conjure."

DN$_1$ ù DN$_2$ ù-dam-me-ki "I conjured you" (Kish 1930, 143 rev.)

na-ʾà-áš LUGAL ù na-ʾà-áš NIN lu tu-mu-at (followed by Subjunctives) "by the life of the king and by the life of the queen may you be conjured" (RA XXIII 25).

TMR? tumrijum?, see $ʾ_x$BR? ibrijum?

TP tuppum "tablet," "inscription."

Written logographically DUB, with or without phonetic indicators.

[i]n DUB li-iš-tu-ru-nim (D 290 rev. x+4)

in DUB-su ù-la ḫu-bu-ut (BIN VIII 141)

DUB ŠE.BA (TA 49, tag; similarly D 155, tag; D 173, tag)

DUB ḫu-bu-lim (D 148, tag)

me-eḫ-ru DUB .... (D 210). In difficult context

DUB PA.TE.SI.KA ÍB.RA (ITT I 1303)

10 GIŠ.KIN.TI ⌈3⌉ GIŠ.TÚG.PI.KAR.DU DUB-bi-su-ni (A 708)

DUB ša-a Ú-gul-la-ni-su (Kish 1930, 170c). Interpr. doubtful

DUB a-ti-nu-šum (ibid.)

ša DUB su_4-a u-sa-za-ku-ni (PBS V 34 x, Lugalzagesi; S iv, xi twice; R xviii, xix, xx, xxi bis, xxiv, xxv, xxvi; R xxvii; RA VIII 136; 139; Mi. passim; NS. passim)

ša za-al-mi-in an-ni-in ù DUB-ba-am ("inscription") ù-ša-za-ku (Morgan, MSP IV 161, Lullubum).

TP$ʾ_x$ tappāʾum "comrade."

Lw. from Sum. TAB.BA.

Sarg. and Ur III PN's:

Written logographically only.

DINGIR-TAB.BA (D+)

Ì-lí-TAB.BA (D+)

Šu-TAB.BA (D)

TAB.BA-.... (D+)

TAB.BA-ba (Kish 1930, 406 iii)

TAB.BA-ì-lí (Boson, TCS p. 28, U; U 2724)

Cf. also some PN's under ṭâbum.

TP$ʾ_x$? tappatum? (a garment).

Akk. lw. in Ur III Sum.:

96 TÚG da-ba-tum (Reisner, TUT 121 v)

88 TÚG da-ba-tum and their weight (Reisner, TUT 265)

17 TÚG da-ba-tum KI.LAL.BI 33 1/3 MA.NA (CT IX 31 rev.)

many examples in UET III p. 172; also Orient. XX 82 No. 134; Barton, HLC Pl. 50, 281; etc.

TPŠK tupšikkum "hod," "basket" (or the like).

Probably a lw. from Sum.

Sarg. PN's:

Dub-si-ga (G+; AnOr VII 372, Sarg.?!)

TAB-si-ga (FM).

TRʾ$_6$ tarāwum "to take away." Cf. also ʾ$_6$Rʾ$_6$ warāwum.

1 NI.GU.ŠA PN it-ru (BIN VIII 144 ii)

animals PN it-ru (BIN VIII 146)

persons PN it-ru (BIN VIII 251; 254)

animals Gu-ti-ù it-ru-ù (JRAS 1932 p. 296:23 and 31)

chariots and animals PN's it-r[u?-ù]? (HSS X 206:18)

[.... l]i-it-ru-ù-nim (D 290 rev.).

TRʾ$_x$? tirûm? "personnel" (or the like).

ŠU.NIGÍN 30 LAL 3 ti-ru IGI.GAR ("inspection") um-ma-nim (MDP XIV 24 end)

distribution of liquids among various professions comprised as ti-ru (MDP XIV 25 end).

Sarg. and Ur III PN's:

Ti-rí-tar (G+)

Ti-ru (MDP XIV 6 v)

Ti-ru-um (D+)

Ti-ir-su (MO).

DN in Sarg. and Ur III PN's:

Šu-Ti-ru-um (D; U 2700)

Ti-ru-ša-ki (G)

Cf. Elamite DN Ti-ru in Cameron, HEI p. 160.

Sarg. MN:

Ti-ru (D 287; Kish 1930, 404 rev.). For OB usage cf. Ti-ri-im and ^{ITI}Ti-ri in Langdon, BM pp. 16f. and UD Ti-ru-um-ŠÈ in TA 1931, 326. Month named after the plant ṭîrum?

TRʾ$_x$.

[4 KÙŠ]? ù ti-ru [ru-up]-⌈šum⌉? (HSS X 156:7). Parallel to si-ir-i?, q.v.

TRḪ tirḫatum "bridal price." For the root cf. Goetze, Orient. n.s. XVI 240ff.

so many things ti-ir-ḫa-[dam] PN$_1$ .... u-bìl (D 169 ii 5)

AB+ÁŠ.⌈AB+ÁŠ⌉ ti-ir-ḫa-ti PN$_1$ a-na PN$_2$ u-ub-lu (iii 9).

TRḪ turāḫum "mountain goat."

PSarg. PN:

Me-me-tu-ra-aḫ (UET II Pl. L 49). Meme is a DN.

TRḪ.

Sarg. and Ur III PN's:

x ESIR.É.A NÍG.DÍB Tu-ru-ḫu-um (JRAS 1939 p. 32 ii 3, U)

A-li-tu-ru-uḫ (D+).

TRK? tarākum?

PN_1 DUMU PN_2 PN_3 ARÁD-zu li-da-ar-ga-am-ma iš-dè PN_4 li-su-zé-áš-su-ni "may he (Egud) TRK PN_1 son of PN_2 (and) PN_3 his slave and may he cause them to go out with PN_4 (RTC 78).

Sarg. and Ur III PN's:

I-da-ra-ak (FM+)

I-da-ra-ak-ì-lí (UET III p. 16+, U)

I-da-ra-ki-[lí]? (Orient. XVIII 26:29, U)

It-ra-ak-ì-lí (AnOr VII p. 26, U; Fish, CST p. 160x, U; PDTI 653, U).

DN in Ur III PN:

Šu-^{d}La-ta-ra-ak (U 708). Cf. ^{d}La-ta-ra-ak and ^{d}La-ta-rak in Deimel, PB No. 1809.

TRK? turkum?

Sarg. PN:

Du-ur-kum (E+)

For possibilities as DRK cf. Da-ri-kum in VAS VII 6 seal and ^{f}Da-ar-ka-tum in Iraq VII 37, both OB.

TRKL tirkullum "pole."

20 dir-ku-lí (FM 33:22).

TRR? turrum? (part of a structure).

....-zi ù tùr?-ra-tim É.BABBAR lu u-ud-di-iš (CT XXXII 1 iii 7, CM). On ṭurru, turru cf. Meisner in MAOG XI 1/2 50ff.

TSKR taskarinnum "boxwood."

da-as-ga-ri-ni (Kish 1930, 143 rev., in broken context)

Elsewhere written regularly GIŠ.TÚG.

TTR? titurrum? "bridge."

Sarg. PN:

Ti-tu-rí (G+).

In Ur III DN:

^{d}Be-la-at-Ti-tu-ri-im (PDTI 563 i). Cf. OB PN Warad-Ti-tu-ri-im in YOS VIII 156:22 (ref. from Dr. Oppenheim).

TTR? tutturum?

For a discussion of this word in EA and Qatna cf. Bottéro in RA XLIII 20 n. 3.

Sarg. PN:

Tu-tu-rí (G).

Ṭ

Ṭʾ$_7$B ṭiābum "to be good."

Ur III PN:

I-díb-ši-na-at (Nies, UDT 91 vi; AnOr VII 48; TCL II 5484; UET III 272 i). "It was pleasing to them." Cf. lá i-ṭí-áb-šu-nu (Acc. with Dat. meaning) in Capp. (AAA I 61:10)

I-ti-ib-si-na-at (A 5508)

I?-dí(b)-ib-si-na-at (PDTI 434). Doubtful.

ṭâbum "good."

In PN's written logographically or syllabically.

Outside PN's written logographically only, as in NI.DÙG or NI.DÙG.GA; NI.NUN.DÙG or NI.NUN.DÙG.GA; SAG.DÙG; UŠ.DÙG; etc.

PSarg., Sarg., and selected Ur III PN's:

A-bí-DÙG (D+)

A-bí-da-ab (ITT IV 7597, U)

A-pù-DÙG (E)

A-bu-da-áb (Barton, HLC III Pl. 107, 203 ii, U)

A-KA-da-ab (ITT IV p. 63, 7610, U)

A-ḫu-DÙG (G+)

A-lí-DÙG (MDP XIV 72 iv; BIN V 302:37, U; CT XXXII 34 ii, U+)

A-lum-DÙG (CT XXXII 7 iv, PSarg.)

ARAD-da-pum (D+). See note under wardum

ARAD-da?-bu-um (Arnold, ABTR 9, U)

Be-lí-DÙG (D+)

Be-lí-da-ab (Barton, HLC III Pl. 129, 307 rev., U)

Be-lí-DÙG-ab (Jacobsen, CTC 9 rev., U)

Be-lí-da-bum$_x$(BALAG) (OIP XIV 102)

Da-bi-a (TCL II 5617, U)

Da-bum$_x$(BALAG) (PBS IX 111 ii 5)

Da-pum (OIP XIV 109)

Da-a-bu-um (Pinches, AT p. 183, U)

Da-bu-um (Barton, HLC III p. 37, U)

Da-bu-šu-ba-at (U 765; AnOr VII p. 22, U; CT XXXII 34 i, U). Ununderstandable. But cf. Dam-ku-zi-ma-zu

DINGIR-DÙG (D+)

DINGIR-su-⌈DÙG⌉ (ITT I 1372)

DÙG-a-ḫi (D+)

DÙG-bi-ti-iš-zu (YOS IV 285, U)

DÙG?-DINGIR (Kish 1930, 149)

DÙG-ì-lí (U 2726+)

Tab-ì-lí (FM). Interpr. doubtful

É-a-DÙG (JCS I 348 b)

Ga-li-iš-DÙG (G+)

Ga-lí-iš-DÙG (FM)
Gal-iš-DÙG (D+)
Ì-lí-DÙG (TMH V 174 i, PSarg.?)
La-da-bu-um MAR.TU (PDTI 335)
Pù-su-DÙG (D+)
PÙ.ŠA-DÙG (BE I Pl. VIII)
PÙ.ŠA-su(d)-DÙG (CT XXXII 8 iii, PSarg.)
Sar-ru-DÙG (ITT I 1080+)
Sar-ru-zu-da-bàt (UET III 754 ii, U)
Tab-be-lí (RA XIX 37, U; A 4710, U)
Tab-ì-lí (see above)
Tab-la-la-ki /Ṭâb-lalâki/ (A 3026, U)
DÙG-ša-ri (U 2732+)
Tab-ša-a-ri (Boson, TCS 340 rev. i, U)
Um-mi-DÙG (D+)
Um-mi-da-bàt (Chiera, STA p. 32, U)
Um-mi-da-bat$_5$ (TMH n.F. I/II p. 24+, U)
Zé-lu-uš-DÙG(wr. KAM) (RA IX 45). Cf. also TA 1931, 463, OB.

Written -da-ba in Sarg. and Ur III DN's:
Si-da-ba (D+)
Šu-da-ba (RTC 324+, U). Cf. also tappāʾum
Cf. A-bi-da-ba (Wiseman, The Alalakh Tablets p. 125, OB) and Am-mi-da-ba (p. 127).

Written -da-bi in Sarg. and Ur III PN's:
A-bu-da-bi (YOS IV 185, U). Cf. A-bu-ta-bi in MDP XXIII 218:18 and A-bi-ṭà-bi in MDP XXIV 331:21 and XXVIII 528:6, OB
Be-lí-da?-bí (VAT 16441 i)
DINGIR-da-bi?(wr. GA) (Nies, UDT 58:46, U)
^{d}KA-da-bi (Chiera, STA 16 rev., U; Oppenheim, CCTE p. 77, U)
Šu-da-pi (UCP IX p. 210, 89). Cf. also tappāʾum
For the formation cf. PN's with da-ni under DNN?
Cf. also ^{d}EN.ZU-ta-bi in PBS VIII/1 77:2, OB.

ṭâbātum "goodness."
Ur III PN's:
Da-ba-ti (AnOr I 88 ii)
Da-ba-tum, wife of a MAR.TU (PDTI 335).

ṭubbum "to make good," "to heal?"
ti-ib da-ad-ga "heal? thy beloved!" (Kish 1930, 143:11). Interpr. doubtful.

Ṭʾ$_x$R, see under TRʾ$_x$.

$ṬB^{\text{ʾ}}_{4}$? <u>ṭibuttum</u>? "seal ring."

X ù ti-bu-ut-tum sa-ap-da-su (Kish 1930, 143 rev.).

ṬBḪ <u>ṭabāḫum</u> "to slaughter."

UDU .... ⌈iṭ-bu⌉-ḫu (D 178 twice)

GANAM .... i-da-ba-aḫ-si-ma (MDP XIV 90).

$ṬM^{\text{ʾ}}_{7}$ <u>ṭemîtum</u> "yarn" (or the like).

Sarg. PN:

Te-mi-tum (D). If the name is fem. interpr. possibly as "weaver."

$ṬP^{\text{ʾ}}_{6}$? <u>ṭapāwum</u>?

For various possibilities cf. von Soden, Orient. n.s. XVI 72-78, esp. p. 77.

ma-sa-ak-su in 7+7+7 woods li-it-bu "may he rub its skin with x woods" or "may he stretch out its skin on? x woods" (MDP XIV 90 rev., inc.). The verb is clearly ultimae $^{\text{ʾ}}_{6}$.

<u>ṭuppûm</u>?

^{d}En-líl u-da-bí-su MU-su i-bí "E. has .... him and has called his name" (M xxviii).

ṬRD <u>ṭarādum</u> "to send."

ṭu-ur$_{4}$-da tu-ur$_{4}$-da-ma (Kish 1930, 143).

Z

$Z^{\text{ʾ}}_{x}$M? <u>zîmum</u> "mien," "appearance."

PSarg., Sarg., and Ur III PN's:

Zi-mu-dar (PSarg. king; De Genouillac, FT II Pl. LIII AO 13015, U)

Zi-mu-um (D).

Ur III GN:

Zi-mu-dar^{KI} (CT XXXII 20 iii+).

$Z^{\text{ʾ}}_{x}$N? <u>zaʾānum</u>? Or $Ṣ^{\text{ʾ}}_{4}$N? Or ʾṢN, cf. Ta-aḫ-ZI-in-At-mu in RA L 66, OB

Ur III PN's:

I-zi-in-^{d}Da-gan (A 29365)

I-zi-in-^{d}Šul-gi (ITT V 8212+)

Te-zi-in-Ma-ma (Boson, TCS 142)

Te-zé-in-^{d}Ma-ma (Boson, TCS 170)

Te-zé-in-Ma-ma (Boson, TCS 145; 218)

Ta-zé-in-Ma-ma (Oppenheim, CCTE p. 202).

$Z^{\text{ʾ}}_{x}$N? <u>zînum</u>?

Sarg. PN:

^{d}Ma-lik-zi-in-su (MO). Cf. DINGIR-zi-nu-ú-a, DINGIR-zi-nu-ú-šu, DINGIR-zi-i-ni, DINGIR-šu-zi-i-ni, etc. in PBS XI/2 Nos. 448f.,

457f.

Z'$_{6}$R?

a-ti /addî/ za-wa-ar-su ù za-wa-ar-ki (Kish 1930, 143 rev.).

Z'$_{7}$R? ziārum? "to hate."

Sarg. PN:

I-zi-ir-gul-la-zi-in (MO). Interpr. doubtful. Stamm, ANG p. 105: Iṣṣēr-kullassin "Über ihnen allen (den Schwestern)."

Z'$_{x}$R? (a profession).

ŠU.NIGÍN 31 GURUŠ UGULA PN za-ru (D 232). Za-ru refers to all the workers.

Z'$_{6}$Z *izuzzum "to stand," "to stand as a witness."

Written syllabically; GUB occurs only in late copies.

DÙL-su .... IGI.ME ^{d}En-líl i-za-az (R xxvii)

PN i-za-az "PN stood as a witness" (MDP XIV 44)

people maḫ-rí-iš Sargon i-za-zu-ni, Subj. (S iv, ix)

2 PN's li-za-zu-ma (Cop. 10055 rev.)

[m]a-am-ma-an [la iz-z]i-za-am [la ka-d]a-a-am (CT XXXII 1 ii) = ma-am-man la iz-zi-za la ka-da-a (RA VII 180 ii) in CM

maḫ-rí-iš ^{d}En-líl e GUB, referring to person (PBS V 34 x, Lugalzagesi; S ix, xi)

maḫ-rí-iš ì-lí-su e GUB (R xviii, xxiv; UET I 274 iv, NS.)

maḫ-rí-iš ì-lí-su a GUB (UET I 276 ii, NS.)

DÙL-mi ma-ḫa-ar ^{d}EN.ZU li-zi-iz?(wr. it) (UET I 275 iv, NS.).

Ur III PN:

I-za-az-mi-sar, PN (UET III 1034 ii). Cf. the Kassite PN Iz-za-az-kit-tum in Stamm, ANG p. 194.

muzzazum "witness."

PN's mu-za-zu (AnOr VII 372 iii, Sarg.?!).

*šuzûzum "to set up" (a statue).

DÙL-su ma-ḫa-ar-su uš-zi-iz (MDP IV Pl. 2 ii)

za-la-am-su .... uš-zi-iz (Morgan, MSP IV 161, Lullubum)

ALAM uš-zi-iz (ibid. p. 158, Lullubum)

[....] ^{d}UTU u-sa-za-za-su$_{4}$ (BE I 12, unknown king). Interpr. doubtful.

manzaštum or manzattum "station" (or the like).

Akk. lw. in Ur III Sum.:

animals for ma-an-za-áš-tum ^{d}Innin (PDTI 544)

animals for ma-an-za-tum ^{d}⌈Innin⌉! (PDTI 273, collated).

Z'$_{6}$Z zuāzum "to divide."

[a-na] še-na [lu a]-zu-uz (CT XXXII 1 ii) = a-na še-na lu-u a-zu-uz

(RA VII 180) in CM.

ZB?

Akk. lw. in Ur III Sum.:

579 zi-ib-tum_x KUG.GI SÁR.DA (UET III 686)

zi-ib-tum 15 ŠE TA 121 ŠÈ (UET III 626; similarly 630).

ZB...?

6 za-bi-[....] (RA XVIII 98). Among objects of metal.

ZB$^{ʾ}_{x}$? zibîtum? (a grain).

Akk. lw. in Ur III Sum.:

x QA ŠE zi-bí-tum (Pinches, AT 69 passim; ITT II 892 iv; V 10011 ii; RTC 307 iv; RA X 64 No. 14 iv; Barton, HLC III Pl. 112 ii, iv; Nikolski, Dok. II 341 passim; Chiera, STA 11 ii; Fish, CST 719; UET III 900; 1082 ii; PDTI 387)

ŠE zi-bí-tum-BI (Boson, TCS 364)

Ú.ŠE zi-bi-tum (RA XVIII 60, Voc. prat.)

ŠE zi-bi-[tum] (UET III 282)

[ŠE zi-b]í-tum and [ḫu-r]í-um (MDP XIV 22, Sarg.).

ZB$^{ʾ}_{x}$, see also ṢB$^{ʾ}_{x}$?

ZBB$^{ʾ}_{x}$N, see ZZB?

ZBḪ?

Sarg. PN:

Zi-bu-LUM (D). Cf. 1 DUG? zi-bu-ḫu-um in TA 1931, 35, OB.

ZBL? zabālum? "to carry."

za?-bí-lu .... (FM 43:20, school text).

ZBL zabālum, see SPL supālum.

ZBL?

Ur III PN:

Za-ba-la-núm (TMH n.F. I/II p. 26).

ZBL?

Ur III PN:

Zu?-ba-la-tum (CT X 16 L.S.).

ZBN? zibnum?

Ur III MN:

ITIzi-ib-[nu]-um (TA 1931, 591; also passim in the OB texts from Diyala).

ZBQ?

Sarg. PN:

Za-bu-ga-núm (D). For the root ZBQ in Semitic PN's cf. the examples cited by Gelb in RSO XII 240.

ZBZR?

12(GUR) [g]a-gi$_4$-a-am zi-ib-zi-ir ANŠE.ZI.ZI?-im (CT XXXII 1 i = RA VII 180) in CM.

ZBZR?

Sarg. PN:

Za-ba-zi-rí (D). Thus clearly on tablet; not Ḫa-ba-zi-rí as one might expect.

ZD'$_x$?

Ur III GN:

Zi-da-núm^{KI} (Gelb, HS p. 104)

Zi-da-nu-um^{KI} (ibid.)

Zi-ti-an^{KI} (PDTI 466 rev., in connection with Ra-ši who is ensi of Zidānum)

Zé-ti-an^{KI} (MDP X 125 = MDP II p. 131, in connection with Ra-si)

PN LÚ.KIN.GI$_4$.A LÚ Zi-da-ni-um^{KI} (PDTI 473).

ZGDḪ? zigiduḫum?

Akk. lw. in Ur III Sum.:

1 DUG GAR 2 QA zi-gi$_4$-duḫ-ḫu-um "flour for z." (UET III 71; 1128 three times; 929 written zi-gi$_4$-duḫ-um)

What is the meaning of "1 gur d'aš-an zi-gí-šu-um" translit. in ITT IV p. 46, 7411? Is ŠU misread for DUḪ?

ZGR?

PN's za!-gi!-ru (Kish 1930, 144a rev. ii, collated).

ZḪN? zaḫannum?

Akk. lw. in Ur III Sum.:

20 GIŠ ⌈3⌉ KÙŠ TA za-ḫa-LUM É.DA (RA XVI 19 vi)

6 GIŠ 3 KÙŠ TA za-ḫa-LUM-ŠÈ (ibid.). Woods for making za-ḫa-LUM. Cf. zaḫannu in ŠL II 443.

ZḪR, see SḪR and ṢḪR.

ZK? zikum?

A location? in Ur III texts.

Akk. lw. in Sum.?:

x ANŠE .... MU 3 LÚ zi-gúm (Radau, EBH p. 382)

ŠÀ.GAL ANŠE zi-gúm (RA III 135)

ŠÀ.GAL ANŠE zi-ku-um (Nakahara, ST 6)

ŠÀ.GAL ANŠE zi-gúm-MA (ITT III 5443 rev.; 6099; Reisner, TUT 298)

ŠÀ.GAL ANŠE zi-kum-MA (YOS IV 260 iii twice)

ANŠE zi-ku-um-MA-ŠÈ (Orient. XLVII 462). Cf. also MCS II 56, 113092

PN UGULA zi-gúm(-MA) (ITT II p. 57, 1021; RA XIX 18)

GIŠ.GIGIR zi-gúm(-MA) (BIN V 107; Fish, MCS I 53, 105753)

ANŠE.ARAD zi-gúm (Nies, UDT 69; Reisner, TUT 43 v twice; 93 i twice;

CT V 21 ii; 23 viii; 27 i, iii; VII 44, 17766; etc.)

zi-gú(m)-um^{KI}-MA-ŠÈ (Fish, MCS I 53, 105713, translit. only)

zi-gúm(-ŠÈ) (BIN V 199; BRM III 49; 51; Nikolski, Dok. II 202; RA XIX 42 Nos. LXV and LXXIII; 43 No. CXI)

Cf. also ZÍD zi-kum (ITT II/2 p. 41, 5675; V 9281; Geneva MAH 16670 ii).

ZK$^{\prime}_{7}$? zakjum? "pure."

Sarg. PN's:

A-bí-za-[ki]? (D)

Be-lí-za-ki (G+). Goetze, BASOR XCV 23:13 compares this name with OB EN-za-ak-kum, which he translates "the lord is power."

ZKL, see SKL.

ZKR, see SKR sikkūrum.

ZKR zikarum "male."

Written logographically as UŠ or syllabically (only in names).

DN's UŠ ù MU [a] i-ti-na-šum (UET I 276 ii, NS.; BE I 120 iv?, NS.)

UŠ [?] ù [MU]-su [a i]-ti-na-šum (UET I 274 iv, NS.; cf. also R xviii)

UŠ É Ù TA MU ú-.... (MDP VI Pl. 2, 1 ii). Ununderstandable

DINGIR-mu-ta-bíl UŠ KALAG.GA (CT XXI 1c, Dêr)

⌈^{d}Ni-id-nu-ša⌉ UŠ KALAG.GA (YOS IX 62, Dêr)

a-na ^{d}Innin UŠ, Dat. (RA XXXI 140, Mari, PSarg.). The male Innin?

^{d}Innin UŠ, Dat. (RA XXXI 142, 143, Mari, PSarg.).

Sarg. and Ur III PN's:

Šu-mu-zi-ga-ar (Coll. De Clercq I 100, U?)

Zi-ik-ru-u[m] (UET III 1126 rev. ii, U)

Zi-gàr (E)

Zi-gàr-su (MO+).

Ur III GN:

Bu-úḫ-zi-gàr^{KI} (CT XXXII 19 iv; PDTI 448, read thus against translit.). Division doubtful.

ZKR?

Sarg. PN:

PN SAL.Ú.ḪUB$_{x}$ ša-at Za-ga/bi-rí-im (Ward, SCWA Fig. 217).

ZKR? šutazkurum?

1 GANAM MI la ba-ti-tum in dub-ga-ti É uš-da-za-ga-ar-si-ma "he will .... 1 black virgin ewe in the corners of the house" (MDP XIV 90).

ZKT, see ZQT.

ZL, see S$^{\prime}_{x}$Ḫ saḫum and ṢLL ṣallum.

ZLL, see ṢLL.

ZLL zilullûm (a low-type person).

Sarg. PN:

Zi-lu-lum (D+).

ZLMḪ, see SLMḪ silammaḫum.

ZMD, see ṢMD ṣimdum, SMD simdum, ʾ$_6$SM simtum.

ZMR zamārum "to sing."

Sarg. PN's:

I-za-mar (D+)

I-za-mar-^{d}Tišpak (D).

šuzmurum "to make sing."

NAR-e .... ù-sá-az-me-ir "he made singers .... sing" (MDP IV Pl. 2 iii).

ZMR?

Sarg. PN:

Za-am-ra-an (D).

ZMRʾ$_x$ zamirîtum, see MRʾ$_x$ mirîtum.

ZNʾ$_x$.

600 BA ("tortues?") zé-nu-a-tum (ITT II/2 p. 15, 3096, translit. only).

ZNʾ$_x$ zinûm?

6 zi-nu-[nothing?], also KAŠ.SUR.RA, KAŠ.UŠ.SA, etc. (D 129). Perhaps the same word as ZÉ.NA (Reisner, TUT 115 iii, U; BE III 105 rev., U; Barton, HLC III Pl. 123, 267, U) or ^{GIŠ}ZÉ.NA (TCL V 6036 i, iii, rev. vii, U), occurring regularly in connection with words for "palm."

ZNB zibbatum "tail."

Akk. lw. in Ur III Sum.:

x MA.NA zi-ba-tum (UET III 1505 v; 1534). Wool from tails of sheep

x MA.NA zi-ib-ba-tum (UET III 1504 vii; 1505 i, v, viii)

Cf. x MA.NA NÍG.U.NU.A zi/zé-ba-tum in BIN IX 139; 142; 194; 197+, OB.

ZNB?

Ur III PN's:

Za-an-bi (HSS IV 15; Reisner, TUT 156 vi)

Za-an-na-bi (HSS IV 15). Cf. Za-an-na-bu in TCL XI 151:21, OB

Za-an-na-KA (Reisner, TUT 162 ix).

ZNN?

Ur III PN's:

Za-an-nu-um (UET III 15; U 1451)

Za-nu-um (UET III 46)

Za-LUM (UET III 1414). Cf. also ṢLL?

Za-a-LUM (U 1445+).

ZNN?

Ur III PN:

Za-nu-LUM (Nikolski, Dok. II 355).

ZNN?

Sarg. and Ur III PN's:

Zé-na-na (De Genouillac, FT II Pl. LI AO 12992, U)

Zi-na-núm (FM).

ZNN?

Sarg. PN:

Zu-na-núm (D+).

ZNZN?

Perhaps sasannum "whip?" Cf. Sa-sa-nu-um in TA 1930, 238, OB.

Ur III PN's:

Za-an-za-an (UET III 1793)

Za-an-za-ni (U 1452+)

Za-za-na-a (Oppenheim, CCTE p. 125)

Za-za-ni-< (Orient. XVII 163 No. 102, translit. only).

ZQN, see SKL sukkallum.

ZQP? *zaqpum* (kind of wood?).

Akk. lw. in Sum.:

20 GIŠ.GAL zag-bu-um (ITT IV 7820 rev.).

ZQQP *zuqaqīpum* "scorpion."

PSarg. PN:

Zú/Zu-ga-gi$_4$-ip (PSarg. king).

ZQR, see ZKR? šutazkurum.

ZQR *zaqrum* "high."

Sum. logogram AN.ZA.GÀR or rather ^{d}ZA.GÀR in GN's ^{d}ZA.GÀR-DUB.SAR^{KI} (TCL V 6041 i, U), ^{d}ZA.GÀR-^{d}En-líl^{KI} (RA XXXII 170 iv 12, OB) = Ti-ma-at-^{d}En-líl-lá (U, see DM dimtum) may very well go back to Akk. zaqrum.

tizqarum "high," "exalted."

PSarg. PN:

Ti-iz-gàr (PSarg. king).

ZQT?

Ur III PN's:

Za-ga-ti (Fish, CST p. 159 iv)

Za-ga-túm (BE III 4).

ZQT?

Akk. lw. in Sum.:

1 QA zak-tum (BIN VIII 301).

ZQT?

Akk. lw. in Ur III Sum.:

GIŠzi-iq-ti-um GIŠ.BAN (RA XVIII 65 x, Voc. prat.)

ÍB.IAL zi-iq-ti-um KUŠ GUD (ibid.)

GIŠzi-iq-ti-um GIŠ.GÍD.DA (ibid.).

ẒQT?

Ur III PN's:

Zu-ku-ti (Fish, CST p. 159 iii)

Zu-ku-ti-a (RA XIX 32).

ZRʾ$_4$ *zarʾum, zerʾum "seed."

Written logographically, with 1 exception.

Meaning "human seed":

2 DN's SUḪUŠ-su li-zu-ḫa ù ŠE.NUMUN-su li-il-gu-da (PBS V 34 x, Lugalzagesi; RA XXI 66 and 71, S.; S ix, xi twice, xv; R xviii twice, xix, xx, xxi twice, xxiv, xxv, xxvi, xxvii; RA VIII 136; 139; Mi.; NS.; Škš.; MDP II p. 66; ZA IV 406, Gutium; etc.)

DN SUḪUŠ-su li-zu-uḫ ù ŠE.NUMUN-su li-il-gu-ut (S iv)

DN's SUḪUŠ-su li-zu-ḫu ù ŠE.NUMUN-su li-il-gu-tu (BE I 120, NS.)

DN's SUḪUŠ-[su] li-zu!-[ḫu] ù NUMUN-[su] li-il-gu-du (MDP IV Pl. 2 v)

DN's zé-ra-šu? li-il-ku-du (Morgan, MSP IV 161, Lullubum).

Meaning "grain seed":

ŠE.NUMUN (HSS X 5:6, 24; 185 vi 14; D 69; etc.)

ŠE.NUMUN-su (HSS X 16:5; 17:2)

ÁŠ.NUMUN-su (HSS X 36 iv)

ÁŠ a-na NUMUN (HSS X 75:2).

ZRʾ$_x$?

Akk. lw. in Ur III Sum.:

9 PI-?zi-rí-um (or wa-zi-rí-um) KUG.GI ḪUŠ.A KI.LAL.BI 1 GÍN BA.ZI.IR (UET III 676).

ZRB?

Ur III GN, translit. only:

KA-úr-ba-tu-um (ITT II/1 p. 78, 803). Cf. Zu-úr-ba-ti^{KI} (U, unpubl.)

KA-úr-ba (p. 9, 638).

ZRD? zardûm? (part of a wagon).

Lw. from Sum. ZAR.DÙ, which in turn may go back to Sem. SRD?

x za-ar-[tu]?-ù (D 325). Occurs in connection with x GIŠ.KA ⌈GIŠ. UMBIN⌉, also part of a wagon

1(or 60) UDU.UŠ a-na zar-tim ma-ra-iš nu-ru-am "we brought 1(or 60) male sheep to the .... for fattening?" (D 159). Reading ZAR-tim is also possible.

ZRḪ, see ṢRḪ?

ZRM, see ṢRM?

ZRN? zarinnum?

ZA.RÍ.IN, said of KUG.GI, KUG.BABBAR, UD.KA.BAR, SÍG (UET III p. 186, U) and of SIG_4 (Oppenheim, CCTE pp. 127f., U, where reference to Reisner, TUT 128 vii contains SÍG, not SIG_4).

ZRN?

2 GIŠ.ÙR zi-rí-núm-ŠÈ (Nikolski, Dok. I 284 rev., PSarg.)

1 ^{GIŠ}zi-rí-núm BE GIŠ UD.UD (DP 471 ii, PSarg.)

Cf. PN Ṣi-ir-ri-nu-um in BIN VII 197:17, OB.

ZRQ? zarāqum? "to pour."

GN SAG.GIŠ.RA GA ANŠE.SAL? iz-ru-uq (MDP XIV p. 10 i).

ZRQ zarriqum or sarriqum "squinter" (or the like).

Sarg. and Ur III PN:

Za-rí-kum (Kish 1930, 144a ii 16; Nikolski, Dok. II 460 rev., U)
Za-ri-ku-um (MDP XVIII 219 rev., U)
Za-rí-iq (U 1473+)
Za-rí-gúm (Oppenheim, CCTE G 16, U).

ZRQ? zirīqum (a wooden object).

Sarg. PN:

Zi-rí-kum (G+).

ZRT, see SRD$^{\text{ʾ}}_{x}$ sirdijum.

ZT? zâtum (a kind of flour).

Akk. lw. in Sum.:

x(QA) ZÍD za-tum (ITT II 4382; RTC 127 passim)

x(QA) ZÍD za-tum and x(QA) za-tum (ITT II 4560)

x bread, ZÍD za-tum-BI is x QA (RTC 126 rev. ii)

1 PISAN BAR BA.NA za-tum (ITT V 6854 ii, U).

ZTR? ziturum? (a container).

Akk. lw. in Ur III Sum.:

3 ^{DUG}zé-tu-ru-um KA.TAB.BA (YOS IV 292:19). Among leather containers

3 ^{DUG}zé-tu-ru-um (ITT II 892 rev. iii; RTC 307 rev. iii bottom).

ZZB?

zu-zu?-ub-bi or zu-zu?-ub KAŠ (FM 42:1, school text?).

ZZB? zizibiānum, zibibiānum (a plant with edible seeds).

Akk. lw. in Sum.:

Cf. plant zibibânu (Thompson, DAB p. 385), zibibianni (HSS XIII 353 = RA XXXVI 169), and GN Zi-zi-ba-nu-um^{KI} (RA XXXII 171 vi 27) and [Zi]-zi-bi-a-nu-um^{KI}, Zi-zi-bi-nu^{KI} (Sumer III 61). Cf. also si-bi-bi-a-ni in KAJ 277:10.

x QA zi-bí-bí-a-nu (BIN VIII 123; 128)

1 DUG zi-bí-bí-a-núm (BIN VIII 132; 271)

1 GUR.DUB zi-bí-bí-a-núm (BIN VIII 132)

1 [DUG] na-za-bu zi-bí-bí-a-núm (BIN VIII 267 ii)

3 DUG zi-zi-bí?-bí-a-núm (BIN VIII 276 ii). Scribal correction?

zi-zi-bí-a-núm (ITT I p. 8, 1137; II/2 p. 8, 2943)

x QA zi-zi-bí-a-núm (Reisner, TUT 121 xi; BE III 148 rev.; CT X 18 i, ii; 19 vi; Pinches, BTBC p. 17 i 13; Barton, HLC III Pl. 112 passim, all U)

x QA zi-zi-<bí>-a-núm (RA X 64 No. 14 i, U).

ZZK zazakkum (an official). See also SSK?

Akk. lw. in Ur III Sum.:

PN za-za-LUM to be interpr. as za-za-gúm or ḫa!-za-núm (Orient. IV 59; XLVII 328).

ZZN? zizānum? "locust."

Ur III PN's:

Zi-za-núm (RA XIX 39 No. 11). Cf. Zi-za-nu-u[m] in YOS VIII 96:6, OB

Zé-za-ni (CT X 50, 14344 rev.).

NAMES POSSIBLY AKKADIAN

This list includes a variety of names which for one reason or another have not been entered under the respective elements in the main Glossary. Mostly, they are names which should be considered Akkadian because of the endings, such as Du-šu-um, Ḫu-zu-um, Ma-gu-um, but for which no plausible interpretation could be offered. For other names in the list some questionable interpretation could be given, as in Ḫa-ar-bu-uk-ŠI = Ḫar-buqlim, La-ma-da = Lâ-maʾdā, but the interpretation could not be considered safe enough to warrant inclusion in the main list. Some names, such as Ma-ri-ḫi-DINGIR, Un-nu-ḫi-DINGIR, I-ti-ni-la-a[g]?, Mi-tu-uk-l[i]?, have suspicious and doubtful readings, in others, such as KIL-DINGIR, KIL-um, DINGIR-li-NI, UD-ra-NI, UR-me-a-ni, KA-KA-LUM, the reading of certain polyphonic signs cannot be ascertained. There is no doubt that this list could be enlarged considerably by many more possibly Akkadian names, mainly in the Ur III Period.

A-ad-a-bi (CT X 17 iii 2, U).
Ab-ba-ba-ti (PDTI 313, U).
A-ba-na-ar (ITT IV p. 46, 7411, U).
Ad-da-bi-li-ir (MCS IV 107, AOTc 152, U).
A-du-ba-sum (RTC 16 iv, PSarg.).
A-du-ra-mu (TMH n.F. I/II 132, U).
A-gu-da (ZA XIX 385 rev., U).
A-gu-za-ar (SO IX/1 No. 31 rev., U).
A-ḫa-an-ši-bu (Fish, CST p. 7, U; Orient. XLVII 40 iii, U), A-ḫa-an-si-bu (JCS X 31 No. 11 rev., U).
A-ḫu-si-ra (D).
A-na-d[a]?-rí (Kish 1930, 406 ii).
A-na-ti (Nies, UDT 84, U; MCS IV 89, U; RTC 396, U).
A-pù-ša-a-a (TCL V 6047 i 11, U).
Ar-ki-LUM (2 NT 596 3 times, U). Cf. $ʾ_x$RGN.
Ar-sa-^{d}Da-ga-an (MDP XXVIII 524).
Ar-ša-ba-ni (Orient. XVIII 29 rev., U).
Aš-da-GABA (CT VII 7 ii, U).
Aš-ni-rí (PDTI 257, U).
⌈Áš⌉-te-ni-ib (HSS IV 47, U).
Ba-bi-lum (Contenau, CHÉU 100 iii, U).

Ba-ga-rí (TCL II 5599, U).

Ba-ga-ti (ITT III 6559, U).

Ba-ga-ti-a (TMH n.F. I/II 106:4, U).

Ba-lá-ša-ri (Barton, HLC I Pl. 8 ii, U).

Ba-na-ti (ITT II/1 p. 15, 710, U; CT III 31 i, U; VII 23, 13166, U).

Bí-ig-NI (UET III 1034 ii, U).

Bí-la-ti (CT VII 7 i, U), GIŠ.BIL-la-ti (Reisner, TUT 158 v twice, U), GIŠ.BÍL-la-ti (RTC 400 rev. ii, U).

Bí-ra-NI (BE III 116, U).

Bi-ri-ša-àm (TCL V 6036 ii, U).

Bu-da-ti (Ward, SCWA No. 306, U).

Bu-ti-su$_4$-ba-ḫi (G+).

Bu-uz-kir (Ist. Mus. Nippur 2614).

Da-a-a-ti (U 753+; TMH n.F. I/II 82+, U; CT XXXII 26 iii; 27 iv, U).

Da-bí-NI (Reisner, TUT 16 iii, U; Orient. XXI 84f., U).

Da-bi-um (ITT II/1 3541, U). Meaning "bear?"

Da-bu-uš (Reisner, TUT 159 iv, U).

Da-ga-za-na-ar (ITT IV 7077, U; 7368, U).

Da-nu-da (G+).

Dar-e-tum (D+).

Dar-su-ba (FM).

Dar-ši-num (CT III 38 vi, U).

Dar-u-ma (D+), Da-ru-ma (Cop. 10059).

Da-ti-ti-in (AOF X 362, U).

DINGIR-li-NI (TCL II 5504 rev. i, U).

DINGIR-zu-ga-an (TCL V 6039 iii, U).

Dun-gá-a-ad (Nesbit, SRD 17 rev., U; A 2869, U).

Du-ra-am-ni (ITT IV p. 91, 8100, U). Perhaps Du-ra-am-ì-<lí>.

Du-šu-um (Iraq V 172 No. 17, U).

É-a-lu-bi (ITT IV p. 47, 7425, U).

E-lú-NI.IG (HSS IV 81, U).

E-mu-du$_7$-um (ITT IV p. 66, 7650, U).

E-mu-te-mu-bí (D+).

E-ni-iš-šà-gi (TCL II 5484 rev., U).

A.ŠÀ En-nu-lum-ma (Barton, HLC I Pl. 44, 90 rev.; Pl. 73 iii, U).

EN-tu-bí (ITT I 1448 iii+).

^{d}EN.ZU-lum (D).

E-ra-am-GI (D+).

E-ri-im-^{d}Da-gan (PDTI 340 rev., U).

E-ru-ba-ni (Boson, TCS 305, U).

E-šu-a-LUM (Lau, OBTR 110, U).

EZEN-^{d}Šul-gi (Hilprecht Anniv. Vol. p. 140 No. IV, U).

E-zu-ì-lí (HSS IV 79, U).

Ga-a-an-bu-ri (ITT IV 7727, U).

Ga-za-NI (ITT II/1 p. 41, 904, U).

Gi-nu-ba (E).

Gi-ir-ša-ti (Langdon, TAD 67, U).

Gi-ti-bu (G).

Gi-tu-bu (G).

Gu(d)-ku-la (UET III 1452 rev., U).

Gu-gu-NI (ITT IV p. 95, 8173, U), Gú-gú-NI (ITT II/1 p. 30, 826, U).

Ḫa-da-ti (PDTI 445 rev., U) = Ḫi-da-ti (532 rev., U).

ḪA.LA-ì-lí (ITT III/2 6533, U). Cf. Zitti-Nabû and Zit-ili in Stamm, ANG p. 371, NB.

Ḫa-la-ti (PDTI 443, U).

Ḫa-lu-lu-a (PDTI 703, U).

Ḫa-NI-NI (CT VII 36, 18415, U).

Ḫa-ar-bu-uk-ŠI (AnOr I 280 rev., U). To be compared with Ḫar-bu-uk-ŠI in BE XIV 12:33, name of a horse, and interpreted perhaps as Ḫar-buqlim.

A.ŠÀ Ḫa-šu-um (UET III 1081 iii, U).

Ḫu-da-⌈NI⌉ (Reisner, TUT 205 rev., U).

Ḫu-zu-um (Fish, CST 354, U).

Ib-mu-tum (PBS IX 25).

Ib-ra-nu-um (Gutian king).

Ib-ri-ru-um (Gutian king).

I-gi$_4$-ḫa-lum (Legrain, TRU 110 rev., U; CT XXXII 10 i, U; A 2964:8, U). IGI-ḫa-lum (CT XXXII 20 ii, U; AnOr VII 24, U), IGI-gi$_4$-ḫa-lum (PDTI 37 rev., U), IGI-ḫal-lum (Orient. XLVII 455, U).

I-gi$_4$-ru-maḫ (A 2868, U; U 1593+).

In-gi-tum (U 1741; YOS IV 254:36, U).

In-na-ti (CT XXXII 48, 103448, U).

I-ri-zi-su (A 5441:6). Clear.

I-sar-ni-ḫi-sa-am (Kish 1930, 144a).

Iš-ti-a (ITT IV p. 74, 7789, U).

I-ti-ni-la-[ag]? = Iddin-Ilag? (Barton, HLC I Pl. 33 vi, U).

I-zu-a (ITT IV p. 62, 7588, U).

KA-a-zum (Chiera, STA 16 rev. iii, U; Oppenheim, CCTE p. 77, U).

KA-KA-um (ITT IV p. 20, 7181 twice, U).

KA-KA-LUM (ITT IV p. 8, 7077, U).

KA-KA-tum(-MA) (ITT IV p. 63, 7603, U).

KIL-DINGIR (D+).

KIL-um (JCS X 26 i and p. 16).

KIL-za-an (U 747 passim, also U 748 miscopied).

Ki-ra-ad-du (UET III 24, 26, 27, 28, U) = Gi-ra-a[d-du] (UET III 24 seal, U).

Ku-da-um (RA VIII 155 AO 5660, U).

La-ba-an-sum (Chiera, STA 16 ii end, U; PDTI 507 rev. twice, U).

La-iš-da-al (BIN VIII 121 ii).

La-la-ti (ITT III 4939 rev., U).

La-la-zi (UET III 1, U).

La-lu(l)-LUM (Reisner, TUT 216, U; Lau, OBTR 114 rev., U).

La-ma-da (Moortgat, VARS No. 263, U).

La-me-ù (D).

La-an-ga (ITT III 5276 i twice).

La-ši-sa[r] (RTC 249 rev. i).

La-za-pi (CT III 5 ii, 7 xi twice, U).

Li-ni-si-in (CT XXXII 28 v, U).

Lu-ga-lu-mu-ug (FM).

Lul-lul-NI (Boson, TCS 306, U).

LÚ-pa-du-um (ITT IV p. 42, 7366, U).

Ma-gu-um (BE III 26, U).

Ma-na-na (ITT II/1 p. 33, 855, U). Cf. Ma-na-an-na in TCL XXII 8:26, 29, Mari.

Ma-an-gi, f.n. (ITT II/1 3516, U).

Ma-ni-ki-ni (CT X 30 i, U).

Ma-ra-UD (D).

Ma-ri-ḫi-DINGIR (Boson, TCS 326, U).

Maš-ba-an-núm (2 NT 601, U).

Mi-šu-a-bi-ni? (PDTI 529 x, U).

Mi-tu-uk-l[i]?, f.n. (Cop. 10059).

Mi-za-ti (OIP XIV 74 ii, PSarg.). Cf. Mi-za?(wr. A)-ti, probably a f.n. in MDP XXVIII 410:6, U, and ᶠMi-za-ti in YOS VII 107:7, NB.

GÁN Mi-zu-a-ni-im (MO D ix).

Mu-na-ḫa?-tum (D).

Mu-ru-pi (YOS IV 63, U).

Na-a-a-ti (AnOr I 292:31, U; YOS IV 188, U+).

Na-gu-ri (ITT IV 7845 rev., U).

Na-ki-ba (Jacobsen, CTC 5:4, U).

NI-a-NI-ba-ni (Contenau, CHÉU 25, U).

NI-ba-um (G+). Read Ì-ba-um?

Ni-da-ti (ITT IV p. 89, 8064, U).

Nin-ma-sum (RA VIII 197 seal, U).

Nu-mu-ši-num (ITT II/2 4550, perhaps not a PN).

Nu-úr-gi-ni-du (AJSL XXIX 136, U).

Pù-ba-LUM (MO). Possibly = Puppānum.

Pù-gi-na-ti (TCL V 6047 rev. i 12, U).

Ra-zum-DINGIR (ITT II/1 p. 12, 667, U).

Ri-ik-bu (Speleers, RIAA 117, U).

Si(g)-ig-sa-am (MDP XIV 71 rev. iv).

Ša-al-ma-um (Barton, HLC II Pl. 94, 106 rev., U; III Pl. 104, 168, U).

Ša-ba-da-túm (TCL V 6039 i, iii, U).

Ša-bu-lu-LUM (PDTI 562, U).

Ša-ra-at-NI.MU (TCL V 6039 iv, rev. ii, U).

Ši-ba-la-num (Arnold, ABTR 8 rev. = Lau, OBTR 126, U; Univ. Michigan No. 48, U).

Ši-ga-zi-bí (DP 32 ii, PSarg.).

Ši-gu-da-a (Barton, HLC I Pl. 253 iii, U).

Ši-zu-tum (UET III 1040 rev. III, U).

Šu-da-bu-NI (PDTI 332, U).

dŠul-gi-ur-šu-ru-uk (Contenau, CHÉU 25, U).

Šu-ma-a-AN (TCL V 6167, U).

Šu-ma-za-ba (Kish 1930, 406 ii, collated).

Šu-nu-un-túm (TCL II 5515:2, U).

Šu-ri-num (ITT V p. 54, 9815, U).

Tab-su-ga (Kish 1930, 144a rev. iii 21).

Tab-ša-ḫi (Nikolski, Dok. II 329 ii, U; TCL V 6039 iii, U).

Tu-ul-ga-núm MAR.TU (JCS VII 105 rev., U).

Ú-ar-ra-su-ni (Nikolski, Dok. II 364, U).

Ú-a-ti (YOS 198, U).

Ù-bu-da-ni (TCL V 6039 rev. i, U).

UD-ra-NI (JCS X 26 vi).

Um-te-bu (D).

Un-nu-ḫi-DINGIR (YOS IV 232:23, U).

UR-me-a-ni (CT XXXII 34 ii, U).

Ú-ú-um (ITT II/1 p. 47, 933, U).

Ù-zu-ḫa-lum (RTC 247 end).

Wa-al-lum (ITT II 6559, U).

Wa-mi-rí (Arnold, ABTR 8, U).

Za-la-ku-um (PDTI 252, U).

Za-na-ti (Legrain, UE X 364, U); Za-na-ti-a (RA XIX 32).

Zi-na-ti (RO V 17, U).

Zi-in-gàr (YOS IV 11, U).

Zi-zi-gu(d)-da-ni (TCL V 6039 rev. i, U).

Zi-zi-ig (Arnold, ABTR 19 rev., U).

Zi-zu-ba-al (TCL V 6039 rev. i, U).

Zu-num-ig-mu-um = Sûnum-ekmum? (D).

Zu-za-al (ZA XII 342, U).

Zu-zi-ba-at (ITT II/1 p. 17, 728, U).

Zu(m)-zu(m)-um (Pinches, AT 31 rev. ii, U); Zu(m)-zum (ibid. 113, U).